SCREENING IRELAND

MANCHESTER
UNIVERSITY PRESS

For Matty

SCREENING IRELAND

Film and television representation

LANCE PETTITT

Manchester University Press

Manchester and New York

distributed exclusively in the USA by St Martin's Press

Copyright © Lance Pettitt 2000

The right of Lance Pettitt to be identified as the author of this work has been asserted by him in accordance with the Copyright, Designs and Patents Act 1988.

Published by Manchester University Press
Oxford Road, Manchester M13 9NR, UK
and Room 400, 175 Fifth Avenue, New York, NY 10010, USA
http://www.man.ac.uk/mup

Distributed exclusively in the USA by
St. Martin's Press, Inc., 175 Fifth Avenue, New York,
NY 10010, USA

Distributed exclusively in Canada by
UBC Press, University of British Columbia, 2029 West Mall,
Vancouver, BC, Canada V6T 1Z2

British Library Cataloguing-in-Publication Data
A catalogue record for this book is available from the British Library

Library of Congress Cataloging-in-Publication Data applied for

ISBN   0 7190 5269 6   *hardback*
        0 7190 5270 X   *paperback*

First published 2000

07 06 05 04 03 02 01 00   10 9 8 7 6 5 4 3 2 1

Typeset by
D R Bungay Associates, Burghfield, Berks

Printed in Great Britain
by Bookcraft (Bath) Ltd, Midsomer Norton

Contents

Part I Cinema

LIST OF FIGURES AND TABLES

Figures

Tables

Appendix tables

Preface and acknowledgements

This study has its origins in three connected periods and activities in my personal and professional life. Living in, lecturing on and writing about Ireland have played off each other in myriad ways, this book being but one outcome. I have been tracking back and forth to Ireland ever since I first went to Dublin as a postgraduate in 1985. My thanks go to Declan Kiberd for his formative influence as a teacher during my time at VCD and beyond. For the last seven years, I have been fortunate enough to teach Irish Studies at St Mary's College in London, and convened 'Ireland on Screen', a lively final year undergraduate course on which much of the content of this book is based. *Screening Ireland* is pitched to stretch this kind of student, but also to suggest new lines of enquiry to graduate researchers and stimulate my peers within the Irish Studies community. The book is also intended to be accessible to the intelligent and inquiring non-academic reader seeking a clear and coherent context for better understanding the increasing number of Irish-themed films and television programmes available to audiences. The text of *Screening Ireland* has taken just over two years to research and write. This period has been punctuated by intense bursts of excitement and productivity, but more usually has been characterised by a lonely slog at a desk in front of a computer screen.

In this respect, I owe an immense personal debt of gratitude to my partner, Matthew Daines, who has supported and encouraged me throughout the writing of this book. He has been unfailingly tolerant of my selfish obsession and *Screening Ireland* is dedicated to him. There are several friends and colleagues in Ireland, Britain and the US who have generously given valuable time, expertise and advice by reading chapters of *Screening Ireland*. Marie Ryan meticulously read the entire book in draft. Her intelligence, common-sense suggestions and insistence on deadlines have helped see the project through. Sunniva O'Flynn at the Film Institute of Ireland in Dublin has brought her considerable specialist knowledge, critical acuity and good humour to bear on the text by reading most of part I and chapter 12, improving them immensely. Rob Savage in Boston read and commented on chapters 2 and 7; my good friend Éibhear Walshe in Cork offered perceptive and succinct comments on drafts of chapters 1, 8 and 9; Wolfgang Truetzschler at Dublin Institute of Technology kindly read over chapter 12 to check details of recent Irish and European media legislation; and Brian Lynch of Radio, Telefís Éireann (RTÉ) Written Archives provided vital information on questions about the Angelus and other broadcasting matters. I have enjoyed much debate with Colin Graham (now in Belfast), who responded with speed and precision as well as applying his critical rigour to reading chapters 1, 11, 12. My colleague and friend, Janet Free, at St Mary's read the chapter on sitcom at short notice, and gave me the benefit of her knowledge of the genre to provide much needed clarity to my chosen case studies. Finally, I am especially grateful to the anonymous Manchester University Press reader who made several incisive suggestions for fine-tuning and improving the typescript. To all these people, I am indebted but of course I am responsible for any mistakes in the final text and the views expressed are my own except where indicated in the conventional academic manner.

There are several archivists and librarians to whom sincere thanks are due. Sunniva was exemplary in her assistance at the Film Institute of Ireland, arranging viewing, rectifying my ignorance and suggesting lines of enquiry. Liam Wylie offered cheery advice, set up viewing and cut film; Emma Keogh facilitated me with film stills and gave good advice on seeking permissions; the staff of the British Film Institute's (BFI) Reading Room in London have been courteous and exemplary in their assistance throughout my research period; so too Mandy Rosen, Alison Strauss, Shirley Collier and Mike Caldwell, who have helped me with photos, posters and frame enlargements at the BFI. Bob Monks arranged early film stills and had the answers to historical queries. Gillian Coward and Phylis McKay were great in setting up a viewing session of Northern Irish material at the Film and Sound Resource Unit, University of Ulster, Coleraine. I offer thanks to Stephen D'Arcy of RTÉ, Dublin, for arranging my video viewing; Malachi Moran of the Reference and Illustrations Library for tracking down and checking historical facts; Fergal Cunningham for his assistance with TV stills; Sheila Casey in Audience Research; Malachi Martin at NIFC, Belfast; and Eugene Finn at the BFI in London for all his advice and help, especially with *that* Donnellan film. Other individuals have helped me with particular requests, loans of materials or just given me good advice. They include: Maire Harris at Gael-Linn for the *Saoirse* still; Billy Roarty and Peter Kelly at the *Radharc* archive in Blackrock; David Miller for his Bernadette McAliskey stills; Liam Harte at St Mary's for the *Dublin Opinion* cartoon, his comments on *Glenroe* and sundry other enquiries about Irish culture; Fiona Tait at the Birmingham City Archive and the musicologist, Reg Hall; Eamon Brophy, Sean Campbell, Mary Doran, Shaun Richards, Paddy Hanlon, Jane Roscoe, Brian Neve, Tony Barker, Alun Howkins, Nessan Danaher; Ted Sheehy at *Film Ireland* for the *Dear Daughter* still and his invaluable contacts; Seán Hutton for checking my Irish and the materials on Liam O'Leary; Martin Doyle at *The Irish Post* for the loan of pictures and use of the archive there; Trish Long at Buena Vista (Ireland), Catherine Maguire at Celtic Vision and Cathal O'Doherty at Tara TV; and Ruth Mellor and Beryl Mason at St Mary's for all their help and good humour. There are several film-makers and producers who generously lent me stills, gave permission to use their material and discussed their work with me. I owe a great debt to the following for contributing to the visual look of the book: Cathal Black for the beautiful front cover – reproduced by Bill 'Blowup' Kaye – from *Korea* (1995), John Boorman, Paddy Breathnach, John T. Davis, Phillipa Donnellan and her late father, Philip (who sadly died just before the text was completed), Dave Fox, Peter Flannery, Margo Harkin, Peter Lennon, Louis Lentin, Trish McAdam, Thaddeus O'Sullivan, Robert Walpole and Orla Walsh.

I am pleased to acknowledge and thank the following for giving permission to reproduce visual images: Beacon Communications Corporation, BBC London and BBC Northern Ireland, the BFI, Buena Vista International (Ireland), Carlton TV, Castle Rock Entertainment, Channel Four International, Crescendo Concepts Limited, Esras (Radharc), Faction Films, the Film Institute of Ireland, *Film Ireland*, Gael-Linn, Geffen Pictures, Granada TV and Granada Films International, Hamilton Projects, Hat Trick Productions, Hell's Kitchen Films, Merlin Films, the National Library of Ireland, Polygram Filmed Entertainment, RTÉ Spelling Entertainment Group, Inc., Tara TV, Treasure Films, Turner Entertainment Inc., Universal Studios, Ulster Television and Warner Brothers Inc. The author and publisher have made every effort to obtain permission to reproduce copyright material.

I would like to acknowledge the financial assistance provided by the Research Fund at St Mary's College, the Departmental Research Assessment Exercise Fund and a grant from the Cultural Relations Committee of the Department of Foreign Affairs, Dublin, which enabled me to travel to present the conference paper on which chapter 9 is based. My friend since school days, David Jones, generously helped finance picture costs and some research expenses in Ireland. I would like to thank Jared Rediske for his companionship over the last two years and for distracting me from work in ways that were never strictly uniform. Last, and certainly by no means least, I would like to thank Matthew Frost, commissioning editor at MUP, and his assistant editor, Lauren McAllister, for their encouragement and help in seeing *Screening Ireland* through to publication.

INTRODUCTION

Screening Ireland

This book examines a selection of screen representations of Ireland in films and television programmes spanning the twentieth century. For the sake of clarity the material is organised into two parts. Part I discusses the history of cinema in and about Ireland and analyses key films grouped in terms of genres, themes and historical periods with examples from Irish, British and US cinema. The case studies examine: the reasons for the inconsistent performance of film production in Ireland and the comparatively recent emergence of an Irish film culture; definitions of 'popular' cinema as a site where the lived contradictions of society are contested and re-presented; and, finally, the extent to which Irish cinema (particularly since the 1970s) has successfully in-appropriated and transformed the idea of a national cinema. Part II examines the history and character of broadcasting in Ireland and Britain, exploring Ireland's representation in both popular and more 'serious' formats, from chat show, soap opera and sitcom to documentary, drama and TV film. The case studies illustrate how Irish television has negotiated different, popular Anglo-American TV formats – in some cases successfully indigenising them, inflecting them with particular Irish concerns and circumstances.

The opening chapter of this book attempts to address the needs of those readers unfamiliar with Irish history, politics and the nature of academic debate about cultural production in or about Ireland since the start of the 1980s. Chapter 1 gives a concise introduction to these topics in order to bring the reader up to speed with those who may have a head-start in these fields of knowledge. Readers who consider themselves reasonably well-informed on these areas are still advised to read this chapter. It may refresh your memory, challenge ideas that you already hold and encourage you to consider some new ones as well. Each half of the book is set up with a chapter providing a critical history of the cinema (chapter 2) and television (chapter 7), explaining origins, key features of development and introducing theoretical issues that have a bearing on subsequent chapters and the book as a whole. These chapters give a chronological and critical framework within which the selective analyses of the subsequent chapters may be set. Each chapter is headed by three bullet-pointed questions to direct your reading and act as a focus for discussion.

It makes sense to think of chapters 2 and 7 in tandem since the book operates on the principle that, while each medium has its distinctive histories, economies and textual features, cinema and television can be productively considered alongside each other. Indeed, the final chapter looks at developments in the 1990s, analysing the extent of media interdependence and convergence. With due recognition given to the differences between film and television, much can be gained from this comparative approach. Both media borrow and adapt from each other, but also form part of a web of connections with other arts and cultural forms. It is well to remember that the material and representational synergies of finance, personnel, images and narratives go back further than the 'late' appearance of the discussion in chapter 12 might suggest.

Ireland's diminutive size, geographical location, political past and bilingual culture meant that, dating from their respective origins, the organisation of cinema and the broadcasting system has been penetrated and profoundly influenced by Britain, the USA and, to a lesser extent, Europe. The economic, technical and cultural realities of Ireland's pervasive if problematic links with colonialism and capitalism are etched into the histories of both media, in and outside of Ireland. I have tried to capture this graphically in the front cover image from Cathal Black's *Korea*, discussed fully in chapter 12. Studies of Irish emigrant narratives in US cinema – both the lives of émigré writers and directors and the 'ethnicity' of screen characters[1] – have begun to trace Ireland's contribution to Hollywood and independent film over the last decade or so.[2] The traffic of broadcasters from Ireland to work in radio and television in Britain is so commonplace it goes largely unnoticed, yet a proper assessment of this aspect of the cultural life of Britain's oldest, largest immigrant population is still to be written.

A cultural studies approach to film and television

A cultural studies approach to film and television seeks to combine textual and contextual analysis. Thinking about the text should go beyond noting which kind of images are on the screen, to ask *how* such images are constructed with different textual qualities and connotations, *how* they function as representations and what formal and conventional codes have been adopted by this representation over others. Film and television images are complicated cultural signifiers not simple reflections of reality. Thus, textual analysis should lead to and be set within the kind of social and cultural context offered by this book. Typically, a cultural studies approach seeks to explore the relations between the textual matter of films or programmes and their context, that is, the cultures in which they are produced, viewed and interpreted. If textual analysis is concerned with the formal and connotative nature of audio-visual images, how they are structured and shaped into meaningful sequences, then contextual analysis explores the processes by which images and narratives are made, considering the conditions of a particular instance of cultural production. It is difficult to draw an absolute theoretical distinction between 'text' and 'context' since they interpenetrate one another. For the sake of clarity, I take context to include the economics of media ownership and control, government policy and finance, institutional aspects of production, considerations of genre and format and audience reception. These aspects of context are themselves embraced by broader historical and social conditions within which media representations are produced, distributed and shown. Marshalling both textual and contextual approaches is a difficult task, but I hope that I have struck a satisfactory balance between providing both explanatory context and textual readings of individual and groups of films.

It is important for me to indicate here that this book is a contribution to a diverse and growing field of interdisciplinary research, teaching and publication within what in Britain since the mid-1980s has been termed 'Irish Studies'. Within this ambit, it is possible to identify significant instances of scholarship on the media. Pioneering work on Irish cinema has been done by Kevin Rockett, with co-authors John Hill and Luke Gibbons, in the seminal but now dated, *Cinema and Ireland* (1987), and Rockett's own encyclopaedic, *The Irish Filmography* (1995). The archivist Bob Monks is painstakingly working on a study of cinema in Ireland based on the Liam O'Leary collection and other archival material held at the National Library, Dublin. Incisive groundwork on Irish television has been carried out, particularly by Martin McLoone in three edited collections, *Television and Irish Society* (1984), coedited with John MacMahon, *Culture and Identity in Irish Broadcasting* (1991) and *Broadcasting in a Divided Society* (1996). Mary Kelly and Barbara O'Connor's edited collection, *Media Audiences in Ireland* (1997), assembled a series of essays investigating the significance of audiences in understanding film and television in Ireland. Luke Gibbons's sophisticated cultural analyses of both media are collected in *Transformations in Irish Culture* (1996). More recently, Brian McIlroy has produced a stimulating study of the representation of political conflict in Northern Ireland, *Shooting to Kill* (1998). Indeed, one of the aims of *Screening Ireland* is, within the covers of one book, to synthesise, add to and develop some of the most influential ideas about the nature of representation in Irish film and television over the last decade.

The analyses of Irish film and television presented in the following pages are situated in broader contemporary debates about the continued significance of nationalism in a postcolonial, postmodern and so-called 'global age'. Underpinning this book is the idea that cinema and broadcasting have at different times contributed to the construction, but also contained a critique, of the concept of nation-ness and the national identities reproduced in the relations between Ireland and Britain this century. This is reflected in the representation of the most problematic political divisions and cultural differences that have shaped the contours of Irish history and society, which may be summarised under the following topics: a) empire and nationalism, b) the local/regional versus the centralist/statist, c) class and social inequalities, d) gendered and sexual identities. These material divisions and differences are represented through different cinematic and televisual conventions, some of which are shared with the wider culture, others specific to the media. Thus, questions about the representation of national identity and racial types loom large in films and television related to Ireland. For instance, the setting, narrative structure and iconography of films may be seen to represent different aspects of colonial relations and attitudes. However, since nationalism generally seeks to unify often disparate sub-national affiliations of people and place, we need to also examine how the regional and local are represented within Ireland. Secondly, the representation of class configurations and social inequalities in Irish society are important in understanding the contested redistribution of power following political independence in both Irish states. Thirdly, the process of film and television representation is gendered. That is to say, the behaviour of characters, the outcomes of narratives, the habitual ways in which male and female figures are filmed and the attitudes of the viewing audience derive from socially-constructed forms of power based on gender and, furthermore, commonly privilege male (hetero) sexuality as normative. It is important to remember that these dominant values are maintained and reproduced through the active work of representation to appear 'natural', unimpeachable and 'true to life'.

In *Screening Ireland*, I contend that film is now the preeminent medium through which Ireland both examines itself and projects its image to the wider world. Ireland is not unique in that its daily life has become saturated with media images originating from outside the country. But the particular nature of that saturation and the creative responses to it are worthy of exploration. Ireland has been unusually subject to Anglo-American cinematic and television image-makers over an extensive period of time. Ireland's experience might be seen to anticipate current debates about the 'hyperreality' of postmodern culture where simulacra take on a material existence and status. The title, *Screening Ireland*, is meant to suggest several lines of enquiry through these debates. In the past, images on Irish screens have been subjected to censorship by the state and church institutions, and the British media have 'screened' Ireland in seriously limiting ways, not just in the representation of political conflict in Northern Ireland. Today, however, Irish film-makers and producers, television and satellite companies, have unprecedented opportunities for the business of screening Ireland. This globalisation of Irishness is not without its problems and pitfalls. Moving between the local and the global is a political, cultural and creative challenge; it is part of reimagining Ireland's complicated relationship with modernity.

Notes

1 L. O'Leary, *Rex Ingram: Master of the silent cinema* (Dublin, The Academy Press, 1980); L. Lourdeaux, *Italian and Irish Filmmakers in America* (Philadelphia, Temple University Press, 1990); K. Rockett, 'The Irish migrant and film', in O'Sullivan, P. (ed.), *The Creative Migrant: The Irish world wide, Volume 3* (London, Leicester University Press, 1994).

2 A. Slide, *The Cinema and Ireland* (North Carolina, McFarland & Co., 1988); J. M. Curran, *Hibernian Green on the Silver Screen: The Irish and American movies* (Westport, Connecticut, Greenwood Press, 1989).

PART I
CINEMA

CHAPTER 1

BACK TO IRELAND'S FUTURES

- What are the key features of modern Ireland's historical development?
- What kinds of nationalism developed in an Irish context?
- How did the two states in Ireland develop politically and economically after 1922?

Locating Ireland historically

The Irish experience of modernity clearly demonstrates the problems . . . which lie in either rejecting modernity or embracing it wholeheartedly.[1]

Ireland's historical development has provided the country with an indeterminate, in-between character. Its modern and contemporary history is characterised by an uneven process of emergence and self-definition, economically and politically, socially and culturally. A history of political conflict and division, economic dependency and British colonial policy resulted in the division of the country into two states in 1920. For the Republic of Ireland and Northern Ireland, temporary solutions have lingered and assumed the appearance of permanence. The first two sections of this chapter set out a brief historical overview of this incomplete, complex and hybrid process of development. It provides readers who have little or no knowledge of Irish history with a clear chronological framework and an examination of the term 'nationalism'. The third section is given over to introducing theories of postcolonial analysis and how they have been applied to the Irish case. The fourth section offers a synthesis of historical and cultural criticism over the past decade, showing how the 'modernisation' of Ireland remains open to different kinds of interpretation, particularly around the issue of Ireland's (post)modernity. This material will help the reader not only to understand the subject matter of the films and programmes discussed later but also to appreciate the historical conditions in which they were produced, viewed and discussed. However, to begin locating Ireland historically, we need to consider the extended impact of its colonial history and the continued significance of nationalism.

Ireland's place within the broad canvas of Western politics in the twentieth century is marginal but not insignificant, distinctive but not unique. That politics has largely been concerned with the consolidation and realignment of nation-states in the wake of nationalisms developed over the previous two centuries. The industrial strength of major European powers like Great Britain, France and Germany was based on their political status as centres of imperial rule for colonies spread around the globe. Early in the twentieth century, the USA was able to draw on vast natural resources within its territories and the human resources of its immigrants to build up a modern industrial and technological power base which rivalled Europe and the Soviet Union. Ireland's modern origins and character derive from a combination of its close colonial relations with Britain during a period of imperialist expansion, the influence of European political thought and the counter-flow of ideas from Irish-American emigrants from the mid-nineteenth century onwards.

This book is based on the notion that colonial ideas have structured the economic, political and cultural relations between Ireland and Britain for several hundred years – longer than any other colony – and have consequently informed deep-seated attitudes in both Irish and British people. Ireland had, in fact, been subject to several invasions since before the twelfth century, but was more systematically colonised by the English from the sixteenth century, with Scots Presbyterians and English non-conformists in the plantations of the seventeenth century, managed by an Anglo-Irish ascendancy from the eighteenth century and incorporated formally within the British Empire under the Union of Great Britain and Ireland between 1800–1921. But if Ireland was England's first colony, it also became one of the first to augment decolonisation. As the historian Bernard Porter laconically put it, 'Ireland was where the colonial rot really set in'.[2] The political vehicle for such dissension was Irish nationalism. The political and cultural forms of nationalism expressed in Ireland between 1870–1921 drew threads from France, Germany and the USA.[3] These were taken up under local conditions to challenge and resist British imperial nationalism. It is important to recognise that there were different political and cultural forms of nationalism in Ireland competing with each other at any one moment.

Romantic nationalism in Ireland consisted of ideas largely derived from German artists and thinkers in the nineteenth century. It defined a nationalism that was principally based on a native language and culture; in other words, a shared ethnic identity. This form of national identity is premised on the real and imagined connections between people of the present and their lineage from a distant race that existed in the past, a golden age when the 'people' constituted a socio-political unit, 'the nation'. According to the romantic nationalists of nineteenth century Ireland the land, the peasantry who worked it and their folk culture symbolically provided ancestral connections with past generations who existed before English colonisation.

Nationalist sentiments were to be given political expression and constitutional form by Irish members of parliament (MP) such as Charles Stewart Parnell and John Redmond, who sat in the Westminster parliament in the late nineteenth and early twentieth centuries. Parnell in particular was the charismatic focus for a broadly-based, modern political party that argued effectively for Ireland to progress to a limited form of self-rule within the British Empire. This was popularly called 'Home Rule', after a campaign launched in 1870 by

Isaac Butt. In contrast to this parliamentary tradition within nationalism, Irish republicanism can be traced back to Wolfe Tone and the United Irishmen (1791) who took up alternative continental and anti-colonial models, deriving its principal ideas from the revolutions in America (1776) and France (1789). Philosophically, republicanism was civic, secular and democratic in character since its adherents believed in rights due to anyone born within the nation-state irrespective of ethnic or religious beliefs. Irish republicanism tended to be more future-orientated, radical and egalitarian than conservative, past-centred romantic nationalism, which developed a narrow, exclusive and xenophobic character at the turn of the century, sometimes known as 'Irish Ireland'. In contrast to the liberal limitations of Home Rule, republicanism argued for a withdrawal from empire and a separate Irish parliament. Such policies were effectively promoted after 1916 by a political party called Sinn Féin (which means 'ourselves' in Irish).

It is important to understand that Home Rule and Irish republicanism were developed dynamically in opposition to the forces and ideas of British imperialism. This political ideology can be seen as the expression of a nationalism which developed self-effacingly at the core of the empire and whose *English* character rarely spoke its name. As Bernard Crick has pointed out, the historic task of maintaining the sense of an integrated British national identity required English nationalism to be muted not strident, in the background but in control.[4] The success of Britishness was that it took the political form of a composite, four-nation state (England, Wales, Scotland and Ireland) with a political identity that subsumed territorial and regional differences. The axis of this political formation was decidedly Anglocentric in economic, political and moral terms. It was England that dutifully projected itself as the parent ('mother') country of an extended family of nations, with the United Kingdom of Great Britain and Ireland as the immediate family or 'home countries', which constituted the British Empire.

The stability of this empire was seriously challenged in Ireland by a ferment of nationalism and republicanism between 1870 and 1921 that is known as the Irish Revival. It was led by dissident intelligentsia of the Anglo-Irish, a declining land-owning class, mostly belonging to the Church of Ireland (Anglican), who had supported British rule in Ireland, and a Protestant, professional middle class. Anticipating some form of national autonomy, these groups sought to provide the necessary intellectual and political leadership in Ireland. This bid for power was challenged by a more populous and increasingly confident Catholic middle class in the same period. However, in the more industrialised and urbanised north-eastern part of Ireland a significant cross-class alliance of Protestants (mostly Presbyterians and non-conformist denominations) organised itself to resist the claims of Irish nationalism. Irish Unionists sought to maintain Ireland's political ties with Great Britain. They were proud of their role in the Empire and identified with a British national identity. But it was a Britishness that had a distinctive Ulster stamp. From the date of the first Home

Rule Bill (1886), through the interlinking of the Orange Order[5] and industrial trade unions, business entrepreneurs and sympathetic Conservative MPs in Westminster, Unionism developed into a powerful political alliance. It combined a strong sense of religious and economic supremacism with a popular monarchical allegiance to the British crown and parliament to oppose Home Rule.[6]

A broad intellectual justification for Irish political self-governance, whether by constitutional or non-constitutional means, was provided by a collection of ideas known as cultural nationalism. This is a generic term given to the creative ideas, images and narratives that formed the imaginative underpinning of a national identity distinct from Britishness. An oppositional, anti-colonial ideology, Irish cultural nationalism subsequently became condensed, reformulated and transformed into the dominant ideology of the southern state after 1922. For a generation after this, cultural nationalism deeply influenced attitudes not only to the Irish language, education, the arts and cultural activity, but also informed social and economic policy. In its narrowest forms, the 'ideal' Irish nation would be based on Gaelic models, consisting exclusively of Irish-speaking, Catholic, small farming communities and family businesses in a largely rural country. Cultural nationalism's more cosmopolitan advocates, including writers like J. M. Synge and George Russell, were less sectarian, more inclusive and acknowledged Ireland's variegated cultural heritage. But such pluralism was marginalised by a more dominant political conservatism. Romantic nationalists, like the young W. B. Yeats and Douglas Hyde, looked to the distant past, seeking to combine ancient Celtic models and folk culture as the basis for a national culture, set apart from the industrialisation and modernity negatively attributed to Britain. We can see that the writers and intellectuals of the Irish Revival invented these enabling myths as a form of cultural resistance to British imperial subjection. Exemplifying Gramsci's idea that 'every new civilisation has always expressed itself in literary form before expressing itself in the life of the state',[7] the heroic images and stories that characterise the revivalist phase of Irish cultural nationalism effectively prepared an imaginary future for Irish people, anticipating the violent phase of decolonisation, which took place between 1916 and 1923.

All the forms of nationalism outlined above had supporters who believed political violence was justified in achieving their aims. The Irish Republican Brotherhood (IRB), or 'Fenians', an underground movement founded in 1858, was committed to a republic achieved through arms and later developed into the paramilitary force known as the Irish Republican Army (IRA). From 1912, in response to Home Rule, Ulster Unionists openly organised their own paramilitary Ulster Volunteer Force (UVF) to defend the Union, protect property and people. Meanwhile, the British Army and auxiliary counter-terrorist forces, the 'Black and Tans' (so called because of the two tone colour of their makeshift uniform), were garrisoned and periodically deployed in Ireland to maintain British law and order throughout this period. In response to paramilitary activities in

Ireland, British policy during and after World War I (1914–18) was to introduce repressive measures in those areas that became ungovernable. Republican activities usually consisted of hit-and-run skirmishes in the countryside but in 1916 a pivotal confrontation took place in Dublin between armed republicans and the British military. A week of intense urban conflict at the centre of British rule in Ireland, the Easter Rising (as it became known) resulted in a crushing military defeat but a resounding propaganda coup for Irish republicanism. Public response to the summary executions of leading republican figures led to a Sinn Féin landslide in the British General Election of 1918 ousting the constitutional Irish Parliamentary Party. Between 1919 and 1921, the IRA engaged crown forces in a concerted guerrilla war known as the War of Independence. Meanwhile, in the north-eastern counties of Ulster, Unionists sought to protect their economic interests and political ties within the Empire. In 1920, the government of David Lloyd George, defending a small majority in Westminster, acquiesced to parliamentary and paramilitary pressures by partitioning Ireland into two states. Six northern counties became Northern Ireland and the remaining twenty-six counties became the Irish Free State. This arrangement brought a measure of political independence to both states, but in fundamental terms failed to satisfy Unionists and Republicans and stored up significant resentments against the Westminster government. The parliament of Northern Ireland, later known as Stormont, was based near Belfast and officially opened by King George V in 1921. Later that year, an Anglo-Irish Treaty was agreed between Lloyd George and a republican delegation led by Michael Collins, a minister in Dáil Éireann, the Irish parliament in Dublin. Ratified by the Dáil, the treaty brought the War of Independence to a close and formally created the Irish Free State. However, under the terms of the treaty, this state only had dominion status within the empire, not full independence. This was seen as a defeat by separatist republicans led by Eamon de Valera and a brief, rancorous civil war took place between 1922–23, which was won by Free State forces who endorsed the terms of the treaty. This was but one aspect of 'the carnival of reaction both North and South [that] would set back the wheels of progress' in a partitioned Ireland predicted by James Connolly.[8]

From end of empire to Euro-nation?

Between 1922 and 1932 the government policies of the Irish Free State 'made virtues of continuity and caution'[9] in its political and economic relations with Britain. Economically, the southern state was heavily dependent on Britain as a market and trading partner. Many of the Free State's political institutions were modelled on those of the former regime and the civil service remained virtually unchanged. But between 1932 and 1959, under the almost unbroken leadership of de Valera's Fianna Fáil party (founded in 1926), Irish policy changed. The Irish Free State waged an intense economic and diplomatic campaign against Britain between 1932–38, introducing protectionist policies that promoted Irish agricultural produce, manufactured goods and argued for greater political independence in the international forum of the League of Nations. De Valera supervised the rewriting of the constitution in 1937 along traditional Catholic lines. Church and state (now known as Éire) became closely aligned and a distinctive Catholic ethos was enshrined in public life. Éire remained neutral during World War II (1939–45) and cut its legal ties with the British Commonwealth in 1949. Although it was recognised internationally as a Republic, part of what its constitution claimed as the 'national territory', namely, Northern Ireland, remained within the jurisdiction of the United Kingdom.

These political developments have to be evaluated taking into account the considerable economic, social and cultural difficulties that beset the southern state: limited economic power, high unemployment, poor social welfare provision, social conservatism and, above all, cultural insularity. By the 1950s, the biggest national asset – its people – were emigrating in record numbers. The state's experiment in self-reliant independence was failing the nation. The election of Sean Lemass as taoiseach (prime minister) in 1959 signalled a change in strategy, which has held sway in different guises since. In the 1960s, international business, instead of being discouraged by the high tariffs and taxes of protectionism, was invited to invest in the country. The Republic began a process of gradual integration into an internationalised economic order from a disadvantaged position. This integration brought with it forms of modernisation, industrialisation and tentative social liberalisation. For a short period between 1966–73 the economy enjoyed relative growth, some of its citizens attained limited material prosperity and the emigration tide turned briefly. In 1973, Ireland joined the European Economic Community (now the European Union or EU). This link became an increasingly important source of economic, political and cultural definition over the next quarter of a decade, offsetting the previous dependency on Britain as a source of trade, providing a new set of confidence-boosting connections and accelerating the post-1959 changes.

In Northern Ireland, a solidly unionist government ruled largely without organised opposition from 1921 until the mid-1960s. The manufacturing sector of the small economy was based on engineering, shipbuilding and linen production that had developed as part of the industrial hinterlands of Scotland and north-west England but these traditional industries went into serious decline after World War II. From the mid-1960s, a significant minority of Catholic nationalists structurally disadvantaged by the state began to demand civil rights. Principally, they sought equality in voting rights, housing and employment. Discontent with the pace of reform led to rioting, a serious break down in public order and the deployment of British troops in Northern Ireland (1969). In response, republican and loyalist paramilitaries emerged and the Provisional IRA engaged in a guerrilla war with the British army. The reaction of both the Republic and Britain to the Troubles was to try to contain it within Northern Ireland. In 1972, the British government prorogued a discredited Stormont and imposed Direct Rule from Westminster, which angered unionist voters and inflamed loyalist groups. Further resentment and suspicion among unionists were later provoked by the Anglo-Irish Agreement (1985) and the Downing Street Declaration (1993) because they were made by the governments of the Republic and the UK without formal consultation with the unionist political majority. Since 1972, Britain has continued its policy of financially supporting Northern Ireland in an attempt to assuage political and social problems. Even during the Thatcherite 1980s – when government financial intervention was taboo and terrorism systematically countered[10] – monetarist rhetoric was readily mortgaged in an effort to contain the 'Ulster problem'. The largest sector of the economy in Northern Ireland is that associated with public service expenditure, including social services, unemployment benefit, policing and judicial and prison service provision.[11]

The political ramifications of paramilitary violence in Northern Ireland, especially during the period of the republican hunger strikes of 1980–81, added to the stark economic problems faced by the Republic in the 1980s as a world recession hit its open, free-trade economy. Many multinational corporations that had set up in the previous two decades now pulled out. Its national debt increased and emigration returned with a vengeance, reaching its peak between 1986–88. This exposed the country's dependency and accentuated its 'in-between' status. The Republic was within the USA/European 'core' but as a peripheral region. It appeared to be in the same league as other young EU countries like Spain, Greece and Portugal but also bore some structural similarities to the economies of the Third World countries of Latin America.[12]

In the Republic, the first half of the 1990s witnessed a considerable change in economic, political and social conditions. While the dominant, core nations of the EU (like Germany and Britain) plunged into recession, the Irish economy flourished from a combination of EU development grants and fresh injections of commercial investment from the USA, Japan and Europe that flowed into the country. In 1996, Ireland overtook Britain in terms of economic productivity, its growth rate being compared to the so-called 'Tiger' economies of south-east Asia. The configuration of Irish political parties changed, the country played an integrated and respected role in the EU, the Catholic church's absolute authority faltered under moral scandals, the state's first woman president, Mary Robinson, established a more conciliatory and socially liberal agenda during her period of office (1992–97) and Irish–British relations over Northern Ireland improved. There were outward shows of prosperity and diplomatic *rapprochement*, including, in 1993, the joint Downing Street Declaration in which Britain stated that it had 'no selfish, strategic or economic interest' in Northern Ireland. This came after over a quarter of a century of British political élites pretending to act as neutral, brokering political solutions between Irish extremists. Liam O'Dowd has more accurately described the continuing significance of Northern Ireland, arguing that it remains the most problematical legacy of the British decolonisation process, and Britain and Ireland's attempts to move into a post-colonial age.'[13]

Postcolonial Ireland: 'not only "after" but "going beyond"'

- What is postcolonial theory?

- How might it be applied to Ireland?

- How have contemporary historians and cultural critics interpreted Ireland?

In this section, I want to elaborate on the theoretical bases for a postcolonial interpretation of the historical developments outlined in the previous pages. I then want to examine how postcolonial and other contemporary criticism have interpreted cultural production in Ireland over the last decade. Postcolonial theory is a term that encompasses a range of ideas that have been developed as a direct consequence of the history of European colonialism, particularly in Africa, the Caribbean, the Indian subcontinent and (more controversially) white settler colonies such as Australia and Canada. It is not a single theory but a diverse, interdisciplinary critical discourse, which has been used to explore the economic, social, cultural and psychological relations between coloniser countries and their colonised territories. The 'post' of postcolonial studies (unhyphenated) is slightly misleading since its area of interest is not just confined to countries *after* the coloniser has withdrawn and political independence has been achieved, that is, when they have become temporally and spatially post-colonial (hyphenated). A postcolonial consciousness comes into being as the result of a colonised individual critically recognising their place in the historical structure called colonialism. Colonialism is augmented by violence and proceeds to include the appropriation of land, settlement and expropriation of wealth. Then it moves into an extended phase of restructuring the economy and culture of the colony, a process that contains within it a dynamic for resistance, decolonisation and emergence 'beyond' the colonial. Theorising the development of human consciousness within colonialism, at both an individual psychological and collective national level, includes consideration of the long-term effects on both the colonised *and* the coloniser.[14] Such effects have been demonstrated to extend well beyond the visible departure of the colonial power from the colony and remain influential but in *different* ways within the life of the independent state and the ex-coloniser.

Postcolonial theory as an academic discipline is associated with the writings of those intellectuals who initially documented and reflected on decolonisation particularly in Africa and southern Asia in the 1950s and 1960s. The Algerian resistance of French colonialism formed the basis of such seminal texts as Albert Memmi's *The Colonizer and the Colonized* (1957) and Frantz Fanon's *The Wretched of the Earth* (1961). Fanon had also earlier used his experiences in French-ruled Martinique as the basis for *Black Skin, White Masks* (1952). Yet, as a fully-fledged academic discipline in western universities, postcolonial theory is a relative newcomer emerging only in the 1980s. It includes the work of Ashis Nandy, Stuart Hall and Edward Said. More recently, work by Homi Bhabha, Ania Loomba and Benita Parry, among others,[15] has been influential in post-colonial theory. The validity of postcolonial theory as a way of interpreting relations between Ireland and Britain has been hotly disputed by cultural critics and politicians, not least among the Irish. Before moving on to summarise and contextualise these disputes, it is important to expand on some of the key premises of postcolonial theory.

Colonialism is established by military violence and economic coercion but it is ultimately sustained through cultural and psychological means. Colonialism is based on the 'implacable dependence'[16] of its constituent conceptual parts, the coloniser and the colonised, which need each other in order to exist. Within the particular instance of Anglo-Irish colonial relations, Englishness (coloniser) is defined in a fixed and oppositional relation to Irishness (colonised). Although mutually dependent, this is not a relationship based on equality since colonialism operates a built-in valorisation favouring the coloniser. He (and it is invariably male) occupies a position of power over the colonised (feminised and infantilised), assuming superiority in a God-given, natural state of affairs. According to Fanon, colonialism is 'a systematic negation of the other person and a furious determination to deny the other person all attributes of humanity'.[17] From this follows a series of ideas that direct the policies of colonial management and inculcate deeply-embedded, more popular cultural attitudes among colonisers, colonial settlers and colonised. Ulster Protestants, conditioned by their experience of being a planted population, were not disposed to recognise differences among the colonised peoples that they dominated since 'another sign of the colonised's depersonalization is what one might call the mark of the plural'.[18] However, the coloniser's (English) metropolitan perspective also lacks discrimination. It fails to distinguish between colonised and colonials and considers Ulster Protestants as 'Irish'. Fanon, in *The Wretched of the Earth*, captures well the 'excessive patri-otic ardour' and the 'exaltation-resentment dialectic' (131) of Ulster Protestant feelings towards Britain especially since 1972. When specific identities are acknowledged in Britain it invariably reflects a colonial view. An example of this would be seeing the conflict in Northern Ireland as a 'tribal war' of religious differences between Catholics and Protestants. The core of colonial discourse manifests itself as a superior, dutiful attempt to 'improve' the colonised: 'The objective of colonial discourse is to construe the colonised as a population of degenerate types on the basis of racial origin, in order to justify conquest and to establish systems of administration and instruction'.[19] At the heart of the colo-nial duty to civilise the natives there is a contradiction: how can one 'improve' a race whose inferiority is genetically fixed? According to colonial logic, the colonised can never match its master since the colonised is deemed to possess no worthwhile indigenous culture. 'He represents not only the absence of values, but also the negation of values',[20] and comes to be personified by a raft of negative characteristics, which include being violent, alcohol-dependent, stupid, irrational, dirty, disordered, feminine and infantile. Correspondingly, the coloniser tries to monopolise all the opposite positive attributes such as being peace-loving, sober, intelligent, logical, pure, ordered, manly and adult. These might seem ridiculous caricatures that belong to the less enlightened period of High Imperialism (1880–1914) but they have lingered well into this century and recur in contemporary media representations, from US-produced films like *Far and Away* (1992) to British television serial dramas like *EastEnders*, *Coronation Street* and *Brookside*. Using the insights of postcolonial theory it is possible to view these reductive stereotypes not simply as fixed and irredeemably negative but rather as instances of exploitable weakness within a flawed colonial discourse: 'stress points within a system of representation which is unable to cope with difference and the unintelligible'.[21]

The status of the colonised in this analysis is clearly subordinate but not entirely passive or hopeless. They are forced to take on the language and culture of the coloniser to survive economically and socially. To survive psychically, they internalise the negative projections imposed on them by the dictates of the colonial regime. The maintenance of such a regime is dependent on its bases appearing fixed and ahistorical, but postcolonial theory insists on colonialism's historical contingency. Furthermore, since a non-indigenous language and culture can never simply be transplanted intact into an already existing culture and

1 Hollywood Irish: whimsical backwardness in *Far and Away* (Ron Howard, 1992). Courtesy of Universal City Studios, Inc. Photo: Philip Caruso

2 Irish character, British TV: alcohol and violence Jim McDonald (Charles Lawson) in
Coronation Street (1960–).
Courtesy of Granada TV

its values imposed indefinitely on a social order, the process of absorbing English
and the mimicry of Anglicised culture provides the conditions in which both are
transformed. Through a rediscovery of Irish language and Gaelic culture practised by the writers and intellectuals of the Irish Revival (though much Gaelic
material was circulated and popularised in translated form), literary and cultural
production of this period constituted a sustained moment of postcolonial resistance and opposition. The dominant feature of the Irish Revival was to invert the
negatives ascribed to Irishness and to engage in the collective celebration of Irish
national culture over and against Anglo-British culture. As critics like Fanon have
pointed out, however, in the act of decolonising the largely bourgeois (middle-
class) revolutionaries would inadvertently reflect the regime from which they
sought to disengage,[22] hence James Joyce's image of fractured, postcolonial Irish

culture being like the 'cracked-looking glass of a servant'. In Ireland, those who wished to define the culture of the nation restrictively rather than inclusively won out, preferring to exclude its urban and socialist threads, to marginalise its feminist and Ulster dissenting contributors.

If the achievement of Irish national independence was partial in territorial and political terms, more significantly, it produced a social and cultural revolution that 'ghosted' its former ruler. Both new states in Ireland sustained politically and culturally conservative regimes from their inception in 1921–22 until the 1960s when their apparent homogeneity began to be challenged both from within and externally. They continue to painfully work through the process of decolonising themselves culturally and psychologically, as well as trying to evolve politically and survive financially in a rapidly changing global economic order.

In this account the colonised – the dispossessed native Irish – might be seen as the sole victims of colonialism. This would be the kind of interpretation of Irish history given by traditional nationalist and some Marxist readings. These kinds of interpretation judge British imperialism as the cause of Ireland's wrongs and the English singularly guilty in the dock of history. Ulster Protestants, with their plantation settler origins, are typically cast as victims of an ideological deception, dupes protesting their Britishness when they are 'really' Irish. However, earlier postcolonial writers, such as Memmi and Fanon are now being carefully reread and interpreted by contemporary postcolonial theorists to produce more sophisticated readings, emphasising radical potentials within the earlier work. One such emphasis would be on Albert Memmi's insistence that 'if colonization destroys the colonized, it also rots the colonizer'.[23] It is this insight that distinguishes a liberating potential within postcolonial theory in comparison to traditional nationalist and Marxist applications since it views coloniser and colonised as 'co-victims'[24] in the structure of colonialism, arguing that 'victors are ultimately shown to be camouflaged victims'.[25] Each component is flawed because it exists within the system which degrades and dehumanises. If colonialism is initiated and sustained by coercive force inflicted on the colonised, it also causes long-term psychological disturbance to those who inflict it.[26] The coloniser is damaged because 'what he is actually renouncing [the humanity of the colonised] is part of himself'.[27] Living their internalised repression on a collective scale over generations, the colonisers (English) and those who rationally affiliate themselves to a British imperialist ideology (Ulster Protestants), have developed identities which are flawed by a superiority complex, believing their own sense of power and security long after such material conditions have ceased to exist, its own culture has become deracinated and alienation has set in. As Liam O'Dowd (1990) and Pamela Clayton (1996) have shown, postcolonial analysis is able to rationalise the limitations to national independence in the Irish Republic but also, crucially, to offer a coherent account of the dilemma of the Ulster Protestants in the decolonisation of Ireland and demonstrate the unstable condition of the former colonisers, the English.[28] To argue, however, that Britain and Ireland were restructured by colonialism and that they are both postcolonial does not mean that they are postcolonial in the same way.[29]

We can sum up so far by saying that postcolonial theory is a way of analysing the power relations between two countries within the structure of colonialism. One of its strengths as a body of theoretical work is that it invites comparisons between different examples of colonialism, noting similarities but allowing for the specific differences in each case. This comparative approach refreshingly discourages the view that Ireland's history is unique or idiosyn-cratic. Properly thought through, the logic of a postcolonial critique demands both the critical reassessment of the project for Irish national independence and the compassionate re-evaluation of former colonisers, their ideologies and cultural expression. In its more testing applications, postcolonial theory is not driven by the desire to see colonisers get their comeuppance; instead it attempts, as Stuart Hall suggests, to re-conceptualise the structuring presence of colonialism itself, to imagine 'not only "after" but "going beyond" the colonial'.[30]

Arguing at the crossroads: historical and cultural debates, 1988–98

The handiest definition of a postcolonial society is one whose leaders persistently claim it is not postcolonial.[31]

Since the mid-1980s, it is significant that the idea of applying postcolonial theory to Ireland has been both stubbornly resisted and enthusiastically explored by different academic, media and political commentators. In the final section of this chapter, I want to briefly explore the critical gaps between the vehement denials, the qualified affirmations and the popular, fashionable use of the term to describe Ireland. In doing so, I will examine how some of the key ideas within postcolonial theory discussed in the previous section relate to other modes of historical and cultural criticism that have emerged in the same period. Given the constraints of space, this section cannot offer a comprehen-sive survey of critical debate within or about Ireland since the mid-1980s,[32] but it provides the co-ordinates for understanding the dynamics of Irish cultural criticism. Film and television representations can be placed within this context and more fully understood.

The last decade has witnessed the continued importance of debates, both professional and popular, about the significance of modern history to contem-porary Irish life. A so-called 'revisionist' view of history had emerged in the 1970s, which continued to provoke debate in the 1980s and beyond. Revisionist historians set out to write a kind of politically neutral, less celebratory history than the generation before them. Through empirical methodologies, including the introduction of economic analysis to Irish historiography, revisionists sought to produce a more objective account of the past and act as a corrective to accounts offered by partial nationalist and unionist historians. Revisionism emerged for several reasons: partly from disillusionment with the achievement of dominant political ideologies in post-partition Ireland; partly as a critical, distancing response to the resurgence of political violence in Northern Ireland in the late-1960s; partly because of a liberal squeamishness about the origins of the Republic in political violence earlier in the century. Instead, revisionists tended to emphasise the consensual forces of Irish parliamentary movements and, by implication, favoured the continuities of political models established under British rule. To its critics, revisionism represented a pro-British 'histori-ography of the Irish counter-revolution',[33] but to exponents the process of revi-sion is intrinsic to all historical re-evaluation: 'to say "revisionist" should just be another way of saying "historian".'[34]

Postcolonial theory added mustard to this debate by offering alternative models to explain Ireland's modern development, its relations with Britain and the nature of its European historical context. Advocates tended to come from the disciplines of literature, cultural studies and sociology while many of the detractors were historians and economists who perhaps felt that the integrity of their specialist areas were being corrupted by promiscuous interdisciplinary methods. Some historians disputed suggested colonial analogies but others have been inclined to offer degrees of qualified acknowledgement. For instance, John Whyte argues that although a colonial explanation is partly acceptable it is not appropriate to conditions in Ireland *after* 1921,[35] completely missing the point that postcolonial theories seek to explore the after-life of colonialism. Roy Foster, a *bête noire* figure for traditional nationalists, has been moved to argue, like Whyte, for a qualified consideration of Ireland under the Union (1800–1921) as a 'kind of metropolitan colony',[36] similar but distinct from other colonies. His dissection of the intimate nature of 'connections in Irish-English history' shyly acknowledges the relevance of certain Indian critics to Irish subject matter.[37] Some historians inclined to dismiss the implications of post-colonial theories explored Ireland's past in the context of European history at the same time as the Republic's political establishment were enjoying a more central role in the EU. In the late 1980s and early 1990s, it became *de rigeur* to be European as a badge of the country's post-colonial, self-confident modernity and political maturity. Yet in contrast, Joseph Lee used European comparative perspectives not as an index of modernity but to expose the economic and social failures of Irish nationalism in both its protectionist and open-market phases.[38] Drawing extensively on parallels between twentieth-century Ireland and small, Euro-Scandinavian countries like Denmark, Norway and Switzerland (none of whom experienced imperial colonisation), he writes of Ireland's 'highly unusual colonial-type history' (xiii), 'long centuries of foreign dominance' and the consequent 'dependency syndrome' (627) of the Irish psyche. He concludes with ambivalent satisfaction that Irish history 'cannot be encompassed within conventional categories of either European or Third World historiography. It is none the worse for that' (xiii).

Less surprisingly, perhaps, historians and cultural critics arguing from liberal unionist positions felt that it was 'incorrect' to term Ireland, now or in the past, as '"colonial" or "post-colonial" pure and simple [since] this description excludes perspectives which an appreciation of the European context would allow'.[39] This is to misconstrue complicated historical links between Ireland and Europe's imperial past. Paradoxically, though Ireland was an early objective for English colonial expansion and treated, though disconcertingly close, as a colony, many Irish men and women were active participants in the British imperial project further afield, serving in its military, managing plantations, administering Empire and doing missionary work. Edna Longley has argued that 'although the term "colonial" may fit some aspects of Irish experience, most historians would qualify or specify its uses, and dispute the one-size-fits-all zeal of most [postcolonial] theorists', suggesting instead that the idea of 'internal European colonisation' is a more appropriate term to apply to Ireland.[40] Longley had previously discussed 'the reality of the North [of Ireland] as a frontier-region, a cultural corridor, a zone where Ireland and Britain permeate one another'.[41] Characteristically, those who refute or heavily qualify Ireland's postcolonial status, emphasise the European dimension, stress the benign inter-connections or permeation of Ireland and Britain, and overlook the point that 'openess towards other cultures does not entail accepting them solely on their own terms, all the more so when a minority or subaltern culture is attempting to come out from under the shadow of a major colonial power'.[42] One critic, John Wilson Foster, has made a number of interventions following the Anglo-Irish Agreement (1985) to articulate a liberal-humanist, unionist position. In 1988–89, sensing that Ulster Protestants had become associated with saying 'No' politically, he argued that intellectuals who endorsed unionism had a task 'to promote positive formations out of this distinctive negativity'.[43] His analysis explicitly recognised that there was a 'colonial strand in Ulster's history', that the Britishness of contemporary Ulster Protestants is not simply provincialism but 'some species of colonialism or postcolonialism'.[44] Then, extensively quoting Albert Memmi, Foster details political disenfranchisement (1972 and 1985), the feeling of being negatively 'stereotyped, essentialised' and his sense of cultural impoverishment to argue that the Ulster Protestant 'already experiences in some sense, and exhibits the symptoms of, *the condition of being colonized*' (21, his emphasis). But Foster's use of Memmi is revealing in its partiality. Citing material exclusively from 'The Portrait of the Colonized', he ignores the section about colonialist frustrations and dilemmas ('The Colonizer who Refuses') that are clearly analogous to Ulster Protestants. Foster's analysis robs the clothes of postcolonial theory in order to claim for Ulster Protestants the sole 'victim-status' mobilised so effectively by the discourses of anti-colonial Irish nationalism. In his interpretation, this would shift responsibility for Northern Ireland's political failures away from unionism and back to the postcolonial centre at Westminster. However, this strategy overlooks Nandy's insight that 'theories which fail to acknowledge the degradation of the coloniser are theories which indirectly admit the superiority of the oppressors and collaborate with them' (xv). In fact, Foster's eagerness to become a victim illustrates perfectly Memmi's analysis of the desires of the colonialist who refuses colonialism: he can vainly attempt to 'accept the position of the colonized' thus becoming a 'turncoat'; he can remain silent in dissent; or 'if he cannot stand this silence and make his life a perpetual compromise, he can end up by leaving the colony'.[45] Having been based for several years in British Columbia, it is clear which course Foster was forced to take in order to achieve his own goal of self-realisation.

Foster has taken issue on several occasions with cultural critics who came to be associated with the Field Day project. Founded initially as a theatre company in 1980 by Brian Friel and Stephen Rea, it soon became involved in publishing pamphlets and a notorious anthology of Irish writing (1991). Academics like Seamus Deane and Declan Kiberd, although they criticised the calcified nationalism originating from the Irish Revival, maintained that Field Day's 'analysis of the situation derives from the conviction that it is, above all, a colonial crisis' and that anti-colonial resistance – culturally and politically – was a logical response;[46] that Irish nationalism was itself a far more complex, variegated phenomenon than revisionists often portrayed;[47] that past nationalist violence could not simply be equated with contemporary IRA violence; and, finally, that nationalism contained progressive as well as conservative forces.[48] Moreover, it was those who explored colonial parallels elsewhere in the world who argued that forgetting the past was precisely the symptomatic aporia of Ireland's colonised mentality. The problematic features of these debates were twofold, embracing, first, the extent to which critics of Irish nationalism remained attached to the idea of the nation and, second, the search for a way to adequately account for the sense of Ireland's protracted crisis of identity, of being caught in a 'transitional tension between revivalist and modernist perspectives'.[49]

The notion of postnationalism, an attempt at breaking the circuit and going beyond nation-state nationalism, has been articulated by Richard Kearney, a philosopher closely associated with *The Crane Bag* (1979–85), an influential cultural journal. Since the late 1980s, Kearney has taken up and expanded the terms of revisionist and Field Day critiques of Irish nationalist orthodoxy. Akin to postcolonial theory, postnationalism deconstructs regressive currents within nationalism while emboldening the emancipatory elements within its discourse. Likewise, this dialectic is carried through to a 'critique of [Irish nationalism's] mirror-image, British nationalism … the spectre of Irish nationalism might be said to represent Britain's return of the repressed'.[50] Heady with iconoclastic *brio* from European philosophy and contemporary psychoanalysis, postnationalism healthily gives the lie to Ireland's exceptionality within a continental context. It proposes an overhaul of nationalism's central tenets. Rather than being fixated on a singular identity (Irish), a discrete territory (the whole island of Ireland) whose origins lie in history (past-orientated), postnationalism foregrounds the potentially liberating ideas of multiple identities (regional, federal, communal), the concept of dispersed geo-affiliations (including Ireland's diaspora) and a concern with the contemporary world and its futures. For a decade, Kearney has been an advocate of a 'Europe of the regions',[51] informed by the idea that 'beyond the "modern" alternatives of national independence and multinational dependence lies another possibility – a post national model of [mutual] interdependence'.[52] Kearney's postnationalism asserts that nationalism in Ireland is arrested, held up in its development, while in Britain 'a kind of permanent immaturity was chosen'[53] as a stand-in for nationalism. Postnationalism cuts across nationalism by positing instead the concept of critical regionalism, a federal system of regions within a European grouping. Kearney's published works do explore political practicalities and, for our purposes, it is important to recognise his attempt to give formal expression to identities at a sub-national level, to retain a shared sense of belonging, a desire of people to identify with place.

Some of the most recent work applying postcolonial theory to Ireland[54] intersects at this point producing a confluence of critical ideas. The more radical of Irish postcolonial theorists, borrowing from contemporary Indian and diasporic critics, have argued the need to think beyond the concept of the nation itself. Such an argument is based on the idea that nationalism in Ireland took its character from that of British imperialism; anti-colonial resistance and pro-unionist reaction were twin derivatives, transferred from imperial centre to colonial margin. From a postcolonial perspective, however, all power does not lie with the coloniser, it is provisional and contingent. All ideologies – nationalism included – are susceptible to active re-appropriation and unconscious *mis*-appropriation, thus such ideologies, in the passage from centre to margins, are liable to unpredictable transformations. While it was the case in Ireland and other colonies that the configuration of political power tended to imitate the conservatism of the former rulers, imperfect mimicry took place under the pressure of the local circumstances, often including authoritarian excesses. Furthermore, nationalism 'always creates a spurious image of unity, it tends to deny internal differences'.[55] Postcolonial theorists have interrogated this homogenising tendency by exploring the apparently fixed dichotomy of the coloniser/colonised relationship. In order to dissolve the colonial structure, postcolonialism tries in its critical work to release what it terms the 'subaltern' undercurrents within nationalism. This term spans a diverse and disparate range, including significant percentages of the population such as women, the working class, the unemployed and those in poverty; smaller groupings and individuals articulating political and creative ideas, from artists and writers to republican socialists and dissenting radicals; and subcultures like the Travellers, people of colour, homosexuals and refugees. The subaltern are, or have been, subordinated, suppressed, outcast or rendered invisible in the official versions of the past constructed by both postcolonial Irish states. Although 'the history of subaltern social groups is necessarily fragmented and episodic',[56] by locating and giving voice to the subaltern elements of gender, class, race, sexuality and so on in Irish culture, postcolonial interpretations of Irish culture attempt to cut across the dichotomy of coloniser and colonised, and critically interrogate the post-colonial state.

Within Irish historical and cultural criticism, some of the most influential work undertaken over the last decade has been the analysis of women, gender and, more recently, race and sexuality. Feminist historians like Margaret MacCurtain and Maria Luddy in particular have highlighted the gendered, sexualised nature of colonialism's and nationalism's historical and political discourses. In 1991, historian Margaret Ward argued strongly for 'putting gender into history',[57] stating that research on women needed to move beyond the transitional stage of contribution history to a more radical agenda. In addition to asking what contribution Irish women made to established male political movements and debates such as nationalism and the trade unions, the impetus of a gendered history should be to 'challenge the categories and concepts of periodisation' that have been defined in male terms (19) and question the apparently unproblematic advances that modernisation brought to Ireland, especially for women (21). Above all, Ward argues on behalf of many feminist scholars who do not want research on women to remain ghettoised, separate from mainstream, male-orientated history. Gendered history 'stresses the interrelationships of women and men's lives, using inclusive historical perspectives in order to analyse [their] experiences' (22). Ward is alert to the history of disputed priorities for feminists who are nationalist or republican but does not see them as incompatible discourses. Eavan Boland, a poet, has written of 'the virulence and necessity of the idea of a nation'.[58] She recognises that Ireland as nation has in the past been figured as an essentialised female personage – variously as the Shan Bhean Bhocht (Poor Old Woman), Cathleen ni Houlihan and Mother Ireland. Although these images are flawed and have been used to support a patriarchal order, these are not inherent properties to nationalism. Instead, women writers and intellectuals should engage in repossessing the concept (150), building on the 'emblematic relation between the defeats of womanhood and the suffering of the nation' (148). The highlighting of progressive tendencies within nationalism in an international context has been taken up by Carol Coulter, a writer and journalist. She advocates a postcolonial interpretation of Ireland's economic status 'Between the First and the Third Worlds'[59] and an internationalist feminist analysis of Irish women's experience looking at parallel histories in Latin America and the Middle East, but is sensitive to the dangers of neo-colonial exportation of western values in so doing.[60] She rejects the idea that nationalism and feminism are inherently polar opposites in colonial situations, the one representing a traditional, religiously-inflected strand, the other a modern, secular strand (4). The idea that women are 'doubly marginalised', as females in an ex-colonial state, can be seen by some as a potentially creative position. It 'may yet provide a space in which Irish women can make and say something different of ourselves as women and of the many traditions which are our burden and our inheritance'.[61]

Gerardine Meaney has observed that 'the fundamentalist streak in northern protestantism is just as hostile to feminism as is Catholicism' (193), opening up the notion of feminist alliances between women in the two states and within Northern Ireland, which have not been sustained. Arguing from a position unsympathetic to postcolonial parallels, Edna Longley states that 'nationalism and unionism in Ireland are dying ideologies, death-cult ideologies'[62] borne out of male insecurities and damaging to women. She offers a liberal alternative of 'a feminist "connective"' which eschews 'male polarisation' and allows women 'to inhabit a range of relations rather than a single allegiance ... to admit to more varied, mixed, fluid and relational kinds of identity' (185). Such calls for pluralism have found scant expression in the political dualisms of Northern Ireland. As Ailbhe Smyth has observed, in the obsessive, difficult process of declining Irish identities, 'pluralising identity does not automatically reduce the risk of eternalising and essentialism ... but it does mean that it is no longer assumed to be the same for all'.[63] Working out of the impetus created by feminist writing, a few critics are exploring lesbian and gay dimensions to Irish history, culture and cinema, including a critique of the misogynist and homophobic strands within nationalism, republicanism and unionism.[64] Contemporary research is working eclectically on what postcolonial theories would term the subaltern elements of gender, race and sexuality to interrogate and complicate male-orientated and heterosexist assumptions within established political ideologies and cultural identities in Ireland.

This short examination of Ireland's historical development and critical debates about the most suitable explanatory models and methods (revisionist, postcolonial, feminist, etc.) should be used to reread the economic and social developments outlined in the first half of this chapter. Ireland is a small country. Its indigenous broadcasting, publishing and the newspress networks are intimate. They provide a space for intellectuals to engage in contemporary debate. Some journalists and academics have popularised a particular version of Ireland in newspaper articles and broadcasts as well as their books, pamphlets and teaching. A common view would see the Republic's short history as a unilinear process of progressive maturation rather than one of political conflict and social dynamic. It would foreground current economic prosperity, the reversal of emigration, EU membership, new laws on decriminalising homosexuality and legalising divorce and a burgeoning cultural renaissance as signs that the country has 'come of age'. Other, more sceptical interventions temper this exuberant celebration of modernisation in both of the post-colonial states within Ireland. Such scepticism focuses on continued economic and social inequalities, persistent poverty and homelessness, racism, organised crime, regional under-development and political injustices, north and south.

While it is clear that there is little agreement between intellectuals about how best to interpret Ireland's historical development and cultural production, there is a populist view in the Republic that it is over and done with its colonial past. The liberal consensus view that Ireland became 'modernised' and developed since the 1960s has been challenged over the last decade. Critics like Luke Gibbons, Liam O'Dowd and Declan Kiberd have suggested that using Anglo-American indices of modernisation and benefits may have been misguided. The unquestioning embrace of international capital failed to determine whether it was appropriate to Ireland's circumstances; it also failed to consider the disadvantages of global consumerist materialism. Within such a model of development, Ireland was invariably characterised as backward, a temporal metaphor perhaps for lingering, racial notions of Ireland's primitivism. It is at this point that we can see a convergence of issues: the question of Ireland's postcoloniality becomes closely associated with debates about the nature of Ireland's (post)modernity. A countervailing reading of history might be posited: 'Irish society did not have to await the twentieth century to undergo the shock of modernity: disintegration and fragmentation were already part of its history so that, in a crucial but not always welcome sense, Irish culture experienced modernity before its time'.[65] Economically and politically disempowered by colonialism, Ireland has sustained the social fracture of emigration and its profound cultural consequences, exhibiting the symptoms of modernity before its time. Thus the late nineteenth century can be read as a kind of precursor, suggesting that Ireland's economy and labour had become integrated into an Anglo-American order earlier than the much-vaunted post-1960s. Contesting the idea that the Irish are late in arriving, Kiberd points out that from the late nineteenth century the Irish were among the earliest colonials to resist, decolonise and begin dismantling the empire. Challenging the British colonial self-image of advancement, he argues that Ireland could be seen as 'a crucible of modernity', that postcolonial Ireland is politically more advanced and culturally innovative than its old master, England.[66] Indeed, some would argue that the 'modernisation' of the Republic from the 1960s onwards merely swapped what was left of a colonial dependency on Britain to a dependency on neo-colonial multinationals. The extent of the Republic's foreign debt in the 1980s raised uncomfortable similarities with those of the Third World and it might be argued that adopting a neo-liberal economic strategy has overly exposed the Republic to shifts in global economic systems and to exploitative commercial practices. Fintan O'Toole has written trenchantly about the Republic's 'Black Hole', where foreign businesses import materials but export products and profits to leave marginal benefits for the Irish economy.[67] Dependent on massive subventions from the UK exchequer, the economy in Northern Ireland has been likened to a Victorian work house, reliant on fiscal charity to compensate for a lack of a self-sustaining productive base.[68]

It is pertinent for us to ask what kinds of cultural production and social identities are produced under the economic and demographic conditions experienced in Ireland? At one extreme, Ireland's embrace of the international was proof to some of its disintegration into oblivion: 'Ireland is a nothing – a no-thing – an interesting nothing, to be sure, composed of colourful parts, a nothing-mosaic. It is advertising prose and Muzak,'[69] a nostalgic yearning for the fullness and unity of the past. An altogether more optimistic interpretation is suggested by the *Irish Times* journalist, Fintan O'Toole, who sees Ireland as often 'something that happens elsewhere'. For O'Toole, a postmodern Ireland exceeds the physical bounds of the island; it exists both 'here and there'. Through his journalism, published collections of essays and broadcasting, O'Toole has become one of the best known and articulate commentators on Ireland's postmodern condition. He argues that Ireland's development has been unusually accelerated, missing out the middle industrial/manufacturing phase associated with European modernisation to 'become a post-modern society without ever fully becoming a modern one'.[70] While the historical condition of postmodernity is cause for anxiety or exasperation in some, postmodernist critical theory and cultural expression celebrates in the face of adversity. O'Toole explores the cultural possibilities of Ireland's radically open, 'ex-isle' status, arguing that the grand narratives of nationalism and religion have been subverted by the permanent impermanence of emigration. Thus Irish people have had to be physically adaptable and develop mental mutability. Ireland's globalisation means that its culture *is* its production. To retain its dynamism it is necessarily a hybrid of culture and kitsch. Habitually, the new and the now butt-end with the old and the then. Accelerated by media saturation to an unusual degree, time and space become confused, the distinction between reality and image is blurred; irony and iconoclasm, once deployed as weapons of the subordinate, now excel in intertextuality and experimentation with narrative. O'Toole as a postmodernist can even claim that 'in the late twentieth century, the metaphor of margin and centre no longer works',[71] qualifying a key term in postcolonial critique by saying that the globe is now multicentred.

While there is much that is accurate and even liberating about considering Irish culture in postmodern terms, others question the idea that 'the unstable and the open-ended are virtues in themselves' and maintain that international recognition for films, music and literature 'is not quite the same as allowing the transnational corporations to walk all over you'.[72] Enjoying the trappings of consumerism and the kudos of internationally recognised cultural achievement should not distract one from objecting to continuing inequalities between major powers and peripheral states. In 1980s Ireland it was possible to see that contact with multinational corporate economies also brought cultural values, which acted catalytically to activate new forms of fundamentalism in conjunction with residual strains of conservatism in Irish society. One of the strengths of postcolonial analyses is that they always see that such cultural contacts may stir the progressive and radical potentials in what appear to be residues of discredited and rejected ideas such as nationalism. Gibbons has made the telling point that 'modernisation is not solely an external force, but also requires the active transformation of a culture from within, a capacity to engage critically with its own past'.[73] This retains the notion of agency within subordination rather than passive subjugation under economic and media imperialism. In a fascinating essay on broadcasting and Irish identity, Martin McLoone combines postcolonial insight with the postmodern politics of 'critical regionalism', a term coined by Frampton, to consider the future for Irish cultural production.[74] Occupying a curious post-colonial location in a global structure, 'the arrière-garde has the capacity to cultivate a resistant, identity-giving culture while at the same time having a discreet recourse to universal technique'.[75] The excitement but also the difficulties inherent in emergent cultural activities in a global economy come from being at the intersection of the local and the universal. If cultural production expresses an individual and collective response to economic forces and social pressures, it is not a direct relationship but one mediated by differing degrees of human agency and political power. Dominant and subordinate groups – at transnational, national and sub-national levels – all attempt to control their representation in the world. We can read in the different screen representations of Ireland all the antagonisms of nationalism, gender, region, class and generation, but to do this we have to consider the particularities of their histories – to think locally and globally simultaneously. This strategy is not an altogether novel one, but it enables us to better gauge the particular condition of Ireland's cultural production. Temporally, there is a sense of going back to the future; spatially, there is the conviction that 'for a small island, Ireland is a very big country'.[76]

In this opening chapter, we have critically examined an outline history of Ireland, concentrating on the twentieth century but acknowledging the roots of forces and ideas from earlier periods. We have seen how Ireland may be located historically and culturally as an 'in-between' country and that this is due to the nature of its economic and political past. Intimately connected to the British empire and the United States of America, through waves of permanent immigration and more transitory back-and-forth migrations, Ireland and Irish identities exemplify all the contradictions and possibilities of postcolonial and postmodern development in a century dominated by the political ideology of nationalism. In analysing the cultural debates of the last decade, we have seen how a postcolonial interpretation of history has been disputed. One of the chief benefits of postcolonial theory is that it offers a critique of Irish nationalism without denying that ideology's historical origins, characterising it as colonially imitative and flawed, but a necessary stage in deconstructing colonial definitions of the relationship between Britain and Ireland. It is a central argument of this book that, following independence, although cultural production in the form of radio, film and television did mainly serve to represent mirror-images of British and Irish nationalism, north and south, these media also contained and became the conduit for the creative critique of nationalism itself. Technological innovations, economic dependencies and cultural borrowing in the after-life of colonial relations meant that broadcasting and cinema in both parts of Ireland were forced to adopt Anglo-American models of these modern media. But picture house, wireless and television set were adapted to indigenous, Irish conditions, never simply imposed. These media represented Ireland's modernity, a complex collision of a global Anglo-American culture with a local, native culture that was itself already bifurcated politically, demographically and culturally. It is the history of cinema's uneven and problematic but nevertheless pervasive influence on Irish cultural life in the twentieth century that we examine in the next chapter.

Notes

1 M. McLoone, 'National cinema and cultural identity', in J. Hill, M. McLoone and P. Hainsworth (eds), *Border Crossing: Film in Ireland, Britain and Europe* (Belfast, Institute of Irish Studies, 1994), 155.

2 B. Porter, *The Lion's Share: A short history of British imperialism, 1850–1983* (Harlow, Longman, 1984), 255.

3 R. Kearney, *Postnationalist Ireland: Politics, culture, philosophy* (London, Routledge, 1997), 1-12.

4 B. Crick, 'An Englishman considers his passport', *The Irish Review*, 5 (Autumn 1988), 5.

5 The Order was founded in 1795 in Derry and takes its name from a Dutch monarch, the Protestant, William III of Orange, who fought a decisive battle to defeat the Catholic, James II, at a crossing on the Boyne River. Today its numerous local societies organise a season of public demonstrations and marches to celebrate the historical tradition of Protestant religion and power in Northern Ireland.

6 D. G. Boyce considers Unionism to be a form of 'Ulster political Protestantism: not a nationalism'. See 'Marginal Britons: The Irish', in P. Colls and P. Dodd (eds), *Englishness: Politics and culture, 1880–1920* (London, Croom Helm, 1984), 242.

7 A. Gramsci, *Selections from Cultural Writings* (London, Lawrence & Wishart, 1985), 117.

8 J. Connolly, 'Labour and the proposed partition of Ireland', in P. Beresford Ellis (ed.), *James Connolly: Selected writings* (London, Pluto Press, 1988), 275.

9 C. Ó Gráda, *A Rocky Road: The Irish economy since the 1920s* (Manchester, Manchester University Press, 1997), 4.

10 L. O'Dowd, 'Development or dependency? State, economy and society in Northern Ireland', in P. Clancy *et al.* (eds), *Irish Society: Sociological perspectives* (Dublin, Institute of Public Administration, 1995), 133.

11 D. Harkness, *Ireland in the Twentieth Century: Divided island* (Basingstoke, Macmillan, 1996), 121, states that in 1990, 68 per cent of GNP in Northern Ireland came from the services sector compared to 4 per cent from agriculture and 28 per cent from industrial production.

12 Compare the perspectives offered by D. O'Hearn, in *Free Trade or Managed Trade? Trading between two worlds* (Belfast, CRD, 1994) and L. Kennedy who argues against the validity of such parallels in 'Modern Ireland: post-colonial society or post-colonial pretensions?', *The Irish Review*, 13 (Winter/Spring 1993), 107-121.

13 L. O'Dowd, 'New Introduction', in A. Memmi, *The Colonizer and the Colonized*, tr. H. Greenfeld (London, Earthscan Publications, 1990), 48.

14 For example, see the perspectives of two Scottish writers, T. Nairn, *The Break-up of Britain* (London, Verso, 1981) and the journalism of Neal Ascherson. For a seminal application of colonial theory to the study of Irish cultural production, see D. Cairns and S. Richards, *Writing Ireland* (Manchester, Manchester University Press, 1988). For

more recent theorisation, see B. Parry 'Resistance Theory: Theorising resistance', in C. Barker, P. Hulme and M. Iversen (eds), *Colonial Discourse/Postcolonial Theory* (Manchester, Manchester University Press, 1994), 180-93.

15 A. Nandy, *The Intimate Enemy: Loss and recovery of self under colonialism* (Oxford and Dehli, Oxford University Press, 1983); E. Said, *Orientalism* (Harmondsworth, Penguin, 1978) and *Culture and Imperialism* (London, Vintage, 1993); G. Spivak, *The Post-Colonial Critic: Interviews, strategies, dialogues* (London, Routledge, 1990); H. K. Bhabha, *The Location of Culture* (London, Routledge, 1994); A. Loomba, *Colonialism/Postcolonialism* (London, Routledge, 1998).

16 Memmi, *Colonizer*, 7.

17 F. Fanon, *The Wretched of the Earth*, tr. C. Farrington (Harmondsworth, Penguin, 1985), 200.

18 Memmi, *Colonizer*, 151.

19 Bhabha, *Location of Culture*, 70.

20 Fanon, *Wretched*, 32.

21 L. Gibbons, in K. Rockett, L. Gibbons and J. Hill, *Cinema and Ireland* (London, Routledge, 1988), 249. There has been considerable debate among the Irish in Britain about the way to interpret English soap opera deployment of Irish characters and story lines that feature traits, behaviour and narrative outcomes offensive to some audiences. See M. Doyle, 'Is this really the face of the Irish?', *The Irish Post* (11 April 1998), 20–1; M. Free, 'Liberal with stereotypes', *The Irish Post* (13 March 1999), 17.

22 Fanon, *Wretched*, 180.

23 Memmi, *Colonizer*, 15.

24 Nandy, *Intimate Enemy*, 99.

25 Nandy, *Intimate Enemy*, xvi.

26 Fanon, *Wretched*, 215-16 and 253.

27 Memmi, *Colonizer*, 86.

28 O'Dowd, 'New Introduction', 47, P. Clayton, *Enemies and Passing Friends: Settler ideologies in twentieth century Ulster* (London, Pluto Press, 1996).

29 Loomba, *Colonialism/Postcolonialism*, 19.

30 The phrase is Stuart Hall's from 'When was the post-colonial? Thinking at the limit', in I. Chambers and L. Curti (eds), *The Post-Colonial Question: Common skies, divided horizons* (London, Routledge, 1996), 253.

31 D. Kiberd, *Graph*, 13 (Winter 1992/Spring 1993), 7.

32 See also W. J. McCormack, *Battle of the Books* (Dublin, Lilliput Books, 1986), for a short, trenchant account of cultural debate from the 1960s to the 1980s.

33 D. Fennell, *The Revision of Irish Nationalism* (Dublin, Open Air, 1989), 66.

34 R. F. Foster's short article, 'We are all revisionists now', *The Irish Review*, 1 (1986), 1–5, calmly states the case for revisionism. For an example of the emphasis of revisionism, see R. F. Foster, *Modern Ireland: 1600–1972* (London, Penguin, 1989), Ch. 18, 'The "New" Nationalism'.

35 J. Whyte, *Interpreting Northern Ireland* (Oxford, Clarendon, 1990), 179.

36 R. F. Foster, *Paddy & Mr Punch: Connections in Irish and English History* (London, Penguin, 1993), 86.

37 Foster, *Paddy & Mr Punch*, 368, fn 4. The critic in question is Ashis Nandy, the book *The Intimate Enemy*.

38 J. J. Lee, Ireland 1912-85: *Politics and society* (Cambridge, Cambridge University Press, 1989).

39 B. Walker, 'Ireland's historical position – "colonial" or "European?"', *The Irish Review*, 9 (1990), 38.

40 E. Longley, *The Living Stream: Literature and revisionism in Ireland* (Newcastle Upon Tyne, Bloodaxe Books, 1994), 30.

41 E. Longley, 'From Kathleen to anorexia: the breakdown of Irelands', in *A Dozen LIPs* (Dublin, Attic Press, 1994), 195.

42 L. Gibbons, *Transformations in Irish Culture* (Cork, Cork University Press, 1996), 179.

43 J. W. Foster, 'Radical regionalism', *The Irish Review*, 7 (Autumn 1989), 12.

44 J. W. Foster, 'Culture and colonisation: A view from the North', *The Irish Review*, 5 (Autumn 1988), 22. Citations from this article are shown in parenthesises in the body of the text. A useful exegesis of Foster's critical work is provided by R. Kirkland, *Literature and Culture in Northern Ireland since 1965: Moments of Danger* (Harlow, Longman, 1996), 98–102.

45 Memmi, *Colonizer*, 109.

46 S. Deane, 'Introduction', *Nationalism, Colonialism and Literature* (Minneapolis, University of Minnesota Press, 1990), 6.

47 L. Gibbons, 'Challenging the canon: revisionism and cultural criticism', in S. Deane (ed.), *The Field Day Anthology of Irish Writing, Volume 3* (Derry, Field Day, 1991), 568.

48 D. Kiberd, *Inventing Ireland: The literature of the modern nation* (London, Jonathan Cape, 1995), 642. Liz Curtis ably demonstrates the variegated nature of the Irish Revival period politics, including suffragist and nationalist feminism, agri-co-op organisation and pacifist and socialist strands, as well as the parliamentary and extra-parliamentary activities set against British imperialism in Ireland. See *The Cause of Ireland* (Belfast, Beyond the Pale, 1994), 160–80.

49 R. Kearney, *Transitions: Narratives in modern Irish culture* (Dublin, Wolfhound Press, 1988), 10.

50 R. Kearney, *Postnationalist Ireland: Politics, culture, philosophy* (London, Routledge, 1997), 9 and 11.

51 R. Kearney, *Across the Frontiers: Ireland in the 1990s* (Dublin, Wolfhound, 1988), 7–28. See also Kearney, *Postnationalist Ireland*, 180–8.

52 Kearney, *Postnationalist Ireland*, 60.

53 T. Nairn, *The Enchanted Glass: Britain and its monarchy* (London, Picador, 1990), 137.

54 See C. Graham, 'Post nationalism/post-colonialism: Reading Irish culture', *Irish Studies Review*, 8 (1994), 35–7; G. Smyth, 'The past, the post and the utterly changed: intellectual responsibility and Irish cultural criticism', *Irish Studies Review*, 10 (1995), 25–9; C. Graham, 'Rejoinder: the Irish "Post"-? A reply to Gerry Smyth', *Irish Studies Review*, 13 (1995/96), 33–6; K. Barry, 'Critical notes on post-colonial aesthetics', *Irish Studies Review*, 14 (1996), 2–11; and B. Grey, 'Irishness – a global and gendered identity?', *Irish Studies Review*, 16 (1996), 24–8. The following paragraph is particularly indebted to C. Graham's lucid exposition, '"Liminal Spaces": post-colonial theories and Irish culture', *The Irish Review*, 16 (1994), 29–43.

55 Kiberd, *Graph*, 7.

56 A. Gramsci, 'Notes on Italian history', in G. Nowell-Smith (ed.), *Selections from Prison Notebooks* (London, Lawrence & Wishart, 1971), 54–5.

57 *The Missing Sex: Putting women into Irish history* (Dublin, Attic Press, 1991), 18. Subsequent references to this essay are indicated by page numbers in parentheses in main text.

58 E. Boland, 'Outside History', in *Object Lessons* (Manchester, Carcanet, 1995), 125. Subsequent references to this essay are indicated by page numbers in parentheses in main text.

59 C. Coulter, *Ireland: Between the First and the Third worlds* (Dublin, Attic Press, 1990).

60 C. Coulter, *The Hidden Tradition: Feminism, women and nationalism in Ireland* (Cork, Cork University Press, 1993). Subsequent references are indicated by page numbers in parentheses in main text.

61 G. Meaney, 'Sex and nation: Women in Irish culture and politics', in *A Dozen LIPs* (Dublin, Attic Press, 1994), 203.

62 E. Longley, 'From Kathleen to anorexia', 183.

63 A. Smyth, 'Declining identities (lit. and fig.)', *Critical Survey*, 8:2 (1996), 148.

64 Three texts are useful introductions to an emergent field of research: K. Rose, *Diverse Communities: The evolution of a lesbian and gay politics in Ireland* (Cork, Cork University Press, 1994); Í. O'Carroll and E. Collins (eds), *Lesbian and Gay Visions of Ireland* (London, Cassell, 1995); and É. Walshe (ed.), *Sex, Nation and Dissent in Irish Writing* (Cork, Cork University Press, 1997).

65 Gibbons, *Transformations*, 6.

66 Kiberd, *Inventing Ireland*, 645.

67 F. O'Toole, *Black Hole, Green Card: The disappearance of Ireland* (Dublin, New Island Books, 1994), 11-12. See also D. O'Hearn, *Free Trade or Managed Trade?* (Belfast, CRD, 1994).

68 Bob Rowthorne, 'Northern Ireland: an economy in crisis', in P. Teague (ed.), *Beyond the Rhetoric* (London, Lawrence & Wishart, 1987), 117-26. See also Mike Tomlinson, 'Can Britain leave Ireland? The political economy of war and peace', *Race & Class*, 37:1 (July-September 1995), 10–14.

69 Vincent Buckley quoted in Fennell, *Revision of Irish Nationalism*, 91.

70 F. O'Toole, *A Mass for Jesse James: A journey through 1980s Ireland* (Dublin, Raven Arts Press, 1990), 35.

71 F. O'Toole, *The Ex-Isle of Erin: Images of a Global Ireland* (Dublin, New Island Books, 1996), 158.

72 T. Eagleton reviewing O'Toole's, '*The lie of the land*' *The Observer* (22 February 1998). For a succinct dismissal of postmodernism on empirical and theoretical grounds, see D. Strinati, *An Introduction to Theories of Popular Culture* (London, Routledge, 1995), 222–45.

73 Gibbons, *Transformations*, 3.

74 M. McLoone, 'Inventions and re-imaginings: some thoughts on identity and broadcasting in Ireland', in M. McLoone (ed.), *Culture, Identity and Broadcasting in Ireland* (Belfast, Institute of Irish Studies, 1991), 2-30.

75 K. Frampton, 'Towards a critical regionalism: six points for an architecture of resistance', in H. Foster (ed.), *Postmodern Culture* (London, Pluto Press, 1985), 20.

76 B. Quinn, 'Imagining Conamara', in P. Brennan and C. de Saint Phalle (eds), *Arguing at the Crossroads: Essays on changing Ireland* (Dublin, New Island Books, 1997), 44.

CHAPTER 2
A CENTURY OF CINEMA IN IRELAND

- What do we mean by a 'national cinema'?
- What are the six key phases in Irish cinema history?
- What kind of film culture exists in Ireland today?

From the margins to the millennium?

National cinemas do not only persist as a means to counter or accommodate Hollywood, they are sustained and shaped by local purposes of a social, economic, cultural and national nature.[1]

This chapter identifies and analyses six phases in Irish cinema history to provide a context for the case studies of films in chapters 3–6. It begins by briefly considering the concept of national cinema and how it relates to the issues of political nationalism and national identity discussed in the previous chapter. It moves on to examine why a national cinema did not emerge in Ireland until the 1970s. In common with many other cinemas in Europe and elsewhere this century, Ireland has had to contend with the economic power of California-based studios. While not the only producer of film in the country, Hollywood is the preeminent force in the cinema of the USA, and was at its height in the anglophone film world between the 1920s and the late 1950s. Ireland's cinematic development was also shaped to a lesser but significant extent by the proximity of Britain's economy and its film industry. These factors, in combination with local economic, political and cultural conditions in both Irish states, contributed to the hybrid nature of cinema in Ireland. This chapter provides an analysis of this cinema's historical development focusing on film production and the wider cinema culture in Ireland, including the emergence and tentative consolidation of both since the 1970s, particularly in the Republic. Born out of the historical conjuncture that saw the rise of nationalism and the *fin de siècle* of colonialism,[2] the chequered development of Irish and other marginal cinemas around the world might offer models for the development of film in a new audio-visual era and alternative political identities in the new millennium.

The idea of national cinema

Given that the twentieth century's major political disputes and wars were over national territorial disagreements, it is not surprising that the development of popular cultural forms such as cinema became an extension and re-presentation of conflicts within and between different nation-states. The basic pattern for cinema's development was conferred by the pivotal event of World War I. Its aftermath provided the economic, political and cultural contexts within which film technology, production and distribution took on its characteristic organisation into national industries, dominated in the early 1920s by US films made and marketed most effectively by Hollywood studios.[3] The beleaguered position of European national cinemas was even more sharply manifest in Ireland since it was geographically peripheral, economically dependent and politically subordinate. To examine the screen images of a nation leads us to consider how cinema has contributed to the construction of the concept of the nationalism itself. From the discussion in chapter 1 we will remember that it is a relatively modern idea, achieving its apogee in the late nineteenth century. Its enduring political significance in the twentieth century and its power to 'command such profound emotional legitimacy'[4] is due to the fact that nations are 'imagined political communities – and imagined as both inherently limited and sovereign'.[5] Anderson's explanation for the ideological potency of nationalism hinges on the point that the bond felt between individual and nation seems natural and inviolable precisely because they are *imagined*. A national identity affects cohesion because it is *limited* to a people whose distinctive characteristics are derived in relation to other, different nationalities. The right of a nation to determine its territory and defend its polity is *sovereign*, autochthonous and indivisible.

These abstract issues of political theory have been translated into debating and defining the idea of national cinema. Traditionally, the existence of a national cinema has been predicated on the extent to which a country creates and controls the means to its own film production. However, other accounts suggest that this cannot be a litmus test since 'at some time or another most national cinemas are not coterminous with their nation states'.[6] This is true of the small and medium sized national cinemas in Europe and Australia, for example. In Ireland, where the nation-state remains a matter of dispute and the 'people-nation' has (with few exceptions) been serially depleted, defining a national cinema is particularly problematic. For long periods both Irish states effectively ignored the question of indigenous cinema industry or conceived of it in terms that were unrealistic given the dominance of Anglo-American cinema. However, since the 1970s, the idea of national cinema has been revisited and its traditional terms challenged by emergent and smaller nations. If the nation is not a pre-ordained, originary form of political organisation but 'imagined', that is, the outcome of a complicated ideological constructive process, it is subject to historical change and human agency and is a more heterogeneous, diverse and 'messy' structure. A national cinema used to be based on the idea of homogeneity, representing a common, unitary and distinctive identity to the exclusion of other national cinemas and also to the exclusion of those *within* who did not conform to this identity. This narrow, restrictive definition has been challenged by an important insight. If nation-ness is 'imagined', then a national cinema arguably plays a significant part in fabricating a collective screen fiction, acting as a powerful ideological institution.

Undoubtedly national cinemas have at times been involved in mobilising dominant forms of nationalism, but they also contain dissident, subversive forces and can open up the nation to scrutiny. Cinema can provide the focus for more liberal, diverse and inclusive identities. Indeed, it can be argued that films and film-makers in emerging and developing nations, unequally located within an international industry, are positioned to problematise the idea of the national by '"trying on" successive identities, holding together apparently incompatible national and cultural objectives and using the nation as a means of questioning and interrogating its very national possibility and merit as such'.[7] Close fiscal control over film production has been a central aim of small-scale, emergent cinemas (Australian, Irish, Spanish) as well as more established but still vulnerable cinemas (British, French).[8] But contemporary scholarship suggests that to examine national cinemas sensitively, a range of different factors beyond film production must be taken into account and analysed. This is to recognise that it is a difficult enough task to establish which films make up the corpus of a national cinema, and begs the question on what basis are films included or excluded? If a film is funded by Warner Brothers but based on native creative writing, acting and directorial talent, to what extent is it an Irish film? Does a film by an Irish writer or director have to be set in Ireland to qualify as part of a national cinema? As a commercial activity, film-making is funded on the basis of financial agreements, distribution deals and tax legislation that provide a set of material parameters within which creativity takes place. But aside from the core issue of financial control, a national cinema may be identified by the narratives that occur in the films themselves. Are there particular narratives which recur and become synonymous with Irish cinema? Do particular national cinemas have certain genres with which they become associated? Are there generic elements, specific audio-visual codes and conventions, which signify Irish locale and character in films? Are there particular codes of physical behaviour, accent, expression and performance that signify national characteristics in film acting? How do certain performers become film stars and do they, by association, become bearers of a national screen identity?[9] The answers to these questions will be explored in the present and subsequent chapters. Cinema in Ireland has been forced to take on and represent historical, political and social issues not addressed in the public realm in an open way. Its character as a national cinema is grounded in its subordinate status, its disorganised negotiation with dominant external forces and reactionary internal conditions, and the necessity of adapting narratives and genres to its own local purposes as best it could. In doing so, that cinema has performed a critique of the nation-ness which it initially adopted to define itself against Britain and America.

Early cinema in Ireland and the silent rise of Hollywood

Film became technically possible and profitably popular in Ireland during a quarter of a century of significant political change that decisively shaped the development of the medium. For the first decade or so of its existence, cinema in Ireland, as elsewhere, consisted of short, simple film presentations with live musical accompaniment in music halls and variety theatres. By about 1909–10, purpose-built cinemas in Ireland were showing a mixture of multi-reel, complex narrative fictions and non-fiction newsreels. Watching film projection rapidly became a branch of a commercially-driven popular entertainment industry in urban centres like Dublin, Belfast, Cork and Galway.[10] In the first two decades of the century of cinema, the nature of film-going and viewing conditions in Ireland were broadly comparable to those in Britain and other European countries. However, in terms of production and distribution, Ireland's island status, its growing political recalcitrance, the comparatively small market and lack of a developed industrial infrastructure meant that it was susceptible to the uneven development of the growing world cinema industry in which feature-length, Hollywood movies became the dominant product from about 1915 onwards. Indeed, 'more fiction films were produced about the Irish by American film-makers before 1915, when the first indigenous Irish fiction film was made, than in the whole hundred year history of fiction film-making in Ireland'.[11] While Britain, France, Germany and Italy directed their

3 Early cinema in Dublin: Dorset Picture Hall (1911).
Courtesy of the National Library of Ireland

economic resources to fight World War I, the centre of the USA cinema industry shifted to sunny California and developed its international networks to greatest advantage, capturing overseas markets in a celluloid distribution war.

In pre-1922 Ireland, the most notable entrepreneurial figures of film production tended to be Irish-North American or British. One such, the Kalem Film Company, employed Canadian Sidney Olcott, who visited Kerry periodically making films between 1910–14, including the popular *Lad from Old Ireland* (1910) about a successful returned Irish emigrant. Another short-lived company, set up by Irish-American lawyer, James Sullivan, called the Film Company of Ireland (1916–20),[12] reworked a popular nineteenth-century novel into a highly successful film of the same name, *Knocknagow* (1918). Kevin Rockett has convincingly argued how Fred O'Donovan's film represented a decisive moment of political hegemony for Irish nationalism.[13] Documentary and newsreels were made by the dominant producers Pathé, Topical Budget and Gaumont but there was one significant if short-lived indigenous company, General Film Supply, set up by Norman Whitten. With experience in the film industry in Britain, Whitten was responsible for a series of newsreels under the title of *Irish Events* (1917–19) and one fiction feature with quasi-religious subject matter, *In the Days of St Patrick* (1920). Given the contemporary context of Anglo-Irish relations, it is not surprising that certain films produced political friction and that cinemas sometimes became the site of popular disturbances. Nationalist women organised protests against British newsreels advocating military conscription in 1913–14, films with overtly nationalist themes, such as Walter MacNamara's *Ireland a Nation* (1914), were censored and *Irish Events* compilation newsreels of Sinn Féin activities were banned in 1919 by the British authorities as 'seditious'.[14]

Within a short time of its introduction into Ireland, watching films quickly became a popular activity. By 1916, there were some 150 cinemas and halls showing films, including about thirty each in Belfast and Dublin.[15] This produced socio-political tensions that were as much about class differences as nationalist politics. While cinemas in the USA and Britain were consciously gentrified by owner-managers to make them more acceptable to the values of middle-class patrons, in Ireland the reverse happened. Apart from certain select cinemas, like the Metropole in Dublin, cinemas developed large working-class audiences,[16] which were viewed with suspicion by an emergent Irish middle class exercising a morally inflected authority. Film historian Liam O'Leary reflected on how a licence for Sunday screenings at a cinema in Dame Street, central Dublin, was refused because 'lower classes coming out of it would inevitably mingle with the better class coming from their religious devotions at nearby Christ Church Cathedral (Protestant) or the Friends' (Quaker) Meeting House in Eustace Street'.[17] Following partition and independence in the early 1920s the question of an Irish national cinema was brought sharply into focus. Tensions developed between popular appetites and what the state and the church thought fit subject matter for audiences: 'many in the Government would have been opposed to film *per se* or judged it in purely Catholic moral terms, as was demonstrated by the speedy passage of the Censorship of Films Act, 1923'.[18] The content of Anglo-American films and the opportunities for unsupervised social activity between the sexes in going to the cinema meant that churchmen of all denominations were wary about the popularity of cinema. The Dublin Corporation's plan to institute a public health committee, including six Catholic priests and six Protestant ministers, to oversee its cinemas was unworkable and it was replaced by a single, government-appointed censor, James Montgomery, and an appeal board. The censor's job was to protect cinema-goers from 'indecent, obscene or blasphemous material' or that which he deemed 'contrary to public morality'. The new government was seeking to establish political and cultural stability after what had been a traumatic period of intense conflict and disruption. Such centralised control measures have to be understood in this context and showed the post-colonial state flexing its muscles, taking over from cultural bodies like the Gaelic League and forming alliances with the churches to exercise power. Earlier that summer, the government had imposed import taxes on unprocessed film stock and prints. This increased costs for existing distributors and would-be producers, but created a tidy source of income for the state from a popular pastime. Within the industry itself there was discord in the form of a two-month strike by Dublin's one thousand cinema employees in the summer of 1923 against a 15 per cent wage cut by management who claimed that workers in the Free State were overpaid in comparison to those in Northern Ireland.[19] While cinema-owners were keen to profit from film's growing popularity, the economic austerity of the times meant that private businesses and the state finances were inclined to be especially prudent, encapsulating a recurring paradox in the newly-independent state. State or private funding of indigenous film production was a low priority for economic reasons, yet, the understandable impulse to produce distinctively Irish films to counteract the popular foreign product entailed using the very medium which to many represented the modernity, 'Californication'[20] and un-Irish values from which the Irish Free State sought to distance itself.

Cultural and economic protectionism, 1922–57

The problem was that between the 1920s and the 1950s cinema-going remained one of the more popular leisure pastimes in Ireland. In 1934, there were 190 cinemas in the Irish Free State with 18,250,000 admissions. By 1954, the peak of cinema's popularity, annual admissions totalled 54,100,000.[21] Although cinema visits per capita were lower than other comparable countries, many people were going twice or more a week and recent studies have demonstrated the significance of cinema in people's daily lives.[22] But it was a form of social activity and interaction that was treated with suspicion and monitored by the state's film censor, the churches, educators and lay religious groups, such as Catholic Action. In the first forty years of operation, the censor banned about 3,000 films and made cuts in 8,000 others. In Britain in the 1920s and 1930s, cinema also became an extremely popular medium dominated by Hollywood films. The British state was driven to adopt protectionist policies more for the purposes of national economic reasons than because of moral strictures although censorship of a political and social nature was exercised on all films. The 1927 Cinematographic Films Act partially revived the economy of British cinema in the interwar years by imposing a system of quotas on foreign imported films. Exhibitors were required to increase the percentage of British films shown in their cinemas from 5 per cent in 1927 to 20 per cent in 1935. In Northern Ireland, however, the 1930s and 1940s saw Ulster Unionist resistance to calls for its cinema industry to be unionised and regulated in line with British protectionist policies.[23] As in the Free State, opposition to cinema in Northern Ireland was also periodically generated by Church and lay religious groups on the grounds that:

Those cinemas which display sensational films are an added source of danger to the moral and social well-being of the younger generation. The increase in juvenile crime in Belfast is most alarming and is in some measure due to the gangster films.[24]

Rather like the situation in Dublin, local authorities in Northern Ireland enacted by-laws to keep cinemas away from churches. The Belfast Corporation prohibited the building of cinemas within a 360 foot radius of a house of worship.[25] Religious groups and local authority antipathy to cinema was echoed in parliament. At the height of British film production in the mid-1930s, and with 122 cinemas operating in Northern Ireland,[26] Stormont debated but rejected the idea of establishing its own trade board for a cinema industry in the province.[27] During 1936–37, Paramount Pictures co-produced some comedies and musical features using the home-grown talents of Northern Irish singer and actor, Richard Hayward, but these were productions that worked just within the 1927 act's definition of British films. These 'quota quickies' were so-called because they were made with minimal budget and produced to a tight time scale. Similarly, it is no surprise that US studios such as RKO and MGM tried to exploit the exhibition and distribution market in Northern Ireland for a short time in the post-1945 period.[28] But surveying a broader postwar period in terms of production, Geraldine Wilkins observes that 'no indigenous feature was made in Northern Ireland between the 1930s and the 1980s'.[29] Instead, it remained an occasional location for London-based films such as *Odd Man Out* (1947) and *Jacqueline* (1956), both produced by Rank at Pinewood Studios, or *The Gentle Gunman* (1952), produced by Ealing Studios.

In the Irish Free State, following the logic of a cultural nationalism that stressed Ireland's exclusivity, the government undertook to protect the nation from foreign films but did little to encourage native production. From an official perspective, Hollywood films represented an unwholesome trio of excessive materialism, criminality and sexuality, and many British films projected demeaning stereotypes of Irish characters and life in comedy films like *Oh, Mr*

Porter! (1937). However, instead of supporting and encouraging Irish-made film production to creatively combat these cinematic 'evils', successive Irish governments, bishops and Catholic groups enacted legislative and lay campaigns to prohibit film.[30] The Censorship of Films Act (1923) amended the powers exercised by local authorities under the old 1909 act (introduced by the British Parliament) and the film censor tightly controlled public film exhibition.[31] The dominant cultural view saw cinema not only as a carrier of values that were corruptive and antithetical to those promoted by the state but that cinema itself was the agent of an unwelcome modernity. Such incursions were resisted by a state that prided itself on its recent, hard-fought independence, its Christian values and a distinctive language. Through its control of the educational syllabuses (from 1922), the national radio station (1926), the Censorship of Publications Act (1929) and licensing of dance halls (1935), Free State governments actively endorsed conservative forms of popular, native cultural activities associated with rural communal life such as storytelling, Irish dancing, music and singing. Cinema and jazz (that is, contemporary dance hall music) were demonised and racialised as cultural invasions that threatened the social and moral fabric of Irish life:

instead of visiting and story-telling, there are cinemas and night walking, often with disaster to virtue. Instead of Irish dances we have sensuous contortions of the body timed to semi-barbaric music.[32]

The 1930s saw the implementation of policies of economic protectionism to encourage Irish agricultural production and stimulate industrial development that were to last until the late 1950s. In such a climate, the state's failure to support indigenous film production in either the English or Irish language is significant. A nationalist cultural insularity and an authoritarian unease with a comparatively new form of popular culture (evident in other countries at the time), combined in the case of Ireland with the macro-economic factors of cinema market domination and extreme fiscal penury of an ex-colonial country. With the coming of sound film in the 1930s, Ireland was even more vulnerable to aggressive US distribution than non-Anglophone European countries. Irish cinema screens were filled with westerns, gangster movies and musicals from Hollywood as well as British costume dramas and musical comedies. However, as Martin McLoone has observed, it is not surprising that 'in a climate where the official culture was so repressive, these "foreign" images became positively life-enhancing' for the popular Irish audiences.[33]

Comparing pre- and post-partition cinema in Ireland, it is apparent that during the 1910s many of the films produced in Ireland were engaged, albeit via historical topics and literary sources, with Ireland's contemporary political concerns in oppositional ways. But from the 1920s until the 1970s, indigenous feature film production was almost non-existent in both states due to cultural and macro-economic factors. Such films that were produced indigenously, like

4 A night at the pictures: Dublin's Metropole Cinema (c. 1938).
Courtesy of the National Library of Ireland

Irish Destiny (1926), *The Dawn* (1936) and the documentary *Mise Éire* (1959),
were individually inspired efforts, the result of private enterprise, local amateur
groups or cultural activists. The notable aim shared by these films is the
attempt to put the recent past into moving pictures, the desire to engage in the
expression of an Irish nationalist project on the cinema screen.

While in partitioned Ireland neither state was economically well-placed to
finance film production nor were the dominant cultural politics supportive,
throughout the 1930s and 1940s arguments were in fact made by leading and
enthusiastic figures within the theatre, church and political establishment to
support film production particularly in the Free State. Plans by the Abbey
Theatre in 1937 and the internationalist playwright, George Bernard Shaw, to
use Ireland's theatrical resources as the basis for an Irish film studio in 1948
went unaided by the state and came to nothing.[34] This was despite the fact that
Irish dramas and acting talent were popular on US screens and with Irish audiences at home. Contrary to the idea that all the clergy were anti-cinema, plans
for an Irish film studio commissioned by de Valera in 1938 were anonymously
drawn up by an astute Jesuit priest, Father Richard Devane. Although not published or acted upon, *The Film in National Life*[35] (1943) indicated that elements
within the church felt that controlled involvement in film production was
better than rejecting the medium outright, as would be the case with

television a decade or so later. Indeed, two years later Devane was closely involved in the establishment of the National Film Institute, which strategically 'concerned itself with the provision of films for schools and educational centres. It [also] produced instructional films for governmental departments and organised schools of film appreciation'.[36] In Northern Ireland, lackadaisical policies towards cinema were criticised in Stormont debates in 1942[37] and a pro-cinema lobby existed among some religious representatives in the north, which 'urged co-operation with film' producers.[38]

Arguments surfaced from within the Dublin Government to combine public and private money in the financing of an Irish film studio in 1946–47, promoted largely by Sean Lemass, the minister for industry and commerce. These were countered by Frank Aiken, the minister for finance, as too costly and likely to encourage foreign producers at the expense of Irish film-makers. Lemass's plans eventually came to fruition in 1958 shortly before he became taoiseach, but Aiken's premonitions came true in the following decades. It was Lemass who is generally credited with directing the changes in the Republic's ideological stance and economic strategy from isolationism to internationalism. As Table 1 shows below, a decline in popularity of cinema-going was already underway by this time and not confined to Ireland. This period saw the restructuring of the Hollywood studio system and the re-emergence of national cinemas in Italy and France, for instance. It also saw the spread of the television as a rival popular medium and, more generally, changes in popular leisure patterns, which offered alternatives to cinema.

From Ardmore Studios to the Irish Film Board, 1958–87

Lemass's plans for a permanent studio facility were part of a strategy for film production under the auspices of the department of industry. The policy of

Table 1 Cinema's decline in popularity: Ireland, 1950–80

Year	Audience figures (millions)
1950	46.1
1954	54.1
1955	50.9
1960	41.2
1965	30
1970	20
1975	15
1980	9.5

Source: *Encyclopaedia of European Cinema* (1995),
Cassell/ British Film Institute

founding a national studio on a commercial, profit-generating basis rather than on cultural or artistic grounds dominated film production in Ireland for a generation. Although the establishment of Ardmore Studios in Wicklow, south of Dublin, promised much in terms of indigenous production, employment and training of film trades (from electricians and carpenters to editors and designers), it became fairly quickly a hireable facility monopolised by British and US studios as a production space. The plan to base indigenous film production on successful Abbey theatrical adaptations was ill-conceived and soon gave way to commercial pressures, British distribution controls and trade union practices, which excluded Irish technician grade workers. *Shake Hands with the Devil* (1959) was a notable first international picture but between 1963–73 the studio constantly ran into debt and was buoyed up by state funding initiatives and different kinds of private business takeovers. RTÉ, the national television broadcaster, effectively ran Ardmore for two years until, in 1975, it was renamed the National Film Studios of Ireland (NFSI). It survived under the chairmanship of English-born film-maker John Boorman until 1982, when it went into liquidation again. By this time, the Irish Film Board (IFB), or Bord Scannán na Éireann, had been formed in 1981 and it is worthwhile examining the factors that brought this about in relation to Ardmore.

Ironically the failures of the national film studio experiment provoked a creative response that laid the foundations on which the current generation of Irish film-makers have been able to build. By the mid-1960s, in constructive reaction to Ardmore, a native community of film-makers and cinephiles began to lay the plans for alternative forms of state support for indigenous production and a different kind of national film that would be more pluralistic and critical and would be generated by artistic rather than commercial interests. The impetus for this was cradled by the brief period of relative economic wealth experienced between 1966-73 and the accompanying social change in Ireland. Different kinds of political radicalism in the late 1960s led to a more self-confident questioning of Ireland's national past, which combined with Ireland's new relationship with Europe as a member of the EEC (1972) and the need to find in film a means of creatively evaluating these changes.

The Arts Council of Ireland had been empowered by legislation since 1973 to assist film in Ireland but it was not until 1977, by providing a film script award for indigenous writers, that this institution provided serious support. The first product of this initiative, *Poitín* (1978), directed by Bob Quinn, was an Irish-language short film that set out to debunk the idyllic portrayal of the west of Ireland so revered by traditional nationalists. The efforts of other committed people formed part of a campaign fought over the next two years to lobby for a state-supported national film board to organise film production in Ireland, to secure funds for a national archive and develop film culture through exhibition and education. Independent film-makers, trade unions, producers and some receptive politicians drew up plans for the Irish Film Board Bill (1980). Despite some short-comings, this legislation meant that the board should 'have regard to the need for the expression of national culture through the medium of film-making',[39] echoing phrasing borrowed from the 1960 act, which legislated for Irish television.

The IFB's achievements in its six years of existence (1981–1987) were mixed. Some notable films were produced under its auspices but from the start the period was riven with controversy and contradictory developments.[40] In the same week as NFSI went into liquidation, the IFB allocated its first budget to help fund Neil Jordan's debut feature, *Angel* (1982) – a film executively produced by the IFB's own chair, John Boorman. The film board was itself short-lived, unceremoniously wound up in 1987 by a short-sighted government anxious for immediate profit and with little interest in sustained development for cultural reasons. Broadly speaking, film-makers in the 1980s fell into one of two camps. There were those who insisted that the primary aim of state assistance should be to fund a variety of modestly-budgeted projects that critically explored Irish society and history and challenged artistic and cultural norms, including previous cinematic representations of Ireland. Others felt that Ireland's contemporary life would be best served by fewer, big budget, commercial films employing a hard-hitting social realism that would attract both home and foreign audiences. As Rockett points out, the record of Irish government film sponsorship shows that it has repeatedly been driven by a commercial rather than an aesthetic imperative and 'the post-1987 film environment … witnessed the restoration of the ascendancy of the industrial model for film production over a culturally engaged, critical cinema in Ireland'.[41]

Interregnum in Irish film, 1988–92

In this period, the government in the Republic accentuated once again incentives to foreign investment in film production, principally through the tax concessions in Section 35 of the Finance Act (1987). However, this was also a time when Ireland became politically and culturally more integrated in the EC. It signed up to the Single European Act in 1987 and the Maastricht Treaty in 1992 and Dublin thrived as the European Capital of Culture in 1988. In the absence of Irish state support, indigenous film-makers were forced to approach European sources for funds. They also explored alternative methods and media, such as video, and exploited new links with television, principally with Channel Four in England but also the BBC in Belfast.

The years 1988–1992 saw some excellent films released, many of which employed native talent, not just in terms of acting, scripting and directing but also in the technical and craft-skilled aspects of the industry such as lighting and make-up. Table 2 (page 41) shows how films produced in and about Ireland were funded by British film or television or secured with US production and distribution finance. Under the inevitable influence of foreign executives, Ireland presented and exploited itself as a picturesque location-base (despite the weather) for US and British productions to send over visiting directors and crew enticed by favourable tax relief. Some Irish-directed productions, like Joe Comerford's *Reefer and the Model* (1988), began with IFB money but were completed with private finance from Hemdale Films. Other productions replayed the dynamics of Anglo-American intervention that have characterised Irish cinema history. John Huston filmed a version of Joyce's short story, *The Dead*, mostly in California, with some location work in Dublin, while Ron Howard's star-vehicle romance, *Far and Away* (1992), featured nineteenth-century emigration to the USA in its narrative. A returned emigrant precipitates the conflict in another period drama and literary adaptation, *The Field* (1990), directed by Jim Sheridan, funded wholly by Granada Films, a subsidiary of the English Granada TV. Two screenplays set in contemporary Ireland, *The Commitments* (1991) and *Into the West* (1992), used considerable creative and performance talent but were driven by Anglo-American funds and directed by Englishmen, Alan Parker and Mike Newell respectively. Both narratives deal with forms of escape from the urban modernity of late 1980s Dublin. In Parker's film, escape is the dream of rock 'n' roll success for a group of working-class Dubliners who find that soul music speaks to their predicament in contemporary Ireland. In Newell's film, the escape is an inward, westward displacement, suggesting that Ireland's marginalised Traveller community (who traditionally live in caravans) can find solace from the brutalising state by rediscovering the values of a mythic past and its aboriginal culture. These films suggest the enduring idea that the American Dream and the Irish Myth have represented the two poles of Irish identity for most of this century. Events at the end of 1992 and early 1993 described in the next section created the conditions that demonstrated Ireland's liminal position between these poles.

Indigenous film production in Northern Ireland was very limited in the post-1945 period and the policies of the British Film Institute (BFI), whose remit was to support film as a cultural practice and educational tool in Britain's regions, excluded Northern Ireland. Production in the 1970s and 1980s was left to a few independent film-makers like John T. Davis and David Hammond and groups like the Derry Film and Video Collective (1984), the Belfast Film Workshop (1985) and Belfast Independent Video (1990). As British film production slumped in the mid-1980s, momentum was generated in Northern Ireland by the Independent Film, Video and Photography Association to commission a study, called *Fast Forward* (1988), which examined the audio-visual infrastructure in relation to Britain and the Republic. Following the recommendations of the report, the Northern Ireland Film Council (NIFC) was set up in 1989 to encourage the development of film, television and video in the region. From its origins as an unfunded, voluntary organisation, the NIFC attracted state finance from the department of education and in 1992 another report recommended more support for film via a revamped Northern Ireland Arts Council. The most influential contribution to film from television up to this point was made by Channel Four, which commissioned film and video projects, notably DFVC's first feature-length production, *Hush-a-bye-Baby*

Table 2 Selected details of film production in Ireland, 1986–92

Film title (Origin, date)	Director (Scriptwriter)	Production company	Distributor	Budget(a)
Eat the Peach (Ireland, 1986)	Peter Ormrod (John Kelleher/ Peter Ormrod)	Strongbow Films, Film Four International (UK)	IFB (Ir), Columbia/ RCA (USA)	1.3
The Courier (Ireland, 1988)	Joe Lee (Frank Deasey/ Joe Lee)	City Vision	Palace Pictures (UK)	1.0
Reefer and the Model (Ireland, 1988)	Joe Comerford (Joe Comerford)	Berber Films	IFB, ZDF (Germ), C4 (UK), RTÉ (Ir)	1.0
The Field (UK/Ireland, 1990)	Jim Sheridan (Jim Sheridan)	Sovereign Pictures Granada Film (UK)	Granada (UK), Miramax (USA)	4.5
The Commitments (UK/USA, 1991)	Alan Parker (Dick Clement/ Ian La Frenais)	First Film, Sovereign, Twentieth Century Fox (USA)	Twentieth Century Fox (USA)	$12.0
Into the West (Ireland/UK/USA, 1992)	Mike Newell (Jim Sheridan)	Little Bird, Parallel Films, Majestic Films Film Four International (UK), Miramax Films (USA)	Miramax (USA), Film Four International, (UK)	£5.0
Far and Away (USA, 1992)	Ron Howard (Bob Dolman)	Imagine Films for Universal Pictures	UIP (USA)	$50.0

Source: British Film Institute SIFT data base and *Screen International*
(a): Budget figures (millions) shown in Irish punts unless otherwise indicated.

(1989). Ulster TV, based in Belfast, also put modest funding into Thaddeus O'Sullivan's *December Bride* (1990) and BBCNI contributed impressively to the BBC's *Screen Two* drama-on-film slot.

Towards a cinema of national questioning, 1993–97[42]

In the Republic of Ireland a number of factors came to a head in 1992–93 that brought about the relaunch of the IFB and the crystallisation of a more vibrant, inquisitive cinema culture. These developments may be set in the context of a growth in the number of people attending the cinema in both the Republic and Northern Ireland in the early 1990s as shown in Table 3 overleaf.

This consolidation should be seen in the light of wider economic and political conditions that existed at that juncture. The economy of the Irish Republic

Table 3 Irish cinema attendance, 1991–96

Year	Republic of Ireland	Northern Ireland
1991	8,084,100	2,313,000
1992	8,258,700	2,452,000
1993	9,310,100	3,490,000
1994	10,422,500	3,829,000
1995	9,836,700	3,436,000
1996	11,480,200	3,801,800

Source: Cinema Media/Taylor Nelson AGB/Gallup, January 1997

remained buoyant with an average volume growth rate of 5.7 per cent for the period 1990–95, compared to the UK's 1.2 per cent, Germany's 1.7 per cent and Australia's 3.3 per cent.[43] Following initial discussions between constitutional nationalist John Hume and Republican Gerry Adams, Anglo-Irish relations improved such that Taoiseach Albert Reynolds and Prime Minister John Major could make the Downing Street Declaration in December 1993. The ceasefires announced by paramilitaries in Northern Ireland between 1994–96 and the on-going peace process under a British Labour government have enhanced the climate for film releases in and about Ireland. Moreover, there were important political shifts within the Republic in the early 1990s, which included the diminution of Fianna Fáil's power, the dominant nationalist party in the state, involving its forced coalition with the Irish Labour Party.

One direct outcome of the Republic's political shifts was a new ministerial appointment in the figure of Michael D. Higgins, a progressive and liberal politician, who directed policy on the arts, culture and the Gaeltacht (Irish-speaking areas) between 1992 and 1997, and argued passionately against Hollywood domination: '[Culture is] the last frontier. It is where the power to resist will be fought out … It is surely wrong that all the images of the world should come from one place'.[44] Several elements came together at the beginning of his term of office, which saw the culmination of efforts by a native film-making community who had been campaigning in the interregnum period. *The Film Production Industry in Ireland*, a government-sponsored report on the future of the Irish film industry was published in 1992, and plans for an Irish National Film Archive (INFA) and an Irish Film Centre (IFC) came to fruition in Dublin when the Friends' Meeting House site was opened in September of the same year.[45] The IFC provided a focus for several kinds of activity associated with an emergent film culture. The INFA was the first such in the history of Irish cinema, a place in which the country's film deposits could be preserved, catalogued and studied. In the IFC's two cinemas, films could be viewed from all round the world; support and practical advice were provided by Film Base who took up residence in 1992 at the IFC. Since the late 1980s, Film Base had hired out equipment, collated information resources, provided a focus for 'wandering' film-makers and published *Film Base Magazine* since 1987, which was retitled *Film Ireland* in 1992.

Neil Jordan's *The Crying Game* was one of the opening films in the IFC's programme. Its box-office reception in the USA echoed the success of Jim Sheridan's *My Left Foot*, which generated distributors' interest in Irish-themed films in the 1990s. Jordan's film was produced by English independent, Palace Pictures, with no Irish finance, but achieved phenomenal 'cross-over' from art house to mainstream in the USA. Its Oscar for Best Original Screenplay in 1993 provided the occasion for a dramatic announcement by Higgins for the launch of a new IFB. The policy for film steered a tricky course between commercialism and culture. Support for Irish film would continue to be based on largely Anglo-American investment, but state funds were made available, disbursed by the IFB, and increased activity within the EU networks were the order of the day. Thus, 1993 saw the extension until 1999 of Section 35 tax incentives begun in 1987 under the Finance Act – which also allowed co-production funding – as well as efforts to build on Ireland's participation in the original MEDIA '92 (1988) initiative. By joining the EURIMAGES, a co-production fund programme, in September 1992, Ireland was positioned to obtain maximum benefit from such funding projects and the EU structural funds.[46] These projects were part of a larger plan to support film-makers in developing regions within the EU, countries in Scandinavia and those countries with more established industries like France, Germany and Italy. The existence of these supports ran parallel to the protracted negotiations under GATT (the General Agreement on Tariffs and Trades) involving the USA and European countries, which started in 1986 and were only acrimoniously concluded in late 1993. Led principally by French delegates, Europe maintained its position that the audio-visual sector required special protection from USA audio-visual products since such items constituted an important component of the national cultures of European countries.[47]

The other major changes provided for at the time of the new film board concerned the relations between the big and the small screen. Under amended legislation from 1993, RTÉ was required to fund independent production by commission, similar to the successful model used since 1982 by Channel Four TV in Britain.[48] Since the early nineties, RTÉ and BBC Northern Ireland have worked symbiotically with a growing number of independent production companies in Ireland, north and south.[49] This has stimulated a great deal of short film production, animation and documentary material, as well as features. Television has provided a valuable showcase for the best of new film-makers in series such as *Short Cuts* and *Northern Lights*. The fact that the Cork (1956) and Dublin (1985) film festivals have been joined by festival venues in Derry (1987), the Film Fleadh in Galway (1988), Belfast (1990) and Limerick (1995) are signs that there is a healthy growth in film culture. In addition, students are increasingly attracted to the burgeoning number of media courses and film schools, picking up skills in such ancillary services as marketing, finance, publicity and journalism. The argument about sustainable film culture is now less about production and more about post-production facilities (editing and sound) to keep films in Ireland. Many film-makers are concerned about the effective distribution and marketing of their films in niche US independent cinemas, video rental and retail sales and television rights.

The bigger picture?

From their origins in the 1920s until the 1970s, neither state in Ireland was supportive of cinema in economic terms or sympathetic to film-makers for cultural and moral reasons. Many indigenous Irish film makers have tended to be artistic and political dissidents, non-conformists critical of the status quo and therefore unlikely to receive state moneys. We have seen that an Irish cinema does exist in its broadest sense but it is a cinema that no longer aspires to attain a unitary form of national culture and which questions the validity of this definition of national project. Intermittently, film production in Ireland has been promoted as an industry. This was both an inaccurate description and a questionable aspiration on the part of policy-makers, since films have social significance and cultural capital as well as exchange-value as commodities. As veteran film-maker, Bob Quinn, has said, 'we don't have an industry in Ireland, we have film-making activity'.[50] He and others, like Joe Comerford, Pat Murphy, Margo Harkin and Cathal Black, have consistently emphasised the cultural dimension of Irish film-making and its importance to the well-being of Irish society. The often make-shift nature of Irish cinema has to be seen in the context of changes to the dominant forms of corporate organisation and ownership in the world audio-visual sector of which film is now but one product. Independent film production companies, screenwriters and producers exist in the gaps between the interests of huge transglobal conglomerates, diversified to incorporate audio-visual studio production, TV satellite franchises, DVD and VHS cassette manufacture and book publishing interests. Not unlike the temporary, mobile film shows from the beginning of the century, Irish independent producers and directors join the travelling circus of the festival circuit, chasing European funding agencies, national television rights and international distribution deals in order to survive and produce the next film. The film industry in the USA has undergone periodic change and restructuring since World War II. In the 1950s, audiences shrank due in large part to television. In the 1970s studios were hit by increasing financial overheads and corporate mergers took place in the 1980s. Finally, a new economic order, technological synergies and transglobal mergers were distinguishing features of the 1990s. Even if 'a mammoth amalgam still identifiable as Hollywood retains the dominance of the moving image industry that it established in the 1920s',[51] the 1990s do provide some encouragement for independent Irish production, despite the fact that distribution beyond the festival, art-house cinema and tele-vision remains a problem. But, as Rod Stoneman has made clear, 'the argument is not against American culture but against the hegemony of American market-driven cultural products'.[52]

This chapter has examined the history of cinema and film production in Ireland in six phases and analysed the significance of complicated forms of economic and cultural domination. Nevertheless, the evaluation is guardedly optimistic, based on the evidence that film-makers and audiences in Ireland have responded creatively to their circumstances. In adopting but adapting the dominant cinematic forms made available – until most recently – in harsh economic and cultural conditions, a growing number of films are being produced in Ireland which express the specific and local concerns of people in Ireland. The living generation of film-makers' work has tested a monolithic definition of a national cinema to encompass a more vibrant and dynamic process, which derives its energy from the diversity of stories, hybridity of genres and playfulness of its cinematography. As Luke Gibbons has put it:

A vigorous national cinema must be judged not solely on its economic performance, or in terms of establishing a native film industry (crucial though these are), but also on its capacity to engage with the multiple national narratives preoccupying a society, and its specific ways of telling its own stories.[53]

Ireland's diminutive status within the cinema world (producing 0.5 per cent of the world's films) does not necessarily mean that it has capitulated to an Anglo-American neo-colonialism. In a process of active transformation, film-making in Ireland has developed strategies to combat its subordinate status and it has produced a distinct film culture. Its better screenplays engage critically with its fractured past and the disparate elements of modern Irish life; its writers, direc-tors and technicians have migrated to America, Britain and around Europe; and, since 1993, Irish governments have countered the state's appalling record of support by innovative funding and encouraging investment in the audio-visual arts to an extent that Ireland has become a model for other European coun-tries.[54] According to some, the tax incentives, the lateral structures, adaptability and networks of collective ingenuity in Ireland hold the future for European cinema.[55] Ireland's position may be marginal and subordinate in relation to Hollywood and other established European cinemas but its experience of polit-ical and cultural struggle now offers narratives that speak – albeit with different inflections – to Irish, European and global audiences.

Notes

1 T. O'Regan, *Australian National Cinema* (London, Routledge, 1995), 65.
2 S. Hayward, *French National Cinema* (London, Routledge, 1993), 14.

3 J. Wyver, *The Moving Image* (Oxford, Basil Blackwell, 1989), 20.

4 B. Anderson, *Imagined Communities: Reflections on the origins and spread of nationalism* (London, Verso, 1991), 4.

5 Anderson, *Imagined Communities*, 6–7.

6 O'Regan, *Australian National Cinema*, 71.

7 O'Regan, *Australian National Cinema*, 69.

8 See the published and forthcoming volumes in Routledge's 'National Cinemas Series', including S. Hayward, *French National Cinema* (London, Routledge, 1993), Ch.1 'A brief ecohistory of France's cinema industry, 1895–1992'; S. Street, *British National Cinema* (London, Routledge, 1997), Ch. 1 'The fiscal politics of film'; and Tytti Sila *et al., Nordic National Cinema* (London, Routledge, 1998).

9 Hayward, *French National Cinema*, 8–9. These questions have been prompted and adapted from Hayward's typography of French cinema.

10 A. Brouder, 'The history of cinema-going in Galway', *Film West*, 22 (July 1995), 20–3.

11 K. Rockett, *The Irish Filmography: Fiction films 1896–1996* (Dublin, Red Mountain Press, 1996), i.

12 T. Downing, 'The Film Company of Ireland', *Sight and Sound*, 49:1 (Winter 1979/80), 42–5.

13 K. Rockett, J. Hill and L. Gibbons, *Cinema and Ireland* (London, Routledge, 1988), 18–23.

14 A. Slide, *The Cinema and Ireland* (North Carolina, McFarland & Co, 1988), 45.

15 B. McIlroy, *Irish Cinema: An illustrated history* (Dublin, Anna Livia Press, 1988), 16.

16 K. Rockett, 'Aspects of the Los Angelesation of Ireland', *Irish Communications Review*, 1 (1991), 18.

17 L. O'Leary, in G. Fleeton (ed.), *A Seat Among the Stars: The cinema and Ireland* (London, UTV/C4, 1984), 14. The same Meeting House is now the site of the Irish Film Centre and Archive with two cinema screens, a neat historical irony. In Northern Ireland there were similar fears and strong objections to the proximity of cinemas and churches. One trade magazine reported that the construction of a cinema next to a church was halted due to local pressure. See *Today's Cinema,* 44 (11 May 1935), 110–14.

18 Rockett *et al., Cinema and Ireland*, 40.

19 'Events of the Year [1923]', *Kinematograph Year Book 1924*, 12–26. Censorship of films in Northern Ireland continued under the 1909 Cinematograph Act, which empowered local authorities to close cinemas on safety grounds and in practice ban films if not certificated by the British Board of Film Censors.

20 This description of Hollywood cinema is attributed to James Montgomery, the Irish film censor, by Oliver St John Gogarty, a poet, surgeon, Irish senator and unreliable autobiographer. My thanks to Bob Monks of the National Library's 'Liam O'Leary Archive', for telling me about this witty if somewhat apocryphal coinage.

21 T. J. Beere, 'Cinema statistics in Saorstat Éireann: a paper for the Statistical and Social Inquiry Society of Ireland', 28 May 1936. This document is held in the IFC Library, Dublin. There are no figures for 1944. The 1954 figure comes from the *Encyclopedia of European Cinema* (London, Cassell/BFI, 1995).

22 H. Byrne, '"Going to the pictures": the female audience and the pleasures of the cinema', in M. J. Kelly and B. O'Connor (eds), *Media Audiences in Ireland* (Dublin, UCD Press, 1997), 88–106.

23 For a concise analysis of the British film industry, including details of the terms of the 1927 act, see Street, *British National Cinema*, 4–27.

24 *Today's Cinema* (5 June 1936), 24, citing a report by the Presbyterian Church, which linked juvenile crime to the influence of cinema. *Today's Cinema* (5 September 1945), 29, reported the launch of a Sabbatarian Campaign against Sunday screenings at cinemas.

25 *Today's Cinema* (11 June 1935), 110–14.

26 *Kinematograph Weekly* (3 December 1936), 24.

27 *Today's Cinema* (3 June 1936), 10.

28 See: *Kinematograph Weekly* (18 October 1945), 11, on MGM extending into Belfast and *Daily Film Renter* (31 October 1945), 3, reporting on visit of RKO executives to Ireland.

29 G. Wilkins, 'Film production in Northern Ireland', in J. Hill, M. McLoone and P. Hainsworth (eds), *Border Crossing: Film in Ireland, Britain and Europe* (Belfast, Institute of Irish Studies, 1994), 140.

30 Slide, *Cinema and Ireland*, 15.

31 *Censorship of Films Act* (Dublin, The Stationary Office, 1923), Section 10:2, 15.

32 Bishop Gilmartin from 1927, quoted in Rockett, 'Aspects of Los Angelesation', 19.

33 Hill, *Border Crossing*, 150.

34 Rockett et al., *Cinema and Ireland*, 95–8.

35 Rockett et al., *Cinema and Ireland*, 96 and 122, note 3 explains that no copy is extant.

36 L. O'Leary, *Cinema Ireland: 1896–1950* (Dublin, National Library of Ireland, 1990), 30.

37 *Today's Cinema* (5 August 1942), 110–114.

38 *Today's Cinema* (20 June 1945), 24.

39 Quoted in Rockett et al., *Cinema and Ireland*, 118.

40 For a contemporary account, read Michael O'Dwyer's, '10 Days that shook the Irish Film Industry', *In Dublin* (8 April 1982), reprinted in *Film West*, 30 (August 1997), 24–8.

41 Hill, *Border Crossing*, 127.

42 The phrase is from M. McLoone's essay, 'National cinema and cultural identity: Ireland and Europe', in Hill, *Border Crossing*, 168.

43 OECD *Economic Survey: Ireland* (Paris, OECD, 1997), 'Basic Statistics: International Comparisons'.

44 On the occasion of a public lecture at the National Film Theatre, London, October 1995.

45 H. Linehan, H. Oram and J. Comskey, 'The Irish Film Centre', *The Irish Times Supplement*, 22 September 1993.

46 The IFB currently receives 48 per cent of its money from the EU structural funds. See *Film Ireland*, 60 (August–September, 1997), 8.

47 See J. Caughie, *The Companion to British and Irish Cinema* (London, Cassell, 1996), 177, for a brief analysis of the significance of GATT. His point is that the USA was prepared to allow the audio-visual sector to be excluded on this occasion because the newer technologies of delivery such as satellite, DVD and Internet may well outstrip the concept of national boundaries, which formed the practical basis for the culturalist argument of 1986–93.

48 In 1993, RTÉ allocated IR£3.5million for independent production which rose to IR£5million in 1994. It is projected that IR£12.5million will be budgeted by 1999. RTÉ also created the Independent Production Unit (IPU), dedicated to the commissioning of such material.

49 *Ireland on Screen* (Dublin, Film Base, 1997–98) indicates that the independent produc-tion sector in Ireland is still growing. Its listings show that 143 companies existed in 1996–97 and that this had grown to 192 in the year 1997–98.

50 'Imagining Irelands' conference at IFI in Dublin, November 1992.

51 Wyver, *Moving Image*, 279.

52 Rod Stoneman, 'Nine notes on cinema and television', in J. Hill and M. McLoone (eds), *Big Picture, Small Screen: The relations between film and television* (Luton, John Libbey Media, 1996), 130.

53 L. Gibbons, 'The esperanto of the eye? Re-thinking national cinema', *Film Ireland*, 55 (October–November 1996), 22.

54 'Britain adopts Irish model for film', *Guardian* (4 July 1997).

55 Hill, *Border Crossing*, 2.

CHAPTER 3

IRELAND AND POPULAR CINEMA: FROM SILENT ADVENTURE TO ROMANTIC COMEDY

- In what ways can popular cinema in Ireland be defined from the 1920s to the 1950s?
- What were the different cultural and cinematic contexts for Irish films in the period?
- How do screen representations of Ireland and the Irish compare across this period?

The textual terrain of cinematic representation

The text is a kind of battleground for competing and often contradictory positions.[1]

The previous chapters have outlined some key contexts for understanding cinema and television by considering the historical and theoretical dimensions to the cultural representation of Ireland. In this chapter I want to examine cinematic representations of Ireland in a selection of popular films in consecutive decades from the 1920s to the 1950s. The opening sections of the chapter define what I mean by popular cinema over this period. They also discuss the interplay between cinema and existing cultural representations of Ireland and the Irish in the 1920s in relation to *Irish Destiny* (1926) and briefly examine Irish-themed films of the 1930s in Britain and the USA. This sets up the detailed discussion of three key films, *The Dawn* (1936), *Odd Man Out* (1947) and *The Quiet Man* (1952). The respective heroic, tragic and comic narrative modes of these films explore perhaps the three major political and social topics in Ireland post-1921: the Anglo-Irish and Irish civil wars; the partition of Ireland and the problematic status of Northern Ireland; and the continued haemorrhage of emigration and its significance to Irish culture.

So the approach to the study of film adopted here, then, is two-fold. Firstly it seeks to combine the contextual knowledge of films with analyses of their formal nature as texts. Secondly, it seeks to compare films from different production contexts and different historical periods. In the films discussed in this chapter, we compare Irish, British and Irish-American examples. The films are 'read' as the textual terrain across which a battle for interpretative position and control is fought bearing in mind that, although no interpretation is ultimately definitive, 'it is untrue that all individual opinions have "exactly" equal weight'.[2] A cultural studies approach recognises that particular interpretations of films become dominant and accepted widely, but that these are nevertheless subject to change. There is always space to critically challenge and offer alternative or oppositional readings. This is done by exploring contradictory elements or addressing absences, bringing different contexts to bear and making new connections between films. Before we move on to explore our three main examples, we need to understand what is meant by 'popular cinema' in the era of Hollywood studio production.

Defining popular cinema in the Hollywood studio era

In the simplest sense, popular cinema produces films that sell a lot of tickets at the box office and make a profit. This quantitative definition is central to the mainstream fiction films considered in this period. Such films usually succeed because they are popular in a second sense: they are made to be widely-liked. That is, they address viewers across a range of differing class, gender, generation and national identities as a collective audience. This is achieved by mobilising readily-recognised character types (goodies and baddies) in narratives of inter-personal conflict featuring a problem, its complication and (usually) its resolution. Popular films assemble audio-visual images in order to create the illusion of verisimilitude, by cinematographic methods and generic patterns internationally circulated by repeated and extensive use. The conventional expectations of the classical Hollywood cinema became second nature and were integral to the pleasure experience of going to the cinema itself.[3] The essential features of this experience became axiomatic for most of the anglophone world, and 'in village hall and city cinema in Ireland the 1930s was the decade of an enthusiastic discovery of celluloid dreams from California'.[4] A high-cost business, film-making followed an industrial model in the USA, becoming a tightly integrated system during the studio era, dominated by five major companies. They specialised in supplying, marketing and controlling the worldwide exhibition of westerns, gangster movies, musicals, romances and so on. This system produced films with generic topics, narratives and visual images within a restricted repertoire but with sufficient variation to maintain a profitable popularity.

There are other ways in which the word 'popular' might be applied to cinema and ways of making films which complicate the first two definitions. 'Popular' retains a sense that suggests cultural activity by people not professionally involved in film production. It can carry the sense of expressing the efforts and aspirations of people with limited capital and not normally in positions to control cultural production. Such activities are based on limited resources and often in defiance of more dominant modes of production. This is exemplified in the production of Tom Cooper's *The Dawn* (1936), discussed below. However, the idea that culture made by ordinary people, amateur film-makers, is somehow more spontaneous or worthy than that supplied by large commercial organisations, especially foreign-based studios, is attractive but problematic. How exactly do you define who the 'ordinary' people are? Though their cultural resources and some practices differ from corporate, mass-produced methods, are the representations they produce necessarily more authentic or legitimate? From these problems, a fourth way of defining popular cinema can be developed. This view holds that popular cinema is not a simple case of an industrial product being imposed on a docile, mass audience who are duped into enjoying film, but neither is it enshrined in local, alternative amateur production. Instead, it argues that films may be defined as popular because of the ways in which they function as a site of struggle between different kinds of social and political subordination and resistance in a culture at given historical moments.[5] In the images and narratives on the screen, indeed in the social experience of cinema-going itself, the lived contradictions of the audience's experiences are imaginatively projected, represented and reconstituted.[6] This is a more flexible and analytically useful conception of popular film because it recognises that films must at some level engage their audience's interests and desires. Further, this conception suggests that the meaningfulness of films does not lie solely in the texts of the films but in the communicative exchange between film and audience. Finally and most fruitfully, it also implies that films form part of a wider social and ideological process of signification.[7]

Existing popular cultural representations

In the first quarter of the twentieth century the medium of film tended to feed off and rework pre-existing popular representations of Ireland and Irish character in Anglo-American culture. There was an uneven transfer and transformation of imagery from stage melodramas, vaudeville or variety acts, illustrated travel guides, popular ballads and novels in the emerging cinema. In Britain, popular visual representation of Ireland and Irish character worked in a potent, ambivalent fashion. 'Irishness' as place or person could be seen as either dark, dangerous and different, or backward, curious and ridiculous, depending on the precise contexts of its expression. As we saw in chapter one, this ambivalence characterised the nature of cultural interchange between Ireland and Britain.

In the same period, Irish representation in US culture witnessed a shift that suggested a more dynamic inflection that was carried over into films. In the first decade of the century, film types of the Irish tended to be comically drawn and burlesqued, reflecting a residual, unflattering portrayal of the Irish from the previous century when Irish immigrants faced considerable discrimination, particularly those who were Catholic.[8] But a transformation took place between the silent shorts and the coming of sound. This change reflected the relative growth in social mobility and political power of Irish immigrants in comparison to other ethnic groups who could be marked out by skin colour, looks, language and customs.[9] By 1924, the USA enacted legislation to curb immigration and, according to one commentator, 'Hollywood elected the Irish to serve as the models of assimilation to other immigrants'.[10] Thus, most of the 1920s films were about recently arrived immigrants and how they made out in the new country. Universal Pictures produced a lucrative series of comedy films featuring New York Irish and Jewish characters and their families: a grocery store owner, Jacob Cohen, and a policeman, Patrick Kelly. Beginning with *The Cohens and the Kellys* (1926), the series ran until 1933. In 1929, Paramount tried to cash in on a film of an extremely successful stage play, *Abie's Irish Rose* (1922), in which comedy ensued from the familial confusion when Rose Murphy marries Abie Levy. As policemen, professional boxers and construction workers, the Irish screen male 'championed law, social order and hard work' while the often more socially and class mobile Irish female 'was the safest guide for WASP (white Anglo-Saxon protestant) filmgoers unsure about the urban ethnic ghetto'.[11] Thus American-produced Irish films of the 1920s focused on the Irish immigrants rather than offering nuanced portrayals of Irish history or featuring contemporary life in Ireland itself.

Irish Destiny (1926)

A rare example of indigenous Irish production in the silent era, *Irish Destiny* (1926) was written and produced by Dr Isaac Eppel, a Dublin cinema-owner. The film takes an historical theme being set during the War of Independence in rural Ireland. Hero Denis O'Hara discovers an intelligence message on a dead British serviceman, joins the IRA and races by horse and motorbike across the countryside to warn his comrades in Dublin of a planned ambush. During the course of the film 'he is shot, wounded and imprisoned, but escapes in time to save his fiancee, Moira, from the clutches of the evil poitín distillers'.[12] In political terms, Eppel's screenplay was populist and pro-Irish. In cinematic terms, it was popular in the senses discussed above since it mixed amateurs with professional actors and production personnel. It featured location-shooting in Glendalough, Wicklow and Dublin – the city filmed from the back of a motorbike – but interior scenes were shot in Shepherd's Bush Studios in London. Hand-tinted colour sequences signified the burning of the Customs House (red) and a remarkably dramatic reconstruction of the Curragh prison camp nighttime escape (dark blue). It also incorporated newsreel footage of British troops in Dublin and the remains of Cork after burning by the Black and Tans. *Irish Destiny*, made just five years after the Anglo-Irish War, clearly represented events in a heroic mould and played to packed houses in Dublin. It was banned from exhibition in England for these very same qualities.[13] When it was shown in New York a year later with newsreel of the St Patrick's Day Parade in New York tacked on to the end,[14] a mainly Irish audience was treated to a pre-screening speech by a prominent Irish-Boston politician. A contemporary review records that the film 'elicited constant waves of applause. The spectators manifested their enthusiasm when the Black and Tans fell, and they hissed, as in the

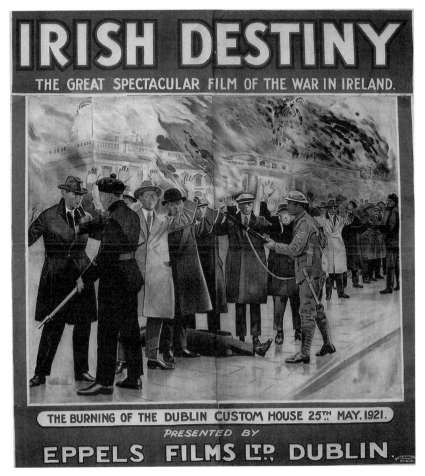

5 War of Independence action narrative: *Irish Destiny* (1926).
Courtesy of the Film Institute of Ireland

days of old melodrama, when a Black and Tan bullet struck an Irish volunteer'.[15] This suggests that, although enjoyed, it looked faintly old-fashioned by contemporary US standards. However, the narrative thrust of heroic action and sentimental romance, the editing of the chase sequences and clear moral message (illegal poitín stills are evil) are all imitative of Hollywood's mores and methods in the 1920s. But the *New York Times* was withering about the film's technical achievement: 'the photography is deficient' and 'the acting in this picture is very amateurish as is also the direction'.[16] The *Variety* review argued that 'the political propaganda of the Celt' meant its 'box office value … as a general release … cannot get far because of its limited appeal',[17] suggesting that films with overtly political themes tended not to be favoured for commercial reasons.

With the proliferation of sound in the 1930s, American accents and the content of Hollywood films were increasingly attacked by nationalists and moral guardians in Ireland, one of whom declared: 'We cannot be the sons of the Gael and citizens of Hollywood at the same time ... The influence of cinema is ... one tending towards more artistic and intellectual degradation'.[18] This echoed the concerns about cinema's morality in the USA itself. 'Irish' characters and second-generation Irish actors came to represent ambivalent, often conflicting values in one of the decade's most popular genres.[19] On the one hand, James Cagney as Tom Powers epitomised the corrupt evil of the gangster (*Public Enemy*, 1931), but this was often set against priest-figures (Pat O'Brien in *Angels with Dirty Faces*, 1938) or narratives that featured family values and virtue tested by circumstance, symbolised in the pivotal Irish mother character (Beryl Mercer in *Public Enemy*) or chaste young female. Voluntary measures by the US film industry to censor itself were stiffened under pressure from the Catholic-backed National League for Decency in 1934 with the formation of the Production Code Administration (PCA).[20] Sentimental Irish-themed films in the 1930s turned to music and dance in orchestrations of popular tunes featuring singing stars and elaborately choreographed routines far-removed from Irish folk contexts. The Vitagraph/Warner short, *Dublin in Brass* (1935), subtitled 'a Broadway Brevity', typifies how such Irish material was hybridised in Hollywood film, anticipating the phenomenon of *Riverdance* by several decades. Such historical and politically-themed films as were produced, notably *Beloved Enemy* (1936) and *Parnell* (1937), took Republican Michael Collins and the eponymous Irish parliamentary nationalist as central figures in their respective narratives. Irish literary works were adapted in film by Irish-American directors, foremost among whom was John Ford, who made the Oscar-winning *The Informer* (1935) and a disastrous *The Plough and the Stars* (1936). Ford's adaptation of Liam O'Flaherty's Irish civil war novel (published a decade earlier) remains a memorable film for the changes wrought in adaptation and its expressionist style. O'Flaherty's *The Informer* is set during the civil war (1922–23) but Ford crucially sets the film in 1919–20, simplifying narrative antagonism to a war against the 'occupying' British army. Secondly, Ford avoids the awkwardness of Gypo's lover betraying him to the IRA. These changes work to shift focus away from Flaherty's interest in the dissensual, internal conflict implicit in civil war, substituting it with an overarching narrative solution of Catholic redemption for the individual moral weakness of Gypo. On the whole, Irish history in Hollywood films provided a simplified backdrop for action that concentrated on the dilemmas of character and community rather than social comment or political analysis.[21]

The British film industry in the 1930s sustained a short-lived period of activity under legislative protection: quickly-made films to quota specifications in the Cinematograph Films Act (1927). However, domestic production in the form of empire films, historical costume dramas and working-class comedies tended to ignore or indirectly address the complexities of the still-fractious relationship between Britain and the Free State/Eire before World War II.[22] The darker side of Anglo-Irish history was avoided by the almost complete emphasis on its corollary: light-hearted, slapstick and whimsical (often musical) comedy. Donovan Pedelty (producer and scenarist) and Richard Hayward (actor and singer) were involved in a series of three quota-quickies with Irish subject matter. All three featured unlikely plots with likeable victims of circumstance, and elements of romance, song and comedy. *The Luck of the Irish* (1935) is about an Irishman's eventually successful attempts to save his ancestral home from wrack and ruin by betting on the fortunes of his race horse. *Irish and Proud of It* (1936) was billed as a romantic gangster comedy while *The Early Bird* (1936) was 'a comedy set in Ireland where villagers rebel against a puritanical woman'.[23] The energies of Irish-born movie migrants were involved in the production of popular Irish-themed films. Brian Desmond Hurst emigrated from Antrim and worked with Ford in Hollywood in the 1920s. Having migrated back across the Atlantic in the 1930s, he directed a rare British-funded film about the Anglo-Irish war, *Ourselves Alone* (1936).[24] In a somewhat improbable plot, a Royal Irish Constabulary (RIC) Inspector takes the blame for an English army officer who has killed an IRA leader in order to allow the victim's sister and the officer to develop a love relationship. But for the most part, British films preferred to give Irish locations and scenarios a comic treatment. Just as US movies had used comedy as a vehicle to explore immigrant inter-racial relations and the assimilative process, so British comic films provided opportunities for testing out cultural differences between the Irish and the English.

Cinemas in Britain continued to feed off but assert supremacy over variety and other stage acts as popular forms of entertainment in the 1930s. *Oh! Mr Porter* (1937) was a star-vehicle film for Will Hay, playing an incompetent railway worker who is expediently promoted to station-master in Buggleskelly, where the local conditions are rather peculiar. A remote side-line station on a comic and political border, the music, the map graphic, the mise-en-scène (dilapidation, proximity of livestock to humans, dress) and screen brogue dialogue, all signify its Irishness despite being in 'British' Northern Ireland. A supernatural sub-plot contributes to the mayhem, mystery and madness that is 'Irishness' in these comedy films. Initially, Will tries to run the station according to the company rules, but his incompetence travesties British officialdom. His ineptitude allows him to inadvertently thwart an attempt by the 'local football team' – heavily disguised as an IRA gang (wide-brimmed hats, overcoats and eye-patches) – from transporting guns across the border. Another popular performer, Dubliner Jimmy O'Dea, was able to transfer his comic talents to the screen and radio throughout the 1930s and 1940s.[25] In *Let's be Famous* (1939), he is a rural Irishman travelling to urban(e) London, which provides a comic displacement. Jimmy Houlihan, village shopkeeper and tone-deaf singer, dreams of fame at the BBC. On the way to give what he mistakenly thinks is an invited performance he meets and falls in love with Betty Pinbright (Betty

Driver) – her name signifying her honest, cheerful working-class origins – who has some genuine singing talent. The films opening and establishing scenes in Ballymunnock provide the staple elements of popular film representations of Ireland in the lilting musical score, the Celtic cross, a cow in the shop and the comic word-play dialogue. Ambitious Houlihan is verbally and visually absurd but the stuffiness and class-bound BBC is also gently mocked and the narrative reassuringly closes with romance. Female-impersonator Arthur Lucan successfully transferred his stage act in a series of fifteen *Old Mother Riley* films between 1936-52, providing much slapstick comedy. Both Lucan's eponymous Irish washerwoman mother and her daughter (played by Kitty McShane, his real-life Irish wife) are working-class Irish emigrants in northern England who stand up to authority figures in their films, puncture class snobbery, create anarchy and temporarily challenge existing power structures. Many critics agree that British film contributed to the interwar social consensus through its popular, home-produced genres.[26] But working-class concerns, regional characters and the Irish in Britain all represented forms of difference that posed non-conformity and potential disruption.[27]

'A landmark without successors': *The Dawn* (1936)[28]

The Dawn, stands out as both emblematic and exceptional in Irish cinema history. It was made in rural Kerry in 1934–35 by a group of amateurs, local people led by the owner of Killarney's garage and cinema, Tom Cooper. It was made collectively on a tiny budget using a makeshift studio and borrowed equipment. Its unusual production circumstances underline the lack of state-organised or corporate-funded film production in Ireland and the finished film reveals the unconscious internalisation of Hollywood's popular film aesthetics. In its representation of the Anglo-Irish war of 1919–21, it expressed a heroic sense of self-determination and independence that was central to a populist nationalist ideology developed in government from 1932 by de Valera's Fianna Fáil party. Viewing the film now, it is important to note that such 'green nationalism'[29] contained within it a subordinate socialist, internationalist republicanism, developed in the wake of civil war by people like Peadar O'Donnell[30] and expressed by those Irish who joined the International Brigade against Franco in the Spanish civil war (1936–39).

A reawakened continuation of a historic struggle is suggested by the film's title, the republican rising sun graphic and the intertitle exhortation that opens the film: 'let every English man who sees this film remember that no nation which oppresses another cannot itself be free'. The film closes dramatically at a paramilitary funeral shot in silhouette and ends with a call to arms: 'the fight will go on'. These obvious, anti-imperialist messages are literally spelled out on the screen but the film-text also works at a visual and discursive level. *The Dawn* redeploys cinematic stereotypes in its representation of the IRA, the RIC and the Tans, inverting the English/Irish polarities of a colonial discourse. The

6 Irish film in heroic mode: *The Dawn* (1936).
Courtesy of the Film Institute of Ireland

IRA men of the 'flying columns' of Kerry are presented as decent, honest and heroic while the Tan officer is shown as drunken, lascivious and murderous. In contrast to the uncouth and immoral Tans, Dan O'Donovan (played by Tom Cooper himself) is a respectable property-owner who dutifully commands an IRA unit that is presented as hierarchical yet democratic. They are shown to have close support and are indeed part of the rural community; the IRA men are at one with the countryside which they inhabit. In one scene, a small group of armed men are framed in idyllic repose in a sunlit glade, singing, relaxed and waiting for orders. When his house is raided, O'Donovan is able to unhurriedly open his back door and escape with a few steps into the countryside.

Like *Irish Destiny* a decade earlier, Tom Cooper and his group had unconsciously adapted the narratives of US cinema to Irish historical material. As a narrative, *The Dawn* contains two problems for its male protagonists: namely, Ireland's fight against the British forces, the RIC and the Tans, and the patriotic commitment of the Malone family's sons. These themes share some similarities with Ford's *The Informer*, released to acclaim a year earlier in the USA but initially banned in Ireland. In contrast to Ford's movie, which invites us to side with an informer, the narrative of *The Dawn* transforms suspected informers into national heroes. The film opens in 1919 with the mustering of the IRA from the local men, but Brian Malone is soon expelled because it is rumoured that he is an informer. A prologue flashback imputes that his grandfather had turned informer during the failed Fenian rising of 1867. Brian and his lover, Eileen O'Donovan, are seen courting, joining in the traditional road-side dancing and, more controversially, kissing in the parlour. Duly their engagement is announced, but this romantic plot development is blocked by his IRA expulsion. The latter raises a question mark over his patriotism and undermines his suitability as a husband. Brian's brother, Billy, is also seen to be of dubious character because he refuses to take any part in the IRA mobilisation. These problems are further complicated when the rebuffed Brian joins the RIC and goes off to train with the enemy in Dublin. But resolution and closure is achieved when his communal and family loyalties are stirred, forcing him to warn the IRA that they are going to be ambushed by the Tans. His credentials proved, he reunites with family and the waiting Eileen. In a subtly indicated sub-plot, it transpires that the pacifist Billy was really an undercover IRA agent all along. Although Billy is tragically shot, his death restores the honour of the family.

The Dawn presents Irish society as ordered, stable and united against British military forces. The film does not represent the degree of discord within Irish politics and society either in the 1919–21 period or during its production. It is not surprising that Fianna Fáil were happy for its political slogan to be used in posters advertising such a popular film that appeared to endorse its stance. Less an organised propaganda film, it is more a case of an astute political party latching on to and incorporating populist feeling and praising amateur enthusiasms. A small-town business proprietor, Tom Cooper was likewise happy to nurture this association and expand his ownership of cinemas following the film's success. For all its anti-Treaty origins, once in power, Fianna Fáil strategically combined republican rhetoric with the practical statecraft of a party uneasily reliant on Labour for its parliamentary majority. Extremist republicans were arrested in 1932 under legislation passed the previous year when Fianna Fáil were in opposition. In 1934 – the summer in which production of The Dawn began – there were some 451 state prosecutions of IRA members. In 1936 – the year the film was released – the IRA was proscribed altogether, its leadership interned.[31] The same government periodically suppressed republican newspapers, which explored Marxist socialism. Indeed, the 1930s were a time of heightened Catholic activity in Ireland. Agrarian radicalism or urban worker organisation was denounced in populist terms as communism and atheism. The rhetoric of the film chimed in with a populist nationalism that became increasingly imbued with a Catholic–Gaelic asceticism as the decade progressed. De Valera made full capital out of the opportunity provided by visiting Papal prelates during the Eucharistic Congress in June 1932.[32] Such was the climate produced by the mutually supportive ideologies of Fianna Fáil and the Church that left-leaning, modernist or social-realist intellectuals and artists wishing to comment on Irish society were marginalised, forced to emigrate or subjected to censorship.[33] In this context, the apparent simplicity of The Dawn belies ideological torsions particular to its historical conjuncture: its narrative is shaped both by suppressed internal political tensions and the adopted cultural form of cinema.

The Dawn was a low-budget, artisan and localised production. If participant accounts of its making are true, it was a genuinely popular, collective event.[34] It expressed a strikingly clear-cut version of recent history, one that generated considerable authenticity by the fact that some of the participants (including Cooper himself) were surviving members of the Kerry IRA. But in the textual work to project an image of a community naturally unified in the fight against the British it dissolved nascent social or class tensions in Irish life. These are signified in contrasting the accents of the polite middle-class voices of the Donovans and Malones with the unaffected Killarney dialect of the local volunteers; the mise-en-scène of respectable domestic interiors; the presence of servants and some of the stilted, drawing-room dialogue. The film was politically and morally acceptable, aside from the implied sexual urges of a living room kiss and the Tan officer's molestation of a woman. In Britain, reviews in the critical and trade press noted *The Dawn's* achievements, 'but throughout the film [it] is reminiscent of an amateur production. As such it is very good; as a professional production it is not so good'.[35] Most Irish reviewers praised the film and overlooked its technical deficiencies – poor sound quality and some pedestrian camera work during interior scenes. The acting and the photography of the natural environment were praised but one claim that 'it establishes not the possibility but the certainty that Ireland will be able to compete in film production with Hollywood'[36] was ridiculously idealistic. Imbued with Hollywood's cinematic values and de Valera's populist republicanism, it is hardly surprising that Irish audiences found considerable pleasures and pride in the film. Yet even as an exceptional amateur achievement, *The Dawn* highlighted the dismal show of corporate or state support for film production in Ireland, which was symptomatic until the late 1950s.

Making partition permanent: *Odd Man Out* (1947)

Carol Reed's *Odd Man Out* sets out to be an apolitical film, exploring the mental landscape of the principal character, Johnny (James Mason) and lamenting Kathleen's (Kathleen Sullivan) hopeless love for her IRA leader, fatally injured while robbing a textile mill pay-roll in Belfast. Its preferred perspectives on human moral frailties and expressionist angst can be questioned by carefully rehistoricising its contexts and analysing the film's textual elements. Studying Reed's 'taste for the heterogeneous'[37] in film method can provide insights into the key issue of how Northern Ireland became cemented awkwardly into the UK by the 1949 Ireland Act.

In the immediate aftermath of World War II, the British film industry's largest cinema conglomerate, owned by J. Arthur Rank, had ambitious plans to step up British film production, expand US distribution through Universal and challenge the Hollywood hegemony of British screens.[38] Part of this broader strategy

involved expansion in the Irish cinema circuits to control exhibition in the
nearest available market.[39] Two Irish-themed films were part of this campaign:
Odd Man Out and *Captain Boycott* (1947), the latter a historical drama set at the
time of the Land War of the 1880s in which Kathleen Ryan played opposite
Stewart Granger. With cinema admissions close to their all-time peak (163.5 million in 1946), *Odd Man Out* was seen by the trade press as 'a superlative general
booking'.[40] Marketed as a popular gangster film starring James Mason with a
strong Irish supporting cast, it was recognised by reviewers in New York to be 'ter-
rifically tense and dramatic on a purely visual-emotional plane' and comparisons
were made with Ford's *The Informer*.[41] While *Odd Man Out* was popular it was
also seen to offer 'absorbing entertainment for *discriminating* audiences, with
outstanding star appeal for all and a further notable achievement for British studios'.[42] To film intellectuals it was seen as 'a sign that our native cinema is reaching
maturity',[43] that 'British cinema has at last come of age'.[44]

Not unlike *The Dawn* in Ireland, this film was taken to embody the qualities of
a British national cinema, but what is interesting about *Odd Man Out* is that its
Britishness is revealed in the process of trying to conceal aspects of problematic

7 The graphics of the crime poster: *Odd Man Out* (1947).
Courtesy of Carlton TV

Irishness. John Hill has observed how a tragic narrative typifies the way in which serious British films deal with the political history of Anglo-Irish relations.[45] Johnny is the leader of the 'Organisation' (the IRA) recently released from prison, with doubts about the continued use of violence to further republicanism.[46] Loyal to his ideals and indifferent to Kathleen's pleading, he determines to undertake one last robbery to raise finances. Predictably this goes wrong, he accidentally kills a man, and is mortally injured himself. On the run from the closing circle of the police, he wanders through the shadows of the city as evening draws in, reluctantly assisted by sundry eccentric people through chance encounters. But nobody wants to be associated with him except the increasingly desperate Kathleen and Father Tom, the local priest. Midnight approaches and, despite the priest's warnings, Kathleen follows her heart by hatching an escape plan for herself and Johnny. The doomed pair are cornered by the police at the dockside. Kathleen deliberately causes the police to kill them in a hail of gunfire and they are united in their joint death on the stroke of midnight.

Odd Man Out observes the classical unities of narrative time and place to give the film a recognisably tragic dimension. The insistent tempo of William Alwyn's musical score and the careful deployment of incidental sound contribute to a sense of fate exerting its forces on the protagonists. The prologue's scrolling text seeks to replace historical specificity with the human and universal, but the film contains a countervailing current of geopolitical detail which led most previews and reviews to identify the Belfast setting by name. Against the grain of most films about Ireland, the urban setting of *Odd Man Out* is established from the titles superimposed on a drawing of docks, followed by an aerial sequence of an industrial city, dissolving to a ground level shot of factory gates with the unmistakable gantries of the Harland and Wolff shipyard in the background. The documentary veracity of these establishing shots help to reinforce the film's immediate postwar realism: trams are destined for the Falls Road, rows of terraced housing have been blitzed, gangs of children play on bomb-cratered wasteland; Johnny hides in a disused air-raid shelter; extras are uniformed sailors and soldiers, or ex-ARP wardens. In the decade of film-making prior to *Odd Man Out*, which included wartime propaganda films, Carol Reed had established a reputation for capturing the 'realism of ordinary lives and everyday settings',[47] so it is not surprising that he chose to feature the authentic dialect of local children in the film, even if their words are made to take on a sinister, expressionist chant.

In fact, his casting and film style reveals a curious eclecticism in Reed as a director. He mixed English film actors (James Mason) with complete unknowns (Kathleen Ryan), also employing non-professional locals, distinguished Irish theatre actors and a Canadian film actor. Reed's film borrows stylistically from various popular film genres and movements. Some of the exterior sequences are reminiscent of Italian neo-realist films like Rossellini's, *Rome, Open City* (1945) and *Paisà* (1946) in the use of bomb sites and non-professional actors to achieve a compelling authenticity. Yet Reed's film

8 British *noir* in Belfast: *Odd Man Out* (1947).
Courtesy of Carlton TV

draws on European expressionist film and borrows elements of American film *noir*, itself derived from émigré European writers and directors in Hollywood. Contrary to the classical Hollywood method, Reed avers the unobtrusive, natural lighting of scene and actor, relishing instead a low-key, chiaroscuro lighting, habits of frame composition and a mise-en-scène that express the emotional state of characters and major conflicts in the narrative. *Odd Man Out* is notable for its juxtaposition of high contrast between light and dark, cramped or disorienting framing and its dramatic use of shadows. While most scenes are edited with the continuity of a tightly chronological plot in mind, some edits go beyond this functional approach and montage sequences suggest Johnny's mental state at several points during the film. Reed was one of the best British directors of his time, managing to combine popular appeal with the detailed art of film-making, showing that craft and commerce could co-exist within Rank's stable of independently-minded directors.

Odd Man Out was shown in Britain when cities like London and Coventry were in ruins, food rationing was still enforced and VE euphoria had given way to postwar exhaustion. Belfast had suffered Blitz like much of beleaguered Britain and contributed greatly to the war effort. But despite this shared experience and sacrifice (differentiating it from Éire's neutrality), Northern Ireland remained an anomalous part of the British state. Under the 1920 Ireland Act, partition and Stormont remained temporary provisions. Constitutionally and politically, Northern Ireland was the 'odd man out'. Its government responded to political manoeuvres by the new British Labour government during 1946–48 to secure Northern Ireland's position within the UK.[48] Remember that months after *Odd Man Out* was released, India was partitioned and two years later it asserted its independence, but significantly it chose to remain within the British Commonwealth. By contrast, in 1948, Éire's new coalition government declared that it would accede to the status of republic and withdraw from the same Commonwealth. John Hill's canny point that *Odd Man Out* does not so much omit the political as displace it onto a human or abstract level[49] may be detected in a contemporary review, which observed that the film was 'a portrayal of a passage in the long battle … between *conflicting and unintegrated rights* – between *majorities and minorities*, between law and the rebel'.[50] A thinly-veiled reference to internal political division within Northern Ireland, namely the Catholic nationalist population, is presented as a universal conflict between the law and a rebel, criminal gang. Such critical language is not neutral but neither does it exhaust the possibilities for interpretation. A British crime film narrative insists on the fate of Johnny and Kathleen because they use violence to oppose the state in the person of the RUC inspector (Denis O'Dea), who stands for law and order. A tragic narrative, the reluctant, passive IRA man and the over-riding fatalism associated with the film's stylistic preferences, coincide neatly with the dominant British view of Anglo-Irish political history. However, there is enough force in the contemporary historical detail within and surrounding the film to provide an alternative reading, to examine why the film narrative insists that some forms of political violence are punished while others are legitimated. Demonstrations at screenings of the film in London by the Anti-Partition League, formed in early 1947, showed that the continued existence of the Irish border was disputed on the streets even as Northern Ireland's status within the UK was being hastily renegotiated by the Cabinet. When carefully historicised, the stability of the state and the moral invincibility of the law represented in the film narrative is critically shadowed by the anxious, contingent authority exercised by Stormont during 1945–48. Given that 'the rude surgery of partition was being used all over the world to "solve" problems',[51] it is not difficult to read *Odd Man Out* as imaginatively prefiguring and morally underpinning the legislative incorporation of Northern Ireland into the British state.

'This is Ireland, Sean, not America': *The Quiet Man* (1952)

One of the most popular cinema representations of Ireland celebrated the coming home of an Irish-American during a decade when nearly half a million Irish left. In Connemara, where the film was made, on average about 18 per cent of the population emigrated in the 1950s.[52] The film's enduring popularity may be explained by the way its comic excesses articulate the trauma of this loss, and by the way it portrays the romantic reintegration of an Irish émigré. It unashamedly celebrated a way of life that was actually being rejected by Ireland's sons and daughters. The traditional basis of community held dear by a conservative Irish-American had been disappearing between 1946–51, assisted ironically by the USA's Marshall Aid Programme. Ford's arrival in Cong, County Mayo, was timely; as he started filming in the summer of 1951 the village had yet to be plugged into the national electricity grid. But by the end of that summer Cong had been irrevocably connected and electrified. The film unit's presence provided lucrative, if short-term employment for tradesmen and a longer-term focus for cultural tourism. On release, the film became an international advert for Ireland just months before the state's new tourism agency, Bord Fáilte came into existence in July. Although it had some Irish critics, later commentators have noted that for all its 'retreat into a pastoral and horse-driven past',[53] it led the way in the unofficial marketing of Ireland. To consider *The Quiet Man* and the cultural circulation of its after-life,[54] is to explore the notion discussed at the end of chapter one that 'emigration is at the centre of the Irish experience of being modern'.[55]

The narrative of *The Quiet Man* is essentially circular. Sean Thorton (John Wayne) is escaping Pittsburgh and the memory of a prize-fight tragedy to come back to Inisfree to reoccupy his ancestral home, White O' Morn cottage, where he promptly falls in love with fiery Mary Kate Danaher (Maureen O'Hara). While Ford generates humour from the whimsical portrayal of the supporting cast of locals, the serious comic conflict of the narrative derives from Thorton's problematic encounter with the traditions of the village community. Though of local stock, his upbringing in a USA steel-town means that he is tainted with a different code of social values. He destabilises the status quo because he outbids Will Danaher (Victor McLagan) for White O' Morn and struggles to observe the social rituals of courtship for Will's sister, Mary Kate. The transformative action that Sean must perform publicly is to fight Will for Mary Kate's dowry money in the film's setpiece donnybrook fight scene. The propensity for the violence of screen Irish characters is here given a comic treatment, as opposed to its presentation in *Odd Man Out*. Here, instead of sealing the hero's fate, it is the means by which narrative equilibrium is achieved: Mary Kate submits herself to full marital relations and opposing brothers-in-law bond through violence.

This structure and the deployment of stereotypes (both racial and gendered) conforms to popular narrative conventions discussed earlier. If we recall that the Kalem Company's *Lad From Old Ireland* (1910) dealt with a returning emigrant, Ford's film is a remarkable distillation of the history of Hollywood's audio-visual representation of Irish subject matter.[56] From the picture-postcard image of the title sequence – castle among trees, golden sunset, lake in foreground – to the glorious Technicolor photography of the natural landscape of Connemara, the screen is packed with popular imagery, including a pony and trap, Celtic crosses and a red-haired shepherdess in a verdant glade. Victor Young's musical score establishes the comic romance genre mixing string melody (including harp) with interludes of a lilting theme and the action itself features renditions of several popular songs. It is easy to dismiss *The Quiet Man* for offering a false representation of Ireland, a stylised, soft-focus version of Irish life, a product of Ford's émigré nostalgia that is in some way less authentic than Tom Cooper's or Carol Reed's simply because it is American. But this is to miss the point that Ford's film does not seek to be real-istic. Astute critics of popular culture take a different tack by arguing that its

9 Idealised Irish womanhood in a natural landscape: *The Quiet Man* (1952).
Courtesy of Spelling Entertainments Group Inc.

excessive idealisation of the Irish countryside, the exaggeration of character traits (how else does comedy work?) and the elision of actual socio-economic conditions, makes for an assemblage of formal and historical elements whose contradictions offer a reflexive critique of Irish film representation.[57]

Most contemporary reviewers were in agreement that Ford 'goes overboard' (*Variety*) on the picturesque aspects of the scenery and another complained that the film is 'not entirely muscular' (*New York Times*). It is as if the visual excess, softness and sexuality are deemed to be inimical to the great director of masculine westerns. Indeed, 'Ford usually played down eroticism, which he considered inappropriate in males. For that matter he wasn't too wild about it in his female characters either'.[58] It was remarked at the time and has been taken up since that *The Quiet Man* is 'a Western made in Ireland rather than an Irish film'.[59] It is no coincidence that 'the myth of the West in Irish and American Culture' produces many fruitful correspondences.[60] Just as a train and the pony trap criss-cross the screen in the opening minutes, so Ford presents us with a bivalent culture in the process of transition. *The Quiet Man* tries to contain the modern by presenting an imagined past of the short story on which it is based,[61] but in doing so it signals the modifications of 1950s Ireland.

Confronting the difficulties of realising the complex material, cultural and emotional connections between Ireland and the USA, and perhaps self-conscious about its own identity, *The Quiet Man* revels in its formal contradictions and excess. Stunning exterior location photography jars with the two-dimensional studio inserts, breaking the seamless flow of classical editing. The closure normally assured at the end of a Hollywood film is also withheld by the final theatrical line-up of characters, some of whom break the illusion of realism by looking direct to camera. These formal glitches unconsciously prompt us to question the constructed nature of the images in front of us. In case we don't get the point, at the moment when the pastoral vision frames our hero's first encounter with the idealised heroine, Sean asks: 'Hey is that real? She couldn't be'. The Reverend Mrs Playfair's quip that 'only an American would think to paint it [the cottage] emerald green' is a self-deprecating Fordian joke. In Ireland, audiences knew it was 'a fairy tale version of Ireland shot in a quaint village just off Sunset Boulevard'[62] and consoled themselves that the film brought money and visitors. But the visual pleasures of Hollywood's Ireland contained an underlying melancholy. In cinemas either side of the Atlantic viewers tried to nostalgically reassure themselves that they or their departed relations could return. The significance of Ford's vision is that it signalled that moment when 'the emigrant's break with the past has been internalised within Irish culture, forming popular images of itself'.[63]

This chapter has examined selected cinematic representations of Ireland between the 1920s and the 1950s by Irish, British and Irish-American directors. It has shown how cinema may be variously defined as 'popular' but it has favoured a view that considers such films as the focus for different kinds of social and political tensions in Irish society. Using *Irish Destiny* (1926), *The*

Dawn (1936), *Odd Man Out* (1947) and *The Quiet Man* (1952) as specific examples, I have demonstrated how the texts of these films contain contradictory, masked or omitted features. These can be brought out by contextualising the films using our historical knowledge of each era and applying a politics of cultural representation. We have seen how 'Irish' films – whether by Irish or foreign directors, shot partly or wholly in Ireland – have represented the major political tensions of anticolonial conflict, political division and the Troubles, as well as the social and cultural shifts brought about by emigration and problematic modernisation that have marked Ireland's postcolonial development. It is important to see that these tensions and shifts have been embodied in the very matter of Ireland's cinematic images. We have observed the ambivalent nature of cinematic representations of Ireland and the Irish, which drew on and were integral to broader transformations in the representation of Irishness in British and US culture. We have explored how Ireland's national cinema may be constituted not just in the films produced indigenously by Irish-born directors, but also those (a greater number) made about Ireland by outsiders, and the high percentage of foreign films routinely viewed with enthusiasm by Irish audiences over the decades. This more expansive definition of Irish cinema draws on but also questions and redefines the notion of national cinema itself. In Ireland's case, its national cinema is defined by its subordinate, promiscuous relations and exchanges with Hollywood, British and European cinemas. The dynamics of these relations in fiction films are explored thoroughly in chapters 5 and 6, but in the next chapter we examine the history and nature of non-fiction film in Ireland by considering documentary.

Notes

1 G. Turner, *Film as Social Practice* (London, Routledge, 1993), 147.

2 A. Gramsci, *Selected Prison Notebooks* (London, Lawrence & Wishart, 1971), 192.

3 D. Bordwell and K. Thompson, *Film Art: An introduction* (New York, McGraw-Hill Publishing, 3rd ed. 1990), 70–1.

4 T. Brown, *Ireland: A Social and Cultural History, 1922–79* (Glasgow, Fontana, 1981), 153.

5 S. Hall, 'Notes on deconstructing "the popular"', in J. Storey (ed.), *Cultural Theory and Popular Culture: A Reader* (Hemel Hempstead, Harvester Wheatsheaf, 1994), 459–66.

6 See H. Byrne's, '"Going to the pictures": The female audience and the pleasures of cinema', in M. J. Kelly and B. O'Connor (eds), *Media Audiences in Ireland* (Dublin, UCD Press, 1997), 88–106, for a study of women cinema-goers in Waterford during the 1940s and 1950s.

7 Turner, *Film as Social Practice*, 147.

8 A. Slide asserts that in the 1920s 'while the stage [images] moved forward and away from its past of racial stereotypes (which also prominently included Jews and Blacks), the fledgling film industry embraced such stereotypes for its productions', claiming that 'the audience for the motion picture was far less sophisticated, definitely working class, when compared to that for the stage.' A. Slide, *The Cinema and Ireland* (North Carolina, McFarland, 1988), 74–5.

9   J. F. Watts, *The Irish Americans* (New York, Chelsea House, 1996), 78–9. See also N. Ignatiev, *How the Irish Became White* (London, Routledge, 1995).

10 L. Lourdeaux, *Italian and Irish Filmmakers in America* (Philadelphia, Temple University Press, 1990), 48.

11 Lourdeaux, *Italian and Irish Filmmakers*, 64–5.

12 A. McKeown, 'Programme Note', *Irish Destiny*, n.p. This was a rare screening of a restored print with live orchestral accompaniment at the Barbican Centre, London in April 1997, as part of a festival of cinema, music and culture called 'From the Heart: Innovations in Irish music and arts'.

13 K. Rockett *et al.*, *Cinema and Ireland* (London, Routledge, 1988), 42–4.

14 Slide, *The Cinema and Ireland*, 19.

15 *New York Times* (29 March, 1927). Reproduced in *New York Times Film Reviews, 1: 1913–1931* (New York, Arno Press, 1970), 3834.

16 *New York Times* (29 March, 1927).

17 'Edba', *Variety* (13 April 1927), 23. Reproduced in *Variety's Film Reviews*, Volume 3: 1926–29, (New York, R. R. Bowkers, 1983).

18 G. Fallon, 'Celluloid menace', *Capuchin Annual*, 1937, as quoted in K. Hickey, 'The cinema and Ireland: A short history', *Green on the Screen* (Dublin, Irish Film Institute, 1984), 8. Hickey points out that Fallon eventually became the Irish film censor.

19 K. Rockett, 'Migration and Irish cinema', in P. O'Sullivan (ed.), *The Irish Worldwide, Volume 3: The Creative Migrant* (London, Leicester University Press, 1997), 179–81.

20 J. M. Curran, *Hibernian Green on the Silver Screen* (Westport: Connecticut, Greenwood Press, 1989), 48–52.

21 Rockett's research presented in the film, *Ourselves Alone* (Taylor Black, 1995), discusses a Michael Farrell film, *Some Say Chance* (1934). This dealt with a middle-class Irish mother abandoned by her husband who then turns to prostitution in England to support her daughter's schooling in Ireland. Made but not released in the 1930s, it demonstrates that some film-makers did attempt to address taboo social issues.

22 Certain films were suppressed by the BBFC in the scenario-writing stage such as *Sir Roger Casement* (1934). Casement was an Irish-born, highly placed diplomat who worked for the British government but who became a Republican. He was executed for treason for his involvement in support for the Easter Rising of 1916. See B. McIlroy, *Irish Cinema: An Illustrated History* (Dublin, Anna Livia Press, 1988), 31.

23 BFI Library synopsis, SIFT database.

24 For a synopsis and critical view on the film, comparing it to *Beloved Enemy* and *Michael Collins*, see K. Brownlow, 'Ourselves Alone', *Film West*, 28 (1997), 34–7.

25 P. B. Ryan, *Jimmy O'Dea: The Pride of the Coombe* (Dublin, Poolbeg, 1991). Chapter 6 succinctly outlines how O'Dea moved during the 1930s between variety, pantomime and film in Ireland and England. His independently-produced *Blarney* (1938), about the consequences of a jewel robbery, saw a very successful release in Dublin, even mocking the permanence of the Irish border in the closing sequence. O'Dea starred in the BBC's wartime *Irish Half Hour* radio show. It was made to entertain Irish personnel in the British Services but offended the Controller of the BBC in Belfast.

26 A. Aldgate, 'British domestic cinema of the 1930s', in J. Curran and V. Porter (eds), *British Cinema History* (London, Weidenfeld and Nicolson, 1983), 270–1.

27 S. Street, *British National Cinema* (London, Routledge, 1997), 46–7.

28 L. O'Leary, *Cinema Ireland: 1896–1950* (Dublin, National Library of Ireland, 1990), 26.

29 K. Rockett, 'Notes on some nationalist fictions', *Screen*, 20:3/4 (Winter, 1979/80), 115–16.

30 H. Patterson, *The Politics of Illusion: Republicanism and Socialism in Modern Ireland* (London, Hutchinson Radius, 1989), Ch. 2, 'Republicanism in inter-war Ireland'.

31 J. J. Lee, *Ireland: 1912–1985, Politics and Society* (Cambridge, Cambridge University Press, 1989), 219.

32 Lee, *Ireland*, 177.

33 For an overview of social and cultural milieu in this period, see Brown, *Ireland*, Ch. 5, 'The 1930s: A self-sufficient Ireland?'

34 D. O'Cahill, 'And so we made "The Dawn"', *The Capuchin Annual* (1937), 119–22.

35 A. R., *Monthly Film Bulletin*, 4:37 (January 1937), 10.

36 Maud Gonne quoted in Rockett *et al.*, *Cinema and Ireland*, 66.

37 D. Vaughan, *Odd Man Out* (London, BFI, 1995), 32.

38 R. Murphy, 'Rank's attempt on the American market, 1944–49', in Curran and Porter, *British Cinema History*, 164–78.

39 'J. A. Rank acquires big Irish cinema interest', *Irish Times* (19 January, 1946), 1.

40 *Kinomatogaph Weekly*, 2077 (6 February 1947), 26.

41 B. Crowther, *New York Times* (24 April 1947), 30.

42 L. H. C. *Today's Cinema* (31 January 1947), 19. My emphasis.

43 A. Vesselo, *Sight and Sound* (Spring 1947), 40.

44 B. Wright, *Documentary News Letter*, 6:56 (April–May 1947), 84.

45 John Hill, 'Images of violence', in Rockett *et al.*, *Cinema and Ireland*, 152.

46 The screenplay is based on a successful novel, published in 1945 by F. L. Green, a second generation Irishman, who moved to Northern Ireland from Portsmouth. It should be noted that Johnny's speech about non-violence does not appear in the novel. Other significant changes from novel to film provide the basis for B. McIlroy's interpretation that *Odd Man Out* 'questions the status quo, and implies that the Protestant community in Northern Ireland is akin with militarism'. See Ch. 3, 'The Rorschach test: Anti-imperialism in Carol Reed's *Odd Man Out*', *Shooting to Kill: Filmmaking and the 'Troubles' in Northern Ireland* (Trowbridge, Wiltshire, Flicks Books, 1998).

47 J. Caughie, *The Companion to British and Irish Cinema* (London, Cassell, 1996), 135.

48 G. Bell, *Troublesome Business: The Labour Party and the Irish Question* (London, Pluto Press, 1982), 73–85.

49 Hill, 'Images of violence', 158.

50 A. Polonsky, *Sight and Sound* (Spring 1947), 40. My emphasis.

51 F. S. L. Lyons, *Ireland Since the Famine* (London, Fontana, 1973), 590.

52 G. FitzGerald's 1961 report on emigration as quoted in C. Ó Gráda, *A Rocky Road: The Irish economy since the 1920s* (Manchester, Manchester University Press, 1997), 218.

53 A. Sarris, *The John Ford Movie Mystery* (London, Secker & Warburg, 1975), 135.

54 The film was released by Video Collection International (VC3398) in 1985 and had sold nearly a quarter of a million units by 1990, according to G. McNee, *In the Footsteps of The Quiet Man* (Edinburgh, Mainstream Publishing, 1990), 9. It was subsequently released on another video label to mark its fortieth anniversary in 1992. See *Sight and Sound*, 2:6 (October, 1992), 69. Its theatrical rerelease was announced in early 1997. See *Screen International*, 1097 (28 February 1997), 6. *The Quiet Man* was also the subject of a documentary titled *Inisfree* by a Spanish director, José Luis Guerín (1990).

55 L. Ryan, 'Irish emigration to Britain since World War II', in R. Kearney (ed.), *Migrations: The Irish at home and abroad* (Dublin, Wolfhound Press, 1990), 47.

56 Ford's 1950s film reworked a 1920s setting from a short story first published in 1933, while Jim Sheridan's *The Field* (1989) adapted a 1950s play and set it in the 1930s. There are several parallels between the two films. See fuller discussion of *The Field* in chapter 6.

57 L. Gibbons, 'Romanticism, realism and Irish cinema', in Rockett *et al.*, *Cinema and Ireland*, 221–6 and 237–40.

58 L. Giannetti, *Masters of the American Cinema* (New Jersey, Prentice Hall, 1981), 177.

59 Lord Killanin, quoted in McNee, *In the Footsteps*, 159. See also L. Gibbons's essay, 'Synge, country and western', in *Transformations in Irish Culture* (Cork, Cork University Press, 1996), 23–36

60 This is the subtitle of L. Gibbons's essay, 'Synge, country and western'.

61 Maurice Walsh's 'The Quiet Man' first appeared in the *Saturday Evening Post* (an American newspaper) on 11 February 1933. Ford paid $10 for the story rights. The story was subsequently published in a collection of Walsh's stories called *Green Rushes* (1935).

62 C. Fitzsimons (brother of Maureen O'Hara) quoted in McNee, *In the Footsteps*, 159.

63 Gibbons, *Transformations*, 40.

CHAPTER 4

DOCUMENTS IN CELLULOID: NON-FICTION FILMS

- What are the origins of documentary film?
- What are the main types of documentary and their formal characteristics?
- How have documentaries represented Irish social and political tensions?

Orchid in the land of technology?

The equipment-free aspect of reality . . . has become the height of artifice; the sight of immediate reality has become an orchid in the land of technology.[1]

Photography and the development of film technology anticipated the mimesis of movement that scientifically evidenced 'real life'.[2] The end of the nineteenth century saw photo-chemical process and mechanical engineering come together as the apparatus for cinematography. In the twentieth century, the profound effects of 'the last machine' on the nature of aesthetic production and the perception of reality itself were envisaged with memorable acuity by Walter Benjamin in 1936. But the residual notion of scientific evidentiality in film's general historical development continued to be a fundamental *raison d'être* of documentary. Most documentarists are motivated by the intent of 'claiming the real'[3] as opposed to creating fictional worlds for entertainment purposes. In this chapter we consider the paradox of documentary's 'character as both artifice and evidence'.[4] Without collapsing documentary into a fiction indistinguishable from the feature films of the last chapter, we examine how it represents truths in the historical world and contemporary life. Using selected examples, we can see how non-fiction film has documented, examined and exposed Irish society and politics, featuring notable directors and less well known film-makers. The chapter examines the ways in which documentary-makers from North America, Ireland and the Irish in Britain have represented national archetypes and historical achievement in the 1930s and late-1950s; constructed Irish emigrant histories in Britain; and critiqued the state in Ireland, north and south, in the 1960s and 1970s.

Documentary film: origins and traditions

Early *actualités* – short, static camera films – tended to record the familiar social world of home and work, but cameras were also used to present vicarious explorations of different worlds in exotic travelogues and nature films. Newsreels – short digests of topical events – were programmed alongside the main feature in cinemas, but it was during the late 1920s and 1930s that the term 'documentary' emerged and became consolidated as a film practice. Robert Flaherty, an American of Irish descent, and John Grierson, a Scottish advocate of documentary, were involved in one of the seminal documentaries representing Ireland, *Man of Aran* (1934). Echoing earlier strands of social documentation and travelogue films, their ideas and practice emphasised different aspects of a realist tradition in documentary. 'Realist' here refers to the desire through film to reveal truths about the condition of the social and historical world, to show 'how life is'. Social realists, like Grierson, hailed documentary as an influential means of public information and reform, despite being a 'poor relation' to what he called the 'yahoo individualism' of Hollywood. Emerging during the interwar period, the British documentary movement's politics were a complex and contradictory amalgam of socialism and liberal democratism. There were more radical 'workers' film groups in Britain and the USA.[5] Against these currents, Flaherty was conservative and romantic. His interest in film came from his experience as an adventurer-explorer and he held essentially nostalgic attitudes towards the pre-modern cultures he documented. His was a humane but unselfconscious filmic 'ethnography' whose style masked its method. In contrast, Soviet film-makers such as Sergei Eisenstein and Dziga Vertov, as well as dealing with revolutionary and modernist concerns, are credited with pioneering a realist aesthetics of experimental formalism – notably the montage of visual collision and reflexive, fluid camera work. But, even if the ideological ends and aesthetic means were markedly different, documentary movements in the USA, Europe and the Soviet Union during the 1920s and 1930s were motivated by social, educational and political purposes.

In Ireland, such developments found little fertile ground for growth because of the particular conditions that existed at the time. Lack of dedicated centralised funds, a dearth of equipment and a pervasive, insular conservatism stymied progressive politics and experimentation in cultural forms, including documentary film. The examination of social conditions was avoided by Irish documentary film-makers who 'chose to reproduce in the main both the ahistorical ethnicity represented in *Man of Aran* and its economic off-shoots, the tourist-landscape film'.[6] There were pockets of enthusiastic activity in Dublin and Belfast – under the auspices of the Irish Film Society (IFS) and the Belfast Film Society, both founded in 1936 – as well as in other provincial centres like Cork and Drogheda. These groups screened foreign films, organised lectures, published reviews and articles, tried to promote education through film and had members involved in making short films. In the absence of sustained feature film production, non-fiction film in Ireland during the period between the 1930s and the 1950s was prolific in comparison. A sense of a profusion of talent that was starved of funds and lacked coherent, sustained development is conveyed in Kieran Hickey's retrospective film, *Short Story: Irish Cinema*

1945–58 (1986).[7] However, people like Liam O'Leary, George Morrison, Robert Monks and Louis Marcus learned how to eke out a living on projects commissioned by state departments, cultural organisations like the clerical-led National Film Institute (founded in 1945) and Gael-Linn (founded in 1953), which dynamically promoted the Irish language and commercial projects. It was O'Leary, reporting on the IFS in the 1940s, who summed up the situation by stating that 'the main interest in film here is centred round the possibilities of documentary'.[8] One such possibility – the direct engagement with contemporary politics – was exemplified in an otherwise subdued period by O'Leary's, *Our Country* (1948). A 'startling piece of agitprop',[9] in eight minutes it abrasively questioned Ireland's national achievement. It was a sharp attack, sponsored by a new, progressive political party, Clann na Poblachta (People of the Republic), helping them to force a coalition government with Fianna Fáil in that year's election. But it was not until the mid-to-late 1960s that independent and radical dissent was articulated through more extensive documentary in or about Ireland. This was part of a coincidence of political radicalism in Europe, innovation in sound recording, faster (more light sensitive) film, less weighty camera equipment and the melding of documentary film with the discourses of journalism.

At this point, we should emphasise that documentary films, while premised on connections with and expressions of the real world, are not factual in the sense of objectively presenting observable events. Documentary's reality is constructed through conventions – particular combinations of audio-visual images based on the habitual use of camera, sound and editing – similar to, but different from, mainstream fictional cinema. Like classical Hollywood conventions, those of documentary film are partly to do with the use of various technologies. The most basic of these in mainstream film is that the camera is invisible: actors do not ordinarily look at the camera. In contrast, because of its historical use, the repertoire of non-fiction film allows for the documentary look, when the glance of non-actors confirms the presence of the camera and the veracity of the image. The issue of staging activity for filming, of reconstructive strategies and dramatising events, involve the use of different aesthetic conventions, degrees of fabrication but retaining the notion of realist truth. Some critics have argued that documentary itself is a contingent idea, subject to being read as real. That is to say, 'documentary-ness' might reside as much in viewer expectations as textual form.[10] For example, a popular current misapprehension that documentary should offer a balanced treatment of its subject derives from the genre's almost total absorption into the structures of broadcast journalism since the 1960s, particularly in European countries with well-established public service broadcasting institutions. But in the interwar period, documentarists in Britain and Ireland survived on a varying degrees of state, cultural and commercial sponsorship, and as such notions of balance are anachronistic. Documentary formed an important test-bed for the development of cinema generally during an era of mass audiences in commercial cinemas, but which also fed into educational institutions, myriad local film clubs, as well as the state-sponsored propaganda films between 1939–45.

The social-realist documentary should, according to Grierson,[11] comprise filmed material from 'the camera shot on the spot'. Documentary's strength was its 'capacity for getting around' to capture 'the living scene and the living story'. People filmed doing their work or enjoying pastimes would be more authentic than professional actors performing such activities. The subject matter for films was best derived from actual life rather than imagined and scripted scenarios. Most importantly, he endorsed the notion that documentaries should be made with a sense of social responsibility, for the purposes of national education. Grierson's significance at the head of what became a movement in British documentary, however patronising its films now seem, did put working class labour on screen, highlighted social hardship and presented the case for reform, even if 'running away from social meaning'[12] and fundamental political questions.

Documentary of the so-called recording tradition, has its politics embodied in its aesthetic, in its particular use of audio-visual equipment. According to Paget,[13] such films assemble the facts, show the elements of their subject, allow reality to speak for itself, using an objective, self-effacing method rendering the film-making process transparent. This is to generalise about the diverse practices within documentary film. Even Grierson himself indicated an awareness that simply *recording* profilmic material (raw, unstaged events) does not in itself make documentary when he defined it as 'the creative interpretation of actuality'. The shaping, editing and ordering of material to convey a point and reveal an underlying truth is a process in which the film-maker's preconceptions about politics and society, equipment limitations and understanding of film conventions are crucial in determining how they view the subject in hand and how it should be tackled at a particular historical juncture. The distinguishing features of documentary are that they take 'shape around an informing logic', which 'requires a representation, a case, or argument about the historical world', and that the formal structure allows for gaps and interruptions of flow such as would not be acceptable in the classical Hollywood feature.[14] Though, as we will see, many non-fiction films have a narrative structure or tell the story of their subject.

Alternative and oppositional strands in documentary, constituting what Paget terms a 'reporting tradition', have existed intermittently throughout film history, flexibly defined against dominant strands – such as the social-realist – that have themselves experienced an uneven development. Such film-makers or groups often adopt particular stylistic conventions in order to represent reality differently. Such films often contend that facts and information in society are not value-free, that film mediates its subject and is itself part of the representational process. Film-makers working within the reporting tradition assume that: a) the audience should not only have access to information but the right to question it; b) that the subjects of films should represent themselves rather than be represented by a professional or within terms dictated by official institutions; and c) viewers should be made aware of how documentaries are put together and know how point of view is constructed through formal conventions. This is film-making that seeks to go beyond revealing the truth of social inequalities and political injustice and change peoples' perceptions of how our lives are organised and governed.

It was in the 1960s that documentary in the reporting tradition became politically significant in various national cinemas in Europe and the USA. Making use of light-weight, hand-held cameras and portable sound tape recorders, two methods of documentary film-making emerged known as 'direct cinema' in the USA and '*cinema verité*' in Europe. Elements of their audio-visual techniques were subsequently incorporated into mainstream broadcast documentary. Black-and-white footage, grainy quality film, with hand-held, unsteady framing and uneven sound recording came to signify a popular notion of documentary film. It demonstrates how a way of filming becomes associated with and transformed at a historical conjuncture. In its purest form, direct cinema film-makers kept the camera running and kept editing to a minimum in an attempt to achieve a goal of unmediated representation, the so-called fly-on-the-wall technique. At variance with these ideas and insisting on the material intervention involved in all film-making, early *verité* film-makers drew eclectically from Soviet formalism, European modernism and radio documentary in an attempt to be more formally inventive, aesthetic in method and reflexive in their practice of oppositional politics. This range of documentary is found within the selected examples in this chapter, including *Radharc: Derry* (1964), *The Irishmen* (1965), *The Rocky Road to Dublin* (1968) and *Ireland: Behind the Wire* (1974).[15] From the 1960s, film documentary was largely absorbed into the structures of broadcasting, but a line of radical alternatives continued alongside and from within this assimilative development.

Analysing documentary film

Having considered a condensed history of the main currents in film documentary and how it features in Irish cinema history, it is worth giving some thought to how documentary may be analysed in formal terms as a film text. John Corner's introductory chapter in *The Art of Record* (1996) concludes with a theoretically flexible scheme for analysing documentary discourse. He discusses in some detail the different kinds of image and speech elements that comprise the textual features of documentary and how they may be combined. His aim is to 'identify some of the principle ways in which communication is organised in documentary' but adds that his 'typology is provisional and heuristic'.[16] In this exploratory spirit, I have chosen to represent his ideas in the form of a table (Table 4) as a viewing aid to analysing individual films. In addition to modes of image and speech, one should not forget to consider the function of soundtrack, including music, in different communicative combinations

Table 4 Modes of documentary language

Modes of image	Modes of speech
Evidential 1 (reactive observationalism) Characterised by minimal directorial intervention. It is an indirect mode – typically used in fly-on-the-wall – putting viewer in position of vicarious witness; viewer required to interpret sights and sounds to organise significance. Camera follows action, may not get close-ups and lacks planned moves of other modes. Often edited to emphasise durational values: temporal sequentiality and immediacy. Potentially gripping but dependent on comprehensibility, interest and visual 'strength' being maintained. In the absence of authorial control, can lose coherence and disengage viewer.	**Evidential 1** (overheard exchange) Speech of observed subjects in the pro-filmic action; overheard speech may come close to the coherence and pointedness of dramatic dialogue; the way in which action is objectified and speaker's self-consciousness/performance are both variable in this mode.
Evidential 2 (proactive observation) Largely observationalist but pro-filmic activity is managed to increase range of camera work, more discursive use of mise-en-scène and smoother time compression. The encoding of mise-en-scène, composition and shot may be appear as self-conscious style or be collapsed into observational transparency depending on nature, frequency, directorial choice and function of sequence in overall design of documentary	**Evidential mode 2** (testimony) Interview speech, obtained and used in various ways. It can be read on an axis of objective/true to subjective/partial, depending on how the sound and visuals are edited (including subversive juxtaposition)
Evidential 3 (illustrative) Visual images are subordinate to verbal discourse, supporting ideas and argument (which are frequently only partially confirmed by visual image); narrative drive of visuals is weak, low level of continuity, little attempt at achieving durational values of observationalism. A mode used widely in current affairs and some news.	**Expositional mode** (commentary) Full and partial commentary, presenter direct address, out-of-frame bridging; expositional voice useful to explain abstract ideas, link disparate visuals; voice-of-god objectivity may be replaced by several subjective speakers, seen or unseen.
Associative Visual images engaged in making second order meanings. Connotations and symbolic resonance generated by pro-filmic, shot type and editing can reinforce and coexist with the use of images for more directly referential purposes.	

Source: J. Corner, *The Art of Record* (1996), Manchester University Press

as I do in the case-study documentaries that follow this section. The point about Corner's scheme is that it is not a fixed set of categories of formal features that are always and exclusively found in particular kinds of documentary. The value of his work is that it is alive to the fact that documentary discourse is constantly shifting, its contours shaped by technological factors, social use and historical change. In particular, his analysis reminds us how modes of documentary language are subject to different interpretations and creative combinations by film-makers and, importantly, by viewers. The table is meant to provoke discussion, stimulate further elaboration and test out theoretical categories against actual film examples. It is a useful exercise to heighten critical awareness to check off the different possible combinations of image/speech modes when viewing any of the selected films discussed in the next section. For example, although the proactive mode of image might characterise *The Rocky Road to Dublin* (1968), it also mobilises potent associative meanings. Similarly, the film deploys a mixture of testimonal modes (interviewees) and an expositional mode of speech in the form of a commentary. So, while certain modes of image and speech usually tend to predominate in one kind of documentary, it is possible for several modes to feature in a single film. The kind of analysis suggested by this table complements the text/context model of a cultural studies approach and is supplemented by the historical contextualising material in the case studies that we turn to now.

Making the romance seem real: *Man of Aran* (1934) and *Mise Éire* (1959)

Searching for suitable images for John Hinde's picture-postcards in 1950s Ireland, David Noble tells how on the Aran Islands he came across a white, thatched cottage perfectly set against a picturesque Connemara skyline. Hardly believing his luck, he promptly photographed it only to find out later 'it was the cottage that Flaherty had built for the family who appeared in his film, *Man of Aran*. He'd deliberately chosen the spot to build the cottage because it made a good picture'.[17] This neatly extends Benjamin's point in an Irish context: not only is it impossible for reality to be equipment-free, in some cases the real turns out to be a simulacrum. In the current section we examine the conditions in which *Man of Aran* was produced, analyse aspects of its formal construction and consider the reception of the film on its release and in its afterlife.[18]

Grierson suggested to Flaherty that the islands off the south-west coast of Ireland would be an ideal subject for a documentary in the style of his previous films on Inuits (*Nanook of the North*, 1922) and Polynesian islanders (*Moana*, 1926). A production budget was secured following a meeting set up by Grierson with Michael Balcon of Gaumont-British. Some of Grierson's personnel were involved in pre-production and in assisting Flaherty's small family unit, including Mrs Frances Flaherty, who helped devise the scenario. The group lived on Inis Mor (Big Island) for two years during which time Flaherty shot and

processed over 200,000 feet (thirty-seven hours) of film in a makeshift labora-
tory. Flaherty's trademark method, a kind of ethnography by experimental
filming, involved a high shooting ratio and the final seventy-five minute film
ended up costing Gaumont-British £30,000.

Although shot on location and using local people, these were selected from
a 'group of the most *attractive and appealing characters* we can find, to represent
a family, and through them tell our story. It is always a long and difficult
process, this type of finding, for it is surprising *how few faces stand the test of the
camera*'.[19] Flaherty's desire for photogenic faces arose from a mix of racial attitudes and commercial savvy. He knew what would look good cinematically and
how his central theme of man versus sea needed to be realised in the scenarios
that the archetypal Aran family and curragh (canoe) crew performed for the
camera. The cottage he had built was authentically constructed but on the
more exposed, dramatic side of the island. The islanders obtained their paraffin
oil from the mainland, not from the sharks they are shown to hunt in the
climax of the film. Indeed, experts had to be hired to teach the native people
how to hunt traditionally. Aside from the ethical questions raised by the
dangers to which curragh crews were exposed in the storm sequences,
Flaherty's rationale for this *reconstructive* approach was to creatively document

10 Archetype of family fortitude: *Man of Aran* (1934).
Courtesy of BFI Collections

what he viewed as the essential features of a primitive civilisation – aspects of a life that *had been* – but one that had rapidly succumbed to contact with the changing Irish mainland, its modernising ways and values. Ironically, the production and success of his film helped, like Ford's *The Quiet Man*, to accelerate the contamination of the culture for which both Irish-Americans professed so much admiration.

Structurally and formally, *Man of Aran* is a rich and fascinating but flawed film. Present-day students may be reassured when watching this classic that there were contemporary reviewers on both sides of the Atlantic who found the film tedious and too long at seventy-five minutes![20] 'Lovely to look at – sincere, virile, and understanding' (Lejeune) it may be but 'even beauty should be organised' (Cooke). In Corner's terms, the film clearly uses proactive observation, attempting to achieve the semblance of transparency largely through continuity editing. The overheard speech is poorly synched with the visuals. While we might find it comic, some notable film critics of the time – brought up on silent film – thought that spoken dialogue 'unnecessary',[21] perhaps believing that it devalued the purity of film as a visual art. There is no spoken commentary (Corner's expositional mode of speech) and three intertitles contextualise the action for the viewer. But the opening credits sequence cues a generic Irishness in the typography of Gaelic script and in the music which – we are informed – is based on traditional Irish melodies. Traces of folk authenticity, however, are deracinated by the full orchestral arrangement: cosmopolitan high-culture transforms the indigenous in a London recording studio.

Flaherty has been acknowledged (even by his critics) as having pioneered the treatment of making actuality dramatic in the history of documentary film.[22] However, the action depicted in *Man of Aran* is not organised around psychologically realised characters as in fiction narrative but rather the archetypal figures of father, mother and son. While the sea may be anthropomorphised with different moods, none of these characters functions within a linear narrative, since the film is episodically structured around typical activities (fishing, collecting seaweed, hunting shark) to illustrate Flaherty's universal theme: man versus nature. The film makes it difficult to establish temporal continuity; it lacks an overall 'chronologic'[23] sense of seasonal cycle, period detail or passing of time. The film does use editing techniques that are recognisable from narrative film but this is due to the fact that the film was largely assembled by John Goldman. A tension that exists within the film – between a conventional continuity editing style and Flaherty's more impressionist cutting – is explained in Goldman's account of two very different approaches to camera and edit bench.[24] An early sequence establishes images of the domestic interior of the cottage, the animals and child. The mother's anxious glance out of the window is conventionally match-edited to a shot of the sea swell. Music cues suspense or anticipation. She waits to spot the returning men on the curragh. In contrast, the storm sequences are composed of rhythmically cut shots, repeated racing pans of waves and tiny isolated human figures against massive backdrops of rock and spray.

Man of Aran is a tangle of connections and cultural cross-overs characterised by its production history, its formal tensions and reflected in its divergent reception on release. Flaherty was an Irish-American adventurer, a self-styled cinematic poet, who unconsciously deployed a colonial discourse in representing native Irish people, undifferentiated from Invits and Polynesians. His predilection for seeking out primitive man in a state of nature is a romantic conception shared by John Ford but with different emphasis.[25] Whereas *The Quiet Man* stressed the convivial, communal and idyllic aspects of Irish rural life, Flaherty dwells on the isolation, austerity and inhospitable aspects of the natural environment. The Irish premiere of *Man of Aran* was greeted by Irish government approval since it was seen to endorse the dominant ideology of self-reliance and ascetic frugality of 1930s Ireland. In Britain it was marketed – with little opposition by Flaherty – as a social realist depiction of life in Aran, with a premier in an art cinema in London. It opened in New York to the full sensationalist Broadway hype and made box-office profit. Although it was given qualified approval by some respected critics[26] and film-makers in Ireland, Britain and the USA,[27] and won an award at the Venice film festival, there were those who compared the film unfavourably to mainstream Hollywood's images of Ireland, arguing Flaherty's 'lie is the greater, for he can make the romance seem real'.[28] Its unquestioning awe of Aran life, the highly selective ahistorical treatment and the limitations of its documentary method make *Man of Aran* a problematic film in many respects despite its undoubted influence.[29]

11 Man of Aran opens at the Criterion Theatre on Broadway (1934).
Courtesy of the National Library of Ireland

If *Man of Aran* was an unwitting endorsement of Fianna Fáil values in 1934, *Mise Éire* (*I am Ireland*, 1959) can be viewed as a cinematic swan-song of nationalism at the end of the 1950s. George Morrison was commissioned to make the film by Gael-Linn, a dynamic organisation keen to revive Irish language and culture through modern means. Dealing with the 1893–1919 period, *Mise Éire* was the first part of an intended trilogy of films. This itself was part of a bigger project, instigated by Morrison in 1952, to preserve and catalogue valuable film sources, most of which were held in archives and collections outside the country. Gael-Linn envisaged the trilogy as an examination of Ireland's recent history through a popular medium, divided into discreet ninety minute films to facilitate projection in schools and clubs. It is significant that only *Saoirse?* (*Freedom?*) followed, bringing the history up to the outbreak of civil war in 1922. Although it generated considerable anticipation in 1961 as 'the epic sequel to *Mise Éire*', it achieved neither the critical nor popular success of its predecessor, probably due to the still discomforting civil war memories.[30] The third film – dealing with Ireland in the 1920s and 1930s – remained untitled and unmade.

Mise Éire was in part the product of a momentum generated by the IFS in the 1940s for film to be recognised as an art form in its own right, but also an important facet of Ireland's cultural history and contemporary life. Morrison's

12 Opening night excitement for *Saoirse?* in Dublin (1961).
Courtesy of Gael-Linn

idea was to compile a documentary from existing newsreel, supplemented with photographs and other visual sources to present 'the resurgence of the Irish nation through the eyes of cameramen who were there when history was made'.[31] Based almost exclusively on 'found' material, it differed in method from Flaherty's location shooting but was Griersonian in its educational thrust and audio track. Its impressive music score was commissioned from Seán Ó Riada, the Abbey Theatre's musical director, performed by the Radio Éireann Orchestra and integrated with a resounding expositional commentary, written and declaimed completely in Irish by well-known RÉ script writers and presenters. Little had changed in terms of production since the 1930s and most of the processing and editing work was carried out in London and Amsterdam. Even this brief detailing of production indicates that *Mise Éire* was the result of considerable indigenous enthusiasms and talents. It drew on a range of the Republic's official cultural and creative resources. However, some of the basic post-production facilities were still wanting in Ireland.

Visual and audio modes of documentary language are closely integrated, leaving little margin for misreading the heroic interpretation of history presented in the film. It is significant to note that Morrison claimed the film was a deliberate critique of a romantic nationalist view of history.[32] Rather like Flaherty, who had chosen the seas around Inis Mor as the symbolic natural apotheosis of Gaelic stoicism, Morrison inserted some curious bridging sequences into *Mise Éire*, which depict the sea crashing against a rocky coast. They stand out as unmotivated links in the actuality newsreel that they join. The eternal forces of nature are linked to the political narrative of nation in a rhetorically powerful romantic image. Although it did not make much international impact[33] because of its all-Irish commentary, *Mise Éire* did well at cinemas in Ireland in 1959. But this success contained a deeper political failure: a nationalist ideology would be severely scrutinised on film by modernisers and iconoclastic radicals over the course of the next decade.

Radical voices: *Radharc: Derry* (1964), *The Irishmen* (1965), *The Rocky Road to Dublin* (1968) and *Ireland: Behind the Wire* (1974)

This clutch of films offer views of Irish history from diverse perspectives but sharing a capacity to unnerve political authority and institutions. *Radharc* were a group of intellectually probing Roman Catholic clerics who were in their day in the vanguard of independent documentary production in Ireland. This section looks at an example of their work that focused on discrimination and political inequalities in Derry well before the civil rights movement in Northern Ireland gained broadcast media attention in the second half of the 1960s. We also examine the work of displaced or disaffected points of view, from a director of Irish descent working for the BBC in England to an Irish newspaper journalist living in Paris and an English film school drop-out. These films are significant in terms of the broader transformation of documentary film sketched out earlier, indicating the cross-fertilisation of film, broadcasting and journalist reportage that took place during the 1960s. Using the technology available to them at the time for their particular social and political visions, these film-makers deploy arresting photography and testimonial speech to powerful effect, and some make significantly innovative use of sound editing[34] and music tracks.

Radharc[35] (meaning 'view' in Irish) came about in the late 1950s as the result of Archbishop J. C. McQuaid's foresight to involve the church in television. As the leading figures of what became an ad hoc production team of priests, Joseph Dunn and Desmond Forristal gained training in independent television in Manchester and in New York before setting up Radharc in 1961 as a unit making films from a religious perspective about Ireland, past, present and abroad. This took place in advance of the establishment of the national television service, RTÉ, in 1962, but with a view to finding a regular scheduled slot in its programming. Joe Dunn's team were in the vanguard of producing films for television when the electronic medium was very new to most Irish people. The archbishop was anxious that the church should continue to have influence over the character of television schedules. McQuaid's pressure had ensured, for instance, that, in 1950, Radio Éireann inaugurated the practice of broadcasting the chimes of the Angelus – a moment of prayer for Catholics at 6 p.m. – every day to remind listeners of their faith during a decade dedicated to the devotion of Mary, the mother of God.[36]

However, at the height of its powers Radharc was far from the tame lap-dog of the archbishop, RTÉ or Irish politicians. Joe Dunn was a maverick and humane priest who astutely helped to produce a body of films that niggled and probed Irish society, linking questions of Christian faith and teaching to the realities of life in Ireland and to Irish involvement abroad. His films inveigled themselves into areas not normally discussed openly at that time. In 1963, his was the first film crew inside a prison (St Patrick's Young Offenders Institution, Dublin) and he made a film about prostitution in Cork (1968) which caused controversy not least because it used hidden camera filming.[37] In the former film, inmates, staff and the Minister for Justice are interviewed. While most of the young men and staff show due deference to the dog-collared interviewer, the Minister for Justice, one Charles Haughey (astute enough to have insisted on viewing the film before interview),[38] criticised the film on camera for emphasising the harsher aspects of the regime. Indeed, the film did employ heightened sound (boot steps on metal gantries, door slamming and key jangling) and framed some interviewees so as to hide their identity, but Haughey himself was then pressed with some awkward questions about the extent to which inmates could be really reformed by such a system and he was repeatedly asked why trade union recognition of the work done by inmates was not forthcoming. As such the film exemplifies the way in which early television broadcasting could be used to question and challenge politicians and force television viewers to examine their own attitudes.

13 *Radharc* film crew at St Patrick's mission, Nairobi, Kenya (1965). Courtesy of Esras Films, Dublin

Radharc managed to film some remarkable international footage, particularly from within Central American countries under military regimes, like El Salvador and Nicaragua, but such successful incursions into world affairs only serve to put into perspective notable instances of the political censorship exercised on *Radharc* by RTÉ. In 1964, departing from its early magazine format, *Radharc* undertook a feature investigation of the local politics of Derry City. Reporter Patrick Cunningham first outlined the historical background of the city and then explained its relationship to the welfare and political systems of the UK. Much of the early part of the film moves between Cunningham on location atop Derry's city wall, simple maps and graphics, still pictorial evidence and archive film footage. The film then moves into a series of interviews, mostly from within the Catholic community and with political leaders holding nationalist views. Their testimonies establish the inequalities of employment opportunity, housing provision, policing and the gerrymandering of voting wards (areas) to maintain power within the city for the Unionist Party, its politicians and Protestant business interests. The film highlighted the sectarian nature of Northern Irish society at a time when Taoiseach Lemass and Prime Minister O'Neill were engaged in tentative diplomacy on economic matters. The various elements of the film are organised to indict sectarianism and the political system that supports it. Moreover, Cunningham is addressed by Eddie McAteer, a nationalist Stormont MP, with polite formality as 'forgive me, an uninformed stranger':

McAteer:	There's a lack of understanding in the south, as to what the problem of living in the north is.
Cunningham:	Would you say there's a lack of interest?
McAteer:	No, I would say that there is a lack of knowledge. I think people are surprised to find out about the curious undemocratic tricks that are played up here ... I keep reminding people, you have no normal democracy here.[39]

The programme implicitly condemned the Irish Republic and its ministers for ignoring political and social injustices in Northern Ireland while seeking to further economic alliances in the cause of modernisation and promote a shallow ecumenism. The film was prescient because it identified the key issues in the civil rights campaign that followed between 1965–68 and tackled a topic little explored by RTÉ's in-house investigative programmes. However, RTÉ senior management at the time judged (possibly influenced by ministerial pressure) that it would be inappropriate to broadcast this particular *Radharc* film because they considered it inflammatory and it was cravenly consigned to the shelves until it was safe to be shown in 1989 as part of a *Radharc* retrospective.[40]

A similar fate met some of the best documentary work by a legendary producer who worked for the BBC in Birmingham during the 1960s. Philip Donnellan was of Irish parentage, had a British Army commission and carved out a distinguished if dissident career at the BBC. His life and work are a confounding collection of influences. He worked in radio features during the 1950s but became interested in making films as BBC TV expanded. *The Irishmen: An Impression of Exile* was a fifty-minute piece shot on 16mm film by Michael Williams for a 'Tuesday Documentary' slot. Although completed, it has never been broadcast nor had a proper cinema release. Like its subject, the Irish navvies of 1960s Britain, *The Irishmen* has been consigned to retrospective film festivals and limited video circulation.[41] It was shot mainly in the work places of labourers in London, but also recorded interviews in their digs (rented accommodation) and Irish pubs. These urban sequences alternate with sequences depicting rural Irish life and a journey to London of an unnamed fisherman (Joesie MacDonagh) from Mason Island off Carna, in the Connemara Gaeltacht (an Irish-speaking area). Donnellan's film gives powerful and proud voice to the Irish emigrant experience in Britain. Using film to represent popular history, it features the testimony of men who are articulate, intelligent and in some cases angry about their circumstances. In his flat, surrounded by wife and children, one interviewee (Jim McHugh, from Edenderry) speaks eloquently of his experiences in England. He criticises the Irish government for letting the country remain 'destitute ... sorry to say it', but the full force of his indictment of English racism – '[the Irish] won't make good in England because from the time they start they're not wanted' – is qualified

14 Giving voice to Irish labour in Britain: *The Irishmen* (1965).
Courtesy of the Philip Donnellan Archive, BFI Collections and the BBC

by another unseen Irishman whose voice-over is brought up over the image of
the increasingly belligerent interviewee: 'The Irish might talk a lot more about
how good they are but in fact, it's all based on a very strong sense of *inferiority*'.
The subjective commentary of a fellow Irishman forms a subtle, qualifying
audio-bridge, which explains the origins of Irish and English attitudes in the
postcolonial terms outlined earlier in this book.

However, the most inventive, memorable feature of the film is the soundtrack, edited by Charles Parker, a creative postwar radio producer and friend of
Donnellan. Folk ballads, such as 'The Rambler from Clare' and 'London Clay',
are arranged and recorded by Ewan MacColl and Peggy Seeger, played by
Seamus Ennis and other noted Irish folk performers such as 'Gabe' O'Sullivan
and Tommy McCarthy. Music forms part of the social life and cultural expression of the workers and on-screen we witness Paul Lenihan sing, solo and unac-
companied, the proud but bitter ballad, 'McAlpine's Fusiliers', in a pub social.
Audio-visual montage is the structural basis of the film, as is demonstrated in
two short sequences. 'Jack of all trades' begins with a quiet introduction of one
or two instruments. On-screen we see men and machines on site preparing to
start work. As more instruments kick in, the tractor jerks forward into motion.
The lyrics tell of Jack's work experience. We see three men balancing a long pipe
on their shoulders as they walk precariously across a bridge structure. The
music is killed and replaced by mechanical noise. Then the visuals show close-
ups of men's boots and their team work as the next verse of the music cuts in.

The tempo of the music and the pace of the editing complements the physical action depicted and the lyrics match the work described. A similar sequence follows to show the ferry-crossing of the young man coming to work in London. The quiet, pulsing opening on accordion to 'London Clay' accompanies shots of Dun Laoghaire port, the ferry at sea and the young man on deck. A horn blast and the deafening sound of drills go with scenes of labourers at work digging clay underground. The music is brought back in for the next verse. The lyric mentions a 'curragh', we see a boat on the beach and the sequence continues alternating and overlapping sound, music and picture in a rousing sequence, which also functions to signify the passing of time.

In stark contrast to these intricately edited sequences associated with work, process and movement, there is one elegantly slow and rather bizarre two-shot sequence that provides a moment for solitary reflection. The first shot begins in a bar after closing time, lighting is low, we hear a solo saxophone playing. Shot from behind the bar counter, a woman wipes the top and moves right out of shot. The camera pans very slowly left, across the bar, past an open door to reveal within the back room a seated man playing the saxophone.[42] The room is dark but he is picked out in a spot light. The saxophone continues into the next shot, overlaying the sound of a train and an almost black screen. Slowly we pan right to reveal the young fisherman asleep in a train carriage. It is a

15 The moment of jazz Irish folk fusion in *The Irishmen* (1965).
Courtesy of the Philip Donnellan Archive, BFI Collections and the BBC

sublime moment in the film, a musical fusion in which a traditional Irish air (Padraic Colum's 'She moved through the fair') is rendered on a jazz instrument. Is the music supposed to signify the young man's dream? Has he left someone behind in Ireland whom he loved? Donnellan's mode of documentary is largely proactive observationalist but in moments like this it moves into the associative realm. It should be noted that it constructs a partial history of emigration, representing it in wholly male, 'southern' and Catholic terms. One female interviewee is used, a few fleeting shots of women appear and there are no Ulster accents. These lacunae are mentioned not to bemoan its lack of 'balance' but to draw attention to the selective processes at work within documentary production. His film catches the emotional range of male emigrant experience, whilst visually celebrating their physicality by photographing men's working bodies. Zooms to close up of male musculature or pull-backs to reveal men operating massive machinery have the effect of heroising them, not unlike soviet worker films of the 1930s. The difference between Donnellan's low-angled shots of labourers and Flaherty's isolated man on Aran breaking stones is that *The Irishmen* is historicised and overtly politicised as well as being aesthetically pleasing. Donnellan's film was deemed too controversial to be aired by the BBC in the mid-1960s[43] because it charged the English for being racist in their attitudes towards the Irish at a time when the British political establishment were only just awakening to the implications of the West Indian presence in Britain following post-1948 immigration.[44] *The Irishmen* remains a poignant document of popular, contributory historiography giving an ignored and embittered diaspora the opportunity to say Ireland was 'destitute', to show the rural west as derelict and lifeless, and that Irish governments were in part responsible for not ameliorating emigration.

Iconoclasm is central to Peter Lennon's mordant but witty examination of the Republic's political establishment, Church hierarchy and the smug materialism of the Irish middle-class at the end of the 1960s in *The Rocky Road to Dublin* (1968). An Irish correspondent for the *Guardian* newspaper's Paris office, Lennon secured funding from USA businessman Victor Herbert to make the film. He employed the cinematographic skills of Raoul Coutard and a music track by The Dubliners, whose version of the film's title opens the film. Footage was shot quickly over sixteen days in Ireland but it is as carefully crafted visually as it is caustic in its critique of the post-colonial Irish state, which Lennon sees as failing the promise of national independence. Lennon himself delivered the voice-over commentary, which assembled interviews with several prominent dissident and liberal voices arguing for revision and change in contemporary Ireland. These include the editor of *The Irish Times*, writer Sean O'Faolain, Conor Cruise Ó'Brien, a trendy priest, Father Michael Cleary, a spokesman from the GAA and sundry ordinary people such as a housewife and school boys explaining sin in a classroom. *Rocky Road* borrows partially from journalism's interrogative, interview style but also from the French *cinema verité* techniques[45] to convey a sense of people hankering for modernity but

16 *The Rocky Road to Dublin* (1968).
Courtesy of Peter Lennon

being held back by staid institutions. Edited in Paris, the film was not declared at customs nor was it put forward to the Irish film censor for inspection before its premiere on 11 May 1968 in Dublin in front of an audience of dignitaries who wrongly assumed it had been certified. As Lennon explained, 'we simply ignored the rules. Film censorship in Ireland is cretinous anyway'.[46] The *Evening Herald* declared it 'ANTI-EVERYTHING' and the *Irish Independent* found the points made against the Church to be 'deliberate discourtesy', but most of the other Irish newspapers felt the film was a passionate if personal view that should be seen and heard. *The Irish Times* was strongest in its praise calling it 'an acute, humane and unsentimental look at this country … if our cinema managers have any gumption at all, they'll be queuing up to book it'.[47] The film hit the revolutionary spirit of the time and, famously, was the last film screened at Cannes that year before the festival was suspended by Godard and Truffaut, who staged a three day debate about cinema and revolution with students. It was also screened by students at universities in Nice, the Sorbonne and to striking Renault car workers in the spring of that year. According to Vincent Browne, 'it paved the way for the development of a critical attitude towards the institutions of the state which was to effect the whole manner in which documentary makers approached their subjects'.[48]

Ireland: Behind the Wire (1974) is credited to the London-based Berwick Street Film Collective, but most of it was filmed by Richard Mordaunt between

1971 and 1973. It is a film clearly committed to examine the reasons for the rise of civil rights in 1968–69, the repressive role of the British military presence in Northern Ireland and the effects of internment (1971)[49] on working class people in Derry and Belfast. Mordaunt, who stayed with families in Catholic nationalist communities during this period found making the film 'an extraordinary experience'. Film school-trained in the mid-1960s, he became disaffected with established career paths and methods and got involved in several collectives well into the 1970s. His collective-based work and his Irish projects exemplify alternative practice and oppositional film politics.[50] *Ireland* was funded by Republican clubs and supporters in Britain, aimed at exhibition through schools, factories and communities, thus side-stepping the kinds of constraint imposed by institutions like the BBC, as experienced by Donnellan. Although attempting to create real social cinema by adopting techniques associated with *cinema verité* and the French new wave, Mordaunt expressed the contradictions of English radicalism when he spoke of the 1960s as a time when fellow collective film-makers learned to 're-engage with Grierson [sic] cinema in terms of documentary'. *Ireland* was an attempt to counteract the institutionalised censorship of Northern Ireland in the British and Irish broadcast news media in the early 1970s. Much of the footage is characteristically *verité* in technique: hand-held camera work, poor sound recording quality, uneven lighting, 'grainy' monochrome film. Other modes of documentary language are used including informative intertitles, subjective voice-over commentary, and powerful, to-camera testimony of police interrogation methods. Northern Ireland appears a bleak, deprived urban area, visualised with gloomy, oppressive skies and cramped interiors. The soundtrack accentuates microphone wind noise and other incidental domestic sounds are harsh, jarring to the ear, reinforcing the representation of a depressing part of the United Kingdom. Like *Rocky Road*, it indicts the complacency and dishonesty of those in power for allowing atrocities like Bloody Sunday to take place and seeks to jolt its viewers into some kind of action. It seeks to achieve its aims outside of the mainstream forms of distribution whereas *Rocky Road* was intended for festival and cinema release and *The Irishmen* for mainstream broadcast. We have seen how, from without and within Ireland, the country and its history have been documented to elevate certain aspects of national character, taking *Man of Aran* and *Mise Éire* as examples. Our other case studies showed that, between 1964 and 1974, more critical representations of Ireland's social and political tensions were made on film, even if not always widely viewed. In Ireland, as elsewhere, the energies of film documentary tended to be gradually subsumed into television, but during the same period the impetus to make questioning alternatives in fictional film representation grew despite the continued domination of mainstream Anglo-American production. We examine these developments and their implications in the next chapter.

Notes

1 W. Benjamin, *Illuminations* (Glasgow, Fontana/Collins, 1973), 235.

2 E. Barnouw, *Documentary: A history of the non-fiction film* (Oxford, Oxford University Press, 1993), 1–30.

3 B. Winston, *Claiming the Real: The documentary film revisited* (London, British Film Institute, 1995), 127–37.

4 J. Corner, *The Art of Record: A critical introduction to documentary* (Manchester, Manchester University Press, 1996), 2.

5 On workers' film societies in the 1930s, see S. Street, *British National Cinema* (London, Routledge, 1997), 154–6. On similar movements in the USA, see Barnouw, *Documentary*, 111–21.

6 K. Rockett *et al*, *Cinema and Ireland* (London, Routledge, 1988), 72.

7 My thanks to Sunniva Flynn for pointing out this particular source.

8 L. O'Leary, 'Developments in Éire', *Sight and Sound* (Summer, 1943), 12.

9 K. Hickey, 'The cinema and Ireland: A short history', in *Green on the Screen* (Dublin, Irish Film Institute, 1984), 11.

10 B. Nichols, *Representing Reality* (Bloomington and Indianapolis, Indiana University Press, 1991), 24.

11 F. Hardy (ed.), *Grierson on Documentary* (London, Faber, 1979). All quotations are taken from 'First principals of documentary', 35–46.

12 Winston, *Claiming the Real*, 35–9.

13 D. Paget, *True Stories? Documentary drama on stage, screen and radio* (Manchester, Manchester University Press, 1990), 39.

14 Nichols, *Representing Reality*, 18–20.

15 All three of these films have received limited theatrical release. Although produced by the BBC, Donnellan's film has never been broadcast but can be purchased on VHS from the James Connolly Association in Northampton, England. Lennon's film made a sharp impact in Ireland and French film periodicals and is shown in retrospective Irish film festivals, most recently at the IFC in April 1998. It can be viewed at the IFA, Dublin. There are few secondary materials on *Ireland: Behind the Wire* but a preservation print is held at the BFI, London. There is no record of it ever having been broadcast on British television.

16 Corner, *Art of Record*, 27–30.

17 D. Noble, as quoted in *Hindesight* (Dublin, Irish Museum of Modern Art, 1993), 38.

18 *Man of Aran* has featured in NFT screenings over the years and in Irish film festivals. It has been broadcast on British and Irish national television. It is available on VHS, released by Academy Video (CAV007), *Sight and Sound* magazine terming it a 'dramatised documentary' (June 1994). The film is regularly shown to visitors at the Heritage Interpretation Centre on the Aran Islands today.

19 R. Flaherty, from 'An account of the making of the film – *Man of Aran*', quoted in Rockett, *Cinema and Ireland*, 91, footnote 3. My italics. Flaherty was not the first creative visitor to be enchanted by the visual presence of the Aran people. Irish playwright J. M. Synge famously wrote in a book read by Flaherty, that 'the peasants have a further intuition for picturesque arrangement and each group is in perfect pose for my camera'. See J. M. Synge, 'The Aran Islands', in A. Price (ed.), *Collected Works: Volume 2* (Gerrards Cross: Buckinghamshire, Colin Smyth, 1982), 54. In his other writings, Synge shows that he was not oblivious to the hardships of Aran, nor was he näive about

the extent to which the modern world had already penetrated island life even at the turn of the century.

20 Jolo, *Variety* (29 May, 1934). This review mistakenly locates the Aran Islands in the north of Ireland! See also C. A. Lejeune, 'A sealed document', *The Observer* (29 April, 1934). L. C., 'A tale of lost opportunities', *Picturegoer*, 3:155 (12 May 1934), 18–19, complained of the highly selective representation of the film, the lack of plot, romance and its repetitiveness, suggesting it could have been edited from seven to two reels.

21 P. Rotha, 'Documentary films: *Man of Aran*', *Sight and Sound*, 3:10 (Summer 1934), 71.

22 Winston, *Claiming the Real*, 99–100.

23 Winston, *Claiming the Real*, 106–7.

24 Goldman is cited at length in, A. Calder-Marshall, *The Innocent Eye: The life of Robert J. Flaherty* (London, W. H. Allen, 1963), 155–7.

25 L. Gibbons discusses the concepts of what he terms soft and hard primitivism in Irish cinema in Rockett *et al.*, *Cinema and Ireland*, 197–9.

26 'One only has a cursory glimpse at the life of a primitive people', W. E. W., *Monthly Film Bulletin*, 1:4 (May 1934), 30. 'One is given the impression that the barren island is cut off from the world altogether … yet the Aran islander enjoys his wireless like the rest of us … For all we can see the inhabitants consist almost entirely of the three main characters who obligingly pose for effective skyline photographs', L. C., *Picturegoer*, 12 May 1934, 18–19.

27 'It is not exactly fashionable these days among European artists and metropolitans generally, but this is to be said for it: Flaherty returned us to the origins of all observationalism'. See J. Grierson, *The Reporter*, as quoted in the 'Film Notes' for a 1957–58 programme including a screening of *Man of Aran*. Paul Rotha gave a carefully qualified review of Flaherty's technique and strategies in *Man of Aran*: 'in its particular sphere [it] represents the furthest lengths to which documentary of this sort has been taken … [it] pursues one of several paths of documentary and must be considered only within those limits', *Sight and Sound*, 3:10 (Summer 1934), 23.

28 I. Montagu, *New Statesman and Nation* (28 April 1934), 638.

29 Winston, *Claiming the Real*, 20–1, argues that Flaherty's was a 'largely imperialist career', tracing his explorer films to those documentaries made for the Empire Marketing Board with Grierson, and beyond with films like *Elephant Boy*. George Stoney made a documentary about *Man of Aran* called *How the Myth was Made* (1978).

30 Rockett *et al*, *Cinema and Ireland*, 88, points out that the premiere of *Saoirse?* was an occasion to signal 'Civil War ecumenism', with politicians and military staff from both sides present and the anti-Treaty 'Old IRA' being allowed to form a flag-carrying parade after the screening. Photographs of this premiere are held at the Gael-Linn Archives in Merrion Square, Dublin.

31 Gael-Linn Press Release (29 September 1959), 1, on the occasion of the Cork Film Festival premiere.

32 Rockett *et al*, *Cinema and Ireland*, 87.

33 *Mise Éire* was screened in London at the NFT and favourably reviewed by M. Ratcliffe, 'Irish Revelations', *Films and Filming*, 9:10 (July 1963), 32, who noted that 'the historical picture is assembled with an impressively restrained anger; the skill with which this has been done has given a perceptive tide to events'.

34 P. Donnellan, 'Memories of the future', *Sight and Sound*, 2:4 (August 1992), 40.

35 J. Dunn provides a witty, informative and reflective account of the early years in his, *No Tigers in Africa: Recollections and reflections on 25 years of Radharc* (Dublin, The Columba Press, 1986). *Radharc Films* is a selected catalogue of productions (RTÉ/Radharc, n.d.) supplied to me by Father Dermot McCarthy. RTÉ produced a thirty-minute obituary programme following Joe Dunn's death, *A Priest Behind a Camera* (21 July 1996), which gives a clear sense of the programme's aims, development and achievements.

36 There had been earlier attempts by lay religious groups to get the Rosary broadcast on radio but this was resisted by the hierarchy at the time. By instituting the Angelus instead – on 15 August 1950, marking the Feast of the Assumption in a Holy Year – McQuaid astutely recognised popular demand but put his stamp of authority on the matter. A decade later, the 1960 Broadcasting Act specified nothing about air-time for religious programming on television, but the Angelus chimes have remained part of the schedules to this day. In recent years, its removal has been hotly debated in the context of uncoupling Catholicism from the state and demonstrating to Ulster Protestants that a Republic would recognise their religious faiths. My thanks to Brian Lynch of RTÉ's Written Archives for this information.

37 Following the death of Joe Dunn in 1996 the archives of *Radharc* have been managed as a Trust, called Esras Films, based in Blackrock, Co. Dublin, and much of its film material been lodged and video-copied at the Film Institute of Ireland where cassettes may be viewed by appointment.

38 Dunn, *No Tigers*, 44.

39 Transcript taken from viewing copy held at the Irish Film Archive, Tape 287.

40 Pat Butler introduced the first broadcast of the film on RTÉ1 in 1989 and then chaired a discussion about the film with Patrick Cunningham, John Hume and Eamonn McCann. Butler concluded the programme by asking 'one wonders if there are other [programmes] lying on shelves here [RTÉ] and elsewhere'. Brian Lynch reports that Dermot McCarthy, formerly of *Raharc* and now Head of Religious Programmes, RTÉ, insists that the decision to pull the programme was taken at 'top level' in Telefís Éireann. I am informed by Lynch that he knows of no documented evidence in RTÉ's Archive to show that there was direct ministerial pressure brought to bear on the management. This decision could indicate a degree of self-censorship but government intervention in the form of a telephone call or 'quiet word' cannot be completely discounted.

41 VHS copies of the film were available from The Northampton Connolly Association, 5 Woodland Avenue, Abington, Northampton, NN3 2BY, England. See also 'At home and over here: Representations of the Irish', NFT Programme (1984). It was most recently screened as part of a festival of cinema, music and culture called 'From the heart: Innovations in Irish music and arts' at the Barbican Centre, April 1997.

42 This man is not credited in the film. Fiona Tait has found a reference in the Charles Parker Archive papers at the Birmingham City Archives that suggests that the saxophonist might be an enigmatically named 'Connolly?' 'The Irishmen', CPA 2/107, 5. Thanks to Alun Howkins, Eugene Finn and Reg Hall for the detective work.

43 P. Donnellan writes of the BBC in the period that 'all the so-called advances were secured against bitter opposition.' Letter in the *Independent* (25 January 1987), 41.

44 T. Sewell, *Keep on Moving: The Windrush legacy, the black experience in Britain from 1948* (London, Voice Enterprises Ltd, 1998).

45 'Peter Lennon's *Rocky Road to Dublin*', *Guardian* (11 May 1968).

46 Quoted in 'How Lennon got around censors and taboos', *Time* (July 1968).

47 All quotations from the press are collected from the BFI Library Microfiche.

48 'The Rocky Road to Dublin', *Film West*, 25 (Summer 1996), 34–6.

49 The BFI Library's Index indicates that a companion film, *Ireland: The Hour Before Dawn* (1974), was made but no copy is available in the National Film and Television Archive. Its title suggests that the topic of the film might very well be internment.

50 M. Ansara, 'Trying for freedom', *Film News* [Australia], 9:4 (April 1979), 9–10. He helped form Cinema Action (1968–70), making a short film about Bernadette Devlin and *People of Ireland* (1970), which filmed inside the Free Derry community of the Bogside during August 1969. Further quotations in this section are taken from Mordaunt's comments quoted in this article.

CHAPTER 5

A CINEMA OF ROMANCE AND EXPERIMENT, 1958–87

- What forces shaped the environment for film-making in Ireland during this period?
- What aspects of Irish society and politics were addressed in indigenous films?
- How significant was the Irish Film Board in promoting indigenous film?

Irish cinema and the 'new' Hollywood

The Irish government ambitiously established a national film studio at Ardmore in County Wicklow in 1958. At state level, Irish cinema opened itself up to an international arena that was still dominated by US production. It is logical, therefore, to understand Ireland's particular developments in relation to the significant economic and social factors that brought about change to this dominant postwar cinema. From 1948, the Hollywood oligarchy of the studio era was forced to restructure as a result of a legal ruling against monopolist practice, falling cinema admissions and rising costs in overheads. Major studios had operated a highly profitable system of vertically-integrated film production, distribution and exhibition (owning key cinema chains). But maintaining extensive properties, plant and personnel became enormously costly over the course of the next two decades and so the majors strategically sold off parts of their assets and gradually switched to a package-system. Under this arrangement, they helped to finance and control the distribution of films made by smaller, independent production companies. It is estimated that even by 1958, 65 per cent of Hollywood movies were made this way.[1] After initial postwar political and social conservatism the USA and many western European economies gradually entered a phase of expansion and consumerism in the 1960s.

However, cinema audiences continued to follow a marked postwar decline for several reasons. Lifestyles changed and became more home-orientated. Television was partly to blame in providing an alternative, *domestic* source of entertainment. During a period of high employment and increased opportunities for extending education, a stratum of young people in society became defined, partly as a result of its disposable spending power. Innovative and cheaper audio equipment popularised dance music on record, transistor radio and the TV. An emerging 'pop industry' thrived on transnational appropriation. Travel became more affordable and people found other ways of spending leisure time than going to the movies.

Initially, cinema responded to this competitive change by making its films bigger (TVs offered small, poorly defined images), more colourful (TV was still monochrome) and more adult in subject matter (TV was constrained by family viewing guidelines). But gradually it entered into a more complex set of symbiotic relations with television. To supplement income some studios made films for television; others began selling their library of old films for TV broadcast, and even making TV series. By the end of the 1960s, 'dangerous rivals were bound by mutual interests'.[2] Most major film studios cut back on production, some withdrew from whole areas of business, others were taken over in finance deals to become part of a conglomerate of unrelated companies, and others again diversified themselves into audio-visual or publishing activities. The 1970s mainstream film was typified by large-budget, big return blockbusters that were heavily advertised and increasingly involved product merchandising to maximise profits. So, although the structural configuration of Hollywood changed markedly between the late 1950s and the 1980s, it maintained its economic dominance of European film markets. As well as absorbing and feeding off the talents of a younger generation of independent US directors, the 'new Hollywood' demonstrated that it was adept at employing British talent, assimilating elements of European art cinema into its production and maintaining its control of distribution.[3] These developments exemplify what we termed the 'fourth phase' of Irish cinema history. It will become evident that historical progress is the result of uneven forces and tensions, often pulling in contradictory directions, under the (dis)organised influence of changing governments, groups and individuals.

Trying to swim with the big fish

The decision in 1958 by the Department of Trade and Industry to establish Ardmore Studios as a substantial base for indigenous film production was a misconceived failure. Its advocates failed to make a realistic assessment of local conditions within Ireland in the context of the broader changes in the postwar cinema industry described above. It may have seemed to some that the breakdown of the studio system in the USA and a less active British film industry in the 1950s would provide an opportunity for Ireland to assume its place alongside other national cinema movements elsewhere in Europe in the 1950s and 1960s. But such indigenous projects produced at Ardmore were by and large dated theatrical adaptations from the Abbey Theatre such as *Home is the Hero* and *This Other Eden* (both 1959). Moreover, the studios were too expensive a facility for small, would-be Irish film investors and there were not the technical staff to crew large-scale productions. Louis Marcus noted ruefully a decade later that IR£1.5 million of public money had been invested in Ardmore, but it had not produced an indigenous Irish film, nor had it nurtured creative or technical talent: 'It cannot produce these because it is a hireable facility and the people who can afford to hire it are the foreign film companies. They aren't there to prove that Irish men and women can make films: they will want to use their own people on these always'.[4] Ardmore was financially insecure and overly dependent on external commercial finance. It stayed afloat by making American TV series, advertisements and Anglo-American funded feature films such as *Shake Hands with the Devil* (1959), *A Terrible Beauty* (1960), *Young Cassidy* (1964) and *The Violent Enemy* (1968). It is ironic and not surprising, then, that at the end of the 1960s impetus for substantial state support of film was to come from John Huston, an American-born Irish director. He very publicly persuaded Taoiseach Jack Lynch to set up the Film Industry Committee with Huston as the chair. In fact, Huston's ideas were grandiose and at variance with the ideas of active and dedicated committee members like Marcus. The final recommendations of the 1968 report, written by Marcus, were to support modestly budgeted films along the lines of other small national cinemas, aimed at the European 'art cinema' market and to support the production of short films, documentary films and commercials. Generally well-received, the report became shelved in a crisis of government in 1969-70 generated by the fraught political situation in Northern Ireland known as the 'Arms Trial'.

However, against the continuing dominance of foreign production in Ireland and the internal setbacks to coherent and sustained state support, the 1970s did witness a considerable dynamic in indigenous film-making; a nascent national cinema was in formation. People like Marcus had worked in documentary for Gael-Linn in the 1950s and 1960s; Bob Quinn, who had been working on television for RTÉ, set up his own small production company (Cinegael) in Connemara in 1973. Liam O'Leary had returned from the British Film Institute in London to work in RTÉ in 1964 and campaigned for preservation as well as production. Pat O'Connor left Ireland in 1965, graduated from a Canadian film school in 1969 and returned to work in RTÉ. In the 1970s, film-makers like Thaddeus O'Sullivan (living in London) and Carlo Gebler started to produce experimental films dealing with the Irish emigrant experience, such as *On a Paving Stone Mounted* (1978) and *Over Here* (1981) respectively. O'Sullivan was also lighting-cameraman on films by Cathal Black and Joe Comerford. These were film-makers whose work was conceived out of an artistic, formally explorative drive, rather than a commercial imperative, and was typically produced on 16mm film, which limited its distribution. Comerford subscribes to the view that art is fundamental to understanding society, that film as a cultural activity is important in redefining a collective sense of identity in a period of change. To varying degrees this was tacitly supported by many of his contemporaries though not perhaps with the same politicised inflection. In retrospect, Comerford has observed of the 1970s that 'there was more wealth, there was less emigration. We simply had choices that people – our predecessors – didn't have … there wasn't a lot of finance to make film, but at least there was the possibility of looking at your own society'.[5] A minuscule amount of state support for film projects came from the Arts Council following legislation in 1973, but greater influence was exerted with the launch of its Film Script Award in 1976. The momentum collectively produced by the film-makers, a broad agreement among trade unions and cinema exhibition associations, and the launch of the Irish Film Theatre (1977–84) helped to make the case for the cultural value of film. This became focused during an intense period of lobbying of Dáil Éireann which resulted in the Irish Film Board Act of 1980. The precise course of the board's action and its rationale for support over what would be the period of its active existence (1982–87) was vigorously debated. From the mid-1970s onwards, it is clear that within indigenous film production there were broadly two views about the way forward, which caused some internal friction, particularly when project funding was sought. One view emphasised the importance of smaller-budget, self-examining and formally explorative films; the other view emphasised larger-budget, more mainstream themes and formats with a view to international distribution. However, throughout this period, large budget, international productions by visiting directors using Ireland primarily as a scenic location continued to be made. We turn now to consider two notable examples.

Big bucks pictures: *Ryan's Daughter* (1970) and *Barry Lyndon* (1975)

The kind of Anglo-American, Irish-themed films against which this nascent indigenous cinema defined itself is exemplified in productions by David Lean and Stanley Kubrick. Lean's sprawling 'gallimaufry'[6] of a film can be read against its own times for what it reveals about contemporary politics and the cinematic exploration of female sexuality in the late 1960s. Kubrick's panoramic and precise picturing of Ireland within a European history arises from both Kubrick's 'deliberate aversion to contemporary [Hollywood] film-making styles'[7] and an American's immigrant outsider sensibility.

Set in an imaginary Irish coastal village called Kirrary in 1916, *Ryan's Daughter* had both literary and cinematic precedents, a cross between Flaubert's novel *Madame Bovary* (1856) and Lean's own *Brief Encounter* (1945). The narrative is centrally concerned with the frustrations of a young woman, Rosy (Sarah Miles), a publican's daughter who finds herself trapped in a respectable but unsatisfactory marriage with the local school teacher, Charles (Robert Mitchum). Rosy's wayward tendencies are heavily presaged from the start in scenes with a paternalistic priest (Trevor Howard). When a wounded British officer, Major Doryan (Christopher Jones), is garrisoned locally, Rosy promptly falls in love with him.[8] The affair becomes public knowledge and she is (wrongly) suspected of being an informant. Rosy is ritually punished by the community and Doryan dies in an explosion (suspected as suicide). Both adulteress and husband are forced to leave for Dublin but it is unclear if they will remain together.

Lean's decision to film what was a small-scale, intimate subject in Ireland as a Super Panavision epic at a cost of approximately £4 million ($13.5 million), indicates both his directorial status and his characteristic method. But this treatment is also symptomatic of a broader history of British cinematic representations of Irish landscape, history and sexuality.[9] A self-declared romantic, who thought that the 'west coast of Ireland is one of the most beautiful wild places I've ever seen',[10] Lean's fascination with Ireland's pre-modern state is informed by a particular colonial and aesthetic outlook. It leads him to adopt a distinctive approach to character, narrative and history. Stunning widescreen grandeur dwarfs his central female character, embodying an aesthetic that sees individual psychology as a function of the natural environment or supernatural forces rather than as a result of active human intervention.

Lean tried to be self-critical of his own proclivities and those of his creative collaborators (Robert Bolt wrote the screenplay): 'we tend to beautify everything we touch – even the ugly – and that amounts to what my dictionary calls "picturesque falsehoods"'.[11] Lean attempted to counteract this tendency by having Kirrary built to authentic specifications at a cost of £100,000. This showed rural Ireland as grimy and muddy, its social system apparently cruel and repressive. But despite the expenditure to produce authenticity, a generation later, the film is indelibly of its time. To be trivial, hair styling is decidedly sixties not 1916; the cut of the IRA leader's leather jacket has more of the Kings Road *couture* about it than Kerry casual. More seriously, Lean's English view of Irish history is motivated by the melodramatic requirement to have 'an outside conflict, something over the hill',[12] rather than by serious attention to historical accuracy.

For Lean, history is a backdrop to and not at the forefront of human activity and the subplot of a German arms shipment to support the 1916 Rising in Dublin is tangential to the main narrative about Rosy. Reminiscent of Flaherty's footage, the stormy night of the arms landing provides a visual *tour de force* (incidentally, filmed by Roy Stevens not Lean) rather than a satisfactory narrative climax to the film. The village mob swarm to assist the IRA, a collective response of film caricature, which misleads about historical realities. The visual spectacle of Ireland's past was in stark contrast to the political storm clouds shadowing the film's release in December 1970 and its run up to the Oscars the following spring. Soon after their arrival in August 1969, British soldiers sent in to protect Catholics in Northern Ireland had become an unwelcome occupying force. By mid-1970, the provisional IRA had begun to organise itself. In this same year, an 'Arms Trial' in the Republic saw prominent members of the Fianna Fáil government unsuccessfully impeached for secretly funding the supply of guns to the IRA. Moreover, the daily antagonisms between a civilian population and a military garrison imagined in Lean's film were witnessed in reality by TV audiences in the Republic and Britain. Network news actuality showed ritualised street riots, known locally in Derry as 'matinees' because they took place on Saturday afternoons like films at the cinema.[13] According to the evidence of Lean's biography and a survey of just about all the English-based press,[14] British cinema-goers seemed blinkered to the contemporary resonance of political violence in his film, convinced that the past puts the problems of Anglo-Irish history safely at a distance.

It is not just political history that sits uncomfortably in the film. In striving to express the nature of Rosy's emotional dilemma, Lean abandoned any semblance of psychological realism, deciding instead to 'change the photography into a mood of wild romance. I went at it full tilt'.[15] This portrayal of sexuality on screen was part of a wider current in the arts at the time, but Lean himself 'did not approve of the new permissiveness that was affecting the cinema'.[16] The link between fictional females and the crucial years of feminist activism in the late 1960s is softened but nevertheless present in Rosy's dreamy insistence that there must be something more to life than marriage. In one gothic sequence, Rosy is captured in moonlight by an outhouse surrounded by impossibly white lilies and Doryan's silhouette is dramatically set against the skyline. Lean taps further into romantic iconography by having the horse-riding lovers meet in secret on a cliff topped by a ruined tower and making love in a shady, bluebell wood. Their sexual passion is signified in a remarkable sequence of visual plenitude and aural excess: trees creak, leaves rustle, a spider's web threads across the screen, the lovers' bodies glisten and dandelion heads shed their seeds to signify climax. Having witnessed an unpleasant, stilted nuptial scene earlier, this highly stylised section[17] veers between a nature film and sixties

17 Landscape and romance: *Ryan's Daughter* (1970).
Courtesy of Turner Entertainment

underground camp. In narrative terms, Rosy's sexuality harbours a threat to the gender-structured roles of village society but she is doubly punished since she is wrongly condemned as an informer too. Charles is ostracised with her because he failed in his role as husband. *Ryan's Daughter* demonstrates how a cinematic colonial discourse conflates racial and sexual images when representing Ireland as an eroticised female (as compared to the 'Mother Ireland' figure). The film clearly bears the marks of 'British attitudes imposed on an alien though proximate culture'.[18] Lean was both fascinated and fearful of the landscape and the heroine he so lovingly filmed.

Sequences of wild romance and stylised cinematography were deplored as undisciplined or indulgent 'jumps in style' by English reviews (*Daily Telegraph* and *The Times*). They complained that the film was too long, that it had a 'fatuous story line' (*The Spectator*), that characters were undeveloped and that it was like women's 'pulp fiction' (*The Observer*). The film was 'divided against itself' (*Films and Filming*) and it collapsed under 'the aesthetic euphoria of the scenery' (*Monthly Film Bulletin*), criticisms that were levelled at Ford's, *The Quiet Man*. But, as with examples discussed earlier, instances of formal tics in the text and visual excess are significant to cultural studies critics and not to be reductively dismissed as mistakes. Irish film historian Kevin Rockett noted the fact that despite its critical reception the film, was successful in Dublin cinemas,[19] due in large part to the pleasure and pride amongst Irish cinema-goers at seeing Ireland on a large screen. The film's historical setting also had resonant contemporary connections that must have struck a chord with audiences even if unforeseen by Lean and the distributors. The ritual shearing of Rosy by the village mob for adultery and collusion with the enemy echoed the tarring and feathering of women in nationalist communities in Northern Ireland who had consorted with British soldiers deployed there a year earlier. However, the official organ of the self-styled national film establishment, the National Film Institute's *Annual Report* (1971), was appalled by the film's alleged immorality and historical inaccuracy: '[*Ryan's Daughter*] shows Irish country girls in a disgustingly immoral light. Not content with putting on the screen the consummation of [Rosy's] marriage, we see her a few weeks later commit adultery in the woods with the British Major. [It is] a film with … little regard to the *true* [sic] situation of the 1916 period'.[20] Such a reactionary assessment shows how out of touch this body was with popular cinema tastes, social change and how the certainty of 'green nationalist' interpretations of Irish history persisted in the face of revisionist ideas. The film's immorality was a marketing problem in the USA, but MGM managed successfully to protest against an R (Restricted Viewing) rating initially imposed on it by censors concerned about the sympathetic portrayal of adultery.[21] US critics Pauline Kael and Vincent Canby savaged the film but grudgingly noted that it might appeal to a popular audience.[22] Having invested $13.5 million in the film, MGM were keen to maximise their return and carefully orchestrated a distribution plan spanning from Christmas 1970 to the Oscars the following spring.[23]

Despite its production problems and bumpy reception by critics,[24] *Ryan's Daughter* won Oscars, grossed $80 million in the USA between 1970–79[25] and has sustained a significant critical afterlife.[26] It also had a transformative impact on the local economy of the Dingle peninsular beyond the location filming. Lean proposed that Kirrary be left standing as a tourist attraction but this offer was declined by Dingle Council, though sepia-tinted postcards of the village were produced before demolition took place[27] and the school house was left intact. One entrepreneur was able to run helicopter flights between Dingle and the Blasket Islands because 'so many visitors want to capture the scenery used in the film with their own ciné-cameras'.[28] Such opportunist tourism could not replace the work lost in the already declining herring fishing industry and agricultural jobs. In this regard, it is has been suggested that the film helped to accelerate emigration because a year's inflated wage-rates offered by MGM to local people made the marginal existence of traditional occupations unattractive and many younger people left the Dingle hinterland.[29] As contended earlier, film making does have material effects on micro-economies, productions can become part of the cultural history of localities and become cinematic referents for subsequent films. A generation later in 1992, 'the legacy of *Ryan's Daughter*' was recognised at the time of the release of *Far and Away*.[30]

Barry Lyndon (1975) is Kubrick's adaptation of Thackeray's picaresque pseudo-memoir novel, *The Luck of Barry Lyndon* (1844). Using the device of a voice-over narrator (Michael Horden) the film version relates the story of Redmond Barry (Ryan O'Neal), an Irish orphan ne're-do-well who fights as a mercenary in the Seven Years War (1756–63) then fraudulently rises in society through impersonation, gambling and an astute marriage to Countess Lyndon, only for his success to end tragically with the loss of his own son. Kubrick painstakingly photographed scenery and period architecture in Ireland, England and Germany to produce a remarkably pared down film with minimal dialogue and little conventional narrative energy or dramatic conflict. The film tests the viewer's concentration in sequences that come close to cinematic tableaux. Typically, a close up shot of a figure is very slowly zoomed out to make them gradually form part of a larger canvass of manicured rural landscapes or architectural cycloramas. The film was scored to an inventive compilation of European classical pieces and Irish traditional music (specially recorded by The Chieftains).[31] The film was instantly disliked by most of the British tabloid press,[32] generated only dutiful, appreciative respect from some broad sheet critics (*The Sunday Times*) but was generally seen as a 'disappointment' (the view of film critic Andrew Tudor in *New Society*). In the USA it won Oscars for cinematography, music, art direction and costume design, but the 'elegant and handsome adaptation' had problems in finding an audience.[33] The death-knell to box office came with Pauline Kael's judgement that it was 'a coffee table movie ... a masterpiece in every insignificant detail'.[34] *Barry Lyndon* was a commercial failure, making only $9.5 million at the US domestic box office but was selectively rereleased in 1981 and went to video in 1982. More recently it has been shown on Sky Movies

(November 1995), broadcast on Britain's Channel Four TV (June 1996), which has a reputation for showcasing art films, and has been favourably reassessed within the Kubrick canon.[35] It remains a curious amalgam of sensibilities about a wandering Irishman, out of country and out of class, made by a New York film-maker with lowly Austrian-Jewish origins who lived in England from 1961 until his death in 1999 and who obsessively espoused artistic values at odds with Hollywood's mainstream. At the core of the film is Barry's sense of displaced identity, captured in the scene where Barry confides in the Chevalier, himself an Irish émigré posing as a French gentleman gambler. Lacking a father, Barry craves fatherhood, but is indirectly responsible for killing his own precious son as the film grinds to its tragic conclusion.

Indigenous experimentation

Internationally renowned directors like Lean and Kubrick were able to exercise their considerable talents on large-budget, panoramic pictures about Ireland with major studio distribution. But at the same time, a smaller grouping of Irish film-makers slowly began to construct an alternative set of cinema images of Ireland, made with modest funds but equally ambitious and challenging goals. It is significant that the first feature film to benefit from Arts Council film funding (*Poitín*, 1978) set out to demythologise those romantic representations of the west of Ireland manifested in much of the Literary Revival, popular theatre and Anglo-American cinema discussed above. This new Irish cinema did not revere its national history nor its traditional institutions, like the Catholic Church, marriage and the family, all of which were scrutinised on screen. The latter institutions were seen less as bulwarks of Irish social stability and more as arenas for conflict and questioning. Ireland changed rapidly and experienced a period of brief affluence in the first half of the 1970s, but these films explored the experience of people pushed to the margins of this new Ireland. By putting Travellers, unemployed people, homelessness, homosexuality and urban lives on screen the fault-lines of modernity in Ireland were exposed. The discussion of Northern Ireland, a key issue from the early 1970s, was seriously curtailed by the broadcast media in the Republic as well as Britain, but it was addressed if sometimes obliquely by some of the film-makers in this grouping.

Bob Quinn's *Poitín* was all the more remarkable in that it was made entirely in Irish when Irish-language film up to the 1970s had been largely confined to the output of Gael-Linn. From the opening shot of a cottage by a lake we know we are located in Connemara, but familiar narrative expectations are confounded by a hard-nosed but humorous story of an old poitín-maker (Cyril Cusak) getting revenge on two unemployed men who try to cheat him out of money made from selling the illegal liquor in the local community under the eyes of the Gardaí (one of whom is played by Mick Lally). The film shows us a rural Ireland of bleak landscapes, chronic unemployment, a black economy, petty officialdom, brutality borne of frustration and domestic sexual abuse. In a drunken state, one of the men (Niall Tobín) screams in the pub: 'A dead place for dead people', which effectively summarises Quinn's deglamorised view of his part of the world without dehumanising it.

Institutionalised dehumanisation is central to Cathal Black's exposé of the brutalising role of the church in the Irish education system, *Our Boys* (1980). Dermot Healy's screenplay evokes a 1950s Christian Brothers school by using monochrome, dramatised sequences showing lessons, beatings and the lives of the boys and brothers in a narrative about the school's imminent closure. The film shows how the effects of violence can last over generations. A priest (Mick Lally) has so badly beaten a boy that his father (a former pupil himself) is urged by his wife to complain but the father's reply is. 'It won't do him any harm. It'll make a man of him'. The long-term effects of this violence are witnessed in contemporary graphic accounts of beatings by former pupils, given to camera. A brother is interviewed, giving a lame defence of the past: 'I don't think it fair to unroll … no more than you can unroll that film back to recast it again, to go over what you've done. We [the Christian Brothers] can't do it either'. Recasting the past is precisely what Cathal Black has done by ironically counterpointing drama, interviewees and newsreel footage. He intercuts actuality from the 1932 Eucharistic Congress and the devotions at a St Patrick's Day parade from the 1950s. The film ends with the school being closed, a Madonna statue is unceremoniously loaded into the back of a van and a worried-looking priest glances back at the old institution, which has fallen into ruin. Such potent, dissenting metaphors have to be understood in the context of the film's production at the end of the 1970s when Catholicism in Ireland was boosted by a papal visit in 1979. The enormous outdoor mass in Phoenix Park recalled similar religious occasions alluded to in Black's film. So sensitive was the subject matter that RTÉ – one of the film's backers – did not broadcast it until 1991 when the church had proved its infallibility through highly publicised cover-ups of child sex abuse, revelations about clergy fathering children and national television discussions of the lesbian sexuality of some nuns.

Joe Comerford directed *Traveller* (1982), based on an Arts Council-funded screenplay by Neil Jordan, which focused on the dark story of a newly-wed Traveller couple, Michael (Davy Spillane) and Angela (Judy Donovan). It is an arranged marriage and the fight at the wedding meal suggests acrimony between the families. Like *Poitín*, Comerford's opening – the sound of 'tinkering' (metal beating) and traditional caravans in a country lane – soon gives way to harsher realities of the Travellers' existence in contemporary Ireland. Michael and Angela take a van from Limerick to the north to smuggle back televisions for sale in the Republic. They become embroiled with Clicky, a man with republican connections, and with whom Angela will eventually emigrate. The journey over and back across the border (punctuated with map graphics) is fraught with incident: the van is crashed, Michael opportunistically robs a post office, and Angela – via a voice-over device – confides in Clicky that she was imprisoned for hitting her incestuous father with a bottle. On the run, any semblance of the young couple's partnership dissolves and Michael returns to murder Angela's father. The film's significance is in its portrayal of dysfunctional marriage and the percipient representation of Travellers. Comerford used non-professional Travellers to act in a film that showed how this outcast group in Irish society was often the target of social prejudice and state harassment by Gardaí. The film's pre-title assertion that 'an ancient, intimate and dark connection exists between murder and politics' is opaquely explored through the character of Clicky, his voice-over about the impact of the Hunger Strikes (1980-81) and the device of having 'Troubles' footage (*Ireland Behind the Wire*) in shot on TV screens.

A film which tackled the political question of the north more cogently though no less inventively, *Maeve* (1981), was made by Pat Murphy and John Davies. It addressed what had become a forbidden topic by provocatively linking it to the gendered nature of power and historical discourse. The eponymous character's name comes from a warrior queen of the *Táin*, whose place in literary history Revivalist scholars had softened over the previous century. Murphy's heroine certainly challenges this and, moreover, *Maeve* was also innovative in that it departed from conventions of realist linear narrative, trying to find an alternative form of filmic expression. Murphy was dissatisfied with both broadcast media representations of Northern Ireland and mainstream cinematic language. Her screenplay applied the formal aspects of 1970s feminist politics to specifically Irish subject matter with considerable success.[36]

Maeve (Mary Jackson) returns from London to her native city of Belfast and the film explores how she confronts the male control of historical and political discourses, embodied in her father's (Mark Mulholland) insistent habit of story-telling, the political rhetoric of her boyfriend's unbending republicanism and the sexual harassment by British soldiers. Maeve engages in a process of reinhabiting the landscape (a hill-fort) and symbols associated with local allegiances and political histories (Cave Hill) that have been occupied (the streets of Belfast) and controlled by men. She does this by recalling her memories and reforging relationships with her sister and her mother, culminating in a drunken party on the Giant's Causeway on the Antrim coast. The film was distinctive in the way that it used unmarked flashbacks, direct address to camera and sequences of non-naturalist dialogue to disrupt a stable point of view and invite an interrogative rather than an identificatory position for the viewer. *Maeve* appeared at a time when the Hunger Strikes were at the forefront of Irish political concerns but the film provided a challenging critique of traditional, male forms of nationalism and republicanism. Murphy went on to make a formally more conventional film, *Anne Devlin* (1984), about the life of the woman who refused under interrogation to inform on the nationalist figure, Robert Emmet. Using its historical setting, the film clearly dramatises and reclaims Devlin as an active, intransigent and alternative figure of femininity rather than simply an adjunct to Irish history.[37]

18 Feminist confrontation in Belfast: *Maeve* (1981).
Courtesy of BFI Films

Circumstances meant that some inexperienced film-makers like Murphy had to take funding from where they could. *Maeve* received most of its budget from the British Film Institute (£73,000), no funding from the IFB and a small amount of backing from RTÉ (£10,000). However, Arts Council and later Film Board finance was crucial to many indigenous Irish films over a ten-year period (1977–87). Neil Jordan's *Angel* (1982, *Danny Boy* in the USA) received £100,000 from the IFB but needed a distribution deal worth £400,000 with the newly formed Channel Four TV in London to secure its budget. Set in contemporary Northern Ireland, *Angel* is a revenge narrative in which Danny (Stephen Rea), a saxophonist in a show band, witnesses the murder of an innocent mute girl by a paramilitary gang. Driven to retribution and circumventing the police, Danny exchanges his sax for a submachine gun in order to kill the members of the gang one-by-one. In the denouement, it turns out that the leader of the loyalist killers is in fact one of the police detectives, though British reviews tended to read the gang as IRA by default. Its spare, elliptical dialogue, stylised lighting and startling visual impact take the film away from mainstream realism but it generated considerable critical debate due to the nature of its representation of political violence. Richard Kearney argued that Jordan was seeking a stylised, non-naturalist approach to deconstruct the political mythologies which under-pin the Troubles by showing their psychic roots.[38] Countering this, John Hill argued that Jordan's approach, focusing on the hero's personal, almost meta-physical condition, dehistoricised and removed the action from its socio-polit-ical context, continuing a tradition in British films like *Odd Man Out*.[39]

Cathal Black's, *Pigs* (1984), based on an original screenplay by Stephen Brennan might seem to open itself to the charge of beautifying squalor,[40] but this would be to misread the film's underlying critique of the Irish state and social attitudes in Ireland. Jimmy (Stephen Brennan) is a gay man, separated from his wife and squatting in a Georgian tenement in inner-city Dublin. He is a lone but tolerant man who seems to attract around him an alternative family of social misfits: mentally disturbed Tom, the down-at-heel northerner, George, a Jamaican pimp, Orwell, his girl, Mary, and an aimless youth. Jimmy is the home-maker and carer but receives little back for his trouble. He is shown picking up a man at a gay bar but is beaten up in the squat by friends of a young punk in the house. The Gardaí call, not to make enquiries about his injuries but to arrest him on suspicion of false social security claims. As in *Poitín* and *Traveller*, the police are vindictive, humiliating Jimmy for his supposed lack of masculinity and taunting him: 'How can you live in all this filth – living like pigs?' Slowly paced, artfully shot (by Thaddeus O'Sullivan) and moodily scored, the film quietly exposed the insensitivity and cruelty of Irish society in the wake of economic and political crisis in the 1980s.[41]

Competing commercially?

By the mid-1980s a palpable sense of momentum had developed amongst indigenous film-makers. Script development funds from the Arts Council and small but significant loans from the IFB allowed Irish producers to pitch for commercial film and television rights abroad with the imprimatur of state confidence in the project. Strongbow Films and City Vision were two indige-nous companies that attracted financial backing for *Eat the Peach* (1986) and *The Courier* (1987) respectively. While *Traveller*, *Pigs*, *Maeve* and *Eat the Peach* were made on 16mm gauge film, *The Courier* and *Joyrider*s were shot on Super 16mm, a stock that is more easily and cheaply blown up to 35mm, the standard gauge for commercial cinema distribution.[42] These productions exemplify a move by producers to compete in a commercial market for film. It is instructive to analyse these productions in cinematic and production terms, given the previous decade's formal experimentation and exploratory themes.

The idea for *Eat the Peach* came from the news story about an enterprising Longford man who had built himself a motor-cycle 'wall of death'. Peter Ormrod developed a script and John Kelleher agreed to produce the film. Development finance for the film was raised from the IFB (IR£120,000), the British National Film Development Fund (£10,000) and broadcast rights were sold to Channel Four TV (£320,000).[43] Shot in the midlands of Ireland, the film made the most of a different Irish landscape: the flat, bare, industrially-worked turf bogs owned by Bord na Móna to feed electricity power stations and to provide a site for a Japanese electronics factory. The narrative follows a conventional problem–complication–resolution format and a central male relationship. Vinnie (Stephen Brennan) is dissatisfied with his work on the bog and Arthur (Eamon Morrisey) has been made redundant at the factory. They see an Elvis Presley film (*Roustabout*) at the local bar and devise a plan to make money from a home-made 'wall of death'. Vinnie becomes obsessed with this project and his wife Nora (Catherine Byrne), pregnant with their second child, leaves him. This scheme comes to naught and the lads become involved in some shambolic cross-border smuggling. The film brings about a kind of closure, reuniting Vinnie and Nora but the hero is left dreaming of an ambitious plan to build a helicopter. Most judgements praised several aspects of the film, managing as it did to offer a storyline close to the concerns of an Irish audience but also offering a narrative about a struggle against adversity more universally recognised by Hollywood,[44] as well as a quirky, small film product for European distributors.[45] Paddy Woodworth criticised the film for the 'blandness with which elements like unemployment and border violence'[46] were treated but noted that this did not invalidate the achievement of the film to produce some novel images of Ireland. Luke Gibbons has carefully argued for the film's recasting of Irish cinematic landscape for the 1980s. The iconography of the Western, the farcical character of Boots (Niall Tóibín) and narrative structure itself attests to the pervasive presence of Americana in Ireland, but Gibbons convincingly analyses the film's creative appropriation and pastiche of American influences and the unreliability of economic modernity, represented by Japanese electronics assembly plants.[47]

A film that tried less successfully to fuse contemporary Irish social concerns with a mainstream TV crime genre film was *The Courier* (1987). It used Dublin city as the setting for a story about a motor-cycle courier. Mark (Padraig O'Loingsigh), the courier, tries to thwart the activities of an inner-city drug-pusher (Gabriel Byrne) who has caused the death of Mark's best friend. Mark struggles to keep his new-found girlfriend (Cáit O'Riordan) from becoming involved in his revenge. The principal writer and director team of Joe Lee and Frank Deasy had plenty of experience of working in community development video with young unemployed people in Dublin but had limited film-making experience. Nevertheless, the script attracted finance from Palace Pictures and Euston Films in London. The unconvincing result on screen 'shuffles the clichés of the genre without animating them'[48] and inexperienced actors played the youthful lead characters.[49] The film went quickly to video sell-through, the packaging making the most of Gabriel Byrne's star image and the contemporary Irish bands featured on the soundtrack. Quotes from one review reproduced on the packing promised that the hard-hitting thriller was 'brutal'. What audiences outside of Ireland did not perhaps know was that this is Dublin slang for 'really poor quality' rather than 'explicitly violent'.

In *Joyriders* (1988), Dublin is seen to harbour all the problems of modern life – urban atomisation, marital breakdown, unemployment, violence and criminality – but a journey into the restorative rural west provides the solution. The narrative brings its two principal characters together by chance to set up such a transformation. Perky Rice (Andrew Connolly), is a sometime car thief (joyrider) and Mary (Patricia Kerrigan), a woman who has taken herself and her children away from an abusive husband. In desperation she places her children in the care of an orphanage run by nuns and escapes to the countryside in a stolen car with Perky. The west is not portrayed as a haven – they meet an old widower farmer, an ageing singer and desperate male bachelors all of whom are lonely and struggling to survive in a depopulated countryside – but the rural setting provides the narrative landscape in which the couple can discover their true selves, fall in love, resolve to rescue the kids from the orphanage and return to the west in a sort of makeshift family unit in an upbeat ending.

The film was funded from several mainly British sources, including the NFDF, British Screen, Granada Film and Film Four. Aisling Walsh developed the original story in the wake of the 1986 Referendum in the Republic, which confirmed divorce as unconstitutional,[50] and the film imagines what avenues are open to a woman who wants to leave her husband.[51] Although it presents itself as 'a voyage of self-discovery against the backdrop of present day society',[52] *Joyriders* falls far short of the feminist films of Pat Murphy. Indeed, Walsh was 'unwilling to make anything of the fact that the film has a woman director and producer' (Emma Hayter) and the latter said, 'I don't believe in women's liberation – I think its a load of old garbage – well, maybe not women's liberation – but the feminist movement generally'.[53] *Joyriders* ended up 'a fairly skewed enterprise, an odd uncomfortable attempt to match realism with whimsy',[54] in which the drive towards resolution somehow rings hollow. Mary and Perky seem to set up an alternative family unit, yet this contains an underlying conservatism about women and the family affirmed in referenda in the Republic in 1983 and 1986.[55]

Joe Comerford's *Reefer and the Model* (1988) is a markedly different film, with radical intent but not without its imperfections. It is an appropriate film with which to close this chapter since, although begun in 1984, it was one of the last productions to receive support from the IFB in this period. Set wholly in and around Galway, *Reefer* follows the fortunes of a motley bunch of people, all peripheral in socio-political terms, marginalised by Irish society. If Comerford's earlier *Traveller* had implied that the disintegration of family and marriage could be seen as a metaphor for Irish political problems, here – rather like *Pigs* – Comerford dramatises the potential for some kind of collective if transient support among outsiders. Mary (Carol Scanlan) is given a lift by Reefer (Ian McElhinney). She has been in London, involved in drugs and prostitution and is pregnant. Reefer is a swaggering, petty criminal, smuggler and armchair republican with a rebelliousness handed down from his gun-toting mother (Eve Watkinson). These misfits team up with Badger (Ray McBride), who is gay, and Spider (Sean Lawlor), an IRA man on the run, to pull off a bank raid. This goes wrong, Badger and Spider are killed in a chase and the film ends with the Model on Reefer's trawler at sea. She begins to give birth or miscarry as the boat heads towards Reefer who has fallen overboard.

Although it received initial IFB funding, *Reefer* experienced difficulties in securing its final production budget late in 1987 after the board folded. Short-falls were met finally by an anonymous Irish backer (IR£200,000) and the millionaire businessman Tony O'Reilly (IR£25,000).[56] Such material problems led to imperfections in the editing stages of the film, which Comerford has acknowledged, but textually the film is deliberately, playfully uneven, manifesting Comerford's concerted critical engagement with the art of film form itself. McLoone has noted that the film incorporates two styles – 'an austere, European art cinema aesthetic, which is his [Comerford's] own preferred style, and a pastiche of the Hollywood chase movie'[57] – that rub against each other creating a self-questioning friction in the viewing experience. The film opened in Berlin, it won the Europa Prize at the Barcelona Festival and Best Feature at the Celtic Film Festival in Wales in the run up to its August 1988 premiere in Galway. Its general release was well received in several European countries, notably France. In a discussion published later that year it was clear that Comerford's non-linear plot, oblique references to the north and lack of detail about characters' pasts, left the film ripe for contradictory interpretations by audiences.[58]

While its annual budget was only IR£0.5 million per annum, the Film Board was a significant indicator that Ireland took its film-making seriously and it helped to secure further funding for many projects. Jointly, over a decade, the Arts Council Script Fund and the Film Board helped to nurture indigenous Irish film-making talent at a time of great social and political change, when other public media, including RTÉ, failed to provide a searching analysis of topics at the heart of national concern. Certainly, the makers of *Reefer* were convinced that 'cinematic stories whether provocative, anarchic or consoling were a necessity for the health of the national psyche, and that this art form required careful fostering in its developing years'.[59] Film commentators declared: 'In uprooting the Film Board, this government has endangered the seed corn of the Irish Film Industry'.[60] In 1982, Ardmore was closed just as the Film Board began its work. Now, the government abolished the Film Board yet introduced statutory provisions ('Section 35') that offered tax concessions to foreign film producers to encourage them to bring their film crews to Ireland. In the next chapter we look at the kinds of films produced in the five year interim before the relaunch of the Film Board in 1993.

Notes

1 J. Wyver, *The Moving Image* (Oxford, Basil Blackwell/BFI, 1989), 180.
2 Wyver, *Moving Image*, 185.
3 For instance, MGM was bought up by a Las Vegas business tycoon in 1969 as *Ryan's Daughter* was in pre-production. It merged to become MGM-United Artists in 1981, but later became part of Turner Broadcasting. This company sold it on but kept the

rights to MGM films for its Home Box Office (HBO) TV channel. MGM is now run by French banking corporation, Crédit Lyonnais. Warner Brothers, who produced *Barry Lyndon*, diversified in the 1960s, getting into TV and into film distribution, culminating in the formation of Warner Communications in 1969. In 1988, it merged with Time Incorporated to become Time-Warner Inc. and is currently the USA's largest entertainment group. See S. Hayward, *Key Concepts in Cinema Studies* (London, Routledge, 1996), 360–2.

4 L. Marcus [1969] speaking in an interview in the film, *Irish Cinema: Ourselves Alone* (Taylor-Black, 1996).

5 J. Comerford speaking in an interview in *Irish Cinema: Ourselves Alone*.

6 G. Millar, 'Rosy', *Listener* (17 December 1970), n.p., means this term to be pejorative whereas I suggest an exploration of its heterogeneity.

7 'Murf', *Variety* (17 December 1975), 23.

8 See E. B. Cullingford's discussion of *Ryan's Daughter* in, 'Gender, sexuality and Englishness in modern Irish drama and film', in A. Bradley and M. G. Valiulis (eds), *Gender and Sexuality in Modern Ireland* (Amherst, University of Massachusetts Press/ACIS, 1998), 167–9. She reads Robert Bolt's screenplay to emphasise Doryan as representing a British empire in degeneration and decline.

9 Luke Gibbons provides a searching critique of Lean's 'hard primitivism' in the context of an essay on 'Romanticism, realism and Irish cinema', in K. Rockett *et al.*, *Cinema and Ireland* (London, Routledge, 1988), 228–31.

10 Lean speaking in a contemporaneous film interview clip in *Irish cinema* (1996).

11 As quoted in K. Brownlow, *David Lean: A biography* (London, Richard Cohen, 1996), 565.

12 Brownlow, *David Lean*, 554.

13 E. McCann, *War and an Irish Town* (London, Pluto Press, 1980), 79.

14 An extensive collection of reviews exists on microfiche at the BFI Library, London.

15 Brownlow, *David Lean*, 589.

16 Brownlow, *David Lean*, 573.

17 Brownlow, *David Lean*, 584, explains that the close up work for this scene was shot several months after the shots of the bluebells in spring time. The art director constructed a living bower of growing plants and water, backed with a cyclorama inside a disused dancehall to film the scene, hence its surreal qualities. This is a case of necessity and intention coinciding in the film.

18 'Murf', *Variety* (11 November 1970).

19 *Ryan's Daughter* ran for nearly a year in one Dublin first-run cinema, Rockett *et al.*, *Cinema and Ireland*, 113.

20 National Film Institute, *Annual Report* (Dublin, March 1971), 5, as quoted in M. P. Hederman, 'Far-off, most secret, and inviolate Rose', *The Crane Bag*, 1:2 (1977), 29.

21 *Variety* (18 November 1970).

22 Pauline Kael, *The New Yorker* (21 November 1970): 'Every idea in it is shop worn … The emptiness of *Ryan's Daughter* shows in every frame, and yet the publicity machine has turned it into an artistic event, and the American public is a sucker for the corrupt tastefulness of well-bred English epics'. Vincent Canby in *The New York Times* wrote two reviews on 10 and 22 November 1970. He complained that the caricatured villagers jarred with realistic detail of the village itself and that the historical background was a 'narrative convenience'. In his second review he said he felt the film had been 'reviewed with more kindness than it deserved', asserted that the film was proving popular with

audiences because they 'dream of a world in which there is still moral order' and, like Kael, suggested that the masses were being persuaded to buy tickets by manipulative marketing techniques. In conclusion, he pulled no punches when he said of the film that, 'the art it represents belongs to that school of very classy calendar art supported by airlines, insurance corporations and a few enlightened barber shops'.

23 *Variety* (16 December 1970).

24 Pauline Kael had led an assault on Lean in person at a meeting of the National Society of Film Critics in New York. For an account of this see Brownlow's even treatment of events, *David Lean*, 587–8.

25 M. Dwyer, 'A suitable case for editing', *In Dublin*, 77 (May–June 1979), reported on how the film was successfully rereleased at the Ambassador cinema Dublin in 1979.

26 It was first broadcast in the UK on London Weekend TV on 13 January 1980, was recently (1997) released in widescreen format on home video by MGM/UA and has featured in retrospectives of Irish cinema.

27 A set of cards exists in the BFI Stills and Posters collection.

28 'In the steps of Ryan's Daughter', *Evening News* (27 June 1972), n.p.

29 Brownlow, *David Lean*, 567.

30 M. Cummins, 'Celluloid Kerry', *The Irish Times* (4 August 1992), 6. Traolach O Buachalla's film, *Spré Rosy Ryan* (Rosy Ryan's Dowry 1997), documents the impact that the film's production had on the economy and social life of Kerry. It includes interviews with extras and locals, outtakes from the film and other archival material, *Film Ireland*, 63 (February–March 1998), 44.

31 V. Davis, 'Film Boost for The Chieftains', *Daily Express* (30 September 1975).

32 A comprehensive selection of clippings is held on microfiche at the BFI, London. Alexander Walker, a close friend of Kubrick's, in *The Evening Standard* was one exception to this general response.

33 'Murf', *Variety* (17 December 1975).

34 'Kubrick's Guilded Age', *The New Yorker* (29 December 1975).

35 John Baxter, *Stanley Kubrick: A biography* (London, HarperCollins, 1997). See Ch. 14, 'Kubrick in the Age of Enlightenment', 268–94, for a full account of the film's production.

36 A copy of *Maeve* can be viewed at the Sound and Film Archive at the University of Ulster, Coleraine, Northern Ireland. For an in-depth interview with the film-maker, see C. Johnston, '*Maeve*: Interview with Pat Murphy', *Screen*, 22:4 (1981), 54–71. For a perceptive analysis of the film, see L. Gibbons, 'Lies that tell the truth: *Maeve*, history and Irish cinema', in his *Transformations in Irish Culture* (Cork, Cork University Press, 1996), 117–27.

37 L. Gibbons, 'The politics of silence: *Anne Devlin*, women and Irish cinema', in *Transformations in Irish Culture*, 107–116.

38 R. Kearney, *Transitions* (Dublin, Wolfhound Press, 1988), 175–83.

39 J. Hill, 'Images of violence', in Rockett *et al.*, *Cinema and Ireland*, 178-81. More recently, Kevin Maher, 'From angel to vampire', *Film Ireland*, 45 (February–March 1985), 16–18, offers a polemical defence of Jordan's *Angel* within his *oeuvre*.

40 T. Byrne, *Power in the Eye* (Lanham, Maryland, Scarecrow Press, 1997), 75.

41 For an analysis of Jimmy's representation as a gay character in contemporary Irish film see my essay: 'Pigs and provos, prostitutes and prejudice', in É. Walshe (ed.), *Sex, Nation and Dissent in Irish Writing* (Cork, Cork University Press, 1997), 256–8.

42 My thanks to Sunniva O'Flynn for this information and clarification of the issues.

43 The video sell-through rights were bought by Columbia Pictures in 1987. *Eat the Peach* has been shown twice on British terrestrial TV. A Channel Four broadcast on 7 April 1988 drew an audience of 3.3 million, while a BBC broadcast on 12 July 1990 reached 1.9 million viewers according to BARB ratings figures.

44 L. Doyle, 'Good reviews for *Eat the Peach*', *The Irish Times* (20 July 1987), summarised USA responses to the film. 'Max', *Variety*, 26 March 1986, praised the film despite its specific nuances and 'confusing sequence at the start involving Japanese industrialists'.

45 B. Glacken, 'Much of Strongbow's success hinges on Cannes reaction', *The Irish Times* (n.d.).

46 P. Woodworth, 'Peachy enough', *The Sunday Press* (16 March 1986), n.p.

47 Rockett *et al.*, *Cinema and Ireland*, 241–3.

48 R. Comiskey, '*The Courier* fails to deliver', *The Irish Times* (n.d.).

49 *The Courier* opened in February 1988 and was the subject of a discussion in *Film Base News* (April–May, 1988), 14–15. Kevin Liddy was deeply critical saying that he 'found nothing good that these people went out and made this disastrous film', while Gerry McCarthy was less dismissive. He felt that criticism of the film itself was 'a side-effect of the hype that too much weight was brought to bear on what *The Courier* should have been and what it wasn't'.

50 Legislation prohibiting divorce was introduced in Dáil Éireann in 1925, divorce was anathema to Catholic doctrine and Article 41 of Bunracht na Éireann (the Constitution) forbade divorce or the remarriage of persons divorced elsewhere. A referendum in 1995 saw the removal of this constitutional ban but only by the narrowest of margins, indicating that many in Ireland feel divorce is morally wrong.

51 K. Sheridan, 'A new film talent takes her bow', *The Irish Times* (13 October 1988).

52 R. Comiskey, 'On set with *Joyriders*', *The Irish Times* (31 March 1988).

53 Emma Hayter quoted in Comiskey, 'On set with *Joyriders*'.

54 K. Newman, *Monthly Film Bulletin*, 56:664 (May 1989), 139.

55 Shaun Richards argues that the film's conclusion is a 'progressive reappropriation of an essentially redundant ideology and its projection into a future which is both hopeful and hesitant', 'Breaking the cracked mirror: binary oppositions in the culture of contemporary Ireland', in C. Graham and R. Kirkland (eds), *Ireland and Cultural Theory* (Basingstoke, Hampshire, Macmillan, 1999), 113.

56 M. Carr, 'The making of an Irish movie', *Evening Herald* (Dublin) (2 August, 1988), outlines the financial details as follows: IFB IR£220,000, RTÉ IR£95,000, Channel Four TV £150,000, Hemdale Films (USA) $300,000. The original IR£1.4 million budget was pared down to IR£1 million in order for Doolan and Comerford to retain control of the film.

57 M. McLoone, 'National cinema and cultural identity', in J. Hill, M. McLoone, P. Hainsworth (eds), *Border Crossing: Film in Ireland, Britain and Europe* (Belfast, Institute of Irish Studies, 1994), 163.

58 S. McBride, 'Reefer Talk', *Film Base News*, 9 (October–November 1988), 12.

59 Joe Comerford and Lelia Doolan, *Reefer Programme* (Galway) (2 August 1988), n.p.

60 P. Woodworth, 'We're only here because of the Film Board … ' *Reefer Programme* (Galway) (2 August 1988) and 'Reefer and the Model – a cast iron case for the Film Board revival', *Cork Examiner* (3 August 1988).

CHAPTER 6

BETWEEN HERITAGE AND HOLLYWOOD, 1988–92

- What is Irish 'heritage cinema' and why did it prevail in this period?
- In what ways did films engage with social and political conservatism?
- What circumstances brought about the relaunch of the Irish Film Board?

Industry's triumph over culture?

The post-1987 film environment . . . witnessed the restoration of the ascendancy of the industrial model for film production over a culturally engaged, critical cinema in Ireland.[1]

Tax legislation introduced in 1987 in the Republic encouraged the in-flow of investment not only from major US studios but an increasing number of comparatively smaller but long-established film production subsidiaries of commercial British television companies and newer independent producers that had grown up in the entrepreneurial 1980s. The period 1988–93 also witnessed the start of a sustained involvement of the BBC and, to a lesser extent, RTÉ, in film production. The pressure of legislation passed in both Ireland and the UK between 1990 and 1993, meant that the interdependence of film, television and video production became more pronounced as the BBC and RTÉ were forced to commission programmes outside their own studios. In theory this was meant to encourage the development of small, autonomous production businesses and hence the diversity of films and programmes. But it took time for this new ethos to take effect – especially within RTÉ – and people wishing to produce films in Ireland without the support of development money from the Film Board had to seek out alternative sources, mostly from private investment.

These changes in economic relations between television and cinema have to be evaluated in the context of the development and proliferation of new technologies for delivering films and changing conceptions of audiences. The anticipation of a more diverse range of outlets for film including cinema, broadcast, the home video sector (rental and retail), laser disks, cable and satellite in international markets, influenced decisions about those projects, which were considered viable by people who held economic capital for investment. In Ireland, limited money could be obtained from bodies like the Arts Council or RTÉ but, emerging from a period of political and social conservatism, projects that sought to probe sensitive political questions, to be formally exploratory or to extend and test traditional social attitudes were less likely to receive funding in a *laissez faire* market. Would-be Irish film-makers were forced to look outside the country in search of development money in Britain, Europe and the USA. Indeed, in this period Irish film-makers were above average in securing financial support for film projects that the EU made available through initiatives under the umbrella MEDIA programme (later MEDIA '92),[2] like SCALE (for smaller countries), SCRIPT for script development and funding for co-productions under EURIMAGES. Overcoming these difficulties, from the critical recognition and popular success of *My Left Foot* (1989) to *The Crying Game* (1992), Irish films proved their box-office potential in the USA, became an attractive investment for British audio-visual investors and, moreover, consistently engaged audiences in Ireland as box-office figures showed.[3]

Heritage film, Irish style[4]

In this context, the dominant kind of films in Ireland in the late 1980s and early 1990s have been collectively classified as heritage cinema, adapting the term used to describe the period-set British films of the 1980s that celebrated Englishness as epitomised by Merchant-Ivory. According to Ruth Barton, Irish heritage films are typically set in the 1950s or earlier providing a distanced scenario – or one with significant historical reference to otherwise contemporary action – that predates changes seen to have been wrought by modernisation in the 1960s. The Irish heritage film is nostalgically uncritical about the past; it displays a longing for a 'pastoral innocence' (often featuring narratives focused on childhood); it tends to have rural settings or eschew modernity; it offers conservative portrayals of gender and sexuality; it endorses the value of family and small community; and it avoids contemporary political violence. The heritage film often has literary or theatrical sources, both in terms of subject matter and the professional experience of its creators. Often formally conservative, using the conventions of mainstream realism, the heritage film is typically (though not wholly) funded by companies with close connections to television, with an eye for a family TV audience, often casting familiar British acting talent alongside Irish. Barton concludes that the visual appeal of these films is aimed at the 'demands of the up-market television tourist and of the Irish tourist trade'.[5] While it is possible to identify many of these traits in a group of films from this period (and continuing into the present day), Barton claims that these films are 'informed by an awareness of early cinematic representations of Irishness', suggesting a degree of critical reflexivity often associated with the postmodern, which is not fully borne out by the evidence of the films. While there are some dangers in generalising about films from a period, it can be productive and this chapter scrutinises selected examples[6] from many cinematic representations in which women's experience is a notable feature. In these popular maternal narratives, the nature of female identity and sexuality is crucial if not central. We also examine the popularity of Irish-themed films with audiences in Ireland based on the evidence available. Finally, this chapter explores the representation of racial and ethnic difference in Irish cinema. This analysis shows how films represent marginalised or taboo areas of Irish culture and society, and how dominant tropes are reinscribed in the film narratives of this period. A key factor explaining this prevalence is the fact that most of these films were produced by private finance looking for profitable returns from a broadly-based audience. However, although heritage films are largely uncontroversial and designed to be safe, the following selected examples show how this cinema did obliquely (and more overtly in some cases) address those institutional and collective silences about sexuality and racism in the public domain, repressed in almost a decade of social conservatism preceding this period.

My Left Foot is based on an autobiographical novel about the childhood of writer Christy Brown (Hugh O'Conor), as seen in flashback from a vantage point of the professional success and emotional achievement of adulthood (Daniel Day Lewis). Born in 1932 with cerebral palsy, Christy is brought up in a large but poor family in Dublin in the 1930s and 1940s, depicted with great period detail. The film celebrates Christy's individual determination to overcome physical limitations and lead a creative life, and shows him to be a complex character, often belligerent, with a sometimes cruel sense of humour. Against this, the film represents the strengths of a close-knit community (an urban village) and, despite its internal conflicts and drunken, authoritarian

19 Brenda Fricker as devout Irish mother in *My Left Foot* (1989). Courtesy of Granada Films International

father (Ray McAnally), the family is anchored in hard times by a long-suffering but resilient and resourceful mother (Brenda Fricker). Indeed, the film reiterates a traditional representation of Irish motherhood and the central relationship of the film is that between mother and physically disabled child. Indeed, Christy's first word, 'M.O.T.H.E.R.' is scrawled in chalk on the floor using his left foot. The film's circular dénouement, where Christy goes off with his nurse (Ruth McCabe), signifies a transfer of Christy's mother-love to that of a 'normalised', sexual love for Mary, symbolised by her popping the cork off a champagne bottle and confirmed by a closing title that informs us they married. To a large extent, then, Sheridan and producer Noel Pearson's recipe for critical and commercial success[7] relied upon on a conventional dramatic structure centred on the true story of an exceptional individual overcoming adversity; carefully crafted design and high production values (IR£1.7 million); and superb performances from a strong ensemble cast centred around the star, Daniel Day-Lewis. A family story and extensive interior scenes of domestic life transferred well to small screen outlets following theatrical success. The film was heavily funded by British television film producers like Granada and Channel Four. This kind of funding source was integral to the realisation of *December Bride* (1990), *The Field* (1990) and *Hear My Song* (1992), all of which were broadcast on Channel Four's premiere series, the first two transferring to video sell-through.

Hear My Song is essentially a romantic comedy in which Micky O'Neill (Adrian Dunbar) has to find out a way of overcoming his apparent inability to declare his love for Nancy Doyle (Tara Fitzgerald). Micky is a down-at-heel concert promoter living in Liverpool on the fringes of the theatrical world. In order to keep his business from going bust and to impress both Nancy and her mother, Kathleen (Shirley Ann Field), Micky sets off home to Ireland to book the legendary Irish tenor Josef Locke (Ned Beatty) to sing at his theatre. Locke had met and fallen in love with Kathleen when she was a minor beauty contest winner in Ireland in 1958 (shown through flashback home-movie footage) before she emigrated to England. Locke followed her and became hugely popular on the entertainment circuit but had to leave the country to avoid imprisonment for tax evasion. Micky tracks Josef down to a village in the west of Ireland and, eventually, in a pivotal scene, is forced to confront his feelings. Micky finds himself at night, having drunk poitín in the ruins of a round tower being dangled over the edge of a cliff by Locke and his cronies. Like *My Left Foot*, the gender dimension of the narrative drive is for a male (Micky) to overcome his inability to articulate his emotional feelings for a female partner (Nancy) and his own mother. The film had opened with a curious monochrome sequence of a boy (young Micky) witnessing his mother's death. His smiling response, directly addressed to us, is 'we all had difficult childhoods, but I think I got away with it', suggesting he is unaffected by grief, but the onset of a nose bleed becomes a recurring motif of emotional stress. As we have seen, the narrative is premised on Micky learning to give voice to his emotions towards women. The echoes in the male/female relationships between Locke/Kathleen and Micky/Nancy potentially signal that history might repeat itself, but for the fact that Micky is forced by Josef to admit he loves Nancy. Drawn by loving mother and daughter, the two men return to Liverpool to stage the comeback concert in a decrepit theatre due for demolition. A policeman with a grudge (David McCallum), who has been obsessively tracking Locke ever since the 1950s, now tries to arrest him but the wanted man is surrounded by the adoring audience and in the climatic mêlée is hoisted to freedom by a demolition crane.

The film's whimsical humour sometimes misses its mark, miscalculating the fine line between playful manipulation of cinematic stereotypes and conventions and relying on them as integral elements to the drive of the comic narrative. The director Peter Chelsom defended the film's mock heroic stance by saying 'it always goes towards the ridiculous with a version of the truth just behind it. It just gets to the point of sentimentality and when ever it's going too far – it undercuts itself'.[8] An example of this might be in a scene where music plays as Locke and Kathleen are reunited, but the camera tracks right to reveal Locke's own backing musicians providing what we initially took to be non-diegetic romantic music. Such moments in the film, where it deconstructs its own cinematic codes, do not guarantee that the film's audiences will decode it this way as Ruth Barton herself admits.[9] The *Film Ireland* reviewer condemned the film: 'we may as well produce plastic leprechauns and garden gnomes as this old tune'.[10] *Sight and Sound* felt that, 'far from making an innovative contribution to British cinema, *Hear My Song* relies for the most part on nostalgia, whimsy and sleight of hand'.[11] While the film is prepared to debunk the shallowness of a local TV journalist (Norman Vaughan), it insists on the idealisation of popular theatre as a cosy realm of authentic entertainment, when in fact both British and Irish culture have undergone profound cultural changes in the postwar period.

A similar nostalgia about the loss of theatrical traditions in the face of cinema and television recurs in *The Playboys*, but this film is grounded in a more substantial sexual politics. Set in 1957 in a border village, shop-keeper Tara Maguire (Robin Wright) becomes an unmarried mother, scandalises the local community by keeping her child and defies Father Malone (Alan Devlin) by refusing to name its father. One young suitor (Adrian Dunbar) commits suicide after being refused by her, but the local Garda sergeant (Albert Finney) is an older, fatherly admirer of Tara and he pressures her to let him 'make an honest woman' of her. This scheme is interrupted by the arrival of a shabby travelling circus who set up their tent on the village common. One of the troupe, Tom (Aidan Quinn), becomes a rival for Tara's affections. Frustrated by the competition of the younger man, the sergeant discloses that he is in fact the father of the child. The circus troupe comprises a bunch of has-beens, only too aware that their itinerant way of life is under threat from Hollywood at the local cinema and the erection of television aerials in the village. Feeding off the popularity of film, the troupe performs a comic send-up of *Gone with the Wind* but at its height this live communal entertainment is interrupted by a fight between Tom and the sergeant over custody of Tara's child. Tom wins, the sergeant wrecks the circus tent and leaves next day. The narrative finds its resolution with Tara, Tom and child riding off to a future in Dublin on motorbike and sidecar.[12] The screenplay's central conflict is that between tradition and modernity: rural Ireland in 1957 was on the cusp of profound economic and social transformation. Tara's defiant challenge to the authority of police, priest and parishioners is significant since unmarried mothers at the time were often forced by their families into harsh institutions run by religious orders, to give up the child for adoption or emigration to Britain for an abortion. Although somewhat marred by the unsuccessful attempt to work in a Troubles theme, by using the *Gone with the Wind* intertextual references and parallels,[13] *The Playboys* is more subtle in its playfulness with cinema than *Hear My Song*.[14]

More art house than heritage, Thaddeus O'Sullivan's *December Bride* (1990), takes maternity as a core narrative issue and generates a more arresting, less cosy film. It is set in and around a rural Presbyterian community near Strangford Lough in County Down at the turn of the century. It tells the story of a servant girl, Sarah Gomartin (Saskia Reeves), who comes to work at a farm owned by Andrew Echlin (Karl Hayden) and his two sons, Hamilton (Donal McCann) and Frank (Ciaran Hinds). Andrew dies in a boating accident, sacrificing his life for his sons and Sarah. Defying her mother (Brenda Bruce) and the mores of the community, Sarah remains on the farm with Hamilton and Frank, becoming sexually involved with both of them. She becomes pregnant, has the child but defies Minister Sorleyson (Patrick Malahide) by not naming the father. The cinematography in *December Bride* presents us with beautiful scenery but in a restrained, austere way that connects character to landscape, showing that visual pleasures are not necessarily incompatible with radical narratives. For the film presents us not with the usual love triangle observed in *Playboys*, but a *ménage à trois* in rural County Down. Sarah fights to be involved in decisions about extending the farm, displaying a sectarian attitude towards Catholic tenants at odds with the elder, more liberal Frank. It is a strength of the film that she is not shown as a paragon of virtue: her sectarianism is juxtaposed with her nascent feminism. Frank reminds her that the land is in the name of Echlin to which Sarah retorts defiantly: 'Name? All about names? Well, my name is Gomartin, and so is his [gesturing to baby] – remember you that'. In time she has a daughter and Frank defends the set-up against the condemnation of the local community and Sorleyson by saying simply: 'Its our way and it works'. Eighteen years on, Sarah's dilemma is that her daughter declares she wants to marry but can't unless she has a family name. On the principal of self-sacrifice taught by Andrew Echlin at the beginning of the film, she agrees to become a belated, December bride, but the film keeps the viewer guessing which of the brothers she marries until the final scene. Its significance as an Irish film in this period is that it tells a story about a strong female character and portrays an alternative version of a heterosexual family allied to a distinctive cinematography and spare but suggestive script.[15]

20 Alternative mothering and marriage: *December Bride* (1990).
Courtesy of Thaddeus O'Sullivan/Channel Four Film International

Confronting taboos: *Hush-a-bye-Baby* (1989), *The Visit* (1992) and *The Snapper* (1993)

Despite the increasingly commercialised nature of film-making in this period, taboo areas of contemporary Irish life were interrogated by film in different ways. It can be shown by retrospective readings of mainstream films but also in productions that determinedly attempted to expose topics that proved difficult to discuss openly in public and in the Irish broadcast media under formal and indirect censorship. The 1980s witnessed several events that provide the context for understanding Margo Harkin's *Hush-a-bye-Baby* (1989).[16] In a referendum in 1983, the Irish electorate voted to introduce a constitutional ban on abortion in the Republic; in Northern Ireland a series of high profile trials using paid informers, known as the 'Supergrass Trials', came to an end in 1984; the Catholic church had to contend with considerable news interest about 'moving statues' phenomena throughout the decade.[17] But perhaps the most pertinent events that occurred were the harrowing cases of infanticide in Caherciveen, known as the 'Kerry Babies' case, and of Ann Lovett, a teenager who died alone while giving birth in a grotto. Margo Harkin had been a leading figure in the Derry Film and Video Collective (DFVC), a workshop group that successfully applied for support from Channel Four in 1984 initially to fund non-fiction video projects. The most notable of these was Anne Crilly's *Mother Ireland* (1988),[18] which analysed the history of the relationship between the female image and Irish nationalism and was promptly banned from broadcast in Britain under new censorship measures imposed in that year. *Hush-a-Bye-Baby* was DFVC's first foray into fiction but it was based on research undertaken locally among women in Derry. It is set in 1984. School girl Goretti[19] (Emer McCourt) is established as a lively teenager brought up in a supportive family, deeply imbued with a Catholic morality through teaching at school and home. She falls in love with and becomes pregnant by Ciaran (Michael Liebmann) but he gets arrested and detained because of his family's republican connections. Goretti goes away on an Irish-language summer school to the Donegal Gaeltacht with her loyal friend, Dinky (Cathy Casey), in whom she eventually confides. Goretti visits Ciaran in prison but he appears not to be interested in supporting her and in desperation she tries first to mask the signs of her pregnancy from her family and then to induce a miscarriage. The trauma at the heart of this narrative is portrayed with insight, humanity and, perhaps oddly, with humour. What the film manages to convey most effectively is how religion, school and family in nationalist Derry shape the fictional characters and condition their responses to events. The abrupt ending pulls up the viewer and is deliberately ambiguous: Goretti screams from a nightmare in which she sees herself as a moving statue of Mary bursting from behind her glass casing. At this point her parents enter the bedroom but we do not know if she is prematurely giving birth or miscarrying. It is important to note that it was

21 Teenage pregnancy in Derry: *Hush-a-bye-Baby* (1989).
Courtesy of Margo Harkin/Derry Film and Video

set in Derry (formally part of Northern Ireland) and funded largely by Channel Four TV in London. Significantly, the narrative brings Goretti across the border to the Republic, out of the city to rural Donegal where she inadvertently tunes into an RTÉ radio discussion (in English) about abortion. Rural Ireland, even with its moving statues, has no miracle cure for Goretti's dilemma and Dinky's aside to a roadside Madonna – 'Don't you fuckin' move' – typifies the topical knowledge that is the basis for the film's rich vein of often sardonic humour.

Orla Walsh's short film, *The Visit* (1992),[20] focuses on the dilemma for Sheila (Magael MacLaughlin), whose husband, Sean (Ger Carey), is doing a twenty-year sentence as a convicted Republican prisoner in the Maze Prison in Northern Ireland. The intimate nature of her emotional state is deftly and economically conveyed in relation to her physical environment and social conditions. The surveillance of her life by the security forces is signified through the low-angled shot showing her caged in by wire and buildings and the RUC barracks in close proximity to housing. But even her own republican community operate a kind of cultural guard-duty on her behaviour: we hear from neighbours of punishments on women who sleep around. Through her part-time work as a teacher, Sheila meets Tom (Brendan Laird), a teacher with whom she has a sexual relationship and becomes pregnant. She decides to have the child but not to go away to Dublin with Tom. She challenges the tradition, having been supportive as a prisoner's wife,

22 Image of incarceration: *The Visit* (1992).
Courtesy of Orla Walsh/Bandit Films

reasoning: 'Now I'll see if he [Sean] has the strength to stand by me'. Walsh deliberately left the ending of the film open: 'Sheila is giving Sean a last chance to listen. In the final scene, he is ready to listen. You hope that through changes and what men are studying, there is hope for the future. I wanted to reflect that changes are occurring'.[21] These two films acknowledged and amplified discussions within particular communities in Ireland, north and south, part of a wider debate about women's control of their bodies, sexuality and other freedoms. What made Harkin's and Walsh's films exciting was that they succeeded in exposing the sexual politics of republicanism and Catholicism, provoking debate at local level[22] about the universally recognised issue of sexual politics without necessarily attempting to address that wider audience. It is also significant that Walsh seeks to acknowledge that masculinity can change, as a result of the pressures of feminist activity and cultural work.

Some indication that Irish masculinity was being redefined was registered in the screen version of Roddy Doyle's 1990 novel, *The Snapper* (1993). Directed by Stephen Frears for the BBC Screenplay series as a television film, it also had a limited cinema release in Ireland and Britain.[23] The film explores the circumstances in which nineteen-year-old Sharon (Tina Kellegher) became pregnant and the reactions of her family, particularly Dessie, (Colm Meaney) her father, and neighbours on a north-side, working-class Dublin housing estate. The baby's (or 'snapper' in colloquial Dublin) father is George Burgess (Pat Laffan), a middle-aged married neighbour, who opportunistically forces sex on Sharon, semi-conscious from alcohol, in a pub car park. The film is as interested in how Dessie reacts to his daughter's pregnancy as it is in Sharon's handling of the social abuse she receives as an unmarried mother. *The Snapper* is especially poignant since it was made during 1992-93, the period of what became known as the X case in the Republic. In February 1992, the Irish Supreme Court ruled that a fourteen year old rape victim (Miss X) did not have the right to travel to Britain for abortion under the parameters of the 1983 constitutional ban on abortion. In the face of huge public pressure, this was quickly reversed on the grounds that the girl's life was in jeopardy, for she had threatened to commit suicide. Angry Pro-Life supporters felt Irish legislation was being undermined, seeing it as part of a wider trend of Ireland's relationship with the EU. Indeed the X case coincided with public debates about the Maastricht treaty, which would mean closer political and legislative integration with Europe. In fact, Europe could not intervene on this issue because Ireland had earlier inserted a clause in a protocol preventing this. The government did resolve to have a referendum on abortion, which was held in November 1992. The voters decided that Irish women should be allowed to have information about abortion and the right to travel for termination but rejected the idea to allow abortions in Ireland except in certain extreme cases.

The film portrays Sharon's parents Dessie and Kaye (Ruth McCabe) as caring and supportive, wanting the best for her. Abortion is not considered.[24] Kaye is concerned that Sharon's younger brothers and sisters should be told that it is better to be married, but Dessie is more concerned to find out the identity of the father and rumours spread that it is Sharon's best friend's dad. Sharon pretends that a young, handsome Spanish sailor had a one-night stand with her, partly to console herself but also as an attempt to ward off her parents' suspicions. Sharon and Dessie's fears of disclosing/discovering the truth about the child's paternity are expressed in a mordantly humorous exchange that touches a raw nerve in the context of contemporary Ireland:

Sharon: What if it's a girl and it looks like Mr Burgess?
Dessie: Oh, feck! Then we'll have to smother it and leave it on his [door] step.

In fact, Dessie becomes a model grandfather to the imminent child, reading up about pregnancy and eventually taking Sharon in to hospital, playfully teased by wife and family.[25] The film ends on an upbeat note. Indeed Doyle's screenplay allowed a mainstream Irish audience to laugh at uncomfortable areas of contemporary experience. Outside this context, however, the representation of Sharon's family is liable to be viewed indiscriminately as a working class family muddling through chaos but coming out well from it.[26]

Box office Irish: *The Field* (1990) and *The Commitments* (1991)

In the absence of both the Film Board and significant funding from RTÉ, it was almost inevitable that Anglo-American film interests would move into the gap to support (and profit from) Irish-themed films. In *The Field* and *The Commitments*, we have examples of a tragedy set in a rural past and a comedy set in the urban present whose narratives have economic marginalisation as a driving force of the drama. In Sheridan's archetypal tragedy and Parker's comic social realism the underlying contradictions of Irish society and culture are represented in a mainstream mode. The common source of dramatic energy in these films is produced by internal conflicts produced by class and race, and by the pressure of external economic and cultural forces.

Bull McCabe (Richard Harris) claims ownership of a field that he and his wife (Brenda Fricker) have long-rented from the widow (Frances Tomelty), a landed Anglo-Irish woman. We learn that the McCabes' first-born son, Seamus, committed suicide – partly as a result of his overbearing father. Bull's single ambition is to pass the field down to his only remaining, though inadequate, son, Tadhg (Sean Bean). But the widow auctions the land to a returned Irish-American businessman, the yank (Tom Berenger), who plans to concrete the field over and build a hydroelectric station. Despite his ineptitude at dancing at the American Wake – a ritual party to mark the departure of emigrants to the USA – a sexual tension builds up between Tadhg and the Traveller woman (Jenny Conroy). He is enticed away, life on the road proving more attractive than working his father's field. Bull, driven by a personal destiny and his own version of a national history, murders the yank. In the tragic denouement of the film he accidentally kills Tadhg in a cattle stampede off the cliffs and then goes mad with remorse wading out into the sea. The complexity of the film's historical resonances were simplified and underplayed in two ways. Firstly, in John Keane's original 1965 stage play, the setting is the late 1950s and the outsider is an Irishman back from England having 'made good'. Bull's begrudging aggression towards an Irishman buying land with English money is absent in Sheridan's film version, being replaced with an emphasis on the yank as a cipher of modernity during the late 1930s. Secondly, Bull represents a generation of small-tenant farmers that typified a class who did not fully benefit from the shift in land ownership between 1879–1903 (the Land War to the Wyndham Act). Bull fervently believes that the law of the land, earned by work and sacrifice, supersedes the law of the Irish state, represented by police and priest. Bull is fiercely independent, scornful of the yank's emigrant forefathers and Travellers alike because they severed their connection with the land during the Famine in the 1840s. The Travellers, who used to be known as 'tinkers', are represented in the film as unruly, savage and a threat to Carrickthomond's sedentary, inward-looking society. A powerful, compelling film with moving

23 Successful screen tragedy of rural Ireland: *The Field* (1990). Granada Films International

performances, some critics felt *The Field* fell short of achieving an epic aspiration towards an Irish *King Lear* or even a reworking of *The Quiet Man* or *Ryan's Daughter*.[27] The film has its own Irish dramatic sources – Yeats's tragic cycle of Cuchulain plays in which the king kills his own son and goes insane in the sea – and other film critics saw the film as effectively marrying Keane's reworked scenario with US influences in both economic and cinematic terms.[28] Materially, to attract US distribution finance, Tom Berenger was cast as a star to sell the movie, but also the Hollywood western was confidently indigenised, with the frontier small-holder versus big business ranchers theme memorably distilled from *Shane* (George Stevens, 1952).

There might seem to be a world of a difference between the USA and northside Dublin, but *The Commitments* not only features characters whose everyday lives are imbued with American ideas, but the narrative of the film itself provides a working example of the American dream of success that occupies a central place in Hollywood films. Yet despite this mixing of cultures there are a number of underlying tensions in the text, anchoring the film in its urban working class milieu, and captured largely in the characterisation, dialogue and setting.[29]

The film is about Jimmy Rabitte's (Robert Arkins) attempt to escape unemployment and bid for rock and roll stardom. He comes from a large family that lives in a corporation house on a deprived northside estate of Dublin. Jimmy takes over the management of his friends' struggling band. He renames them The Commitments, revamps them as a Dublin soul band and imports ageing Joey the Lips (Johnny Murphy) as guru saxophonist. Just as the band gets some gigs and begins to get press interest, musical egos interfere and the dream crashes in a satisfying triumph of failure that Jimmy seems to relish as poetic. Fictional failure with energy, humour and a good soundtrack equals a huge box-office hit, particularly with youth audiences in Ireland and Britain. Two main themes in the film are relevant in this context. Firstly, there is the issue of an Irish urban working-class dream about success in US, capitalist terms. Dublin is portrayed as on the edge of modernity, fast-moving and vibrant if a little noisy, tatty and dirty. For a capital city, it has a local and communal culture witnessed in its markets and pubs, and Jimmy jostles to sell his audio-cassettes alongside a boy busking traditional ballads. As the band's agent, Jimmy is astutely aware of marketing a recognisable image, instructing the photographer not to pose the band against eighteenth-century Dublin architecture: 'I don't want a bleedin' picture postcard, give me urban squalor'.[30] Secondly, Jimmy's image for the band is based on imitating the sound of James Brown and soul. One of the band queries, 'D'you not think we're a bit – white?' 'Black' is substituted for the novel's original use of 'nigger' in Jimmy's oft-quoted retort: 'The Irish are the blacks of Europe, right? An' Dubliners are the blacks of Ireland. An' the northside Dubliners are the blacks o' Dublin. So say it loud, I'm black and I'm proud'. This omits a crucial line from Doyle's novel, 'The culchies have fuckin' everythin',[31] which appeared before the line about

24 Urban squalor chic? *The Commitments* (1991).
Courtesy of Beacon Communications Corp. Photo: David Appleby

Dubliners being the blacks of Ireland. 'Culchie' is a term used by Dubliners to refer to people from the country and this line encapsulates the urban perception that Ireland is dominated by rural interests, economic and cultural. Elsewhere, Ireland is compared to a Third World country and while this identification with oppressed peoples has impact, the omission elides and softens what is a significant insight about discrimination and division between the rich and poor, the rural and urban, within contemporary Irish society. It is an instance of tensions generated by Ireland's ambivalent status as a postcolonial country. It is to such representations of racial and cultural difference that we turn in the next section of this chapter.

Cowboys or Indians? Race and migration in contemporary Irish film

We can see in the production, narrative and intertextual references of *Into the West, The Crying Game* and *Far and Away* that the cultural histories of Ireland, Britain and the USA are profoundly interconnected. The difficulties of determining racial identity, tracing cultural origins and suppressing subaltern histories are common themes to three very different films released in 1992. In *Into the West*, Gabriel Byrne, an Irish actor and producer who now lives in Los Angeles, and Mike Newell, an English director, made a film that attempts to grapple with the discrimination against Travellers practised by settled communities and the Irish state since its formation.[32] It presents a narrative of search and pursuit in which two Traveller boys, Ossie (Ruaidhrí Conroy) and Tato (Ciaran Fitzgerald), learn about the true circumstances of their mother's death and their father, Papa Riley (Gabriel Byrne), overcomes his grief at the loss of his wife seven years previously. The film presents contemporary Ireland at the intersection of tradition and modernity, signified in the shot where Grandpa's horse-drawn wagon and the accompanying musical motif are drowned out by a roaring jet aircraft. The opening of the film shows Papa and the boys living in the urban high-rise housing of Ballymun, north Dublin. This representation of the Travellers' marginalised existence in conditions of social deprivation, welfare dependence and alienation has its basis in the historical reality of social, demographic and economic change since the 1960s.[33] The narrative catalyst is a mysterious white horse, brought to Dublin by Grandpa Riley (David Kelly) who calls it Tír na nóg – so named after the mythical land of eternal youth – and it becomes attached to Ossie. Tír na nóg's *puissance* attracts the attentions of an evil Garda inspector (Brendan Gleeson) who abducts the horse and illegally sells it to a businessman and stud owner (John Kavanagh) for show-jumping competitions. The boys rescue the horse and then ride cross-country imagining themselves cowboys in an Irish wild west: 'It's the Rockies ... Hi ho Silver – away!' The horse leads them to the boys' mother's grave, confirming that she died giving birth to Ossie. In the climax to the film, Ossie is saved from drowning in the sea by a vision of his mother, her spirit can be laid to rest according to Traveller lore by Papa burning their old caravan and the horse mysteriously disappears.

   Within this conventional plot scheme and narrative closure, *Into the West* portrays the history and culture of the Traveller as pre-modern, humane and valid when set against the materialism and alienation of modern Ireland. Indeed, modern life is represented as damaging, cruel and discriminatory. But for the fairness of Superintendent O'Hara (Jim Norton) – 'give these people [Travellers] some peace' – and the bumbling social welfare man, Irish society seems hard-pushed to hold back the harsh exigencies of greedy business men, corrupt policemen and the racism of settled communities, which call the Travellers 'knackers', a term that refers in part to their occupational links with horses. One writer has critically summarised the characterisation of the Travellers as an undeserving dispossessed native 'people without a history, without a homeland'.[34] The film viewer is addressed to sympathetically identify with Ossie and Tato as the pursued. However, the boys are themselves confused as to the nature of their identity and the film oscillates in its inter-textual references so that we are left unresolved about the very parallels to which the screenplay's dialogue and iconography draw attention. For example, near the opening of the film, while watching a TV western, Ossie tries to empathise with the Native Americans, asking, 'Were us Travellers [like] Indians?', only to be told emphatically by his older brother, 'No! *We* were the cowboys.' This exchange is significant, firstly, because they talk in the past tense as if their culture is dead and Ossie has never been on the road; secondly, because of Tato's insistence that cowboys are more appropriate models. The film seems to present the Travellers as being outlaw cowboys, but blurs this into attributes of Native Americans. The film repeatedly and explicitly portrays the Travellers as contemporary Irish 'Indians' in the way that they are marginalised, treated by the Gardaí (cavalry?) and small townsfolk. In order to find the boys, Papa enlists the help of his old Traveller friends, Barreller (Colm Meaney) – complete with leather-tasselled jerkin and stetson – and Kathleen (Ellen Barkin). At their encampment, they dance wildly around an open fire to Irish music. In one shot a television, positioned to the right of the foreground faces us, its presence offering another of the film's visual juxtapositions of indigenous and modern culture. This scene signifies Papa's cultural recuperation but it is threatened by interrupting Gardaí: 'Stop it, stop it, stop it ... dancing like animals'. Following the boys on horseback, Kathleen is shown to retain her native, feminine tracking skills. In a midlands town, a local man abusively calls her a squaw and she retaliates by cursing him.

The Travellers are represented as the 'Other' of mainstream Irish society and its contemporary culture, but the film works to humanise and reclaim them in a liberal gesture as somehow representative of Ireland's postcolonial status, of its confused identity in a postmodern world, saturated with US audio-visual culture. In this context, it is significant that the cinema in which the boys shelter and mischievously reproject a film shows a sequence from *Back to the Future* (1985) with the time-travelling car in the Old American West. *Into the West* attempts to resolves its narrative problems created by an absent mother with a suggestion that Kathleen may replace her, but it remains unresolved on the question of racial status and cultural identity. At the end of the film, Tato asks Papa, 'Are the Travellers cowboys or Indians?', to which Papa replies, 'There's a bit of a Traveller in everybody ... few of us know where we're going'. This line may simply sum up Papa's confused emotional state at this point. But it also evades the issue of the Travellers' displacement within Ireland, elevating it to a more universal sense of disorientation in the modern world. *Into the West* highlights the problems encountered when Irish subaltern differences are expressed in parallels between Irish and native or black American experience, which throw up as many complications as clear links.[35]

Such problems trouble *The Crying Game* (1992), although on release and in its immediate critical afterlife it generated more debate about its representation of gender, sexuality and nationality than it did about its portrayal of race.[36] The film explores the relationship between an IRA man, Fergus (Stephen Rea), and his captive, a black British soldier called Jody (Forest Whittaker). A sexualised intimacy grows between the two men and Fergus is unable to carry out his orders to execute the other soldier. Jody is accidentally killed by one of his own Saracen armoured cars but not before he has set Fergus the task of finding his girlfriend, Dil (Jaye Davidson), in London. The film transfers from rural Northern Ireland to urban London where Fergus (under a pseudonym of Jimmy) hides from the IRA, finds Dil – hairdresser by day, chanteuse by night – and becomes fascinated with Jody's former lover. However, Dil reveals 'herself' to be a biologically male transvestite, initially shocking Fergus. His affections, however, remain strong and he comes to terms with the nature of his own sexuality. In the film's graphically violent climax, Dil – temporarily disguised and masculinised in Jody's cricket whites and shorn hair at Fergus's suggestion – kills Jude (Miranda Richardson), the IRA volunteer cum *femme fatale,* who has hunted down Fergus. In an act of self-sacrifice, Fergus goes to prison for Dil's homicide and in the closing scene 'she' visits him in prison as 'Stand by Your Man' comes up over the credits.

Among Irish critics, Sarah Edge has given the most cogent feminist interpretation of the film, arguing that despite its humane characterisation of an IRA man and 'gender-bending' plot, the narrative is unconsciously misogynist: the only redeemable 'woman' is biologically male.[37] This insight qualifies a gay reading of the film that focuses on the disruptive consequences for Irish republican discourse and a subversive take on Anglo-Irish history.[38] What should be acknowledged is that Fergus, gay or bisexual, remains male and subject to the conditioning masculinity of the society in which he lives. Gay men may be just as misogynist as straight men. Jordan, as the film's creator, has shown himself to be very defensive when questioned about the film's sexual politics, mostly notably in an interview by Marina Burke in *Film Ireland*.[39]

As regards race, according to Jordan, the film attempts to set up an irony that a young man (Jody) whose origins lie in an ex-colony like Antigua should be forced by his economic circumstances in London to join the British Army at war with the IRA in the last colony of the old empire. Jordan's film posits a love between two men, made doubly problematic by Jody's being black and Fergus being Irish and caucasian, since the director claims that 'Irish people have never liked other minorities'.[40] Despite Jody's reports of being racially abused on duty in Northern Ireland and Jude calling Dil 'the wee black chick', there is little ironic play with race in the dialogue compared with the puns and quips about gender and nationality. Jordan's assertion about the racist attitudes of the Irish (for which there is growing evidence in 1990s Ireland) is lost on many white audiences – if my students' reactions are typical – who tend to read the transgressive, (hyper)sexualities of black or mixed race characters as bizarre or weird. Indeed, racial origins confirm such characters' difference from white, hetero 'normality'. The narrative invites identification with Fergus's obsessive fascination with Jody/Dil's otherness, which he finds repulsive yet compulsively attractive. Unlike female desire and power, fears about which are addressed and punished in the narrative, *The Crying Game* does not fully engage the 'fear of the dark' that is projected on screen.[41]

In a land where green is white: *Far and Away* (1992)

Far and Away epitomises a tendency in some Irish-American film-makers to distort not only historical events in Ireland, but simultaneously produce a myopic representation of the Irish in the construction of the US past. Ron Howard believed that *Far and Away* was 'a fairly risky undertaking, and I think it is something I was very afraid of, even while I was working toward realising it'.[42] An awareness of his own Irish forbears and the cinematic heritage of Ford and Lean, was combined with the risk of spending $55 million on a period romantic comedy shot on location in Kerry, Dublin and Montana set supposedly in 1892. Some of these fears were realised at Cannes as 'an assemblage of the world's critics laughed their way through' the indulgent cinematic paddywackery with its clichés and speech anachronisms.[43] Young Joseph (Tom Cruise) seeks revenge against the landlord who has kept his tenant family in poverty and killed his father (Niall Tóibín). The script conflates Irish history since eviction scenes were more typical of the Land War of the 1879–82 period, but 'filmed in wishfulfilmentscope',[44] events in Ireland are made to tally with those experiences of the Irish in the USA. Joseph becomes romantically involved with the landlord's proto-feminist daughter, Shannon (Nicole Kidman). The pair secretly emigrate to Boston where their class and religious differences become socially unimportant. Boston's melting pot of incoming migrants and free African-Americans is captured in the quayside confusion of different languages, races and ethnic dress. In these circumstances, Irish immigrant networks provided accommodation, work and support, but this did not preclude exploitation by unscrupulous fellow-Irishmen (Colm Meaney): Joseph turns to prize-fighting, while Shannon is comically reduced to chicken-plucking. The couple become separated: Joseph goes west, Shannon is rescued by her land-hungry parents and gentleman cad fiancé. But, on the eve of the Oklahoma Land Rush, the romantic leads are reunited. Joseph jostles with other would-be homesteaders (followed in line by an African-American in the

25 Boston's immigrant melting pot: *Far and Away* (1992).
Courtesy of Universal Studios Inc. Photo: Philip Caruso

registry office) to lay claim to the free land of the west. The triumphal finale is technically very impressive. The 70mm widescreen is finally justified; the hunger for narrative resolution is satiated by the improbable reuniting of Shannon and Joseph; the hero gets the woman and land that is his destiny. Here the objectionable politics of the film protrude as we are reminded of the emotional rhetoric of Joseph's oppression by a landlord class at the beginning of the film. The screenplay would have us uncritically admire the spectacle of US neo-colonial expansionism, in which the Irish actively participate. Far from being a fair method of distributing land, this event was the organised expropriation of territory already belonging to native peoples. In the briefest of shots, three Native Americans (one male wearing a cavalry tunic) are shown in the crowd passively witnessing this dispossession. Exactly a century after the event (five hundred years after Columbus's discovery), the film's evasive understanding of the Irish in US national and cinema history is passed off as an ironic, nineties knowingness. Howard's idea, that 'the story of Irish immigration and my sensibility or take on the material, [which] is much more light-hearted and fanciful an approach',[45] belies the fact that *Far and Away* reprocessed an unpalatable episode in the USA's past.[46] The risks Howard mentions in the same interview *could* have involved a more rigorous consideration of his own Irish-American connections. That his film avoided this speaks volumes for the historical facility with which the Irish 'became white'[47] by the end of the nineteenth century in the USA and articulates contemporary white anxieties about native rights, black urban alienation and immigration in US society.[48]

A second coming: the Film Board revived

Back in Ireland, between September 1992 and Spring 1993, a number of events occurred that contributed to the relaunch of the Irish Film Board in March 1993, significantly on the occasion of the all-night Oscar party in the Irish Film Centre (IFC), which celebrated *The Crying Game's* scoop of Best Original Screenplay. A strong, well-organised campaign of film-makers, trade unions, educationalists and academics, galvanised by the shock of the IFB closure in 1987, gave a cautious welcome to the economic findings of the Coopers & Lybrand Report published at the end of 1992. Commissioned by the IFC and business interests in the Temple Bar area of Dublin, this report argued that substantial income could be derived from an expanding audio-visual sector. In September 1992, the status of film as part of Ireland's cultural heritage had been affirmed by the establishment of the Irish Film Institute and the long-planned Irish Film Archive housed in the IFC building in Dublin. Here was a place in which the country's film deposits could be collected, catalogued and preserved; films from all round the world could be viewed in two cinemas; and support and advice to would-be film-makers could be provided through Film Base and the MEDIA desk located in the IFC. The centre provided a focus for Ireland's developing a film culture in the widest of senses, including an active education department. Minister M. D. Higgins spoke of the importance of educating young people about all kinds of music, film and other media not just because it might provide employment for them but because it was crucial to understand how the media controlled people's perception and understanding of the world.[49] Part of the development of a critical stance towards media in Ireland was the expansion of film schools, educational programmes and media courses in higher education in the late 1980s and early 1990s, which encouraged and equipped young people in practical skills and critical acumen. Dun Laoghaire College of Art and Design (DLCAD) instituted a graduate film and video show from 1987 and their work fed into the burgeoning film festival circuit and RTÉ broadcast slots. Indeed, the early 1990s saw the beginnings of change in the relations between the large and the small screen. Legislation in Ireland and Britain had forced broadcasters like RTÉ and the BBC to commission work from independent production companies rather than making them solely in-house.

The budget of 1993 saw the tax incentives of the 1987 Finance Act extended until 1999 to maintain the inward investment of film production in Ireland. Indeed, some sectors of the Irish economy were beginning to expand. This was taking place against the backdrop of a peace process that delivered the Irish–British government Downing Street Declaration (December 1993), affording a degree of stability and optimism in Ireland, manifest in paramilitary ceasefires that followed in the autumn of 1994. Within the Republic, the balance of political power had taken a decisive shift in 1992 when Fianna Fáil had to enter a coalition agreement with the Labour Party, which brought Michael D. Higgins to the fore in the cultural sphere. A progressive and imaginative minister, an intellectual in the European mode and passionate supporter of the arts, he was given a full cabinet position as Minister for Arts, Culture and the Gaeltacht. He appointed the dynamic Lelia Doolan as chair of the Irish Film Board, which was relocated nearer to Higgins' home constituency in Galway. With the revised Film Board, the prospects for the 1990s seemed cautiously encouraging: 'Within five years we could begin – yeah, begin – to see a solid body of Irish work, made by Irish people living and working in Ireland. That might be a reality if this Board is true to the spirit of what Michael D is about'.[50] An assessment of films in the rest of the 1990s is provided in the final chapter of this book. But for the moment our attention turns in Part II to the role of broadcasting and to Ireland on the small screen.

Notes

1 K. Rockett, 'Culture, industry and Irish cinema', in J. Hill, M. McLoone and P. Hainsworth (eds), *Border Crossing: Film in Ireland, Britain and Europe* (Belfast, Institute of Irish Studies, 1994), 127.

2 Mesures pour Encourager le Développement de l'Industrie de Production Audio-Visuelle (MEDIA). Simon Horrocks succinctly describes the EC's involvement with cinema since the 1980s, in J. Caughie and K. Rockett (eds), *The Companion to British*

and Irish Cinema (London, Cassell, 1996), 177–80. K. Rockett points out that 'Ireland does very well from MEDIA' on a per capita basis, getting 3 per cent of MEDIA's total funding allocation while Ireland only accounts for 1 per cent of the EC's population. See Rockett, 'Culture, industry and Irish cinema', 137.

3   Indeed, *The Irish Times* (8 April 1990), carried an article titled 'State has no role in films', which argued that 'the last thing needed is the dead hand of the State'. The success of these prominent films, it was pointed out, 'is likely to have hardened the Government attitude of keeping the State out of the film-making business apart from providing tax incentive breaks to those wishing to invest in a risky business'.

4   R. Barton, 'From history to heritage: some recent developments in Irish film', *The Irish Review*, 21 (Autumn/Winter 1997), 46.

5   Barton 'From history to heritage', 50–1.

6   This genre of film carries forward chronologically with several examples, including *War of the Buttons* (1993), *Widow's Peak* (1993), *All Things Bright and Beautiful* (1994), *The Run of the Country* (1995), *Circle of Friends* (1995) and *Amongst Women* (1998). The latter has not had a theatrical release and was made for broadcast on the BBC, with the tie-in publication of John McGahern's novel and VHS retail video sell-through.

7   *My Left Foot* was reported to have grossed $8.7 million at the US box office after just nineteen weeks on limited release. See *The Irish Times* (28 March 1990). *The Irish Independent* (28 March 1990), 13, ran a feature titled, 'The greening of Hollywood'.

8   Interviewed in *The Irish Times* (3 April 1992), 10. In the same feature, M. Dwyer, 'Stage-Irish and proud of it', reported that the film represented Ireland at the Cannes Film Festival and 'has built up a body of critical support and commercial success in America and London.'

9   Barton 'From history to heritage', 53.

10 I. Palmer, *Film Ireland*, 29 (May–June 1992), 18.

11 T. Charity, *Sight and Sound*, 1:25 (11 March 1992), 47.

12 In the 'Synopsis' provided in *The Playboys Press Release* (Los Angeles, Samuel Goldwyn, 1990), Tom offers to take Tara to the USA but in the final version of the film, they talk only of going to Dublin. See *The Playboys* file held at the IFC Library, Dublin.

13 K. Rockett, 'From Atlanta to Dublin', *Sight and Sound*, 2:2 (June 1992), 26.

14 For contrasting views of the film see M. O'Dwyer, 'Romancing at the cross-roads', *The Irish Times* (n.d.) and L. Francke, *Sight and Sound*, 2:2 (June 1992), 50. O'Dwyer believes the film to 'firmly eschew[s] the patronising stereotypical trappings of most movies set in Ireland and financed from abroad', while Francke argues that 'much of the film revolves around too-familiar rural stereotypes [and that] the film cannot make up its mind whether to be tongue-in-cheek or hand-on-heart. Ultimately, it is that much touted "whimsy factor" that ossifies the project from the start'.

15 For an interview between Thaddeus O'Sullivan and Luke Gibbons, see 'Fragments into pictures', *Film Base News*, 20 (November–December 1990), 8–12.

16 P. Murphy, '"Hush-a-bye Baby": An interview with Margo Harkin and Stephanie English', *Film Base News*, 16 (February–March 1990), 8–10.

17 For an account by Fintan O'Toole, originally published in *Magill* (May 1985), see 'Seeing is believing' in *A Mass for Jesse James: A journey through 1980s Ireland* (Dublin, Raven Arts Press, 1990), 16–22.

18 M. Emerman, 'Derry Film and Video: an interview with Margo Harkin', *Cineaste*, 17:2 (1989), 43.

19 Goretti was a popular name for girls from Catholic families, named after St Maria Goretti, who allowed herself to be killed rather than lose her virginity. Thanks to Marie Ryan for this information.

20 The screenplay is based on a short story by Laurence McKeown.

21 M. Sullivan, 'The Visit, incarceration and film by women in Northern Ireland: An interview with Orla Walsh', The Irish Review, 21 (Autumn/Winter 1997), 37–8.

22 See Margo Harkin's account of the responses to Hush-a-bye-Baby in Derry and Northern Ireland in M. McLoone (ed), Culture, Identity and Broadcasting in Ireland (Belfast, Institute of Irish Studies, 1991), 113–16. The film also played at the Academy Cinema in Dublin and was broadcast on RTÉ and on Channel Four in Britain.

23 It is also available on VHS. For a lengthy and informative interview with Doyle on this project and other work, see Liam Fay, 'Never mind the bollix!', Hot Press, 17:10 (June 1993), 38–40.

24 The family 'accept the pregnancy with baffling equanimity' according to M. Moroney and 'although the abortion option is briefly mentioned at the outset, [it is] then firmly dismissed – which may well be why this is a BBC, rather than an RTÉ film'. See The Irish Times (6 August 1993).

25 Fintan O'Toole has argued that the film recuperates Irish fatherhood from its largely negative portrayal in Irish literature and found the film a progressive reclamation of family values in response to the lay Catholic appropriation of that term during the 1980s: 'Family solidarity', The Irish Times (10 April 1993).

26 The review condemned the film for patronising the working-class lives of Barrytown, Film Ireland, 35 (June–July 1993), 24.

27 J. Gogan, 'The Field', Film Base News, 20 (November–December 1990), 19–20; and N. Floyd, 'The Field', Monthly Film Bulletin, 58 (March 1991), 78–9.

28 M. Dwyer, 'The power and the glory of The Field', The Irish Times (21 September 1990), 10.

29 B. Guckian's review describes it as 'a fine, well-crafted film … an honest portrayal of Dublin and her people', Film Base News, 25 (September–October 1991), 18.

30 A. Parker describes the preparations that went into location searching, casting and choice of music (ending with fifty-two different songs in the film) in his 'Synopsis' to the Press Pack of The Commitments (May 1991), 2–5.

31 R. Doyle, The Barrytown Trilogy (London, Minerva, 1993), 13. In an otherwise interesting article on the film, Timothy D. Taylor notes Parker's substitution of 'black' for 'nigger' in the film version, but he passes over the line about 'culchies', Ireland's own 'niggers': 'Living in a postcolonial world: Class and soul in The Commitments', Irish Studies Review, 6:3 (1998), 291.

32 'This isn't a hymn to the Gypsy [sic] ideal and way of life … to be a gypsy in the 1990s is to live a difficult life because you're torn between your old ideals and your inability to fit into the settled community': G. Byrne, 'Production Notes: Into the West' (n.d.), 14. See also Byrne's comments in 'Take that script and shove it', Hot Press (Special Anniversary Issue) (1992), 17.

33 J. Mac Laughlin, Travellers and Ireland: Whose Country, Whose History? (Cork, Cork University Press, 1995), 1–2.

34 Mac Laughlin, Travellers and Ireland, 5–22.

35 Into the West proved to be a very popular film. It took IR£855,073 between November 1992 and January 1993; in February it was released in Britain and Northern Ireland. See Film Ireland, 33 (February–March 1993), 5. In May it went on

release in the US, marketed very much as a children's film. Miramax reported 'a healthy $1.4 million from 550 screens in its opening weekend': *Screen International*, 926 (24 September 1993).

36 S. O'Hara, 'A crying shame', *The Irish Times* (19 December 1992), 36, Section C., argues that the film reinforces negative images of women in contemporary film culture and society. James, '*The Crying Game* wins at gimmickry', *The New York Times* (31 January 1993), 40, claims the crucial thing about the film was its publicity campaign.

37 S. Edge, 'Women are trouble: You know that Fergus?', *Feminist Review*, 50 (Summer 1995), 181–6. Another devastating exegesis of the film from a feminist perspective is provided by A. Kotsopoulos and J. Mills, 'The Crying Game: Gender, genre and "post-feminism"', *Jump Cut*, 39 (1994), 15–24.

38 L. Pettitt, 'Pigs and provos, prostitutes and prejudice: Gay representation in contemporary Irish cinema', in E. Walshe (ed.), *Sex, Nation and Dissent in Irish Writing* (Cork University Press, 1997), 268–73.

39 M. Burke, 'Celtic dreamer', *Film Ireland*, 34 (April–May 1993), 17–21.

40 Jordan as quoted in Burke, 'Celtic Dreamer', 20.

41 L. Young, *Fear of the Dark: 'Race', gender and sexuality in the cinema* (London, Routledge, 1996).

42 A. Brett, 'All the right moves', *What's on in London* (12 August 1992), 12.

43 D. Malcolm, 'An epic out of its time', *The Guardian* (30 July 1992), 30.

44 N. Andrews, 'Begorrah, 'tis Hollywood himself', *The Financial Times* (30 July 1992), 15. Condemnation of the film's representation of race may also be found in V. Letts, 'It's a free country', *The Spectator* (1 August 1992), 40, and A. Mars-Jones, *The Independent* (31 July 1992), 14. G. Greig, *The Sunday Times* (2 August 1992), 8–9, neatly summarises USA critics' reactions, who explained that the film's 'turkey' status was due to poor timing of release (against *Batman*), the mismatch of Kidman and Cruise, its 'old fashioned, un-hip' look and its failure to 'excite young male movie fans'. See also N. O'Neill's review in *Film Ireland* (July–August 1992), 26–7, calling it 'an essentially dumb, juvenile example of inoffensive dross made with remarkable vulgarity.'

45 A. Brett, 'All the right moves', 12.

46 Andrews, 'Begorrah', 15.

47 N. Ignatiev, *How the Irish Became White* (New York/London, Routledge, 1995).

48 See also the discussion of *Out of Ireland* (1995) in chapter 10 of this book.

49 'The work aesthetic', *Hot Press Magazine* (9 September 1993), 23.

50 Lelia Doolan, as quoted in *Film Ireland*, 34 (April–May 1993), 5.

PART II

TELEVISION

CHAPTER 7

CATHODE NI HOULIHAN:[1]
A SHORT HISTORY OF BROADCASTING
IN IRELAND

- What different kinds of broadcasting systems have developed in Ireland?
- What problems have recurred in Irish television?
- How has television helped to redefine Irish national identity since 1962?

British broadcasting in Ireland, 1924–66

Broadcasting emerged as a practical proposition in Britain at the same time as legislative arrangements were being prepared for the partition of Ireland.[2]

The origins of broadcasting in Ireland are closely related to the momentous political changes taking place around 1920. This part of the book is concerned with television representations of Ireland but initially we need to discuss the history and principal features of the wider term 'broadcasting'. Firstly, we need to appreciate how the shaping of radio provided a context for the adoption of television in the 1950s and 1960s. Secondly, we need to understand how broadcasting in Northern Ireland has always differed from Britain and been distinct from the service offered by the southern Irish state. Thirdly, a brief historical outline will suggest comparisons between the development of broadcasting and the cinema history examined in Part I. Indeed, it might be argued that the intimate involvement of broadcasting systems in defining national political and cultural identities is more direct and pervasive than cinema since it inhabits the domestic space of family lives. What is without doubt is that the broadcast media were instrumental in defining and focusing socio-political change in Ireland at significant moments throughout the twentieth century. From its origins in amateur and military use, radio broadcasting in Europe emerged in the political, social and commercial chaos that followed World War I. Governments in several European countries began to licence radio broadcast services led by the British Broadcasting Company (BBC) in London in 1922, followed by Germany, Belgium and Switzerland in 1923, then Austria and Finland in 1924.[3] The first radio broadcast service in Ireland (2BE) began in 1924 from the Belfast studio of the BBC. This commercial company operated for four years until it was transformed into a national public utility under Royal Charter in 1927 and rapidly grew into a national cultural institution. The Irish

Free State inaugurated its own national radio service (2RN) in 1926, which became known as Radio Éireann (RÉ) from 1937 and whose development we will examine in the second section. The emphasis in this chapter is on understanding historical development and issues central to the nature of broadcasting rather than the analysis of individual case studies of programmes or the discussion of the generic characteristics that comprise chapters 8–12. This chapter will also give more space to the earlier periods in this history since they are probably less familiar than contemporary events and issues. A final section does consider how Ireland is now imaged via satellite and cable for Irish diaspora groups in the UK and the USA. In creating audiences beyond the island of Ireland, and by aiming to reach viewers who might not specifically self-identify as Irish, is this new circulation of media images fundamentally changing the nature of what constitutes Irishness for the next century?

Although challenged since the 1980s, the nature of broadcasting in both Ireland and Britain has been decisively shaped by the notion of its public service broadcasting (PSB) function. The concept of PSB stems from the specific pattern of radio's emergence in the 1920s. The anticipated potential of a relatively new medium (then called wireless) was such that its public role was hotly debated by three kinds of interest group. Firstly, the state – represented by politicians, civil servants and the military – was concerned about the financing, administration, control and influence of radio. In the UK, the non-military use of radio transmitters had been banned between 1914–19 for security reasons. Restrictions were maintained in Northern Ireland until 1924 and in the Irish Free State until 1926 because of the political violence associated with partition and the Irish Civil War. Secondly, commercial interest groups – radio manufacturers, music hall, cinema and newspaper proprietors – were eager either to exploit or limit the potential competitor as a source of news and entertainment. Thirdly, the public was constituted by a small but vocal lobby of amateur enthusiasts or clubs (eager to transmit as well as receive signals in an organised system of broadcasts) and a larger unknown group of potential listeners. In England the BBC began a limited service in 1922 driven by the commercial concerns of a consortium of wireless-set manufacturers. Newspaper owners correctly reckoned that radio would provide them with competition but some in parliament also felt that radio could have an inflammatory effect on listeners just by hearing relayed news on air: 'there were complaints about the reading of extracts from *The Times* dealing with the situation in Egypt ... and Ireland'.[4] Between 1922 and 1926 the debate about the social and political role of radio was refined and the argument was made for its unique place in British life. Under the stewardship of John Reith, who became the new BBC's first director-general, broadcasting shifted its concerns from the commercial to the cultural, from profit to public service. The BBC achieved the status of corporation and with it the autonomy of a public service in 1927.

The BBC received revenue from a licence fee and an annual levy from the state. Unlike the commercial system in the USA, the British system carried no advertisements and the BBC's function was to broadcast programmes in order to inform, educate and entertain its listeners. In recognition of its unique position – effectively a monopoly on broadcasting – the BBC was restricted in parliamentary reporting, had to refrain from making editorial comment and remain impartial in its reporting. It would be a largely self-regulating institution, run by 'the great and the good' for the enlightenment of individuals and acting independently of the government in the national interest.[5] The recent war had traumatised Britain economically and politically. Its leaders became alert to class tensions and regional differences. Cracks of discontent had also begun to appear in the Empire. A great deal of faith was put into radio's bonding potential, as Paddy Scannell writes:

Radio, in an organised social form, seemed to be one significant and unprecedented means of helping to shape a more unified and egalitarian society. Through radio a sense of the nation as a knowable community might be restored by putting people in touch with the ceremonies and symbols of the corporate national life.[6]

The national conditions which determined the shape of the BBC between 1927 and 1939 required cohesive organisation through both restorative and constructive means. Radio was the means by which an elite, high culture was domesticated and brought into middle- and working-class homes. It is significant that annual events like the Grand National (a horse race), the FA Cup Final (a knock-out football competition), the Boat Race (a rowing race between Oxford and Cambridge universities), the Royal Tournament (an indoor team display by the British Armed Services), Trooping the Colour (a military parade marking the British monarch's official birthday), the All-England tennis at Wimbledon and cricket test matches all started live commentary on BBC radio in 1927. The monarchy and national institutions were popularised, and a sense of togetherness and belonging was created and celebrated across geographical and social differences. Daily programmes of music and talk were improving in taste and morals. Radio began the process of connecting the lives of ordinary people and their pastimes as well as creating a new form of leisure activity in itself. The BBC ethos was that of a liberal if patronising institution[7] but it was effective in developing and contributing to a workable social and political consensus in the interwar years in Britain.

The same could not be said for the BBC in Northern Ireland (BBCNI) for 'from its inception in 1924, broadcasting in Belfast was not like any other part of the UK system'.[8] Although constitutionally part of the UK, the same social or political consensus did not exist in Northern Ireland itself since most of the Catholic nationalist population refused to recognise the state's legitimacy. Most of the small BBC staff in Belfast were not from the province and broadcasting was, formally at least, under the control of London. Strained, mutually suspicious relations existed between the broadcasters and the unionist political establishment. Assessing the position achieved during the interwar years, Des Cranston states that BBCNI became 'an integral part of the dominant political, class and business structure'.[9] Official unionist culture wanted to emphasise the Britishness of Northern Ireland in its links to the BBC's main network, reinforcing the political border with the Irish Free State through the assertion of cultural difference. However, sometimes Irish-themed broadcasts received from mainland Britain undermined this because they featured material of a Gaelic, Catholic or broadly nationalist nature, such as St Patrick's Day commemorations or traditional Irish music and song content. The listening majority of unionists were highly sensitive to such BBC blunders. Following the controversy over the content of a programme called 'The Irish' in 1937, a gatekeeping role was formalised by the regional controller of BBCNI. London agreed to editorial procedures whereby Northern Ireland was able to veto material made about the island of Ireland, which it found unsuitable for the local region or the rest of the BBC's national network.[10] This narrowed the view that those outside of Northern Ireland might have of the place and simultaneously prevented alternative political views being aired. Relaxed or tightened, according to the political climate, these procedures became institutionalised by the BBC, demonstrating that censorship about Northern Ireland in British broadcasting has a long history. In the interwar years, the class-biased nature of the BBC meant that popular loyalist marching bands were ignored in local programming in the same way that dance music (jazz) was frowned upon. In this collision of national and class politics, unionism's anomalous position was exposed. Political separation from the Free State and support for the Union was an expression of being British and not 'Irish'. But aspiring to the highbrow metropolitan values embodied by BBC London meant ignoring Ulster's working-class culture and rural values. The unionist establishment was acutely aware of being included in so-called Irish programmes networked from London. On such occasions, they were defensively inclined to reassert the need for broadcasting autonomy and separation. McLoone has pointed out the 'irony in the fact that the loyal unionists sought to break free from the centralised control of the Imperial centre which could not be trusted to guarantee proper representation for its loyal subjects'.[11]

During World War II, the BBC was largely given over to the services of the state in propagandist mode, providing information and entertainment to boost national morale. After the war, the BBC restructured its radio network in a gesture towards the egalitarian mood of the time and reluctantly relaunched a television service in 1946 amidst lingering austerity. This service was extended to Northern Ireland seven years later in the hope that the coronation of 1953 would stimulate patriotic unionists to buy television sets.[12] Northern Ireland secured its constitutional position within the UK in 1949 in the wake of the Republic's exit from the Commonwealth. As a consequence, throughout the 1950s and early 1960s, the BBC's policy in Northern Ireland was more interventionist, attempting to construct a consensus at a local level in a deeply divided society. In the circumstances of declining industries, rising unemployment and growing social dissatisfactions, this was bound to fall short of expectations and frustrate all groups. In addition, the coverage that Northern Ireland received in Britain was of a minimalist, let-well-alone approach and maintained the profound ignorance of people in Britain: 'Northern Ireland did not feature on the [BBC] TV network, except in news bulletins ... so the greater British public learnt little about what was going on its own political backyard'.[13]

Between 1950–54, commercial and political interests argued the case for breaking the BBC's monopoly on broadcasting. In the mid-1950s Britain emerged from rationing, looked towards economic rebuilding and culturally began to experience the beginnings of an Anglo-American consumer boom. The time was propitious for the inauguration of a new kind of television service. Under the aegis of the Independent Broadcasting Authority (IBA), ITV began transmission in 1955. ITV differed from the BBC in that it was a federation of individual production companies based in geo-demographic regions that shared a transmission network for some national programmes. ITV was also different to the BBC in that its licence was granted under an Act of Parliament (not a Royal Charter) but its conditions carried very strict requirements defining a public service function, due impartiality and with a remit to reflect local audiences. The ITV service carried spot commercial breaks, the money from which paid for production. From the beginning, ITV's output brought innovations in style and presentation, which forced the BBC to change its programming. However, a consensus about PSB remained and what developed was a broadcasting duopoly that lasted from 1955 until 1982, when Channel Four first began broadcasting.

The franchise for the ITV licence in Northern Ireland was won by Ulster Television who began broadcasting in 1959, but less disposable income and local loyalty to radio meant that TV set ownership in the region was lower than in the rest of the UK.[14] Potentially, UTV might have addressed itself to the one third of the population whose political concerns and cultural identity had largely been ignored by the BBC but instead the commercial station practised a brand of 'apolitical populism' in order 'to avoid giving offence to unionists or nationalist opinion'.[15] In an effort to keep the issue of the Irish border to the fore of the public mind, a campaign of IRA attacks on buildings and symbolic targets lasted from 1956–62, but during this time the BBC's news reports were brief and UTV did not have a newsroom until 1962. Election coverage (in 1959 and 1963) and current affairs in Northern Ireland involved highly sensitive editorial decisions, which London producers often misjudged. However, Cathcart notes that by the mid-1960s, some BBC journalists were becoming more investigative, probing into areas of life like economic disadvantage, employment, housing and social conditions. In 1965, relations between the governments of the Republic and Northern Ireland appeared to show a growing détente but, on the ground, resentments in nationalist communities emerged as a powerful civil rights movement and the loyalist UVF were reborn in 1966. Cathcart asks pertinently of this period: 'In its drive to develop consensus, to extend the middle ground, had the BBC failed to alert the population to the real division which remained and the extremes on both sides?'[16] The media's response to the crisis that ensued will be taken up after we have examined the parallel development of broadcasting in the Irish Free State/Republic in the next section.

Radio Éireann and national identity, 1926–60

While not forgetting what is best in what other countries have to offer us, we desire to especially emphasise what we have derived from our Gaelic ancestors – from one of the oldest civilisations in Europe, the heritage of the O's and the Mac's who still make up the bulk of our country.[17]

Radio transmitters had been banned in Ireland because of their potential subversive use by paramilitaries under the 1914 Defence of the Realm Act, throughout the Anglo-Irish crisis (1916–21) and during the Irish civil war (1922–23). Strictly speaking, owning a radio was still illegal in 1923 as Irish Free State politicians engaged in parliamentary debate about a national radio service. As in Britain, radio was cautiously introduced into Irish life and regarded with a circumspection previously reserved for cinema, neatly captured in President Douglas Hyde's inaugural broadcast quoted above. The parlous condition of finances in the early years of the Irish Free State provided economic reasons to delay expenditure on a national radio service, only complicated by the new government's desire to counter BBC transmission leakage from Belfast and provide an alternative to the incursion of a planned commercial service backed by British financial interests. After considerable debate, the Dáil decided on a modified British model of PSB,[18] conforming to a tendency towards postcolonial mimicry. The nationalised radio service began transmission in 1926 but with a less autonomous structure than was adopted in Britain the following year. Broadcasting over a smaller area, one transmitter would eventually cover most of the Free State and spill into parts of Northern Ireland, which was regarded as the 'national territory' anyway. Unlike the BBC in Britain, radio in partitioned Ireland was more clearly aligned with and controlled by the state. In the Irish Free State the radio was run as a department in the civil service until 1953 and although ultimate power concerning radio legislation for Northern Ireland lay in London, unionist politicians in Belfast exerted considerable influence over the local BBC station. Even though the BBC received an annual subvention from the state, it maintained a degree of constitutional autonomy from government control. The radio system in the Free State was a monopoly financed by revenue from domestic licence sales and advertising but much of its income came from the import duties charged on radio sets coming into the country. However, after 1932, when the government decided that it would cream off the import tax for itself, broadcasting was increasingly forced to look to advertising for revenue. The state assumed that listeners would unquestionably accept and enjoy the programmes broadcast; it also expected the broadcasters to produce a public service without it being properly supported by the state.

We have seen that the BBC's public service ethic was overtly constructive; it sought to not only integrate but produce new kinds of cultural activity and establish a national identity using radio in the consensus mechanism. Ireland was different, Luke Gibbons suggests, because of the dominant cultural nationalist perspective that continued to frame the consciousness of the political elite post-1922. In their view, the Irish nation already existed in spirit and, therefore, 'the function of broadcasting was not to establish but to revitalise this nation, releasing the cultural energies which, it was believed, had accumulated over the centuries'.[19] There was a misapprehension or unwillingness to recognise that the medium did not simply *relay* already existing, organic Irish cultural forms but that radio was itself an *agent* for transformation and creation of new cultural forms. While radio became instrumental in apparently continuing tradition it was actually reworking it. Radio soon became the organ of an official Catholic, Gaelic-inflected culture that included Gaelic Athletic Association (GAA) sports commentary from 1926, Irish music and language, celebrations of feast days and coverage of the 1932 Eucharistic Congress. Regional dialects tended to be flattened out in announcers' voices, local styles of singing and music-making were tamed by radio, even the provincial differences of sports rules were changed for new national competitions avidly followed by listeners. This was a form of constructive homogenisation to produce the national voice of Radio Éireann (RÉ), not dissimilar to the process by which the BBC assumed the position of being able to speak with what Martin McLoone calls, the 'Big We', the mode of address that has a clear function 'to forge a sense of collective identity across potentially divisive factors of class, gender, regional or ethnic background and a host of other particularities'.[20] As in the north, the authoritarian nature of RÉ was used to bolster a singular, dominant cultural identity, which held sway until the inauguration of television in 1962. Radio was influential in mobilising and maintaining the political vision of de Valera and the cultural-religious views of the church, underpinning a broad political and theocratic consensus in the Free State/Republic. However, there was popular dissatisfaction and non-acceptance of RÉ. Such dissidence came from within and without the state. Where technically possible, RÉ listeners fed up with the exclusion of jazz music, the diet of high-brow classical music and the invented tradition of the radio Ceili band, could and did tune into the BBC, continental European or US Armed Services radio to hear more diverse, contemporary music during the 1940s and 1950s. There were also daring individuals who illegally transmitted 'The Colleen Home Service' radio from a domestic studio during the same period but this offered only a local, limited alternative to RÉ's moribund programming. For most of Ireland, RÉ *was* broadcasting until the late 1950s. By then, technical possibility and political arguments for television had developed to a point at which it was poised to make significant social impact in and about Ireland, representing significant historical crises.

Television's origins, crises and censorship, 1961–88

Overspill television broadcasts from the BBC, the development of British commercial TV during the mid-1950s and the launch of Ulster TV in 1959, provided the context and incentive for discussions about the desirability of a national TV service in the Republic. But the economy of the state was stagnant with little spare funds, emigration had soared and governments struggled to keep up with social provision in comparison with the UK. It was also a decade of unsteady government ending in 1959 with de Valera ceding leadership of Fianna Fáil (FF) to Sean Lemass and assuming the presidency. FF's traditional, conservative ideology had shaped the post-independence generation but Lemass, politically and economically a moderniser, was in fact culturally prudent. Following a report in 1953, civil servants, politicians, various electrical manufacturers (Irish and Anglo-American), special interest lobbies (such as Irish language campaigners) and broadcasters from Irish radio and foreign concerns, spent some seven years debating the pros and cons of a national television service. During this protracted process disagreements emerged within conflicting state departments, their civil servants and politicians offering differing views about the desirability and feasibility of providing a television service. Following a logic similar to the debates about radio in 1920s, some felt that television transmission 'invasion' from Britain and Northern Ireland made an Irish television service an imperative to counter the flow of images and ideas that would tarnish Ireland's unique culture. In 1956, it was estimated by state sources that some 7,000 television sets were already owned by people in the Republic who were receiving British broadcasting.[21] Some within the political class clearly felt that Ireland was isolated in comparison to other western European countries by not having a national broadcasting service and that it was a matter of national prestige to have television. But there were powerful economic arguments made by financial administrators who pointed out that, in the light of the state's limited funds, spending should be directed towards improvements in basic social service amenities. Consumer durables like television sets were seen as unnecessary luxuries that would encourage those with disposable income to spend it instead of investing in government-sponsored savings schemes, thus further weakening the economy.[22] Most positions in the on-going debate agreed that a television service was an admirable idea – even if some suggested delaying plans. No agreement could be found on the question of how it would be organised, or funded, or how it could best serve Irish people. In the end, the pressure of events, the tenacity of civil servants arguing for a public service system and the decisive influence of Sean Lemass produced an Irish television service of a hybrid nature; an independent public service with commercial advertising.

Since the mid-1950s the Irish state had received formal propositions from various British, US and French-based private broadcasting companies offering to set up a television system on its behalf, thus saving the state considerable costs in initial outlay for technical equipment and studio plant. Some of the schemes were very attractive to the department of finance but most required that exclusive or highly beneficial broadcasting rights be signed away to commercial organisations which were not Irish-owned. Gael-Linn, the Irish language organisation, was the only wholly Irish organisation to throw its hat in the ring but it did not have the broadcasting experience or finance to be a serious contender. The rationale for establishing an Irish film studio at Ardmore in 1958 may be seen to be partly echoed in concurrent debates concerning the establishment of a national television station. The nature of broadcasting, its (potentially) continuous projection into a domestic viewing context and the presumed vulnerability of younger viewers, made the discussion even more sensitive than worries about foreign cinematic product, which were subject to strict censorship. Persuasive civil servants in the department of post and telegraphs (P&T), who worked closely with broadcasters in the existing RÉ service, considered that public service television could be a considerable national asset. Despite the political risks, they liaised with and took advice from the BBC and were prepared to argue for the inclusion of BBC programmes in a future Irish system on the grounds that they were of good quality and more improving than the envisaged output of a privately-run station.

However, such were the financial limitations on the state between 1957 and 1959 that while a national television service was desirable, the government envisaged one owned and run by a private company in order to keep the costs to the state to an absolute minimum. In 1958, a television commission was set up to sort out which model would be adopted from the proposals. Lemass as Tánaiste (deputy prime minister) had backed a fully commercial station, but as Taoiseach a year later he endorsed legislation that set up a statutory, independent authority responsible for providing public service broadcasting, funded by licence fee and advertisements.

The 1960 act provided Telefís Éireann (TÉ) with a degree of independence from government control. This was an improvement on the situation endured by RÉ. It was only seven years earlier that radio had formally been extricated from the clutches of the Irish civil service. 'Given the particular circumstances of Ireland [the 1960 act] was a remarkably liberal piece of legislation',[23] but it required that broadcasters 'bear constantly in mind the national aims of restoring the Irish language and preserving and developing the national culture' (Section 17), and that news and current affairs be 'presented objectively and impartially and without any expression of its own views' (Section 18). However, it was still circumscribed by legislation, such as Section 31 of the act, under which a government minister had ultimate power to exert censorship if they so wished.[24] The terms set for RTÉ (as it became in 1966) were public service requirements broadly similar to those in Britain and other European democracies, but MacConghail points out that the charter and acts governing British broadcasting 'described what was a well founded convention. The Irish Act on the other hand intended to define a new relationship which ... was not understood by all the parties involved'.[25] A hint of this was given by the newly instated President de Valera who, like Hyde on radio, gave a cautious welcome to the new medium in an inaugural TV broadcast on New Year's Eve in 1961.[26] He maintained that it had the power to do great good but also warned of its dangerous influences. At the time, about a third of Irish television viewers could already receive British programmes so there was some justification for his worries. Between 1961 and 1966, RTÉ extended its reception coverage to 98 per cent of the country but in areas to the east and north of the Republic, Irish television had to compete with rival national services for two decades until the arrival of new technologies brought alternatives to broadcast television. These historical developments will be dealt with in the second half of this chapter but in the rest of the current section we will concentrate on how television accompanied change in Ireland. We will also briefly note how both Irish and British broadcasters responded to political crisis in Northern Ireland and identify some of the key structural problems for broadcasting in the Republic.

The cartoon (see figure 26) from the *RTV Guide* shows that in the early 1960s television caught the spirit of change and played a causative role in the relative liberalisation of Irish society by providing an arena for inquiry and debate. By the end of the decade, it had developed a less supine and more critical role for both broadcast and print media journalism. The 1960 act made provision for an element of autonomy for RTÉ so that it could begin to report on changes in Ireland and its wider horizons. These included the Second Vatican Council's far-reaching debates on the role of Catholicism (1962–65), the coverage of President John F. Kennedy's visit to Ireland in 1963, the path-breaking visit by Sean Lemass to Northern Ireland in 1965 and the commemoration of the fiftieth anniversary of the 1916 Rising. All of these events galvanised the technical production of the new television service, tested its capabilities as a responsible broadcaster and reflected a more searching approach by its journalists and programme-makers. The decade also saw the innovative development of TV formats, most notably the light entertainment programme called *The Late Late Show* (1962), the establishment of indigenous serial drama in 1965 and the improvement of news and current affairs coverage, with programmes like *7 Days* (1967). Figures of established authority in Irish society – politicians and clergy – changed their initial resistance and hostility towards television to a wary acknowledgement of its potential uses. But Sean Lemass made a speech in 1966, which reveals the extent of residual, authoritarian views on the medium. During the course of a Dáil debate, he said, 'RTÉ was set up by legislation as an instrument of public policy and as such is responsible to the government ... The government reject the view that RTÉ should be ... completely independent of government supervision'.[27]

In the decade following this speech, the Irish state's deep-seated suspicion of television would be highlighted in clashes between politicians and

"O brave New World . . ."

26 'O brave new world': *RTV Guide* inaugurates national television (1961).
Courtesy of Reference and Illustrations Library, RTÉ

broadcasters on international and domestic news stories such as Vietnam and farmers' protests. But it was RTÉ's response to civil unrest and the resurgence of paramilitary violence in Northern Ireland that provoked the full authoritarian anger of government, armed with Section 31 of the 1960 act. It was natural that there was initial genuine concern in the Republic for the human suffering of northern Catholics and political instability within what was still constitutionally-defined as the national territory. But anxious not to jeopardise its own recent prosperity and stability, the emotive involvement of the Irish state hardened into a pragmatic, nationalist (dis)stance. The Irish government used its censorship powers to gradually erect a broadcasting *cordon sanitare* in an attempt to insulate the Republic from the Troubles. It dismissed the entire RTÉ executive in 1972 for allowing a journalist to interview republican paramilitaries. In 1976, legislation was reworded to ban the appearance or the reporting of named paramilitary groups (such as the IRA, UDA and UVF) and anyone voicing support for them from Irish airwaves. In 1982 Sinn Féin, a republican socialist party legal in both Irish states, was barred from taking part in RTÉ party election broadcasts. Northern Ireland was the issue that cast a shadow over the whole of the television service for the next quarter of a century.[28]

The BBC and ITV were initially concerned to report civil rights abuses in Northern Ireland but soon after 1969, when British troops were deployed in the province, broadcast journalism was subjected to different forms of censorship. In comparison to RTÉ, methods appeared less stringent but they were equally insidious. Both the BBC and the IBA implemented a set of guidelines for codes of practice within their organisations. 'Reference upwards' was a system instituted during 1971 whereby journalists and editors had to consult with producers, senior managers and so on up the management hierarchy to get clearance for programme making about any items on Northern Ireland. It was intended to avoid editorial error and minimise potentially life-threatening mistakes. It was operated as a kind of professional code of conduct, a form of self-censorship that mitigated the need for blanket legislative measures and retained the appearance of independence from direct state intervention. In Northern Ireland itself, reporting the Troubles became particularly fraught. Local broadcasters, UTV and BBCNI, were faced with a set of immediate and vexed questions: who to interview or not, how to report events, which topics to investigate and which not? The liberal parameters of the public service television were severely tested during a period of intense political conflict and violence. The 1970s demonstrated the limitations of trying to operate a broadcasting system that assumes a broad socio-political consensus in a society like Northern Ireland, where there is chronic division and dissensus.[29]

In addition to these political issues, there were also insistent trends within the structure of Irish broadcasting, which compromised the stated assumptions and aims of the 1960 act. Basically, the intended aim of RTÉ to function as a public service institution, bolstering a culturally distinctive national identity, was undermined by a combination of internal and external factors. As the table illustrates, there were significant leaps in numbers of 'TV homes' in the Republic between 1966–71 and 1976–81. Television rapidly became a popular consumer durable that provided entertainment as well as news and information. However, other statistics show that since the early 1960s, between a third and nearly half of TV homes have been multi-channel; that is, able to receive British terrestrial transmissions. Well into the 1980s, there was a pronounced regional imbalance, which meant that many homes in the west and south tended to be restricted to RTÉ while those in the east, midlands and north were multi-channel.

Irish viewers of BBC and ITV overspill were exposed to a mixture of populist consumer and liberal paternalist television emanating from a foreign cultural milieu, seen by some as a form of cultural imperialism. But this would be to

Table 5 Growth of television ownership in the Republic of Ireland, 1956–83

Year	Total TV homes (000s)	Single channel (RTÉ1)	%	Multi channel (RTÉ1/ British)[a]	%
1956	7[b]	–	–	–	–
1963	237	123	52	114	48
1966	380	239	63	141	37
1971	536	336	63	200	37
1976	655	367	56	288	44
1981	825	430	52	395	48
1983	843	435	51	408	49

Source: M. McLoone and J. MacMahon, *Television and Irish Society* (1984), RTÉ/Irish Film Institute

[a] From 1978, RTÉ offered a second channel, RTÉ2, now known as Network 2

[b] Estimated figure (Savage, 1996, 48). By comparison there were 127,000 TV households in NI in 1959 (Sendall, 1982, 26)

dismiss all British programmes as negative. The situation of dual-reception did expose the censorship flaws of RTÉ since, after 1976, a viewer at least might see a republican or a UDA representative interviewed on British television. If the shadow of British transmissions were seen as an external threat to the national project of RTÉ's programming, there were also potent internal dissidence and self-inflicted injuries.

We have seen from earlier discussion that the setting up costs for RTÉ entailed a considerable financial commitment from the state. The costs of maintaining a hybrid institution with a public service remit but a significant commercial element to its funding strategy meant that RTÉ was forced to compromise its policy. As a cheaper alternative to making its own programmes it bought in pre-recorded US and British programmes to fill air time. So, ironically, even single channel homes were experiencing the popular culture of Anglo-Americana. This in part explains why a generation of contemporary Irish film-makers often employ intertextual references to US TV westerns and police shows that they grew up with in the 1960s and 1970s. Although the launch of a second RTÉ channel in 1978 suggests production expansion, in fact, by 1980, 70 per cent of RTÉ's television programmes were produced outside of Ireland; the highest proportion of imported programmes in Europe. From the mid-1960s, in the cheaper medium of radio, serious disenchantment with RTÉ's indigenous radio schedules meant that pirate radio stations flourished in Ireland, in marginalised defiance of RTÉ's legalised monopoly. In urban areas like Dublin and Cork, these stations grew into large business concerns with considerable popular following and became known as 'super pirates'. Imitated by RTÉ in community radio initiatives, pirate radio also forced RTÉ to belatedly revamp its mainstream schedules to produce what is now known as 2FM. Eventually, however, even the pirates were accommodated within the changing broadcasting environment at the end of the 1980s. In contrast to the relative laxity allowed for radio, an attempt to start up a commercial pirate TV station in the early 1980s was effectively quashed by the government.

Underlying the programming issues, the fundamental problem for broadcasting in Ireland during the 1970s and 1980s was finance. This was not unique to Ireland and most other European countries with semi-autonomous broadcasting services experienced the same kinds of tensions, including Britain. As production costs soared in the 1970s and the revenue from licence fees was outstripped by inflation, public service broadcasting in Britain was brought to a watershed. In 1977, the government-sponsored Annan Report effectively broke the duopoly of BBC/ITV and made provision for a fourth terrestrial channel but as a *commissioner* not a producer of programmes. Annan also redefined public service by saying that minorities and people with special interests had a right to representation in television, a move away from the patrician ethos of the old BBC and IBA. This brought about legislation to inaugurate Channel Four TV in 1982 with a particular remit to encourage ethnic programming, stimulate and showcase independent film and cater for minority viewing tastes.[30]

In Ireland, RTÉ struggled through the 1970s because it lacked the subventions that the BBC received under its charter to cushion the increases in costs. It was forced to rely more heavily on advertising, to buy in cheaper pre-recorded television packages and fight against censorship in its news and current affairs departments. In 1970, 50 per cent of RTÉ's revenue came from advertising and it had one of the highest licence payment evasion rates in Europe. By 1982, advertising money represented 60 per cent of RTÉ's income.[31] This was the year that RTÉ bought a majority share in the cable franchise for the Republic, Cablelink. While this was another method by which mostly British TV could be relayed to city areas like Cork and Waterford beyond transmission range, RTÉ did at least profit from its own competitors and could control it to an extent. By the mid-1980s, 66 per cent of Irish television viewers could receive British programmes via broadcast or cable relay.

The 1980s saw the gradual shift in broadcasting priorities within the Irish Republic, Britain and the rest of Europe.[32] These arose out of technological possibilities and political shifts. Cable and satellite challenged the idea of a universal provision by terrestrial broadcasters, offering instead the prospect of delivering specific kinds of programmes to audiences conceived as consumers rather than citizens.[33] The uptake and use of VCRs also modified television viewing patterns, popularising the habit of time-shift viewing and the hire or purchase of VHS cassettes as alternatives to scheduled programmes. Politically, the 1980s saw British and Irish governments adopt policies that opened up established institutions like the BBC and RTÉ to the challenge of commercial broadcasting. Old style control under charters and acts of parliament were compulsorily deregulated but then reregulated in the terms of economic neo-liberalism. It is significant that both national governments in the mid-1980s commissioned reports, which examined the nature of broadcasting and signalled changes. In 1985 the *Stokes Kennedy Crowley Report* (SKC) analysis of RTÉ marked the start of deregulating the station's monopoly. Among other things, it recommended that reductions be made in staff costs (which involved voluntary retirements and redundancies), greater activity in co-production and emphasis on international sales. But its most significant recommendation was that RTÉ be required to broadcast independently-produced material up to a quota of 20 per cent of the programming. Likewise, the *Peacock Report* (1986) on the future of the BBC noted that the corporation should exploit its reserves of old programmes in international sales and the burgeoning VHS market. It also noted that, since 1982, Channel Four TV offered an alternative model of broadcasting as a 'publisher on the airwaves' and anticipated the increasing influence of satellites. It recommended that the BBC should resist the use of advertising and be compelled to broadcast up to a fifth of its output derived from independently-produced programmes.

Perhaps because of the particular human geography of the island, the fact the Irish system was smaller and less financially secure, and already more 'opened up' to non-indigenous production, the Republic took to the emerging alternative technologies like cable and satellite more quickly than Britain. Once again, in *arrière gardist* fashion, Ireland in the 1980s presaged what occurred to Britain in the 1990s. The new technologies forced old political ideas to be rethought. If the intention in the 1960s and 1970s was to use broadcasting to promote a collective cultural identity for a national community on the island of Ireland, the 1980s and 1990s has seen the notion of policeable national boundaries evaporate. European and US satellites and the Internet operate transnationally and target increasingly refined audience-groups and individuals rather than nations and families. It should be emphasised that Ireland assumed this stance due to insistent pressure of circumstances and not as the result of engaged public debate and clear policy-making by legislators.

As we have seen, the 1980s was a hard decade for the Republic: domestic political problems associated with the economy and emigration were more pressing than a coherent programme of broadcast legislation. In 1988 Minister Ray Burke did grasp the nettle of pirate radio and the Dáil set up a legal alternative in commercial radio station franchises, mostly local but including one national radio station, Century. Under the regulation of the Independent Radio and Television Commission (IRTC), privatised broadcasting was made legal in Ireland for the first time in the state's history. In Britain, 1988 saw a Conservative government implement its most overt form of censorship following so-called 'irresponsible journalism' in Thames television's, *Death on the Rock*, which investigated the killing of IRA members by the SAS in Gibraltar. In parliamentary debate justifying the ministerial order, Home Secretary Douglas Hurd cited the Irish case of Section 31 and RTÉ as a pre-existing model of a more stringent form of censorship.[34] Rex Cathcart's prophesy brought the decade to a gloomy close: 'when the history of the BBC over the past twenty years comes to be written in the light of the full record, it will be found that Northern Ireland has provided the means by which the professional broadcasters have steadily been brought to the government's heel'.[35]

Beyond broadcasting: reregulation and new technologies, 1989–95

1989 saw the adoption of an EU directive called *Television Without Frontiers* in most of western Europe. This was an attempt to establish by 1992 a workable set of agreements between countries in a single market for European audio-visual material. This was seen to be necessary in order to combat the increasing domination by US films, television programmes and other audio-visual products, which would become the central issue for debate in the General Agreement on Tariffs and Trade (GATT) negotiations in 1993. As a smaller country within the EU, Ireland was set to gain a great deal from closer relations, including access to development money and co-production and distribution deals. It also meant that Ireland could not erect barriers against other EU products. It is in this context that Ireland's legislative changes to broadcasting need to be evaluated.

If the 1988 act had legalised private broadcasting within Ireland for the first time, the 1990 act accelerated the dismantling of RTÉ as a public service broadcaster. Both acts chimed in with the emphasis in *Television Without Frontiers* on unfettered competition within the EU's audio-visual sector and the encouragement of independently-produced material. The government in Ireland at the time was pursuing a neo-liberal economic policy that aimed to reduce costs in public sector spending. This included the deregulation of state-sanctioned monopolies such as RTÉ. In the current of swift technological change, these pieces of legislation, in conjunction with the EU directive, were a way of breaking down a unitary public broadcasting institution and drawing up new legal regulations in favour of private enterprise. It has been astutely observed of Irish policy that 'in many respects these [governmental] initiatives have been a reaction to, not an attempt to construct, the broadcasting environment'.[36] The significant feature of the 1990 act was that it diverted finances from RTÉ towards private broadcasting and distribution services such as cable, satellite and small production companies. This was achieved by ordering the reduction of air-time RTÉ was allowed to use for advertising and also by setting an annual maximum amount of money that RTÉ could earn from this source. This cap on advertising revenue-generation forced RTÉ to make further cuts in staffing (about 10 per cent in 1991), curb its own production expenditure and seek finance by other means, such as selling its existing programmes to disapora audiences via cable and satellite in the USA and Britain. Although RTÉ continued to argue for the centrality of its public service function in the 1990s, the radically altered broadcasting environment has continued to expose the difficulties in fulfilling this role. As Table 6 shows, at the end of the 1980s the TV audience share in the Republic was significantly marked by the incursions of foreign terrestrial (54 per cent in total) and satellite television (11 per cent in total) with the national terrestrial broadcaster (RTÉ) securing only 35 per cent of TV viewers between its two channels.

Although supporting the concept of public service in Irish broadcasting, amendment legislation in 1993 meant that RTÉ was forced to set aside a proportion of its annual budget for the commissioning of independently produced programmes, rising from IR£3.5 million to IR£10 million or 20 per cent of its total programme expenditure between 1995–99, although the capping and advertising restrictions were dropped.[37] Table 7 shows that RTÉ clawed back its share to over 50 per cent, that the other terrestrials lost ground and satellite increased its share slightly. In mid-decade, research showed that the top-ten rated programmes in Ireland were mostly of indigenous origin or were Irish-related. They included one of RTÉ's soaps (*Glenroe*), its main chat show (*The Late Late Show*), the Eurovision Song Contest, a special edition of a sitcom (*Father Ted*) and a controversial documentary (*Dear Daughter*).[38]

Broadly similar structural changes were taking place in broadcasting in the UK during the same period. The 1990 Broadcasting Act changed the commercial arena and had a knock-on effect for the BBC. From 1991, the IBA became the Independent Television Commission (ITC) but was less an authority (like RTÉ) and more a regulator. Individual companies within ITV were required to comply with the conditions and legal responsibilities of the new act with the ITC overseeing activities. The rules governing applications and conditions for ITV franchises were changed and in the bidding process some well-established companies lost out. One such was the London-based Thames Television,

Table 6 Television audience share in the Republic of Ireland (1989)

Channel	%
RTÉ1	28
RTÉ Network 2	7
BBC1	25
UTV/HTV	18
BBC2	6
Channel 4	5
Sky TV	5
Other satellite[a]	6

Source: PETAR (1989)
[a] Includes Lifestyle, Screensport, Super, MTV, Children's

Table 7 Television audience share in the Republic of Ireland (1997)

Channel	%
RTÉ1	40.8
RTÉ Network 2	17.7
UTV	9.3
BBC1	8.8
C4/S4C (Wales)	4.9
BBC2	4.3
HTV	1.1
TnaG (Irish language)	0.9
Satellite	12.1

Source: *Eurodata–TV Statistical Yearbook* (1998), Office of Official Publications of the European Community

allegedly as much to political pressure over *Death on the Rock* as to the quality of its bid. ITV companies were also required to compete with the cable and satellite channels for advertising revenue. Although the BBC seemed to remain relatively unscathed by the 1990 act, developments set in train by the Peacock Report began to expose the corporation to the increasingly competitive economies of the television market. Leading up to 1996, the BBC had to fight its corner as a PSB institution as its charter came up for renewal. Under its conditions, which last until 2001, the BBC was required to ensure that not less than 25 per cent of its programme output was derived from independent production companies. Like RTÉ, the BBC was having to take on a publisher–commissioner broadcasting role in addition to the integrated production and diverse scheduling expected of a national public service provider.

Irish broadcasting has developed a hybrid character due to the particular combination of economic, social and political factors over its seventy-year history. Its growth has been shaped by its situation in a small, mixed, capitalist economy that has been dependent on larger economic systems for much of its existence. Like film activity in Ireland, the broadcasting system was profoundly influenced by the larger, financially well-endowed audio-visual industries of Britain and the USA including, in the last decade, the development of cable and satellite technologies. A recent RTÉ report points out that its station's entire broadcasting services budget for radio and television of IR£1.36 million (1995) was less than that of the BBC's drama department alone. RTÉ budgets are minuscule when compared to fully-commercial companies in an international context: London-based Carlton TV is valued at IR£3 billion, the satellite company BSkyB at IR£5 billion, the US News Corporation at IR£6 billion and Time Warner at IR£10 billion.[39]

Ireland's core broadcasting values of public service built around a legalised monopoly in a liberal democratic polity have, in Irish contexts, been unusually subject to the authoritarian strictures of state control typical in postcolonial countries. The radio service was closely aligned to the interests of the state up until 1953. The achievement of the 1960 act, which ushered in television, was comparatively liberal. It tried to combine the ideals of a state-owned but independent public service model (exemplified by the BBC) but with advertising adding to revenue raised by licence. However, these potentially liberal democratic strains were emasculated by inadequate resources, strong external competition and political censorship. The public service ethos of Irish broadcasting has gradually succumbed to the transnational pressures of a reregulated, openly commercial system that combines terrestrial, cable and satellite forms, actively encouraged over the last decade by successive Irish governments and the EU. However, it is important to point out that because of its geo-political situation, the Free State/Republic has always received overspill transmissions from Britain, Northern Ireland and continental Europe. The idea that national cultures remain within the politically defined bounds of the nation-state was challenged even by the early technology of broadcasting. The particular development in Ireland exposed the futility of trying to contain the airwaves. In the 1990s, both Irish and British states have made their PSB institutions accommodate commercial imperatives while trying to retain the notion of control in the national interest. Bell and Meehan point out that the difference between Ireland and Britain was that Britain had a fully-fledged independent sector whereas Ireland only had a tiny number of radical film-makers active since the early 1970s.[40]

The state in both parts of Ireland has generally been more authoritarian and liable to enact censorship on the broadcast media than in Britain. More covert, self-imposed forms of control and censorship have been the norm on British television since the early 1970s, which reflects the nature of the 'hidden wiring'[41] of the British polity. Between 1988–94, censorship measures in Britain became more overt, similar but not quite as stringent to those in the Republic, but both countries dropped some measures in 1994. While television systems with a public service remit are instrumental in projecting and maintaining national cultural identities, attempts to unify and embrace all kinds of internal social, political and racial differences have proved to be problematic. As a clear instance of this, broadcasting in Northern Ireland has always operated differently to the rest of the British networks precisely because social and political consensus did not exist in the province. Since the rebirth of political violence in the late 1960s, conflict in Northern Ireland has tested the limits of broadcasting in liberal democratic states. Both Britain and the Republic enacted statutory legislation and broadcasters used tightly defined codes of practice for reporting and representing the Troubles. Although both Irish and British broadcast media like to stress the degree to which they are independent of government, it might be argued that even by taking an impartial stance they tend to tacitly support the political status quo. However, there are notable instances over the past thirty years where individuals, programmes, editors and controllers have seriously questioned the accepted frames of reference for representing Northern Ireland and affected policy. Early 1994 saw the lifting of Section 31 restrictions from Irish broadcasting in a period of political dialogue and in anticipation of ceasefire announcements by the main paramilitary groups in the autumn. Britain belatedly withdrew its 1988 restrictions in October 1994 after the ceasefires. This assisted the conditions in which political agreement was reached in Northern Ireland early in 1998, but – as David Miller has argued – through uncritical reporting of British government briefings, television journalists effectively became part of the tortuous negotiation process itself.[42]

Television futures? Tara TV and Celtic Vision

Since the 1980s, the future of PSB has been changed irrevocably. While it remains central to terrestrial broadcasting in both Irish and British systems,[43] new technologies are changing the delivery of audio-visual images and the nature of their consumption is being restructured, segmented and delivered as part of broader leisure, culture and information services via satellite, cable, home video, video disk and of course cinema. The configuration of audiences is changing. While still largely domestic, it might not be a family group viewing. Satellite, cable and video have begun to construct new audiences, with a capacity to market and distribute images of Ireland abroad. Irish cinema and television reflect the fact that significant numbers of people have migrated from their country of birth, complicating the idea of a homogenous audience, based in one national territory. Such demographics set in train cultural transfers and borrowings, not always on an equal basis, but which have manifested themselves in a kind of nomadic, hybridised audio-visual culture, producing what one critic has termed the cinema of 'non place'.[44] Dislocated from home, the Irish in Britain and the USA watch music concerts and sports fixtures in pubs and clubs not just because of distance or individual satellite subscription costs but as socially meaningful events. Launched in 1990, Setanta TV is well established in Britain as a provider of Irish sports in Britain. Although the 1990s has seen a strong shift towards developing viewers as consumers rather than citizens, there is a less pronounced but nonetheless countervailing development of media-literate viewers educated to critique representations of themselves as an ethnic-grouping on terrestrial television, particularly in programmes like *Coronation Street*, *EastEnders* and *Father Ted*.[45]

In this respect, it is interesting to consider how broadcast TV has catered for the Irish community in Britain. Channel Four TV, acting on its remit to represent minority communities in Britain, engaged with RTÉ in the scheduling of programmes for a packaged slot called 'Irish Angle' which ran between 1982–87. For instance, it showed an edited version of *The Late Late Show* on Monday mid-afternoons followed by a documentary programme from RTÉ/UTV. This was a pioneering effort to bring Irish-produced television to Britain. A decade later, Tara TV's £10 million-funded cable/satellite station was launched on 15 November 1995 to serve the considerable Irish communities in Britain's urban areas like North London, Birmingham, Teeside and the south-west of England around Bristol. Tara is 75 per cent owned by United International Holdings and RTÉ, who own 20 per cent shares in the business. RTÉ in Dublin beams a wide range of its schedule to Tara in England, including *The Late Late Show*, both RTÉ's soap operas, *Ros na Rún*, RTÉ news, racing, Gaelic and other sports. This is then principally cabled to subscribers, but from October 1998, Tara became available on Skydigital satellite too. In its short life, Tara TV has changed its marketing strategy. Early in its campaigns, it targeted the Irish as Britain's single largest ethnic group (over 10 per cent of the population), stressing the range, familiarity and quality of its programmes as 'the best of television from Ireland'. Two years later, it was attempting to attract viewers other than those self-identifying as Irish with the idea that Tara represented 'the best of Ireland for all of Britain'. Another slogan read 'From Ireland, for Britain: it comes across brilliantly'. Reaching 20 per cent of Britain's cabled homes, Tara's strategy is to 'resist being a niche, premium package' and to play up its strengths as a balanced schedule of high production television with 33 per cent consisting of

27 Television futures: Tara Television logo (1995).
Courtesy of Tara TV

live programmes. With a budget that is greater than that of Channel Five TV, Tara's executives claim that they are 'really Britain's sixth terrestrial channel'[46]and clearly do not see themselves in a minority ghetto. There are obvious commercial reasons for this, but it is also due to the cultural confidence of the Irish middle and professional classes in 1990s Britain.

Based in Boston, with an office in Dublin, Celtic Vision is a cable service that began on St Patrick's Day in 1995, but aspires, like Tara TV, to go beyond what is termed ethnic minority channel status in a highly competitive USA cable market.[47] Celtic Vision carries programming from RTÉ, the BBC, UTV and Scottish National TV but makes its own continuity and occasional live programmes in a studio in Dublin. It aims primarily to reach the 44 million Irish-Americans, among others of Celtic descent, but sets itself apart from ethnic channels narrowly defined by non-English language. Instead, Celtic Vision claims in its promotional material to be part of 'a wave of arts and entertainment that's rippling throughout the world. From "Riverdance" to "Braveheart", Van Morrison to Frank McCourt, Enya to Liam Neeson: a cultural phenomenon is occurring and it's offering an unprecedented opportunity'.[48] In seeking to export Celtic-themed programmes to Americans via cable, Celtic Vision represents another phase in the history of the transatlantic translation of Irishness, reinventing new viewers' identities in a process that goes beyond the exigencies of national broadcasting.

Historically, the PSB broadcast media have been vital in defining and representing the polity and culture of Ireland and Britain. As such, they have not remained static; they have reshaped themselves to the new contours of the societies of which they are an integral part. From being national institutions, stations like RTÉ and the BBC have now to operate transnationally. To remain economically viable and culturally significant, they have to engage with supranational structures and postmodern ideas. The rest of this book examines television in Ireland and Britain, exploring how TV helped to shape social and political changes since the 1960s. From chat show to soap opera, and from sitcom to documentary and drama these examples trace how Ireland has been represented on the small screen.

Notes

1 The phrase was coined by Eamonn Andrews, an Irish broadcaster and RTÉ executive, perhaps best known for presenting the British television interview programme, *This is Your Life*. Andrews chaired the broadcasting committee that drafted the legislation that became the 1960 act.

2 R. Cathcart, *The Most Contrary Region: Northern Ireland and the BBC* (Belfast, The Blackstaff Press, 1984), 11.

3 P. Mulryan, *Radio Radio: The story of independent, local, community and pirate radio in Ireland* (Dublin, Borderline Publications, 1988), 11.

4 A. Briggs, *A History of Broadcasting in the United Kingdom, Volume 1: The birth of broadcasting* (London, Oxford University Press, 1961), 23.

5 P. Scannell, 'Public service broadcasting: The history of a concept', in A. Goodwin and G. Whannel (eds), *Understanding Television* (London, Routledge, 1990), 13, points out that 'the definition of broadcasting as a public utility, and the mandate to develop it as a national service in the public interest, came from the state'.

6 P. Scannell and D. Cardiff, *A Social History of British Broadcasting, Volume I: 1922–1939 – Serving the nation* (Oxford, Basil Blackwell, 1991), 13.

7 M. McLoone, 'Inventions and re-imaginings: some thoughts on identity and broadcasting in Ireland', in M. McLoone (ed.), *Culture, Identity and Broadcasting in Ireland* (Belfast, Institute of Irish Studies, 1991), 11.

8 D. Butler, 'Ulster Unionism and British broadcasting journalism: 1924–1989', in B. Rolston (ed.), *The Media and Northern Ireland: Covering the troubles* (Basingstoke, Hampshire, Macmillan, 1991), 100.

9 D. Cranston, 'From Portland Stone to River Foyle: The decentralising and democratisation of BBC Radio', in M. McLoone (ed.), *Broadcasting in a Divided Community: Seventy years of the BBC in Northern Ireland* (Belfast, Institute of Irish Studies, 1996), 39.

10 Cathcart, *Most Contrary Region*, 278–81.

11 M. McLoone, 'The construction of a partitionist mentality: early broadcasting in Ireland', in McLoone, *Broadcasting in a Divided Community*, 27–8.

12 Cathcart, *Most Contrary Region*, 174.

13 Cathcart, *Most Contrary Region*, 193.

14 B. Sendall, *Independent Television in Britain, Volume 2: 1958–68 – Expansion and change* (London and Basingstoke, Macmillan, 1982), 25; and Cathcart, *Most Contrary Region*, 181.

15 Butler, 'Ulster Unionism and British broadcasting', 105.

16 Cathcart, *Most Contrary Region*, 201.

17 D. Hyde in 1926, as quoted in L. Gibbons, 'From megalith to megastore: Broadcasting and Irish culture', in T. Bartlett *et al.* (eds), *Irish Studies: A general introduction* (Dublin, Gill & Macmillan, 1988), 222.

18 R. Savage, *Irish Television: The social and political origins* (Cork, Cork University Press, 1997), 4-5.

19 Gibbons, 'Megalith to megastore', 222; and D. Bell, 'Ireland without frontiers', in R. Kearney (ed.), *Across the Frontiers: Ireland in the 1990s* (Dublin, Wolfhound, 1988), 226.

20 M. McLoone, 'Inventions and re-imaginings', 10.

21 Savage, *Irish Television*, 46.

22 Savage, *Irish Television*, 81.

23 D. Fisher, *Broadcasting in Ireland* (London, Routledge & Kegan Paul, 1978), 27.

24 The Broadcasting Act (Dublin, Stationery Office, 1960), 23 and 35–6.

25 M. Mac Conghail, 'The creation of RTÉ and the impact of television', in B. Farrell (ed.), *Communication and Community in Ireland* (Cork, Mercier Press, 1984), 67.

26 The National Library of Ireland has produced *Ireland from the Press*, a useful facsimile series, one of which includes newspaper reports of the first night's programmes and readers' letters which indicate the content and reaction to it. See also L. Doolan, J. Dowling, B. Quinn and M. Leonard *Sit Down and Be Counted* (Dublin, Wellington Publishers Ltd, 1969), for an account of the first night.

27 *Parliamentary Debates* (Dublin, Dáil Éireann, 12 October 1966), columns 1045–6.

28 B. Purcell, 'The silence in Irish broadcasting', in B. Rolston and D. Miller (eds), *War and Words: A Northern Ireland media reader* (Belfast, Beyond the Pale Publications, 1996), 261.

29 Dick Francis, a former BBCNI controller offers a very clear statement that reflects the core elements of such a liberal view of broadcasting on Northern Ireland, 'Broadcasting to a community in conflict', in Rolston and Miller (eds), *War and Words*, 56–66.

30 A. Crissell, *An Introductory History to British Broadcasting* (London, Routledge, 1997), 191–4.

31 M. McLoone and J. MacMahon (eds), *Television and Irish Society* (Dublin, RTÉ/Irish Film Institute, 1984), 7.

32 V. Porter, 'Broadcasting pluralism and the freedom of expression in France, Germany and Ireland', in P. Drummond *et al.* (eds), *National Identity and Europe: The television revolution* (London, British Film Institute, 1993), 51–70.

33 Bell, 'Ireland without frontiers', 225.

34 *Hansard* (London, House of Commons, 19 October 1988), column 893.

35 'Hearing no evil', *Fortnight*, 267 (November 1988), 7.

36 E. Hazelkorn, 'New technologies and changing work practices in the media industry: The case of Ireland', *Irish Communications Review*, 6 (1996), 29.

37 *Broadcasting Authority (Amendment) Act* (Dublin, Stationary Office, 1993), 8 (c), 5.

38 M. Mac Conghail, 'The key to RTÉ's survival', *Film West*, 31 (January 1998), 58–9.

39 *RTE's Response to the Government's Green Paper* (Dublin, RTÉ, 1995), 18.

40 D. Bell and N. Meehan, 'Cable, satellite and private TV in Ireland', *Media Culture and Society*, 1:1 (1989), 107–8.

41 The phrase is from P. Hennessy, *The Hidden Wiring: Unearthing the British constitution* (London, Indigo, 1996).

42 D. Miller and G. McLaughlin, 'Reporting the peace in Northern Ireland' in Rolston and Miller (eds), *War and Words*, 434.

43 See the terms of the BBC Charter renewal (1996) and the Irish government's *Fócas Géar/Clear Focus* (1997), 43–4.

44 A. Scallan, 'Non places: Irish cinema from another perspective', *Film West*, 32 (May 1998), 22–4.

45 M. Doyle, 'Is this really the face of the Irish?', *The Irish Post* (11 April 1998), 32–4. This article surveyed the negative stereotypes of Irish characters in British soap operas following the controversial portrayal in an *EastEnders* special 'week in Ireland' story line. The prime time programmes only seemed to feature Irish characters who were alcoholics, aggressive and neurotic. The BBC were inundated with complaints, were criticised on air by Edward Barrington, the Irish Ambassador in London, and were forced to broadcast an apology before its Sunday omnibus edition.

46 The information for this paragraph was derived from Tara TV's presspack, marketing surveys and promotional material kindly supplied by Cathal O'Doherty at Tara TV, London, interviewed by author on 12 October 1998.

47 E. Casey, 'Shamrógery in America', *Film Ireland*, 56 (December 1996–January 1997), 21–2, discusses the pioneering effort and difficulties faced by Celtic Vision, but maintains that 'there are opportunities for a regular international Irish television service in the United States or at the very least a regular presence on American television screens'.

48 'Celtic Vision: The Opportunity', *Press & Promotional Pack*: *Television with an Accent*, kindly supplied by Celtic Vision, Boston. Catherine Maguire of Celtic Vision, Dublin, interviewed by author on 21 October 1998.

CHAPTER 8

THE CIRCUS IN THE FRONT ROOM:[1]
POPULAR TELEVISION IN IRELAND

- What characteristics define popular, entertainment television?
- How have *The Late Late Show* and RTÉ's serial drama mediated change in Ireland?
- In what ways is *Eurovision* significant to Irish television?

Talk, soap and song: television as entertainment

In this chapter we explore the televisual terrain of popular entertainment programming on RTÉ, concentrating on contemporary examples but situating this analysis in an historical context. In selecting the live talk show, serial drama (soap opera) and the Eurovision song contest, this chapter shows how forms of television originating from cultures outside Ireland have been successfully indigenised. By this, I mean that the structures and conventions of TV formats developed in the USA, Britain and elsewhere have been adapted to the contours of Irish society, making the programmes meaningful and distinctive to members of that culture. Luke Gibbons has persuasively argued that 'soft' areas of programming on Irish television like light entertainment and serial drama (less prestigious than single plays) provided innovative production and effectively challenged the status quo more than the 'hard' news and current affairs programmes, which have been subject to stringent scrutiny.[2] During the economic recession, increased emigration and social conservatism of the 1980s, deep-seated tensions caused by marginalisation and exclusion bubbled up on popular television. Church pronouncements and state legislation on marriage, family and sexual morality were only gently being teased out in *Glenroe* (1983),[3] a discussion on abortion prior to the referendum in 1983 was banned from *The Late Late Show* and, under pressure from RTÉ executives, the programme's normal format was altered for discussing divorce in 1986. This chapter applies Dyer's idea of 'utopian sensibility' to *The Late Late Show* and *Eurovision*, popular television forms that have survived from the 1960s, and extends the work by O'Connor on Irish soap opera to this genre in the 1990s.

At this point, before dealing with specific programmes, it would be useful to recall the definitions of the 'popular' outlined in chapter 3 in order to extend and apply them to television. Popular television can mean those programmes watched by significant numbers of viewers in a domestic situation (quantified as TAM, or television audience measurement). It appeals to viewers within the family across different generations and genders, and across different classes and

regions: in short, 'something to suit every taste'.[4] From the early days, Irish schedules used pre-recorded USA series such as *Buckskin* and *Dragnet* to economise on
production costs, invoking complaints that these were foreign and of inferior
quality to indigenous, home-produced material, such as *Siopa an Bhreathnaigh*, a
children's Irish-language serial set in a grocery shop. The first director-general of
Telefís Éireann (as RTÉ was known at the time) was an American who defended
the station's policy: 'We are buying only what is necessary and it will be of the best
quality available', going on to point out that 'in the area of live programming we
are relying almost 100 per cent on the Irish people on our staff'.[5] Serial drama and
chat shows from Britain, the USA and, more recently, Australian TV – like
Coronation Street, *Dallas*, *Wogan* (an Irish broadcaster working in Britain) and
Home and Away – have remained permanent fixtures in Irish viewing ever since,
but RTÉ's *The Late Late Show*, *Glenroe* and *Fair City* regularly top audience ratings. These programmes are popular in the sense that they adopt modes of
address and offer audience pleasures that are generic to universal TV formats but
which have been unequivocally indigenised and intimately imbued with the concerns of Irish viewers at different transitional moments in Ireland's contemporary history. Although RTÉ had become a bureaucratic institution for modern
Irish culture by the end of the 1960s, it also had to contend with what one critic has
characterised in another context as 'an emancipatory accessing of voices and
releasing of energies from below'.[6]

   This was made possible largely because the cultural forms adopted by
popular television in Ireland and the textual structure of particular formats
lend themselves to more open-ended and ambiguous readings by viewers. Such
readings are allowed and encouraged, producing the kind of pleasurable
decoding that characterise non-serious, entertainment television in ways that
are less 'permissible' (but not impossible) in news and current affairs programming. *The Late Late Show* was broadcast live. It created a sense of immediacy,
informality and unpredictability in its use of a participatory studio audience,
often discussing issues forbidden in Irish society. The programme's regular
weekly slot, combining topicality and entertainment, gave the show's audience
its memorable, communal pleasures, generated discussion the following day
and built up a compelling sense of anticipation for the show's next broadcast.[7]
Some of these points also lie at the heart of serial drama's popularity, which we
will deal with in a moment.

   It might be thought that the pleasures derived from popular TV are simply a
kind of vicarious observation, or (especially with American and Australian
soaps) a form of escape from lived reality into a world of fantasy, a kind of coping
strategy on the part of the viewer. But although popular television is primarily
about entertainment and relaxation, its viewers do remain socially and culturally
engaged, even if this is different from watching a serious documentary. Some
critics have pressed this further to argue that popular television operates as a site
where conflicting ideas are contested, to refine and maintain forms of social and
political hegemony.[8] Others again have argued specifically that entertainment

works at an emotional level as well as cognitively, offering the pleasure of imagining what a better world would *feel* like, not just considering what it would *be* like.[9] Dyer's concept of the 'utopian sensibilities' used to discuss Hollywood musicals has been applied to other forms of entertainment television, including variety, talk shows and soap opera. Popular television is not simply the kind of programme imposed on viewers by executives (Edward Roth), producers (Noel Curran of RTÉ's *Eurovision*) or professional performers like Gay Byrne or Michael Flatley, nor is it a mode of escapism; rather, entertainment works and is enjoyable precisely because it 'responds to real needs created by society'.[10] According to Dyer, the economic system of international, commodity capitalism produces social tensions, inadequacies and lacks which are experienced as 'modern life', including: the *scarcity* of poverty and underdevelopment; *exhaustion* caused by alienated labour; the *dreariness* of poorly planned urbanisation and the monotonous predictability of dominant cultural forms; *manipulation* by agencies such as the church and the media, particularly regarding social roles for women and men; the *fragmentation* produced by persistent emigration and the disintegration of organic communities and extended families. It was just such an economic system into which Ireland entered in the late 1950s. Even the so-called boom periods, such as the 1960s ('the best of decades'[11] as one journalist termed it) and the first half of the 1990s[12] contain an undertow of negative characteristics, which require what Dyer calls 'utopian solutions'. The entertainment of popular television offers representations of ideal changes, imagined circumstances of abundance, energy, intensity, transparency and community[13] epitomised in the personality of Gay Byrne, the form of *The Late Late Show*, the bravura performance in *Riverdance* and the spectacle of *Eurovision* in the 1990s.

Soap opera had its origins as a popular day-time US radio genre specifically targeted at women who worked in the home. Academic interest in women's broadcast fictions from the late 1970s was led by feminist scholars like Tanya Modleski and Christine Geraghty and gay cultural critics like Richard Dyer,[14] who focused on television serial drama. The serial as a genre is premised on establishing a set time in the schedules to build up an audience who become familiar with fictional characters' involvement in domestic scenarios and communal locations with unresolved multi-story line narratives. Based on cumulative character identification, the pleasures soap typically invoke are expectation and endlessly deferred closure. Feminist analysis explored the openess of soap structure and its modes of address – often offering multiple identificatory possibilities in male and female characters. They also distinguished how female viewers tended to watch the interrupted, never-closing stories in a distracted fashion due to the multiple roles involved in being a home worker and carer. Women orientate themselves towards narrative and character in particular ways that were usually concomitant with their socially constructed gender roles and other cultural competences, ascribed by class, race and age, for instance. Soaps have tended to occupy the ground of the personal and emotional aspects of family life: its intimate relations, its

28 Domestic gossip in communal space: *Fair City*'s McCoy's Pub (c. 1991).
Courtesy of Reference and Illustrations Library, RTÉ

problems, romances and betrayals, marking the life boundaries of birth, (heterosexual) courtship, marriage and death. But soap narratives engage playfully in the forbidden, disruptive aspects of these bonding and unifying social markers with their plots about disputed parental identity, hidden sexualities, adultery, divorce, incest and homicide. However, since the earliest work on women and soap was published,[15] significant changes to women's economic, political and social roles have taken place. The world of paid work has slowly become feminised in Ireland to such an extent that, in 1991, 32 per cent of the labour force was female. Women also have gradually entered formal political structures – although, in 1992, women comprised only 12 per cent of members elected to the Dáil – as well as continuing in their activist roles, and it is beginning to be more socially acceptable for women not to have their lives defined solely by marriage, housework and child-rearing. Such changes are reflected at the level of character and theme in indigenous Irish soaps. In terms of audience, it remains the case that Irish women tend to watch more prime time evening soaps than men. This leads to the next question: how do men feature in the academic analysis of soap opera? Research confirms that most men prefer watching factual programmes (news, sport, current affairs) and realist fictions (serious drama) rather than soap or light entertainment, some saying that they felt that their masculinity was compromised.[16] O'Connor's (1990) research showed that although large numbers of Irish men did watch both US and Irish soaps they did not engage with them like women viewers, due largely again to

29 Taboos tested: gay sexuality on primetime RTÉ's *Fair City* (1995).
Courtesy of Reference and Illustrations Library, RTÉ

their socially defined male roles. This picture of gendered viewing is nuanced further when we consider that the 'utopian solutions' presented by RTÉ1's broadcasting of Granada TV's *Coronation Street* (the top British soap is usually in the top five places in Irish ratings), *Fair City* and TnaG's *Ros na Rún* have offered additional attractions to gay males in Ireland. While the venerable British soap does not feature gay characters, it has an established gay following (apparently identifying with strong Mancunian 'divas' like Bett Lynch). The Irish soaps have Hannah Finnegan (Pat Leavy), have introduced credible homosexual characters like Eoghan (Alan Smyth) and screened Irish television's first gay clinch for a prime-time soap. Representations or discussion of such desires have largely been absent or marginalised from the Irish small screen, save for the occasional space offered by *The Late Late Show*, whose impact we now examine.

Mid-wife to contemporary Irish liberalism: *The Late Late Show*?[17]

Television in general and *The Late Late Show* in particular will be mentioned as having been a tremendous force for change.[18]

In August 1998, Byrne announced that his association with *The Late Late Show* would come to an end the following year, thirty-seven years after the programme began as a cheap, summer schedule-filler.[19] History has indeed demonstrated the young presenter-producer's estimation of his show to be substantially correct. The key to its longevity and popularity has been how 'Gaybo' introduced liberal ideas to his viewers without seeming to completely reject their existing cultural values. The idea for a live talk show on Telefís Éireann was imported from Canada by Tom McGrath, a young producer who sought to adapt the format to a country whose people prided themselves as hospitable talkers:

The show should, as far as possible in the admittedly artificial environ-ment of a television studio, reflect the atmosphere of an evening round an Irish country fire. The young master was having guests and it was there-fore his job to entertain them.[20]

This fusion of homely tradition and modern technology needed a personality vehicle and Gay Byrne fitted the bill. A Christian Brother-educated Dubliner, by the early 1960s, he was a young, confident, professional broadcaster who had been a jobbing-presenter for Radio Éireann, had achieved some success as a compere for Granada TV in England and was established as a quiz show-host on RTÉ's own *Jackpot*. *Dublin Opinion*, an influential satirical magazine of the time, graph-ically captured the sense that overspill television from Britain already distracted Irish people from native, oral traditions epitomised by the hearth-side *seanachi*

30 Television's threat to indigenous oral culture: *Dublin Opinion* (1960)

"Bí ꝼeaꞃ ann ꝼaꝺó aguſ ꝼaꝺó a bí——— will ye listen to me?"

(story-teller), and that Irish television would compound this problem. In fact, the first four weeks of *The Late Late Show* starting in July 1962 were disastrous since (due to the absence of clear advertising) its audience had expected a TV variety show. They found it difficult to adjust to a hybrid programme that did not 'handily fit into any of the categories they could cope with'.[21] The programme became liked for its unpredictability and the fact that it:

was so obviously disorganised, so blatantly unprepared, so casually presented ... There was no effort at production, the cameras were seen, and camera men and sound crews joined in. If someone wanted a microphone, a soundman just walked on set and handed him one.[22]

From this description it seems that *The Late Late Show* was displaying its television aesthetic in a postmodern fashion from its origins while other stations strove to be professional. This was partly due to production inexperience and practical necessity caused by limited funding, but also as a result of calculation based on previous knowledge of the medium by its creators and presenter. As Byrne took over a producer-presenter role from 1965, the show's format of talk from his guest panellists, song and entertainment began to be more channelled, though spontaneity was assured with the programme's live status and Byrne's technique of questioning from minimal information so that he asked what the man-in-the-street would ask if they were meeting the guest. Byrne aimed to 'discuss a serious subject but not kill it stone dead with seriousness' and actively tried to chip away at RTÉ's organisational divisions between light entertainment and news and current affairs. Without being in any sense radical, Byrne was 'groping for a way of breaking down this over-protective guardianship of large segments of Irish society' and as such he can certainly be understood as a product of his times.[23]

The Late Late Show was shifted to a Saturday night slot where it ran (apparently open-ended) from 11.00p.m. until about 1.00a.m. It was directed by an American, Burt Budin, but it was 'Gaybo' and his researcher who plugged into Irish life, establishing it as the most-watched programme in Ireland, becoming an 'outlet for popular impatience',[24] the focus of debates that were central to Ireland's modernisation in the 1960s and beyond. Initially, its informal, populist approach to serious topics, its involvement of the panellists in face-to-face debate with politicians and clergy, witnessed by a participating studio audience, astonished and angered those in power.[25] Byrne's show challenged authority, which public figures had hitherto *assumed*, and tackled the shibboleths of Irish society in a domestic forum that was disarmingly open for its time. Programmes provoked discussion within Irish homes, in the national daily press and Dáil Éireann. Byrne's technique was to ask the questions people secretly wanted to ask themselves and to do so through a medium that created a kind of intimacy of exchange not known in Irish culture. Its mode of address ('to whom it may concern' is the off-camera voice introduction to the show)

31 Gay Byrne works his studio audience on *The Late Late Show* (1962–).
Courtesy of Reference and Illustrations Library, RTÉ

and the performance style of Byrne epitomised the idea that if someone with a point of view wanted to express it, *The Late Late Show* would provide the forum. Over the years, through thorough planning, careful research and constant minor innovation within a basic format, the show honed a style that was deceptively casual, distinctly Irish and occasionally devastating.[26]

In the 1960s, *The Late Late Show* was notable for contentious programmes on the Irish language, criticism of the Bishop of Galway and the infamous incident known as the 'Bishop and the Nightie' in which a harmless game about a married woman's nuptial nightwear (or lack of) became the object of protest from a bishop, which in turn sparked controversy in the press and RTÉ. The impact of the show is recalled by Colm Tóibín: 'Down in Enniscorthy when I was a lad we all sat glued to it. We were often glued by embarrassment that someone was talking about sex: there were older people in the room who didn't like sex being talked about.'[27] The show is credited with broadcasting RTÉ's first four letter swear word and displaying condoms in the studio in 1979 at a time when they were not widely available. According to one study,[28] *The Late Late Show* has not just aired topics but has been influential in changing social and moral attitudes. It has provoked legislative change and shifted the boundaries of taboos in Irish social discourse on a variety of topics, including unmarried mothers, Travellers' rights, infanticide, different kinds of sexuality,[29] marriage and clerical celibacy. Controversial shows on politics included debates on topics ranging from farmers' taxation, Dáil salaries and Northern Ireland. In doing so, Byrne has attracted almost as much flak internally from RTÉ executives as from politicians, the public and clergy.

By the 1990s, *The Late Late Show* had itself become an institution to RTÉ and its viewers, though Byrne admitted that it was 'probably safer and more bland now than we were 30 years ago'.[30] Viewers who were young and eager to see change in the 1960s, had aged with the show and now formed 'a loyal core of middle-aged and elderly watchers'[31] on its new Friday night slot. However, despite the glut of chat shows on television, radio phone-in programmes and the audience's acclimatisation to controversy, the weekly show managed to hold its own against the competition, attracting 822,000 viewers or nearly a quarter of the population of the Irish Republic (6 September 1998).[32] However, as one letter writer to the press noted 'having a consistently high TAM is not always symptomatic of quality broadcasting'.[33] Byrne showed himself out of touch in October 1994 and reluctant to respond to the mood of the times when, at a crucial stage during the peace process, he pointedly refused to shake the hand of Gerry Adams on his show, having long been a staunch opponent of Republicanism.[34] It was an historic irony that the church, which so vehemently attacked the programme in the past, agreed to air its concerns about falling mass attendance and dwindling vocations; the pressures on clerical celibacy in the light of revelations about Bishop Casey's fathering a son; the ordination of women; and the tide of public concern about paedophilia in care homes run by the church. Cardinal Daly's extended interview in November 1995 produced memorable reaction shots of priests in the audience shaking their heads and hisses of dissent from the female laity in the studio.[35] Because of its ratings popularity, *The Late Late Show* represents a considerable source of direct income to RTÉ. Syndication to Channel Four TV in Britain was reported to be worth £140,000 (1996), recent franchising of live TV via cable and satellite to Britain (from November 1996) and the USA's Irish populations brings in substantial sums, while advertising revenue to the station is estimated at £50 million.[36] Despite its economic importance, the future of *The Late Late Show* is uncertain but its place in the history of Irish television is undisputed. The 'unique hybrid of American talk-show, part-entertainment, part game-show, part-catalyst for serious change'[37] is probably too closely associated with its original host to continue successfully in his absence.[38]

Agri-soap, urban naturalism, 'súil eile'?[39] *Glenroe, Fair City* and *Ros na Rún*

Good entertainment is a serious business and a good domestic serial drama is a crucial part of RTÉ's public service remit.[40]

Irish television has a distinguished pedigree in serial drama[41] and, despite the co-presence of British, USA and Australian imported serial dramas like *Coronation*

Street, Dynasty and *Home and Away*, RTÉ's two current home-produced soap operas, *Glenroe* and *Fair City*, command immense audience loyalty and have demonstrated themselves to be woven into the fabric of contemporary life in Ireland.[42] Indeed, as the quotation from the head of audience research at RTÉ (1990) suggests, indigenous serial drama is one of the most important forms of popular television and, moreover, seen as a vital ingredient in the justification for a terrestrial, public service model that has typified much of European television.[43] In this section, we offer a brief examination of the history of rural and urban soap opera on RTÉ, provide comparative assessments of *Glenroe* and *Fair City*, and explore how both programmes have engaged with, and been a mediator of, social change in Ireland in the 1990s.

Since the mid-1960s, RTÉ has managed a comparatively small resource base to ensure that it produced two kinds of soap operas, one rural and the other urban. That configuration has changed over the years but even though Ireland became geographically more urbanised, city and country remain significant material and mental divisions in Ireland. RTÉ's first soap was *Tolka Row* (1964–68), written by Maura Laverty, set in inner-city Dublin, while the long-running *The Riordans* (1965–79), devised and written by Wesley Burrowes, was set in a fictional farming community of 'Leestown', supposedly in County Kilkenny.[44] The latter was innovative in that it used outside broadcast television cameras normally used for sports or special events coverage to shoot on location in Dunboyne, County Meath. *The Riordans* was conceived 'to get across surreptitiously ideas about good farm management and farm practices',[45] but its scope went much further and its strong character-led drama rapidly captured a national audience whose attitudes, especially to sexual morality, were challenged because issues were 'raised with a deeply-rooted authenticity with a long-established sympathy for popular and credible characters'.[46] The current Sunday night soap, *Glenroe* (broadcast since 1983), was linked to the same creative source as *The Riordans*, involving the collaboration of Wesley Burrowes, who devised its scenario, and directors like Brian MacLochlainn and Deirdre Friel. Narrative and character continuity was provided by the characters of Dinny and Miley Byrne (Joe Lynch and Mick Lally) via the spin-off series, the more melodramatic and stylishly produced *Bracken* (1980 and 1982). The last episodes of *The Riordans* and much of *Bracken* allowed an unglamorous but addictive television double-act of Dinny and Miley to develop. Dinny was a small-time sheep-farmer, a *cute hoor* (a rural expression meaning 'secretively clever') who moved off Bracken mountain down into Glenroe village where he became a likeable rogue, playing off his sometime wayward, wide-eyed gom of a son who eventually settles into marriage and parenthood with independently-minded Biddy on an arable farm, but with his father never far behind him. This long-standing triangle of characters has matured in *Glenroe*, providing for fictional father-son and in-laws relationships, whose antagonisms are tempered with unstated affection. *Glenroe's* headline stars developed into instantly-recognised television personae, and the show's characters have

32 The broody Irish male: Dinny (Joe Lynch) and Miley Byrne (Mick Lally) in *Glenroe* (1983). Courtesy of Reference and Illustrations Library, RTÉ

entered the public consciousness of 'subsidiary circulation'[47] through media appearances, press interviews and speculation, talk, jokes and songs.

The essential milieu of each soap is encapsulated in their thirty-second opening titles sequences whose function is to alert the viewer with familiar theme music, visually reinstate the programme's identity and generate narrative expectations about what will happen. *Glenroe's* combines aerial shots of lakes, fields, mountains, farms and housing to establish the location of the serial as being on the border between the counties of Wicklow and Dublin in the fictional 'rurban' village of Glenroe. The title captions in old Irish typography become modernised in stages to spell out 'Glenroe' and the theme music on uilleann pipes is gently lyrical. *Fair City's* (1995) title sequence also favoured aerial views but this time of Dublin city, which are inset with a smaller screen showing streets, a couple in a park, a little girl in a confirmation dress, the exterior of a betting shop, the interior of a pub, a boy with a hurley on the street and elderly neighbours gossiping outside their houses. Columb Farrelly's up-tempo theme is a small orchestra arrangement with strings and synthesised sounds connoting middle-of-the-road modernity.

Despite its consistently high rating positions, *Glenroe* has been subject to criticism in the past and more recently for failing to engage maturely with Irish social life.[48] A decade ago, Helena Sheehan's evaluation of *Glenroe* in *Irish Television Drama* suggested that the programme 'had not done much to face up to the black spots in Irish society', it avoided the real world (except that its characters referred to other foreign TV soaps in dialogue) but that it had been progressive in its representation of women through the characterisation of Biddy.[49] Less overtly educational about agricultural matters and less explosively controversial than *The Riordans* in its heyday, during the 1980s of post-Abortion Referendum Ireland *Glenroe* was a soft-centred serial, affectionately enjoyed by middle Ireland. The 1990s have seen change bubbling up to disturb the surface of apparent conservatism. *Glenroe* is a soap undergoing a process of reinventing itself, trying to retain its original low-key style and play to its established strengths of 'wryly humorous depiction of rural life'[50] but it made some faltering attempts to engage with problems that have emerged as a result of socio-economic changes and challenges to social attitudes that marked the uncertainties of the early 1990s.

An episode from September 1996 illustrates how *Glenroe's* strength in the comedy of personality traits and behaviour may sometimes jar with the effort to tackle issues such as criminal assault. O'Connor (1990) found that viewers of *Glenroe* most enjoy the humour derived from its main characters in social situations. A scene from early in the episode exemplifies how the central relationship between the likeable rogue father and slightly gormless son has worked to make *Glenroe* so popular. It is Sunday morning after mass on the steps of the church. A cheery Father Treacy is trying to revive an old practice of saying mass in people's houses, known as stations. He catches Mr Brennan, Dinny Byrne and Miley on the steps. The scene is filmed combining medium and close-up shots to extract a gentle comedy from observing firstly how Stephen Brennan is passed over as a potential host by Father Treacy. We have a close-up reaction shot of Brennan's face as we hear the priest speak of 'an older more established member of the community' but then see it change as Father Treacy chooses Dinny. This is ironic, since Dinny Byrne is not a native of Glenroe but a 'blow-in' or outsider. Next Dinny is in close-up but his expression changes from smugness at getting one up on Brennan to worry at the actual implications of this honour. The camera cuts back to a medium shot taking in all four men in a line:

Dinny: I can tell you, Father, it'd be an honour and a privilege, but I
                  must tell you that my home is on the small side. Mind you, on
                  the other hand [*turning to Miley*] Miley's plenty of room. Let's fix
                  a day! [*Camera pans along line of faces to Miley*]
Miley: [*horror in close-up*] Ah, now Father . . .
Father Treacy: [*Cutting in*] Excellent, Miley! You know in the area of
                  revitalisation, it's always decisive men who'll lead the way.[51]

The episode went on to follow on the complications of Miley's lame acquiescence to this intrusion in his relations with his wife, Biddy. In part these had been under strain caused by difficulties in trying to diversify their agri-tourist farm into beef production. Miley knows he should have consulted Biddy about the station because she has independent views about the church. The following exchange takes place in the yard, and brings out the comic tensions between in-laws:

Miley: Y'know what I'm thinking?

Biddy: Yeah, we're not going to have enough of this stuff, [cattle feed] are we?

Miley: Blast to hell. We picked a fine time to take a herd of cattle, didn't we?

Biddy: Oh, I know.

Miley: [*Not listening*] The drop in prices, the cost of the feed ...

Biddy: And your father's wages.

Miley: [*Still not listening*] Yeah.

Biddy: Mind you, that's where we could make a few cuts.

Miley: [*Suddenly*] Now lookit, Biddy, in fairness we made a deal with him.

Biddy: Well that was before BSE reared its ugly head.

Miley: [*Feigned decisiveness*] Right, I'll have a word with him, so. [*Exits frame*]

Biddy: [*To herself, half to viewer*] Well, that's something to look forward to.[52]

However, this same episode concluded with a sequence that provoked considerable response from viewers and in the press. The elderly Stephen Brennan is shown being robbed and humiliated at knife point by three teenage girls with Dublin accents.[53] The producer, Briain MacLochlainn justified the scene by referring to the increased media reportage of criminal attacks on elderly people and felt it was worthwhile to explore the issue through drama, demonstrating how soap can function to mediate anxieties about a lack of social cohesion and order.[54] While *Glenroe* had featured its share of extra-marital affairs, the depiction or suggestion of sexual intercourse in the programme was still liable to cause protest. An episode from January 1994 involved a ten-second, bare shoulder in bed scene in which Biddy walks in on her niece Fidelma caught *in flagrante delicto* with Conor Sheehy. Some viewers who telephoned RTÉ thought this inappropriate to show before the 9p.m. watershed for family viewing, but *The Irish Times* critic put such reactions in perspective by pointing out that much more graphic violence and sex is depicted on British channels beamed into Irish homes at 7.30p.m. Art Ó Briain, the series producer, explained the reaction by saying that *Glenroe* presents 'Irish characters with whom the audience is familiar and has an emotional connection, so the scene appears to have offended in a personal sense'.[55] It is characteristic of audiences to identify with favourite characters as their family, but it also showed that a kind of moral double standard still existed for middle Ireland.[56] In a recent perceptive article, Eddie Holt has argued that agri-soap is suffering due to material and social changes in Ireland since its inception and that now it 'faces some of the problems which blighted Irish urban soaps in the past'. His contention is that *Glenroe* can no longer rely on its audience in Ireland identifying wholly with the Mileys and Biddys, but feels that RTÉ should, given its public service remit, 'seek to protect a rural voice and perspective in popular drama'. This point was potentially addressed with the inception of Telefís na Gaeilge's (TnaG) *Ros na Rún* in 1996. Holt concludes by characterising *Glenroe* as 'a soap in transition and [it] has got to remake itself as relevant without losing too much of its traditional, cutesy entertainment'.[57]

Given the historic legacy of Ireland's socio-economic base in agriculture and the dominance of a nationalist ideology that placed great value on rural images of the nation, it is not surprising the history of urban soap opera on television has been problematic and discontinuous.[58] The working-class setting of *Tolka Row* (1965–68) was succeeded by the short-lived suburban *Southside* (1969) and middle-class milieu of *Partners in Practice* (1971). The late 1970s saw a ten-part serial, *The Spike* (1978), set in a post-secondary vocational college in working-class Dublin, aborted by RTÉ mid-way through the series due to phenomenal public and political pressure, ostensibly due to its sexist and crude depiction of nudity in episode five.[59] The only alternative serial to *Glenroe* until the end of the eighties was *Inside* (1985), set in a prison. Launched in 1989, *Fair City* did not have *Glenroe's* advantage of being a spin-off, nor had it the production resources or its star actors, and it was seen as a national joke by RTÉ viewers in its first few seasons.[60] Unlike *Glenroe*, whose exterior scenes are shot on location, *Fair City's* exteriors are shot on a small street set built next to a carpark for RTÉ employees in Donnybrook, Dublin. The ratings for the imaginary northside suburbia of Carrigstown went up following the transfer of executive producer John Lynch (from *Glenroe*) in early 1996. He forged a story-line team to actively address contemporary topics in a rapidly changing Ireland, particularly those of concern to a younger, urban audience that enjoyed the naturalism characteristic of British soaps. However, Lynch notes that *Fair City* began by mistakenly trying to imitate the 'in-yer-face' style of British soaps, *EastEnders* (set in London) and *Brookside* (set in Liverpool), which relentlessly piled on highly dramatic incidents between characters who were very confrontational. *Fair City* has achieved its success, according to Lynch by rescheduling the programme so that it did not compete with *EastEnders'* air-time, eschewing this British style 'because it doesn't fit in with the Irish way of communicating',[61] but maintaining its attention to contemporary themes and concentrating on strong, character-led story lines, the bread and butter of soap opera. A recent, much praised addition was the introduction of a gay student character, Eoghan (Alan Smyth), which has been developed in storylines about his coming out in 1995, his work as a teacher and subsequent relationships with Liam (Peter Warnock),[62] a bi-sexual married man, in 1996 and Andrew (Peter Vollebregt), a gay man whose partner, Simon (Raymond Keane) has HIV/AIDS. Ireland's gay viewers have thus been able to tap into the more traditional camp humour of *Coronation Street* and enjoy *Fair City's* contemporary engagement with contemporary realities for gay men in Ireland following decriminalisation and legalisation in 1993.[63] *Fair City* topped *The Late Late Show*, *Glenroe* and *Father Ted* in the Nielson ratings for the first time in 1997,[64] and the programme now commands a position in the top five with a twice-weekly, half-hour, early prime evening slot on Tuesday and Thursday at 7.30p.m. *Glenroe* remains a Sunday evening primetime half-hour at 8.30p.m., currently tucked in between *Upwardly Mobile* and the British-produced, adaptation of Deirdre Purcell's popular novel, *Falling for a Dancer*. Barbara O'Connor, in calling for RTÉ to produce an urban soap in 1989 just before *Fair City* appeared, argues that indigenous serial drama 'creates a crucial space in which we can engage with our own society and the needs and pleasures of its audiences'.[65]

Television occupies the central battleground of consensus and domesticity at two levels. Television was developed as a technology for family entertainment; it literally became part of the furniture at home. In terms of its representational function, it is axiomatic to dramatise family life and its dysfunctional variants, emphasising the emotional aspects of interpersonal relations. The serial drama in Ireland has mediated observable changes in family structure, social patterns (such as the increase in marital breakdown) and the emergence of lifestyles (such as single, professional career women and gay relationships) that contest with traditionally defined, Catholic, male-oriented and heterosexual norms. Mary Halpin, a scriptwriter for *Fair City*, makes the point that to remain connected with their audience, serials have had to develop over time: 'soaps have grown with the Irish public',[66] who are now more willing and prepared to explore the less pleasant aspects of life, including rape, crime and injustice. Critic Barbara O'Connor has argued that serial drama has been more effective in producing attitudinal change than areas of schedule formally designated for information and education because soaps represent the lived experiences and explore the common sense attitudes of its audience.[67] This would seem to be confirmed by counselling professionals who argue that 'consciousness can be raised through soaps because people will watch them, whereas they might turn off a documentary'.[68] It is significant that as part of its package of programmes TnaG felt it should direct its finances to produce *Ros na Rún*, a fifteen minute serial set in the Gaeltacht. It indicates the importance of popular drama for an Irish language station that is not only trying to provide watchable programmes for native speakers but attract people outside the Irish language areas (a subtitled repeat is also shown on RTÉ). TnaG is recognised to have made considerable effort to lose the purist, hair-shirt Gaeilgor image sometimes associated with Irish language enthusiasts. Indeed, TnaG has embraced other popular television formats such as studio dating shows like *Blind Date* (UK) and *Love Connection* (US). Its own *Cleamhnas* – meaning 'match' or 'marriage arrangement' in Irish – uses a person to act *on behalf of* the chooser. Instead of a contestant questioning and choosing his/her partner from behind a screen, the match-maker uses his or her knowledge of the person (it could be a son, daughter, nephew or friend) to select the best suited mate from the three people available. The tradition of match making or arranged marriages existed in the modern period from post-Famine times. It survives today as a tourist event in Lisdoonvana, but *Cleamhnas* tries to reinvent it as an entertainment spectacle on television, exemplifying how Irish indigenisation adapts media formats to local conditions. This process, with a history in television terms that dates back to the introduction of the medium in Ireland, is amply illustrated by the role of *Eurovision*.

Staging a TV spectacle: RTÉ and *Eurovision*

I love the *Eurovision Song Contest*. I love it for its magnificent foolishness, its grand illusion that it brings together the diverse peoples and cultures of Europe on one great wing of song, when all it makes manifest is how far apart everyone is.[69]

The Eurovision Song Contest (*Eurovision*) was inaugurated in 1956 as a televised competition that was intended to encourage fellowship and unity through popular entertainment within what was called the European Economic Community (now EU). Ireland applied to join this economic club in 1961, finally becoming a member in 1973, but entered its first *Eurovision* in 1965.[70] Apart from sports coverage, *Eurovision* is a rare trans-European television viewing experience that continues to confound its critics. In Ireland, a country with a deep history of native music, song and performance, it is affectionately derided as trivial and culturally inferior,[71] but the annual broadcast is a significant television entertainment spectacle.[72] Underneath the humorous 'slagging', Irish people take great pride in the national performance, winning the competition a record seven times, including four victories between 1992 and 1997. Having won in 1993, Ireland's financially-stretched RTÉ was required to host the show in 1994, costing around £2.5 million, which provided a show-stealing interval act at the Point Depot, Dublin. In seven minutes, *Riverdance* produced a memorable moment in Ireland's contemporary image-making. *Eurovision* became transformed into 'Éirevision' as upwards of 100 million television viewers watched worldwide. This section will examine how *Eurovision* exemplifies the principal features of 'utopian sensibility' in entertainment TV, the significance of *Riverdance* in redefining Ireland's media image in the world and argues that *Eurovision* represents a complex bundle of contradictions in Irish society and culture as it jostled for position and exerted its political influence within Europe.

Eurovision is quintessential light entertainment TV and puts an enormous strain on RTÉ's resources in terms of technical support, personnel and finance. The costs are partly subsidised by the European Broadcasting Union (EBU) but in 1994, RTÉ committed £1.0 million out of a total budget of 2.5 million. RTÉ supplied the on-stage presenters Gerry Ryan and Cynthia Ní Mhurchú, whose job it is to provide the conventional sincerity to presenters and performers from the other TV stations around Europe,[73] as well as communicate with the live audience and Irish viewers. The set design at the Point was an eclectic mix of skyscrapers, lighting towers and Celtic imagery. Its scale, the way it was lit and filmed exuded graphic abundance, corollary of the Republic's economic success and political self-confidence. The interval act was a spectacular performance by Irish-Americans Michael Flatley, Jean Butler and a chorus of young, energetic dancers

33 TV's spectacle of hybridity: *Riverdance* at The Point Depot during *Eurovision* 1994. Courtesy of Reference and Illustrations Library, RTÉ

who had been choreographed to combine traditional Irish set dancing, ballet and contemporary movement in an exhilarating, bravura show the intensity of which was heightened by Bill Whelan's stirring musical score. The technology of television applied conventional techniques to connote emotion (close-ups) in carefully rehearsed shot sequences and the exhilarating swoop of boom-crane camera work. Pat Cowlap, who directed the show for television, innovated by using a sports coverage tracking camera on the front of the stage to capture the line-up finale of *Riverdance*. *Eurovision* offers entertainment in the communal interactions and response of audience to performers. The roar of approval that greeted *Riverdance* was shared in homes and television lounges in pubs. Much comment was made about the fact that Ireland was embracing the talents of the diaspora in Flatley and Butler to produce a strong, vibrant culture which an *Irish Times* editorial commented 'has the confidence to borrow and adapt from others, while valuing what is native to its own, can rise head and shoulders above the bland Euro-American pap'.[74]

Riverdance went on to become a worldwide theatrical success and the show became emblematic of Ireland's revitalisation of traditions that had become hidebound. Fintan O'Toole makes the important points that *Riverdance* not only reclaimed the hidden folk and pagan elements in Irish traditional dancing before it had been purified by church and prudish middle-class revivalists, but it recognised the Irish contribution to the Broadway musical genre.[75] Its postmodern, hybridised Irishness relies on very fluid, some argue, vacuous notions of 'celticism'. Flatley and Butler were seen to be part of Ireland's diaspora much publicised by President Robinson and *Riverdance's* spectacular melange of music, dance styles and set design chimed in with *Eurovision's* idea of inclusivity.[76] Yet, *Eurovision* as a competition sanctions a kind of playful xenophobia. Expanded from eighteen to twenty-five competitor countries, *Eurovision* represents an idealised EU, a notional space without borders, but in actuality one in which the flow of people from the newer, eastern states and non-EU immigrants is increasingly monitored and policed by older EU states.[77]

Eurovision became heavily commercialised in the 1990s. During Ireland's successful run of first places in the mid-1990s, RTÉ executives were hard-pressed financially since the station advertising revenue had been capped between 1990–93 and it was forced to commit money for independent commissioning in a deregulated environment. Successful staging of *Eurovision* reiterated its position as the largest single audio-visual resource in the country and underpinned its case for being retained as the principal Irish broadcaster. Although by 1997 *Eurovision* was staged at a cost of £2.8 million (£1m from RTÉ, £1m from sponsorship and balance made up by EBU), the spin-off money generated in advertising and publicity was enormous.[78] Through television, *Eurovision* became a marketing opportunity on a national scale. In 1997, the organisers affected an image shift 'to move away from nostalgic Celtic themes and instead embrace a modern contemporary Ireland'.[79] The show was themed on 'culture and communications', designed to embody the notion of cyberspace, and co-presented by RTÉ's youthful Carrie Crowley and Ronan Keating, of the pop group *Boyzone*. RTÉ executives heaved a sigh of relief at Ireland's runner-up place: 'Honour without responsibility' as one put it.

The significance of *Eurovision* extends beyond its primary function as a popular song contest spectacle. Corporate Ireland and state agencies have claimed it as an audio-visual showcase event to promote tourism and business. But *Eurovision* exhibits tensions brought about by economic policies dominated by an enterprise culture fostered within the EU and producing rapid cultural hybridisation. *Eurovision* remains a popular entertainment show, whose most ardent Irish fans view it as ridiculing the political amities and modernity it is supposed to represent. In the Irish presidential elections of 1997, Dana – ex-*Eurovision* winner (1970) and now self-styled evangelist Catholic – came a close third in the polls on a fundamentalist Catholic ticket. The winner of *Eurovision* in 1998 was the parodically-named Israeli transsexual singer, Dana International, demonstrating that popular entertainment television remains a cultural space where all kinds of everything – the real toleration of social difference – have to be vigorously contested.

Notes

1 This phrase comes from L. Doolan, J. Dowling, B. Quinn and M. Leonard's acerbic and analytical assessment of RTÉ in the 1960s, *Sit Down and Be Counted: The cultural evolution of a television channel* (Dublin, Wellington Publishers, 1969), 4.

2 Luke Gibbons discusses *The Riordans* (1965–79) and *Bracken* (1980–81) in, 'From kitchen sink to soap: Drama and the serial form on Irish television', in *Transformations in Irish Culture* (Cork, Cork University Press, 1996), 44–5.

3 H. Sheehan's 1987 evaluation of *Glenroe* was that 'there has been little to challenge the status quo, whether of Church or State, in any sort of fundamental way'. See H. Sheehan, *Irish Television Drama: A society and its stories* (Dublin, RTÉ, 1987), 365.

4 *RTV Guide*, 1:2 (8 December 1961), 4–5.

5 Edward J. Roth, Jr., *RTV Guide*, 1:2 (8 December 1961) 3. The island of Ireland was already criss-crossed by overspill broadcasting from Britain and the European continent, so the importation of pre-recorded material intensified an already existing phenomenon. Ireland became a comparatively heavily cabled country in the 1970s and from the mid-1980s was penetrated by satellite.

6 J. Corner (ed.), *Popular Television in Britain: Studies in cultural history* (London, British Film Institute, 1991), 11. It was just such voices, energies and creativity that radical RTÉ employees felt were being irrevocably damaged by creeping institutionalisation during the course of the 1960s. See Doolan *et al.*, *Sit Down and Be Counted*, especially 'Two Notions of Authority', 303–16.

7 J. Corner, *Television Form and Public Address* (London, Arnold, 1995), 5, discusses the way in which television works both 'centripetally' and 'centrifugally' in relation to wider society and culture. He talks of the 'sheer capacity of television for *cultural ingestion* and the way in which so much in the culture necessarily bears some relationship to what is "on" television', but also television's tendency 'to *project* its images, character-types, catch-phrases and latest creations to the widest edges of the culture, permeating if not dominating the conduct of other cultural affairs'. Italics in original.

8 M. O'Shaughnessy, 'Box Pop: Popular television and hegemony', in A. Goodwin and G. Whannel (eds), *Understanding Television* (London, Routledge, 1990), summarises the different positions succinctly, 88–95.

9 R. Dyer, 'Entertainment and Utopia', in *Only Entertainment* (London, Routledge, 1992), 18.

10 Dyer, 'Entertainment and Utopia', 24.

11 The phrase comes from a book of the time by Fergal Tobin, *The Best of Decades: Ireland in the 1960s* (Dublin, Gill & Macmillan, 1984). In fact, the opening up, the temporary staunching of emigration, economic and social changes associated with 'the 1960s' are more circumscribed to a period between 1965 and 1974, the first 'oil crisis' of the 1970s, the collapse of Northern Ireland's parliament and the escalation of political violence.

12 The term 'Celtic Tiger' was coined in August 1994 by investment bank Morgan Stanley comparing the economy of the Republic of Ireland with those in South-east Asia.

13 Dyer, *Only Entertainment*, 24.

14 T. Modleski, *Loving with a Vengeance* (New York, Methuen, 1982); and C. Geraghty *Women and Soap Opera: A study of prime time soaps* (London, Polity Press, 1991).

15 Richard Dyer, *et al.* (eds), *Coronation Street* (1981); Dorothy Hobson on *Crossroads* (1982), Barbara O'Connor on 'The presentation of women in Irish television drama', in M. McLoone and J. MacMahon (eds), *Television and Irish Society* (1984) represent three texts dealing with British and Irish material in what is now a considerable body of work.

16 David Morley's research findings on gender preferences (1986) are discussed in T. O'Sullivan, B. Dutton and P. Rayner, *Studying the Media* (London, Arnold, 1998), 139–42.

17 The phrase is Maurice Earl's from his essay, '*The Late Late Show*, controversy and context', in M. McLoone and J. MacMahon, *Television and Irish Society* (Dublin, RTÉ/Iash Film Institute, 1984), 113.

18 G. Byrne, *To Whom it Concerns: Ten Years of The Late Late Show* (Dublin, Torc Books, 1972), 158. The programme is the subject of a substantial Ph.D, 'Challenging Irish society: *The Late Late Show*: 1962–1997', by F. Doyle-O'Neill of University College, Cork. It was not possible to consult this dissertation but quotations from its author were reported in the Irish press.

19 C. Newman, *The Irish Times* (11 August 1998), 4.

20 Byrne, *To Whom it Concerns*, 21.

21 Byrne, *To Whom it Concerns*, 29.

22 Byrne, *To Whom it Concerns*, 29–30.

23 P. Collins, *It Started on the Late Late Show* (Dublin, Ward River Press, 1981), 27, 50, 56 and 58. Collins became the show's senior researcher.

24 Earls, 'Controversy and context', 109.

25 D. Lusted, 'The popular cultural debate and light entertainment', in C. Geraghty and D. Lusted (eds), *The Television Studies Book* (London, Arnold, 1998), 178–9.

26 An insight into the behind-the-scenes preparation and a sense of the studio atmosphere during transmission is well conveyed by D. Dunne, 'An owling success', *In Dublin* (25 October 1986), 19–21.

27 C. Toíbin, 'Gay Byrne: Irish life as cabaret', *The Crane Bag*, 8:2 (1984), 66.

28 L. Collins, '"Late Late" dying soul of the nation', *Sunday Independent* (9 August 1998), 3.

29 S. Byrne, recalls the evening of 13 September 1985 when the show interviewed two lesbian nuns and the furore it caused in, 'It all happened', *Gay Community News* (September 1995), 6. Byrne notes that the next lesbian who discussed her sexual orientation was Emma Donoghue in 1993.

30 E. Reilly, *The Sunday Business Post* (11 June 1995), 23–5.

31 A. Wholley, 'Is anyone watching at all?', *The Examiner* (Cork) (6 September 1996), 12.

32 *RTÉ Guide*, 'What you watched', 22:40 (25 September 1998), 34. See also: '"Late Late" can still see off the opposition', *The Irish Times* (4 August 1998), 2. This article quotes Doyle-O'Neill's contention that the show is 'an interrogator of Irish life' and remained influential among viewers, even from the younger age ranges.

33 M. J. Cassidy, *The Irish Times* (23 March 1996), 15.

34 T. Humphries, 'Old language fails in a changed scenario', *The Irish Times* (29 October 1994); and on the letters page of *The Irish Times* (5 November 1994), 'Adams on the "Late Late"', on the letters page of *The Irish Times* (5 November 1994).

35 E. Holt, 'Belated modernity clashes with medievalism', *The Irish Times* (6 November 1995).

36 E. Corry, 'Better late than never', *Evening News* (6 September 1996), 17.

37 Collins, 'Dying soul of the nation', 3.

38 F. Walsh, 'G'day Gay', *RTÉ Guide* (28 August, 1998), 64–5.

39 Anne McCabe, commissioning editor at Telefís na Gaeilge (TnaG), described the station's policy as 'súil eile', or providing a different perspective in relation to its drama output whose main production is *Ros na Rún*, a fifteen-minute serial drama.

40 Tony Fahy, 'Introduction', in B. O'Connor, *Soap and Sensibility: Audience response to Dallas and Glenroe* (Dublin, RTÉ Audience Research Department, 1990).

41 Recognised in 1974 by Raymond Williams in *Television: Technology and cultural form* (London, Routledge, 1990). In RTÉ's *Response to the Government's Green Paper on Broadcasting* (Dublin, RTÉ, 1995), the section on RTÉ's television services is headed by its drama rather than its news and current affairs programmes.

42 It is significant that neither BBCNI nor UTV has ever produced a serial drama set in Northern Ireland except for the long-running *The McCooeys* on BBC radio, discussed by Rex Cathcart in *The Most Contrary Region*. Graham Reid's *Billy* trilogy of the 1980s was envisaged as a serial drama.

43 O'Connor, *Soap and Sensibility*. O'Connor's study was part of a larger, European-wide survey to examine how audiences in different countries viewed *Dallas* in comparison with indigenous serial TV fiction.

44 A useful insight into the genesis, original thinking behind and summary of the series is provided by its creator, Wesley Burrowes in *The Riordans: A personal history* (Dublin, Gilbert Dalton, 1977).

45 In this, it was similar in educative project to the long-running British radio soap, *The Archers* (BBC Radio 4). The instigator of this idea was Gunnar Ruggheimer, RTÉ controller of programmes, quoted in Burrowes, *The Riordans*, 2. Irish television in the 1960s was an eclectic, international mix of Irish, USA, British and German television expertise.

46 Sheehan, *Irish Television Drama*, 162.

47 J. Ellis, *Visible Fictions: Cinema, television, video* (London, Routledge & Kegan Paul, 1982), 106–7. Brendan Grace did a popular song about Biddy's tractor for instance.

48 See, E. Devereux, 'The Theatre of reassurance? Glenroe, its audience and the coverage of social problems', in M. J. Kelly and B. O'Connor (eds), *Media Audiences in Ireland* (Dublin, University College Dublin Press, 1997), 231–48. Devereux focuses on the problematic representation of Travellers in *Glenroe*.

49 For a discussion of this topic in Irish television, referring to *The Riordans*, *Bracken* and *The Ballroom of Romance* (a single drama as opposed to a serial), see B. O'Connor, 'The presentation of women in Irish television drama', in McLoone and MacMahon, *Television and Irish Society*, 123–32.

50 O'Connor, 'Soap and sensibility', n.p.

51 Transcribed from RTÉ's viewing tape.

52 Transcribed from RTÉ's viewing tape. Bovine Spongiform Encephalitis (BSE) is a cattle disease that affected herds in Britain mainly but it destabilised the market price of beef.

53 M. Lavery and M. McDonagh. 'Anger at *Glenroe* mugging delights producer', *Irish Independent* (10 September 1996), 4.

54 Columnist Kathy Sheridan felt that the scene was poorly scripted and acted; she felt that it was not integrated well into the story and that it was inappropriate to show this kind of violence when younger viewers were watching. See 'Television soap gets in the eyes of Ireland's dozy hicks', *The Irish Times* (16 September 1996), 14.

55 As quoted in M. Dwyer, 'The valley of the squinting screens', *The Irish Times* (29 January 1994).

56 J. O'Shea, 'TV soaps row has RTÉ in a lather', *The Sun* (Irish edition) (9 March 1996), 9.

57 E. Holt, 'Where there's grit there's life', *The Irish Times* (20 September 1998), 5.

58 M. McLoone examines the television representation of the urban working class portrayed in RTÉ's seven-part serial, *Strumpet City* (1980), but contextualises this usefully

in terms of other dramatic forms and examples, in McLoone and MacMahon, *Television and Irish Society*, 53–88.

59 Sheehan, *Irish Television Drama*, 162–177, gives a thorough appraisal of the serial and makes use of access to scripts that were not broadcast. She concludes that although its objective was to explore attitudes to, amongst other things, sexuality in Irish society, it had neither the production means nor the strength of script to carry these through and speculates that *The Spike* 'may have actually set back efforts to open up drama to the terrain of dealing with the controversial growing points of contemporary Irish society', 176–7.

60 H. Linehan, 'Fair Dues' *The Irish Times*, 'Weekend' Section (5 April 1997), 1.

61 J. Lynch, quoted in D. Doyle, 'The fairest of them all', *Sunday Tribune* (23 February 1997), 63.

62 'Fair City gay scene is likely to give sharp boost to RTÉ soap's ratings', *Cork Examiner* (11 March 1996), 3; and S. Barnes, 'Why *Fair City* is the talk of the town', an interview with one of actors involved in the so-called 'gay kissing scene', *Irish Independent* (23 March 1996), 14.

63 Evidence of this dynamic viewership is provided in Deborah Ballard's 'Media Watch' column of *Gay Community News*. See the following articles to trace the welcome introduction of Eoghan, his coming out and then viewer frustration at RTÉ's reticence to show men kissing on screen before 9p.m: 'Media watch', *GCN* (February 1995); 'Just when you thought it was safe …', *GCN* (March 1996), 11; 'Quare city?' *GCN* (April 1996), 11; 'No sex, please – we're Irish', *GCN* (May 1996), 9; 'Coitus interuptus', *GCN* (May 1996), 11.

64 C. Dwyer, *Sunday Independent* (30 March 1997), 39, reports that ratings for *Fair City* in February 1997 were recorded at 879,000 viewers.

65 O'Connor, *Soap and Sensibility*, 'Concluding Remarks'.

66 As quoted in Carol Flynn, *Irish Independent* (20 April 1996), 5.

67 B. O'Connor, 'Presentation of women in Irish television drama', 131–2.

68 Olive Braiden, Rape Crisis Centre, Dublin, as quoted in Flynn, *Irish Independent* (20 April 1996), 5. Similarly, Eoghan's coming out on RTÉ in 1985 was accompanied by an increased number of enquiries to the Gay Switchboard counselling service.

69 Terry Wogan is an Irish chat show host and presenter for the BBC who has regularly employed his wit to poke fun at *Eurovision* even as he presents it. Quoted in F. Ryan, 'All kinds of everything', *Ireland on Sunday* (3 May 1998), 1.

70 RTÉ produced a wonderful spoof of Ireland's first year (1965), called *A Song for Europe* involving the talents of RTÉ's satirical *Nighthawks* team. Broadcast in 1991, this programme went 'back stage' during the preliminary rounds to find Ireland's representative. It sent up much of RTÉ's earnest and self-important image from the 1960s as well as scabrously poking fun at bitchiness and back-biting among crew and performers. My thanks to Eibhear Walshe and Donald Driscoll for drawing my attention to this and letting me view it. *Father Ted* also found rich pickings in *Eurovision* in 'Song for Europe' (episode 2, 1996).

71 It should also be noted that *Eurovision* is a favourite with Irish gay men, being an excuse to have a theme party at home or at a public gay venue. S. Robinson asked his readers to 'relax and enjoy the Eurovision for its banality and bitchiness', 'Euro fever', *Gay Community News* (May 1997).

72 European Broadcast Union figures for 1996 indicated one million Irish viewers watched the show, nearly one third of the population and one of the highest percentage viewer ratios in Europe.

73　D. Lusted points out that there are 'showbiz' conventions for hospitality and sincerity, which it is often funny to see being broken by mischievous compères and commentators (like Wogan).

74　'Editorial', *The Irish Times* (5 May 1994).

75　Fintan O'Toole, 'Unsuitables from a distance: The politics of *Riverdance*', in *The Ex-Isle of Erin: Images of a global Ireland* (Dublin, New Island Books 1997), 149.

76　For a critique of *Riverdance*'s brand of globalised hybridity, see B. O'Connor, 'Riverdance', in M. Peillon and E. Slater (eds), *Encounters with Modern Ireland* (Dublin, Institute of Public Administration, 1998), 51–60.

77　See several of the essays in E. Crowley and J. Mac Laughlin (eds), *Under the Belly of the Tiger: Class, race, identity and culture in the global Ireland* (Dublin, Irish Reporter Publications, 1997).

78　One estimate suggested *Eurovision* was worth £7 million in boosted tourism and business. See the *Sunday Tribune* (27 April 1997), 32.

79　Noel Curran, 'RTÉ warms up for next Eurovision', *The Irish Times* (29 November 1996), 9.

CHAPTER 9

SITUATING IRISH TELEVISION COMEDY

- How significant is Anglo-American sitcom to Irish examples of the genre?
- In what ways does sitcom register social and political conflict?
- How have audiences responded to Irish sitcom in the 1990s?

The empire laughs back?

The sitcom and television in general are concerned with reaffirming cultural identity, with demarcating an 'inside', a community of interests and values, and localising contrary or oppositional values as an 'outside'.[1]

Like other Irish cultural traditions, situation comedy (or sitcom) has an uneven history within Irish television, north and south. This might seem somewhat odd since wit, humour and satire run deep in Irish literary and popular culture. The dearth of sitcom on RTÉ is due to material and organisational factors, not a lack of writing talent. Insufficient finance, incoherent series development and executives satisfied to minimise the risk of controversy and stifle innovation have dogged the Republic's main broadcasting institution well into the 1990s.[2] In addition, Irish sitcom writers inhabit a genre that carries both low cultural esteem and the distinctive subtexts of the dominant television cultures from which it derives; namely, those of Britain and the USA. The first aim of this chapter is to outline the genre's basic formal characteristics and explore the idea that comic disruption in sitcom is tempered by a comedy narrative tendency towards resolution and reparation. Second, this chapter examines the ways in which Irish exponents may be seen to indigenise the genre,[3] using *Upwardly Mobile* (broadcast by RTÉ since 1995), *Father Ted* (Channel Four, 1995–97) and *Give My Head Peace* (BBCNI, since 1998) as examples. Third, it explores the way in which different audiences interpret contemporary Irish sitcom, particularly the ways in which disruption and social change may be simultaneously incorporated and kept outside by the mechanics of the genre.[4]

Before addressing the question of sitcom's historical origins, analysing how it works as a comedy format and how that format functions in a social context, a brief description of the three case studies used in this chapter will be given. Most of the points on the theory of comedy will be illustrated with reference to them so it is important to have some knowledge of each programme.[5] *Upwardly Mobile* is a home-grown RTÉ1 prime-time sitcom that has run to four series with ratings of around 390,000 (September 1996). Originally devised in 1994 by Bill Tierney and written by Thomas McLoughlin from an RTÉ sitcom writing seminar, it was developed further by RTÉ executives Kevin Linehan and David Blake-Knox, and by its third series (1997) was being written by a team of ten named contributing writers.[6] The basic premise was the well-worn domestic sitcom scenario of incompatible neighbours. In this case, work-ing-class, Dublin north-siders Eddie and Molly Keogh (Joe Savino and Catherine Byrne) win £2 million on the Lotto (Irish national lottery), decide to leave de Valera Mansions (council flats) and move to Belvedere Heights next to Pamela and Anthony Moriarty (Hilary Fannin and Niall Buggy), a south-side suburban couple with social pretensions.

Father Ted was produced by Hat Trick Productions for Channel Four TV. It was written by Graham Linehan and Arthur Matthews, initially as a one-off spoof documentary, but reworked as a sitcom which ran to three series. It was highly successful with audiences and TV critics alike in Britain and Ireland, and has been sold to ten countries worldwide, including RTÉ.[7] Selected episodes have been released on home video, *Ted* has spawned fan web sites and a spin-off book. The Christmas Special in 1996 on RTÉ's Network 2 achieved an audience of 975,000, almost a third of the Republic's total population. Set on an imagi-nary, remote Craggy Island (shot on location in Clare), the main setting is a parochial house, home to Fathers Ted (Dermot Morgan), Dougal (Ardal O'Hanlon) and Jack (Frank Kelly), who are looked after by Mrs Doyle (Pauline McLynn), the spinster house-keeper. The priests have been banished to the island parish for various misdemeanours or incompetence and, true to the genre, they are trapped in their predicament, surrounded by eccentric islanders, rival priests on another island and inconveniently visited by bishops and others who threaten the zany equilibrium of their world. The four main characters represent comedic types, composites of sociological categories and actual individuals. Ted is self-regarding, frustrated by his lack of status and aspires to wider recognition in a bigger parish (Dublin or Las Vegas preferably); Jack is an older, wily and grotesque figure, at once foul mouthed, alcoholic and lecherous; Dougal is a childlike, gormless fool who does not understand grown up social propriety or even why he is a priest. Mrs Doyle is a servile spinster who shows due deference to authority, indeed is sycophantic towards bishops. She carries out her housekeeper duties with a mix of motherly duty – we see her bathing Father Dougal – and manic politeness. She often scares her male employers into complicity – clerics wary of female frustrations simmering below the surface of her pious propriety, glimpsed at when she has a crush on the milk delivery man ('Speed 3').

Give My Head Peace, produced by BBCNI in Belfast, is written by Tim McGarry, Damon Quinn and Michael McDowell, three of 'The Hole in the Wall Gang' performance team. It had a six-episode run in the summer of 1998, followed up by a Christmas Special in common with the other two case studies. Like *Upwardly Mobile*, *Give My Head* has a mostly domestic setting but also includes some workplace and location work in and around Belfast. It derives its

34 *Father Ted* cast (1995).
Courtesy of Hat Trick Productions

comedy from the situation of having two working-class families, one republican, one loyalist, related to each other by the mixed marriage between Emer (Nuala McKeever) and Billy (Michael McDowell). Da (Tim Garry) and Ma (Olivia Nash) also have a grown up son, Cal (Michael McDowell), as well as Emer. Billy's family members are absent except for 'Uncle' Andy (Martin Reid), a grotesque, ignorant, loyalist bigot, a permanent layabout house-guest who is actually Billy's biological but unacknowledged father. There is no pretence in the realism of characterisation in *Give My Head*: Cal (Damon Quinn) is too old to be Da's son for instance, and accents, mannerisms and acting style are grossly exaggerated.[8] The script satirises the shibboleths of republicanism and loyalism and exposes the social prejudices underlying sectarianism in Northern Irish society. The series' upbeat, liberal iconoclasm is well captured by the opening titles and theme music by 'The Saw Doctors',[9] a pop anthem for peace during a summer of expectancy and discontent.

Playing with other people's rules

Historically, sitcom developed as 'a televisual form for the presentation of comedy'[10] in the 1950s and, like the soap and chat show, is essentially a cheaply made popular format produced to entertain large, broadly-based audiences in a domestic setting. Its USA origins stem principally from vaudeville routines and radio soap opera series, while in Britain it came about from a fusion of variety act comic sketches, radio comedy series and the broadly-drawn class characterisations of postwar film.[11] Undoubtedly, such low-culture antecedents contribute to the fact that sitcom in Britain and Ireland is made primarily as light entertainment and is not seen as a serious form of television. Yet successful sitcom series are vital to television companies in terms of securing ratings and the buying in of pre-recorded popular USA shows has a long history. In 1955, ITV bought in *I Love Lucy* (1951) to which the BBC responded by transferring *Hancock's Half Hour* from radio to television a year later. In Ireland, exposure to both British overspill transmission and acquired Anglo-American programming on RTÉ schedules meant that from the late 1950s onwards (that is, before the advent of a national TV service) television viewers became very familiar with both British and USA sitcom material. This led to a condition in the 1970s where in RTÉ-produced programmes, 'the foreign sitcoms were given domestic analogues'.[12] The BBC has produced some of the most enduring British examples of the genre within its mixed schedules and its classic sitcoms – *Hancock's Half Hour* (1956–60), *Dad's Army* (1968–77) and *Fawlty Towers* (1975 and 1979) – have become retrospectively elevated and valued as a kind of popular national cultural heritage. While Helena Sheehan could note the importance of satirical sketch shows like *Hall's Pictorial Weekly* (1971–80) from the 1970s on Irish television, RTÉ 's sitcom production is less prolific and memorable.[13] Since the 1980s, several British independent companies have specialised in TV comedy, such as Hat Trick Productions (producers of *Father Ted* for Channel Four) and

Alomo (producers of *So You Think You've got Troubles* for the BBC).[14] In the increasingly commercialised environment of TV production, the potential for spin-off merchandising (such as home video sales and books) from a successful sitcom are as important as securing ratings for broadcast. *Upwardly Mobile's* development by RTÉ in 1994 came about from the perceived need to have a successful, home-produced sitcom on its schedules for competitive reasons, but also to redress RTÉ's poor record and prove that it 'could do sitcom'.[15] Since its inception in 1996, the Irish language station TnaG has not wasted time in producing both an innovative soap, *Ros na Rún*, and a sitcom with the macabre, punning title, *C.U. Burn*, about an Irish crematorium set in Donegal.[16]

(Con)texts, sitcom and society

Sitcom is constituted as a televisual genre by a particular set of textual and contextual characteristics. Each episode usually lasts thirty minutes, is part of a seasonal series (six to thirteen weeks) and is scheduled at a regular, prime time evening slot. Typically, each episode comprises a self-contained narrative, resolved in a circular return to the programme's basic premise. Unlike soap narratives, sitcom does not usually allow its situation to change nor its characters to develop, though there are some examples that allow an element of seriality. Most sitcom characters in the British model are hopelessly entrapped by their situation,[17] but formal rigidity and narrative fixity are distinct from the cumulative familiarity and complex identification with character experienced by viewers of long-running sitcom series. While most actors normally have established careers and personae prior to becoming associated with a particular sitcom, the best sitcoms do enter popular discourse: characters' catch phrases, talk about episodes, impersonations and retellings of scenes are all examples of how sitcom becomes part of everyday talk, though sometimes contained within distinct sub-cultural groups of viewers. These features, the circulation of publicity and merchandising of secondary products form the basis of the cultural significance of sitcom.

The situation of sitcom is usually confined to a domestic environment or work place but the presentation of the setting can range from a social-realist typicality (*Upwardly Mobile*) through to a more stylised, zany, farcical world (*Father Ted*). Characters in sitcom tend to be readily recognised types – open to interpretation by non-indigenous audiences – but inflected with the particulars of the society in which they originate. Moreover, these types acquire particularised visual traits, behaviours and speech habits supplied by writers and performers. Fixed situation and predictable characters are the basis for humour and the pleasure for viewers who watch weekly to see the situation temporarily disturbed, characters' reaction to this change and the premise situation ('the original loop')[18] restored for the following week. Sitcom popularity rests on repetitive narratives, weekly instances of which are paradoxically forgotten by the regular viewer.

A further paradoxical element in sitcom is captured in T. G. A. Nelson's observation that a fundamental tension exists between the potentially disruptive force of laughter, jokes and the comic, and the harmonising principles of reconciliation and social integration implicit in the structure of comedy narratives.[19] Elaborating and analysing the contradictions produced therein has been the basis of contemporary debates about the significance of sitcom to the societies in which they are produced and viewed.[20] This debate seeks to go beyond thinking of sitcom as simply diversionary entertainment, laughter-producing television for large audiences, to consider how it functions as an ideological form in society. For instance, its closed, repetitive structure and its use of crude stereotypes (of class, gender and race for instance) might suggest that sitcom is an irredeemably conservative mode of popular television representation. More convincing arguments can be made for seeing sitcom as an important site where definitional boundaries are set down, fought over, crossed and re-established in an on-going process of cultural struggle between conflicting forces at play in society at any given time. In this cultural process, the production contexts (economic, generic and social) and sitcom's formal, textual features interact with viewers to produce meaning through the recognition of pre-existing comedy genres and the existence of wider social conflict, of which the sitcom is a representation. Thought of in this way, sitcoms may be seen as good indicators of wider ideological patterns and tensions.

Sitcom can be thought of as an institutionalised and extended form of joke telling; television's way of creating a communal experience by addressing viewers in the domestic intimacy of their homes, analogous to sharing a joke with someone. But to tell a joke, to present a situation as funny, assumes a set of ideas and conventions defining what is logical, normal or proper in order to invert, disrupt or transgress them to produce humour and (hopefully) laughter. Seen in this way, sitcom acts to give vent to the transgressive. It performs a socially bonding function constantly redrawing and testing the boundary lines of acceptability. As Steve Neale and Frank Krutnik argue, it creates a sense of us belonging to an inside world as against an outside realm, which is so different and potentially threatening that it has to be ridiculed, made funny and tamed.[21]

Modes of comedy in sitcom

Within the sitcom, there is considerable diversity of humour and comic effect, so it is useful to outline some of the key modes used in order to distinguish between them analytically. Satire highlights, mocks and attacks *social conventions*, particularly those associated with institutions and authority. Typically it works by exaggeration, reversing expectations (of, say, behaviour) or inappropriately treating serious issues such as the peace process, marriage or religion in a trivial way ('That's the great thing about religion, Dougal. It's all so vague and nobody really knows what it means', says Ted). This is where *Father Ted* and *Give My Head* come closest to the overt satire associated with the reputations of Dermot Morgan and the 'Hole in the Wall Gang' outside the sitcom. *Father Ted* scripts made direct, top-ical references to scandals within the Catholic Church (such as Bishop Brennan's 'love child' in the USA, referring to Bishop Eamon Casey),[22] which injected a level of satire for viewers aware of actual events. Linehan and Matthews have claimed (with tongue in cheek?) that 'it's not satirical, we're not trying to make points. We're writing something that's very playful and slapstick. That's all'.[23] Unlike *Father Ted*, *Give My Head* refers to named contemporary figures in Northern Irish politics. Jokes are made about the hair styles of John Hume, Gerry Adams and Ronnie Flannagan (a Royal Ulster Constabulary Chief Inspector). When Ma is arrested and dragged off, she screams, 'quick, Da, phone Joe Hendron' (a nationalist M.P.) and there also are references to Joel Patton (an outspoken Orange Lodge leader). Several exchanges lead up to punchlines that could exist in a topical sketch; combining social satire and astute parody, the dialogue works on several levels. Grand Master of the Kneebreakers Temperance Lodge (George Flannagan) expounds on Catholic in-laws: 'Uncle Andy, you understand the importance of being Protestant. To have one Taig in the family may be seen as a misfortune. But to have two Taigs, means "would you please mind leaving the area?" And we all know what three Taigs in the family is … ?' Andy, in close up, interjects, 'Ay, a republican plot'.

The family paradigm and its gendered power relations has been central to the sitcom genre, exemplified in the husband and wife couple, *Terry and June* (BBC, 1979–87), reversed in *George and Mildred* (ITV, 1976–79) and camped up in *Terry and Julian* (Channel Four, 1992). In *Father Ted*, John and Mary, the arguing hus-band and wife who run the shop on Craggy Island, abuse each other verbally and physically when alone but pretend to be kind and considerate to each other in front of the priests. This parodies the now dated conventional TV representation of domestic couples but also serves as a satire of the traditional image of marriage and its values extolled by the church in Ireland. Parody works through the height-ened imitation of aesthetic categories, exposing the conventions of theatre, film, television and cultural events. In *Give My Head*, an episode titled 'Allo, Allo, Allo', about the RUC, parodied the camera work, music and characterisation of an ITV police series called *The Bill*.[24] In *Father Ted*, the Eurovision song contest and the Rose of Tralee (an Irish national beauty contest) are comically traduced. In another episode, a group of priests gets lost in the women's lingerie section of a department store and invoke the dialogue/characterisation of Vietnam war movies, prior knowledge of which is assumed.

Nearly all sitcom uses some kind of slapstick; comedy derived from physical action and visual jokes. Mrs Doyle falls off a window-sill several times in one episode and in another scene Father Jack's head accidentally catches fire, to which he is oblivious. These are instances of comic surprise events but neither character is hurt by their mishap, as is acceptable in other non-realistic repre-sentations such as cartoons. There is also a strong tradition in sitcom (derived from the medium of radio) for verbal jokes, puns and mishearings. On the arrival of the bishops to give a special mass on the island, Father Ted asks Father

Dougal: 'Have we got any incense?' Initially confused, Dougal offers help as best he can: 'No, but I think there's a spider in the bath.' In 'The Importance of Being Protestant' episode of *Give My Head*, Uncle Andy (a loyalist) is confronted by a confidence trickster posing as Andy's long-lost love child who has become a Catholic priest. At first Andy denies paternity ('I am not your father, *Father*') but in the end he is sorry to see him leave for the missions: 'Good-bye, Father – *son!*' Visual humour and puns are associated with low-comedy traditions (such as pantomime) and much of sitcom feeds off contemporary popular TV culture via intertextual jokes. Mrs Doyle of *Father Ted* brings out a huge pyramid of Ferrero Rocher chocolates to impress the visiting bishops and one of them says: 'Mrs Doyle, with these you are spoiling us', lifting a line from a poorly-dubbed foreign advertisement on British television which viewers will recognise and (in most instances) laugh at.

Sitcoms abound in running jokes and catch phrases that enter into common speech or within viewer groups. Father Jack, the disgusting, ageing priest, exists mainly to demand 'drink, gerls [girls]' and shout 'feck!' [an Irish euphemism]. Mrs Doyle's insistent politeness, 'Ah, go on, go on, go on … ', when pressing someone to have a 'nice cup of tea' satirises Irish manners by an exaggerated repetition that turns into an aggressive imperative, although Linehan has pointed out *Father Ted's* broader appeal to non-Irish viewers. While much British and Irish sitcom remains set in broadly social realist locations, there is a strain of alternative comedy, or anti-sitcom, which incorporates elements of an anarchic, freewheeling surrealism. From BBC radio's *The Goon Show* (1952–60) to television's *The Young Ones* (1982, 1984), *Blackadder* (1983–90) and *Father Ted* (1996–98), all have played with time, created surreal effects and dimensions, and parodied sitcom's own conventionality. In *Father Ted*, Craggy Island has a road that goes backwards and surreal sight gag inserts tend to interrupt or suspend sitcom's own stable reality, no matter how improbable that is itself. Having discussed the historical origins, theory and modes of comedy in sitcom, it is time to consider our three case studies in more detail.

RTÉ comedy: a contradiction in terms? The case of *Upwardly Mobile*

Populist complaints by journalists about RTÉ's lack of home-grown sitcom have periodically appeared in the press over the last two decades.[25] Recalled titles of half-forgotten sitcoms are contrasted with vivid, fond memories of the sketch-based *Hall's Pictorial Weekly* from the 1970s, the one outstanding example of Irish television satire. Formal questions aside, Michael Murphy accurately identified the problem to be not one of a lack of material ripe for satirical treatment nor writers to shape it, but rather 'the poverty and paucity of social and political satire … is a failure of nerve, of imagination, of elementary competence'[26] on behalf of RTÉ, its executives and producers. *Upwardly Mobile* was developed by RTÉ in 1994 in an attempt to produce a sitcom on a limited budget that was popular with Irish viewers and addressed these kinds of

35 *Upwardly Mobile* cast (1998).
Courtesy of the Press Office, RTÉ

charges. In its primary aim, *Upwardly Mobile* has undoubtedly been successful since it weathered a largely unfavourable reception in the press during 1995 and secured top ten ratings positions on RTÉ1 on Fridays at 8.30p.m. in its first season of twelve episodes.[27] It is worth considering the terms in which the programme has been attacked and ask why there is such a cleavage between critical consensus and viewing figures. We can then examine what *Upwardly Mobile* signifies about contemporary Ireland and its television culture in light of the history and theory set out in earlier sections of this chapter.

Early critics of *Upwardly Mobile's* situational premise – a working-class family moving to a middle-class residential area – asserted that it represented an unoriginal 'virtual sit-com-by-numbers structure'.[28] The programme's 'dated [title] and the whole Beverley Hillbillies type premise',[29] suggest twin influences of Anglo-American sitcoms and RTÉ's 'in-appropriation' of these formats. But most sitcoms are formulaic and, indeed, historians of Irish television will know that in 1975 RTÉ had produced *Up in the World*, a ten-part series scripted by David Hayes, a precedent set some twenty years earlier. Ted Sheehy took his objections further by insisting that 'the sitcom format used in [*Upwardly Mobile*] is an irredeemably class-based British model'.[30] What rankled Sheehy was how RTÉ could make a sitcom that – in its representation of the neighbourly tensions between the Moriartys and the Keoghs – reproduced the concerns and interests of its middle-class viewers, as well as uncritically following the lowest common denominator in comic effects – visual gags and verbal innuendo – to do so. First, to wholly attribute the issue of class to British antecedents is to ignore the purchase that comedy *might* have on the class-basis of Irish society. Second, a class analysis should not preclude other forms of social difference, such as gender, being seen as equally significant to the dynamics of a sitcom. For instance, Pamela Moriarty is more offensively class conscious towards the Keoghs and more socially pretentious than her more passive husband, Anthony, who is more accepting of Molly, but not Molly's mother. In this respect, Pamela is a post-feminist retro version of 1970s domineering TV sitcom wives.[31] *Upwardly Mobile* does use a format tradition-ally associated with representations of British class-conflict, but this format – as with other examples of Anglo-American culture – has not simply been trans-posed intact into Irish society. If the sitcom was that alien to Irish viewers they would not be able to engage with it. Rather, I am arguing, sitcom has been mis-appropriated within an Irish social structure that has its own class and gendered conflicts. Using such TV formats, hastily developed within the hot-house confines of an RTÉ sitcom seminar, with the close, hands-on involve-ment of executives armed with audience research,[32] *Upwardly Mobile* is bound to reflect how the structures for supporting sitcom have been developed at RTÉ. At the same time, the programme's ratings popularity are a reminder of how deeply Irish audiences have internalised British TV models as a result of the last generation of production and viewership. They also suggest that popu-lar comedy TV series often depend as much on careful (but not intrusive insti-tutional) script development as on individualised comic writing genius. A more general point is that considerable changes to the structure and nature of class have taken place in Ireland since the mid-1970s.

The phenomenon of social mobility in a class-structured society has a particular resonance in Ireland, undergoing a relatively late and comparatively rapid industrialisation as a European country. This has produced a series of transformations some of which are common and others of which are particular to Ireland. Despite the shift over a generation from a reliance on agriculture to that of employment and income generated in the service sector, despite the gradual feminisation of the workforce and the urbanisation of Ireland, accord-ing to one sociologist writing in the 1995, 'what marks Ireland out as distinctive, in comparative terms [to the rest of Europe], is the *extremely low level of upward mobility*'.[33] The inside/outside realms constructed by the situation, character and narrative of *Upwardly Mobile* acknowledges working-class frustration and resentment with continued blocks to social mobility, especially during a time of rapid economic growth in the mid-1990s following the previous decade in which unemployment and emigration hit unskilled rural and urban labour hardest. But the comedy also expresses the fears that the existing boundaries and markers of class and status (geographical location, occupation, education, accent, social behaviour) are *not* permanent and might change. These are tested out in the central situational premise of the programme. Ordinarily, the Keoghs and Moriartys would not live next to each other. It needs luck – Keogh's winning the Lotto – to bring them into the middle-class world of Belvedere Downs. The definitional premise is that social movement in this direction is incongruous and inherently funny, but that movement in the other direction would not be. Early scripts seemed to veer between celebrating the working-class values of the Keoghs as more authentic, genuine and decent but patron-ised Molly for her aspirations to own a boutique or their still-poor friends who were not lucky enough to win the Lotto. Against this, the middle-class values and behaviour of the Moriartys (particularly Pamela) are portrayed as shallow, affected, social pretentiousness; they are artificial, even un-Irish. Unspoken – in between Pamela's exaggerated attitudes, which represent the social aspirations of a 1990s Euro *nouveau riche*, and the residual fiction of Dublin's decent work-ing class – is the conservative ideology of an unostentatious Irish middle class with its traditional bases, the 'sons and daughters of farmers and the *petite bourgeoisie*', with college educations who want to consolidate the unequal class structure, preserving its immobility in the face of seismic changes.[34] In concep-tion, organisation and production, *Upwardly Mobile* seems to have produced mostly laboured, trite and lame scripts but the programme is not 'completely harmless'[35] just because 'it seems too timid, too afraid to say much that is mean-ingful about class … given that class friction is not always a laughing matter'.[36] That sitcom has the capacity to engage with social change and more consciously with its own history as a genre is demonstrated by the case of *Father Ted*.

More jocular than jugular: *Father Ted*

The scenario of three priests and their housekeeper on a remote island reworked an existing Irish example and yet also exceeded the tradition of clerical comedy in British television. RTÉ's *Leave it to Mrs O'Brien* (1984–86), about the mishaps of the eponymous housekeeper and her priests in a Dublin parish, was a success with audiences but a critical disaster, not unlike *Upwardly Mobile* a decade later.[37] *Father Ted*, however, owes less to *Mrs O'Brien* and more to a longer, stronger tradi-tion of British sitcom that featured the clergy, from *Our Man at St Marks* (1963–65) and *All Gas and Gaiters* (1967–71) to *The Vicar of Dibley* (1994–98). The writers of *Father Ted* and Dermot Morgan have acknowledged the strong influ-ence of British broadcast sitcom, satirical humour and alternative comedy on their careers.[38] We can concur with Linehan's evaluation of *Father Ted* that it exhibits 'the standard vocabulary of television comedy in the Irish vernacular'.[39] Working creatively within such generic bounds, *Ted* mimics its pattern so well as to surpass the original. Its Irish credentials were firmly grounded since it was commissioned by Seamus Cassidy for Hat Trick Productions in London, written by two Irishmen, directed by Declan Lowney and performed by a quartet of Irish performers and well supported by guest Irish acting talent. It was securely Irish, but expressed a strand of expansive, confident identity associated with the Irish in mid-1990s Britain. It addressed the derogatory stereotypes endured over genera-tions by the Irish in English society, exaggerated them and sought to explode them. Its Irishness contained an added piquancy since it was created and produced out of Ireland itself and could be seen to simultaneously engage in the satirical examination of social and cultural changes taking place in the Republic throughout the decade.

To understand the significance of *Ted* in its time, it is important to gauge the intentions of those involved in its production and the responses in different audiences to the series in Ireland, Britain and worldwide. While one of its creators, Arthur Matthews, claimed that it was not conceived as an 'ethnic show, there's no Irish thing in it that excludes people',[40] there are conflicting ideas about *Father Ted's* comic *modus operandi* and its targets. Graham Linehan has said that the main objective was to be playfully funny, gently (almost affectionately) mocking the clergy, for instance, rather than being hostile or purposefully satirical. Ardal O'Hanlon (Dougal) thought that the show had the effect of humanising the priests and that religion was not the butt of jokes. Dermot Morgan, however, had a sharper sense of bringing out an underlying satirical edge to his character, Ted Crilly, and the show as a whole: 'I don't think everything should be anodyne. I don't think people should not be offended sometimes.'[41]

These views and the programme's secure sense of expatriate Irishness, did not insulate *Father Ted* from criticism from Irish viewers in Ireland, Britain and the USA, who claimed that it was 'offensively disrespectful of our clergy and Roman Catholics in general', 'disgusting and degrading to the Irish people', and indignantly proclaimed 'that this racist depiction … perpetrated by Irish people is despicable. Uncle Toms, indeed, who pander to British racism for profit'.[42] Academics in North America and Australia exchanged views on *Father Ted* as it was sold and distributed globally.[43] John Hildebidle thought it a 'brainless and unfunny show … And full of stage Irishry to book [sic]', an estimation with which Ross Chambers concurred having viewed the Christmas Special in 1997.[44] Unlike the BBC serial, *EastEnders*, which presents itself as contemporary, slice-of-life realism or *Far and Away*, which offers itself as a film romance based on historical events, *Father Ted* is overtly non-realist, reflexive and ludicrous in its caricature. As Liam Greenslade has pointed out: 'There is huge difference between being laughed at by the coloniser and re-possessing those jokes for your own purposes'.[45]

Examined in the context of postcolonial theory and TV sitcom history, *Father Ted's* significance makes clearer sense. Its broadcast came in the wake of several notable controversies in the early 1990s concerning the church. With its moral authority in Ireland under question, many of the certainties that had underpinned Irish society crumbled away. Through its comedy, *Father Ted* was able to catch at a growing sensibility amongst the laity within Ireland and the Irish diaspora in the mid-1990s. In an economically buoyant and socially unstable period, reactive anxiousness and a liberating confidence mixed uneasily in viewers' minds. While *Father Ted* contained an underlying satirical current it was formally a relatively safe way of exploring change. It can be viewed as a way for Irish society to get used to the church in a new era and, according to one view, probably did the church 'an unintentional service, *providing a release* for the resentment it has provoked in recent times'.[46]

Yet, the strategy of stereotype exposure was not felt to be workable or justified by some readers of *The Irish Post*. The culturally specific vernacular of
Father Ted could not only be misread by English viewers – reinforcing existing
prejudices – but by first and second-generation Irish viewers in Britain and the
USA who held simplistic notions of how popular media stereotypes circulate.
Such complainants failed to see that there were alternative approaches to positive imaging, and, indeed, that self-directed humour and satire may well be
indicative of assured selfhood and a collective cultural maturity. However,
many Irish viewers did read *Father Ted* correctly, taking up the ludicrously
dysfunctional types and the surreal humour with relish, locating the
programme within a tradition of literary satire and parody associated with
Swift, Joyce and Flann Ó'Brien.[47] The quantitative measurement of such
responses would require careful audience analysis but it is fair to assume that it
would vary depending on location, age, gender, generational status and individual upbringing. The divisiveness of *Father Ted* is ludic, tracing the shifting
contours of postcolonial representation and reinscribing the boundaries of
social conflict. It shows how media texts become meaningful in ways that are
dependent upon specific combinations of residual and emergent representations, and particular cultural cross-overs being interpreted at any given time by
situated audiences within and without Ireland.

Laughing at the peace process: *Give My Head Peace*

'Give my head peace' is a colloquial Northern Irish expression meaning 'leave
me alone, shut up'. The first series of this satirical sitcom was broadcast in early
1998 during the negotiations that led up to the Good Friday agreement and the
second series (discussed in this section) went out in May–June 1998 as the loyalist marching season built up to its climax in July. The punning title of the
show played on and expressed a popular frustration with the halting progress
of political manoeuvring about the Northern Ireland Assembly and the confrontation produced by loyalist marches. Of the case studies discussed here,
this series is perhaps the most culturally specific and although it was received
in the Republic by multi-channel viewers, it has not been networked by the
BBC in Britain because it is seen as too parochial. Steeped in the local detail of
Northern Irish political culture, the particularities of sectarian social discourse
and delivered in a Belfast vernacular, *Give My Head Peace* is not easy viewing
for those lacking the cultural competences necessary to follow it, but it is a
sharp indictment not just of sectarian attitudes within Northern Ireland, but of
wariness or wilful ignorance of the north in England and in the Republic.
Writer Damon Quinn acknowledges that it is 'primarily a local sitcom for a
local audience', but saw that 'the challenge of *Give My Head Peace* was to move
from satire to popular comedy so that it worked on various levels'.[48] Reaching
up to 59 per cent of Northern Ireland's TV audience share,[49] the programme
illustrated how sitcom is part of a social process to demarcate an inside, a

community of interests and values, and through humour identify contrary values as outside and extreme.

The writing and performance team responsible for the series, 'The Hole in the Wall Gang', are well known within Northern Ireland on the alternative club circuit and local radio for their comedy sketch shows and satirical revues.[50] *Give My Head* parodies theatrical, film and television genres, which carry a subversive, satirical charge, aimed at ridiculing the pervasive jargon of the peace process and media representations of the Troubles, which are seen largely to be imposed from outside, and the dominant ideologies of the two main political communities, which are demonstrably inadequate to the demands for peaceful transformation (rather like the residual discourse of the Catholic church in the Republic, failing to keep pace with the emergent ideas of the laity). The show also explores the reasons for the predominance of division in Northern Irish society along sectarian lines, at the expense of addressing the class and gender conflicts that remain in evidence.

A rich vein of humour runs through *Give My Head* that is concerned to highlight the hollowness of the terminology that has been generated by the peace process negotiations and mock its formality and sense of self-importance. This is seen particularly in the way that Da and Cal speak, using the phraseology of political diplomacy in small-scale, domestic matters. In 'An Indecent Proposal', Cal attempts to reconcile his parents whose marriage is temporarily thought to have been invalid: 'Now Ma and Da, I have been up all night working on this draft settlement, which I think forms the basis for the pre-nuptial settlement ... I have adopted a three-stranded approach – giving recognition to the totality of relations within the marriage'. The male republican characters are ridiculed for their tired, repetitive parroting of clichés about Irish history and Catholic ill-treatment under 'imperialist rule' and the 'Orange jackboot'. They are obsessed with protesting against the 'SS' RUC, loyalist marching and forming Concerned Residents Committees. Da seeks recognition from Gerry (Adams) and aspires to the status of an international, media republican. His vanity and pompousness is similar to Father Ted's or Captain Mainwaring's (*Dad's Army*). On the opposite side, Uncle Andy and the Orange Order's rituals are lambasted, their traditions exposed as phoney and their attempts to claim 'civil and religious liberties' a sham. In 'The Long Marching Season' (episode 4), Andy and his stupid friend, 'Big Mervyn', decide to march through the fictional village location of a BBC comedy romance called *Ballykissangel* in the Republic: 'If we march this year – it'll be traditional next year', they explain. Uncle Andy is shown to be vain and desperate to become Assistant Grand Vice Master in 'The Importance of Being Protestant' (episode 1). Despite the topical currency of the series, Andy's caricature (whose physical characteristics bare some striking resemblances to his namesake, UDA leader, Andie Tyrie) is fixed in the 1970s: his clothing, moustache and hair style, taste in music (Elvis) and the attitudes he espouses about women and 'Fenians' signify the backward, unreconstructed nature of male loyalism. The wallpaper and furnishings of Billy's house comically conforms to this time-lag representation of loyalism; even the front door glass is etched with King Billy on his horse and the door-bell plays 'Derry's Walls'. Challenged by Billy that he is work shy, Andy retorts: 'Excuse me, Big Merv has a cousin whose brother-in-law has a mate who works in the shipyard', making fun of traditional (now implausible) myths about the Protestant work ethic. Andy is *Give My Head's* equivalent to Father Jack in his grotesque, anti-social behaviour and blatant, unconscious sectarianism: 'Zero tolerance? You know, that's how I feel about Fenians as well'. Andy cannot comprehend why Billy, a Protestant, has married Emer, a Catholic, but the series makes explicit that there is considerable tension between Andy, his hard-line loyalist associates, and the RUC. In 'Allo Allo Allo' (episode 2), Emer temporarily joins the RUC and rapidly gets promoted to chief constable ('positive discrimination' to reform the force in gender and denominational terms). At home, to her husband, but *about* and *in front* of Uncle Andy, she says: 'He's a civilian, Billy. I don't have powers to order him about'. Andy's retort is delicious, topical satire: 'Ay, Drumcree taught yous that', giving vent to populist loyalist conflict with(in) the RUC,[51] the state's official force of law and order (see chapter 11 for the treatment of this topic in a tragic mode in *Force of Duty*).

Ma, Emer and Billy are the moderate characters; they help to demarcate a utopian inside, to articulate the values of toleration and bridge the gap between the two families and across generations within them. In 'An Indecent Proposal' Ma even temporarily becomes Andy's lover, but the comic loop is joined come the end of the episode when we learn – true to character – that he was only trying to win a bet with Big Merv. Ma is a slightly scatty, well-meaning matriarch who in 'Setting an Example' (episode 5) gives an anodyne interview for the Channel Four TV documentary film crew in a parody of the mother Ulster figure. However, both Emer and Ma rebel against the dependency of the male characters in their domestic spheres, and, in 'Allo, Allo, Allo', Emer briefly assumes a higher status and authority over her Da and her husband in the RUC. But, power goes to her head, she temporarily feminises the RUC's canteen culture but becomes an authoritative Amazon, reducing the ranks to children under her command, arresting her own Da and Cal ('I don't believe this! I'm being harassed by me own daughter!') and eventually Mo Mowlam, the secretary of state for Northern Ireland, for having an out-of-date car tax disk. The humour here is partly in seeing the Mowlam authority figure levelled but also seeing familial gender roles reversed. However, this is a temporary transgression for the comic loop of the sitcom narrative is closed by having Emer dismissed and safely restored to her allotted domestic sphere. Situational stasis is further reinforced because Da and Cal interpret her loss of job as confirmation of their idea that the RUC is irreformable. In *Give My Head*, gender and sectarian conflict are carefully interwoven.

As with *Father Ted* (and many other contemporary sitcoms), *Give My Head* engages in a whole-hearted, parodic assault on other media genres to produce comedy. This tendency towards intertextual referencing may be seen as a part of the postmodern character of much television discourse, which assumes a media-literate viewer to decode and find pleasure in the references. While not inherently radical, the incursion into other genres, the robbing of their narratives and conventions, provides potential for comic disturbance and oppositional readings of representations offered in the original, uncorrupted genres. We have already mentioned how 'Allo, Allo, Allo' spoofs the macho grittiness of a crime series, *The Bill*, but only temporarily replaces that with a hyper-authoritarian female. 'Hollywood on the Falls' (episode 6) parodies cinematic narratives involving US male stars playing Republican gunmen, with 'Mitch Morgan' as a wicked take on Brad Pitt (for his part in *The Devil's Own*?). The parody of Oscar Wilde's play in episode 1 of the second series cleverly subverts notions of essential identities that underpin sectarian social attitudes, since *all* the Orange Lodge members confess to having had sexual liaisons resulting in hidden 'Catholic/nationalist' off-spring, and the episode ends with republican Da about to be convinced he has English connections. In 'The Long Marching Season', Uncle Andy and Big Mervyn go south to march through the BBC fictional Irish village, *Ballykissangel* – to that programme's theme music – and disturb its tourist iconography of bucolic order and peacefulness. The sight of Orange marchers out of context is humorous and a genial Guard (policeman) is lackadaisical about the stand-off that develops between them and the inevitable counter-protest march of Da and Cal. In this episode, as others, Ma, Emer and Billy form a cluster of moderation, appearing as non-violent 'hippies' and establishing a quasi-feminist 'peace' vigil camp, to protest about the protests. In *Give My Head*, all extreme ideas and behaviour are subject to exaggeration and lampooning as outside and unacceptable. Uncle

36 *Give My Head Peace* cast (1998).
Courtesy of BBC Northern Ireland

Andy's bigotry, his excessive hatred of Catholics, is condemned by Billy, but in our laughter we are acknowledging such attitudes. We are drawn in to laugh at the excesses of Uncle Andy, Da and Red Hand Luke, yet the familial situation also represents the capacity for communities to live with, accommodate and tacitly support those extremes at which we are invited to laugh as sectarian, cruel and ultimately inhumane.

The areas of social and political unease addressed in sitcom humour in the case studies in this chapter include those concerned with class and social mobility, religious belief, church authority and political ideologies in Northern Ireland. *Father Ted* and *Give My Head Peace*, in particular, exemplify the idea – noted elsewhere in this book – that the most challenging cultural work is often carried out at political and cultural frontiers (Damon Quinn has referred to BBCNI in Belfast as a 'colonial outpost'[52]) or by emigrant Irish flourishing in the entrepreneurial centres of cultural capitals like London. *Give My Head Peace* articulated popular, local frustrations at the constipated peace process during 1998–99 and a moderate critique of the sectarianism produced by the historical political structure of Northern Ireland. *Father Ted* expressed a new self-confidence about the Irish in Britain in the mid-1990s but it also registered profound changes within the Republic too. In their own ways, both programmes laughed back at the remnants of colonialism in Ireland, making marauding incursions into existing representations and forming part of an emergent vision. They used satire and slapstick to address anxieties deep within the heartlands of Ireland's dominant social traditions and political culture. In the next chapter, some of the same anxieties are represented through one of television's more serious programming strands, documentary.

Notes

1 S. Neale and F. Krutnik, *Popular Film and Television Comedy* (London, Routledge, 1990), 242.

2 It is a *Father Ted* myth – popularly circulated – that RTÉ turned down the script in development. The truth of the matter is that Matthews and Linehan did not offer it to the Irish station, S. Walsh, 'Joking for a living', *Film Ireland*, 54 (August–September) 1996, 19.

3 T. O'Regan on 'Negotiating cultural transfers', Chapter 9, in *Australian National Cinema* (London, Routledge, 1996), is pertinent in relation to theorising how TV genres transfer and pass between cultures.

4 J. Tulloch explores 'comedy's quality to control and subvert' (246), in *Television Drama: Agency, audience and myth* (London, Routledge, 1990), 245–60.

5 *Father Ted* is available on VHS from retail outlets. *Give My Head Peace* can be viewed at the Film and Sound Resource Unit at the University of Ulster at Coleraine and sample copies may be obtained for private research or for classroom use if covered by an institutional licence for educational purposes in the UK. *Upwardly Mobile* may be viewed in RTÉ in the VT Library, but I have also relied on off-air copies made for me by Éibhear Walshe.

6 It has been suggested that some episodes of the first two series were pseudonymously written by Linehan and/or Blake-Knox under the nom de plumes of 'Ted Gannon' and 'James Corry'. See, 'Will the real "James Corry" please stand up?', *Film Ireland*, 55 (October–November 1996), 7. See also Liam Miller's refutation of Sheehy's attack on this and other aspects of *Upwardly Mobile* in *Film Ireland*, 56 (December 1996/January 1997), 38. 'Strong script writing team for *Upwardly Mobile*', *RTÉ News Release* (RTÉ Press and Information Office, 22 September 1997), credits no less than ten named writers for the third series.

7 M. Chiara Benazzi, 'Cult of the irreverent priest', *The Financial Times* (21 October 1996), 18.

8 Tulloch, *Television Drama*, 247, distinguishes between comedies of social realism, naturalistic comedies and farces.

9 'Give My Head Peace' was successfully released as a single with EMI in 1998 in the Republic and Northern Ireland but not in Britain.

10 P. Goddard, 'Hancock's Half Hour: A watershed in British television comedy', in J. Corner (ed.), *Popular Television in Britain* (London, British Film Institute, 1991), 75.

11 Goddard, 'Hancock's Half Hour', 75.

12 H. Sheehan, *Irish Television Drama* (Dublin, RTÉ, 1987), 156–7.

13 Sitcom is to be distinguished from satirical sketch shows exemplified in Ireland in the 1970s by Frank Hall's *Hall's Pictorial Weekly* and Niall Tóibín's acerbic *If the Cap Fits* (1973) and *Time Now Mr T* (1977). See Sheehan, *Irish Television Drama*, 177–81.

14 *So You Think* was created and written by the well-known team of Maurice Gran and Laurence Marks. It starred Warren Mitchell, indelibly associated with his screen character, Alf Garnett, from the Johnny Speight sitcom, *Till Death us do Part* (1965–75). Far from Garnett's working-class racism and sexism, in *So You Think*, Mitchell portrays a middle-aged, liberal, Jewish executive in a sitcom with serial development to it. Kieran Prenderville and BBCNI produced a highly successful series set in a fictional village called *Ballykissangel* (1996–98) but this is more strictly comedy drama than sitcom. Another recent series, produced independently for BBCNI by Witzend Productions, *Safe and Sound* (August–September, 1996), was scripted by Timothy Peager. Set in Northern Ireland, the scenario of two mates working in a garage (see *Film Ireland*, 55 (October–November 1996), 39) had already been used to moderate success in a two-series sitcom, *Foreign Bodies* (BBCNI), co-written by Graham Reid and Bernard Farrell in the late 1980s.

15 Telephone interview, Kevin Linehan, RTÉ, 23 February 1999. In the early 1980s, Dermot Morgan appeared in the television sketch show, *The Live Mike* (1979–91), performing Father Trendy in a precursor of his Father Ted character. Memorably, he co-wrote (with Gerry Stembridge) and played in RTÉ radio's *Scrap Saturday* (1989–91), a sketch show that was sharply satirical of politics and society in Ireland during the demise of Fianna Fáil. See H. Sheehan, 'The parameters of the permissible: how *Scrap Saturday* got away with it', *Irish Communications Review*, 2 (1992), 73–6. Selected *Scrap Saturday* script excerpts appear in D. R. Morgan and B. Morgan, *Our Father: A tribute to Dermot Morgan* (Dublin, New Island Books, 1998).

16 *C. U. Burn* (1996) is produced and directed by Niall Mac Eachmarcaigh at Lios na Sí Productions for TnaG.

17 F. Gray, 'British sitcom: A rather sad story', in *Women and Laughter* (Basingstoke, Hampshire, Macmillan, 1994), 83, points out a distinction between British and US sitcom in this respect: 'If the message of American sitcoms is "we can work it out", that of British sitcom is "you'll never get out".'

18 Graham Linehan in interview with Nicky Fennel, *Film West*, 25 (Summer 1996), 39.

19 T. G. A. Nelson, *Comedy: The theory of comedy in literature, drama and cinema* (Oxford, Oxford University Press, 1990), 179.

20 For other important studies of comedy and sitcom in particular, see J. Cook (ed.), *Situation Comedy: BFI Dossier 17* (London, BFI, 1982); Neale and Krutnik, *Popular Film and TV Comedy*; S. Wagg (ed.), *Because I Tell a Joke or Two: Comedy, politics and social difference* (London, Routledge, 1998); P. Kirkham and B. Skeggs, 'Absolutely Fabulous: Absolutely feminist?', in C. Geraghty and D. Lusted (eds), *The Television Studies Book* (London, Arnold, 1998), 286–98; and Gray, 'British sitcom: A rather sad story', 80–111.

21 Neale and Krutnik, *Popular Film and TV Comedy*, 242.

22 Eamon Casey was a popular and well-respected Bishop of Galway who had to resign in May 1992 when it became known that he had fathered a son with a divorcee in the 1970s and had paid for his upkeep with Church money.

23 *Radio Times* (4–10 April 1998), 129.

24 Many of the titles of *Father Ted* and *Give My Head Peace* played on popular cultural references and genres. 'Ello, ello, ello, ello (what's going on 'er then?)' is a (now dated) phrase popularly attributed to a British policeman beginning an enquiry. Origin not known. *Allo, Allo* (sic), the title of which is supposed to mimic a French accent, was a popular BBC sitcom set in wartime occupied France.

25 M. Murphy, 'Funny business', *In Dublin* (6 February 1986), and P. Howick, 'Irish comedy – it's no laughing matter', *Evening Herald* (8 September 1995), 20.

26 Murphy, as quoted in Sheehan, *Irish Television Drama*, 376.

27 Favourable reviews heralding the second series, extended to sixteen episodes, included: E. Brophy, 'Upwardly soaped – in the best possible taste', *Evening News* (24 June 1996), 23; and A. Coogan, 'The show that's *Upwardly Mobile*', *Evening Herald* (19 September 1996), 36. Coogan explains the show's popularity by asserting that 'it seems that everybody wants to win the Lotto and *Upwardly Mobile* has struck a chord with the TV watching public'. Maintaining his attack for the second series, P. Howick produced a damning account of the show's production, its allegedly excessive 'green room' audience hospitality and subsequent falsity of applause, 'No comedy in this situation', *The Evening Herald* (8 November 1996), 19. In fact, *Upwardly Mobile* was RTÉ's first sitcom to use the laughter of a live studio audience present at recording rather than relying on canned laughter.

28 'Rat Boy', *Film West*, 23 (Winter 1995), 38.

29 Howick, 'Irish comedy', 20.

30 *Film Ireland*, 55 (October–November 1996), 7.

31 One thinks of Mildred (Youtha Joyce) in *George and Mildred* (ITV, 1976–79) and Margot Leadbetter (Penelope Keith) in *The Good Life* (BBC, 1975–80)

32 Liam Miller, director of television programmes, RTÉ, cites IMS research undertaken after the first series, which 'indicated that Irish audiences not only welcomed the representation of class differences … but wished to see these differences more clearly emphasised … This view was expressed most strongly by working class respondents.' See 'Letters', *Film Ireland*, 56 (December 1996–January 1997), 38.

33 C. T. Whelan, 'Class transformation and social mobility in the Republic of Ireland', in P. Clancy *et al.* (eds), *Irish Society: Sociological perspectives* (Dublin, Institute of Public Administration), 1995, 334. My emphasis.

34 Whelan, 'Class transformation', 351.

35 D. Lynch, *Sunday Independent* (29 September 1996), 51.

36 E. Holt, *The Irish Times* (20 September 1997), 5.

37 Originally titled, *The Good, the Bad and the Clergy*, it was devised and scripted by Angela McFadden, an 'ordinary' Dublin housewife. The second and third series were written by Joe Dunlop who had been the first series script editor. For an account of its reception see, Sheehan, *Irish Television Drama*, 374–6.

38 Matthew and Linehan were sketch and script writers for *Alas Smith and Jones*, Alexei Sayle and Steve Coogan. See also, M. Doyle, 'In good faith', *The Irish Post* (9 March 1996), 'The Craic', 3. R. Chalmers interviews Dermot Morgan in 'The father of invention', *Independent on Sunday* (15 March 1998), 16–17.

39 Doyle, 'In good faith', 1.

40 As quoted in Doyle, 'Unholy Trinity', 1.

41 Doyle, 'Unholy Trinity', 1.

42 These quotations are taken from letters in *The Irish Post*'s 'You Say … ' column by K. Dwyer (20 May 1995), J. J. Lavin (6 May 1995), D. Keegan (6 April 1995) respectively. An 'Uncle Tom' is a derogatory remark made of a Black person who is 'servile and cringing' (OED).

43 Bonazzi, 'Cult of the irreverent priest', 18, provides a very good summary of responses to *Father Ted* in Denmark, Iceland, France and Norway.

44 Irish Studies e-mail discussion group, 5 January 1998.

45 Irish Studies e-mail discussion group, 6 January 1998.

46 Linehan, as quoted in Doyle, 'In good faith', 1. My emphasis. See also chapter 10 on the RTÉ documentary, *Dear Daughter*, for instance.

47 D. Carroll, 'You Say … ', *The Irish Post* (13 May 1995), 10. A very funny spoof letter from Feilim O'Deagh in Wolverhampton adopts the rhetoric of the anti-*Father Ted* correspondents in describing his extreme, paranoid preventative measures involving strong paper bags and personal stereos: 'Let 'em try and get past that with their "satire"', *The Irish Post* (27 April 1995), 10.

48 Quinn, interview with author, 13 April 1999.

49 Figure cited by BBC Belfast Press Office for 1998 Christmas Special.

50 Formed in 1989 from university law graduate trio who are behind the writing of *Give My Head Peace*, 'The Hole in the Wall Gang' worked through the early 1990s on live satirical cabaret at the Empire Club, Belfast, took part in the notorious *The Show* (BBCNI, 1989–91) and performed short slots on Radio Ulster's *Talkback*. *Two Ceasefires and a Wedding* (BBC, 1995) was an award-winning TV film comedy that spawned most of the key characters that led to *Give My Head Peace* (1998–99), including a Christmas Special episode and a spoof period piece, *1798: The comedy* (December 1998). Thanks to BBCNI Press Office for clippings.

51 Drumcree church just outside Portadown, Northern Ireland, has become a symbolic and geographical rallying point among loyalists since a major confrontation between dissident Orangemen and the security forces took place in the summer of 1996 in what is known as the 'Siege of Drumcree'. This site has continued to be a flashpoint in subsequent summers with 'Spirit of Drumcree' loyalists like Joel Patton maintaining that Orange marchers have a civil right to walk the mainly nationalist Garvaghy Road to the church, despite this causing offence to the residents.

52 Quinn, interview with author, 13 April 1999.

CHAPTER 10

DOCUMENTING CONTEMPORARY IRELAND

- What are the central issues for documentary in an age of television?
- In what ways has censorship affected non-fiction images of Ireland?
- How have political conflict and social issues been represented?

Television documentary and its hybrids

To those who still believe that documentary has a specific job to do, this mass access to audiences and quick answer is of paramount importance. It is something new in the documentary experience.[1]

In the age of broadcasting and beyond, the core issues of documentary representation resurface but in modified forms, from basic production methods to social, educational and political purposes. Non-fiction film and video-making remains a buoyant activity but it is significant that documentary is now virtually synonymous with television. The majority of documentary projects only become realised with some funding from television, often tied in with broadcast rights. Some practitioners continue to think of documentary primarily as an artistic, expressive activity using film for cinematic exhibition, rather than as an expositional tool of journalism in what Butler calls the 'institutionalised documentaries'[2] typified by current-affairs reports. In this chapter, we re-examine documentary in its diversity taking contemporary examples from Ireland, Britain and the USA and illustrating a variety of different formats and styles. We analyse the representation of Northern Ireland, emigration and contemporary socio-historical issues.

In order to set the context for a range of material, it is useful for us to revisit the term 'documentary' discussed earlier in chapter 4. Examples there included classic observational and expositional films like *Man of Aran* and *Mise Éire*. We also sampled different kinds of politically independent documentary, some of which were produced close to broadcasting institutions or borrowed the discursive attributes of investigative journalism, like *Radharc*, *The Irishmen* and *The Rocky Road to Dublin*. These films were marginalised and censored because of their subject matter and approach, but continued to have an alternative existence at the edge of cinema exhibition and without television screenings. Generally, however, the gradual assimilation into broadcasting from the 1950s kept alive and transformed established modes of documentary, as was recognised at the time by people like Paul Rotha. Modes formulated in the 1930s were challenged by different kinds of observational documentary in the radicalised climate of the 1960s. Using lighter cameras and smaller, portable sound-recorders, North American direct cinema got in close to its subject to produce greater authenticity but did not acknowledge the effects of the documentarist's presence. Recognising the problems with this, the same kinds of technologies were used by European *verité* practitioners to experiment. Proximity to subjects led in this practice to a more interactive, participant relationship with film-makers and more reflexive work.[3] Formal innovation came from reconsidering how new equipment could be adapted to produce documentary for television's home-based, family audiences. The socially integrative purpose envisaged in the 1930s for British cinema's documentary movement was transferred and accommodated in the 1950s at the start of the television era, allowing notions of social responsibility to survive within public service broadcasting.

A generation later, in the 1980s and 1990s, changes in political, institutional and technological conditions produced documentaries that used mixed modes more freely, hybridised new forms and became more reflexive. That is to say, the interest in the documentary is as much about the relations between the maker and the viewer as the viewer and the world that forms the context of the film. Documentaries increasingly integrated several subjective voices to present points of view on a topic, or adopted a first person mode of address. This is associated with the explosion in the use of video by non-professionals, the development of non-fiction programming within a television system whose basic public service tenets have been significantly challenged by commercial pressures. Television has appropriated some of these popular, innovative uses in new programme forms, like the video diary or compilation series. Other voyeuristic, confessional and affective television formats have proliferated, existing for entertainment more than information and education. Less common is the adoption of a poetic mode, as in elements of *Trouble the Calm* (1989), where there is a concern with using audio-visual images in an indirect, associative way to evoke or suggest rather than explicitly state or construct an argument like journalistic reportage.

Although evident from the early 1950s, the application of dramatising techniques and the adoption of dramatic formats to factual material have proliferated in the 1980s and 1990s. Its two main hybrids (in British terms) – drama-documentary and documentary-drama – have shared roots but also distinctive features.[4] Drama-documentaries – like *Shoot to Kill* – while based on events that occurred in real life and verifiable by journalistic documentation, nevertheless, predominantly use the conventions and codes of dramatic discourse. In documentary-drama the emphasis is different, using conventions and styles of filming developed in the 1960s that have come to signify 'documentariness'. Thus, rough sound, shaky framing, overlapping speech and surprised camera movements contribute to the look of documentary with its rhetorical sense of authenticity, keyed into real events. Documentaries like RTÉ's *Ballyseedy* and Lentin's *Dear Daughter*, use extensive, dramatised reconstruction sequences inserted into more conventional formats with vary-ing degrees of success as are discussed later.

This brief summary of some indicative developments in documentary is neither comprehensive nor exhaustive. It should not be taken to suggest a developmental progression or, alternatively, loss of a notional purity in docu-mentary form. The textual qualities of the film and video examples in this chapter are discussed in their own particular historical and political contexts. In its diverse forms, documentary remains concerned to represent truths about people and the real world, either in the past or the present. This may have an impetus that is investigative and campaigning for social reform and political justice or, simply, from the need for personal expression through moving images. A distinguished critic of documentary has observed that 'dramatisation has become a standard element in the popularisation of documentary journal-ism … merging "actuality" with "entertainment" values'.[5] Within this fusion, the integrity of seeking to inform, educate and to show the truth remains a potentially progressive force within democratic societies. *Death on the Rock* (1988) and *Dear Daughter* (1995) – two quite different examples – show that documentary amplifies rather than initiates investigative findings,[6] but in some instances it can nevertheless have significant social and political impact. The routine self-regulation of broadcasting, statutory policing legislation and a flexible ideological containment produce the status quo that some notable documentaries have sought to challenge. These are discussed in the next section on censorship.

Broadcasting, censorship and (Northern) Ireland

Irish and British broadcasting have been subject to different kinds and degrees of direct and indirect political censorship regarding Northern Ireland since the 1920s. News and current affairs have been most closely guarded, but documen-tary and drama have also been subject to constraint. The drive to censor has emanated internally, from within broadcasting institutions themselves, and externally in the form of statutory powers enforced by the state. For example, within the BBC, the controller of BBC Northern Ireland retains the right, estab-lished in 1937, to be consulted about and to veto transmission within Northern Ireland any Irish-related programme produced by the BBC.[7]

The Irish Broadcasting Act (1960) also had specific provisions – most notably within Section 31- that allowed a government to exercise stringent and blanket powers of censorship regarding Northern Ireland with punitive results for infringements. There are also similar statutory requirements on broadcast-ing in both Ireland and Britain to observe impartiality and balance in program-ming in a way that tends to support a dominant ideology and limit the range of political views that may be represented about contentious issues. For instance, from the early 1970s, Britain and Ireland developed different legislative and institutional codes to restrict the range of representation possible in news, current affairs and documentary features about Northern Ireland.[8] This censorship did not take the form of a classic totalitarian kind but it is the indeterminate and indirect forms that have done most to create a culture of censorship in Ireland and Britain in which considerable restriction is acceptable to many and a positive requirement to others.[9] While Section 31 in the Republic and the British restrictions of 1988–94 are the most overt examples, legislation not directly related to the media, such as the Prevention of Terrorism Act (1976; amended 1989) in the UK and the Offences Against the State Act (1939) in the Republic,[10] has been used by the police and law courts to harass, dissuade and, in some cases, imprison journalists who withheld their sources or material of sensitive investigations. In a wider context, the commercialisation of a public service broadcasting (PSB) system has produced an increasingly market-led, cautious and litigious climate in which the media operate. Indirectly, but no less decisively, this has skewed the kind of programmes that are commissioned, made and broadcast tending towards safer topics and less penetrating analysis of politically contentious subjects.

In the Republic, Section 31 had lain dormant for over a decade before it was invoked in 1971 by Gerry Collins (minister for posts and telegraphs) to forbid the transmission of 'a particular matter or any matter of a particular class [which] would be likely to promote or incite to crime or would tend to undermine the authority of the state'.[11] When the RTÉ authority (its executive officers) stood by its decision to broadcast an interview with an IRA spokesman, the entire authority was dismissed and a journalist served a four-month prison sentence. In 1976, Dáil Éireann approved an amendment whereby RTÉ was prohibited from broadcasting 'an interview, *or report of an interview* with a spokesman'[12] (my italics) from a list of paramilitary and political organisations, including several proscribed organisations in Northern Ireland. This effectively prevented the public from seeing, hearing or *hearing about* the ideas of people, including elected local and national politicians; a bizarre situation in a democratic state. Ironically, it also gave definitional power to a state (Northern Ireland), which, according to the constitution of the Irish Republic, had no legal status. Section 18, which prohibits incitement to violence on television, was invoked in 1987 by RTÉ itself against journalist Nell McCafferty after she explained that she supported the IRA. According to one commentator, the response in the Republic since the 1970s 'was generally in sympathy with the curtailment of journalistic freedom',[13] even though this undermined the credibility of broadcast journalism. The ban introduced specifically to deal with the treatment of Northern Ireland has had effects on other issues because Sinn Féin politicians, even if wishing to comment on unrelated matters, were prevented from appearing or being reported on RTÉ. The pervasive effect of the ban while it operated was to make all news and current-affairs programmes restricted and nervous because programme-makers tended to err on the side of caution. Section 31 contradicted and superseded RTÉ's other obligations to be impartial and objective. The fact that Irish multi-channel viewers could receive British transmissions meant that between 1976–88, the ban was circumvented and Section 31 was open to ridicule. The pernicious effect of the ban in the Republic, which was removed early in 1994 following the Downing Street Declaration, was to create a climate in which those who expressed opposition to it were demonised by implication as being pro-IRA.[14]

A similar state of affairs was reached in Britain by the late-1980s but by a different route. Liz Curtis has detailed how, since 1971, the BBC and ITV companies effectively censored themselves through internal working procedures gnomically termed 'reference upwards'.[15] The institutions strove to protect their status as an independent fourth estate free from government interference, while journalists were required to internalise a set of guidelines. Before engaging in any preliminary research or planning for a programme, let alone seeking an interview with a paramilitary group, journalists were required to consult formally with producers, who then contacted their seniors, and so on up the line of management to controller and senior executive level. The result was to act as a retard mechanism, to hold hostage journalists' professional integrity and inculcate inhibition. It was a form of self-censorship that was all the more effective and deleterious because, unlike the overt legislation exercised on RTÉ, it was a less obvious and low-key British way of operating.

The 1980s saw considerable friction develop between the British government and broadcasters over Northern Ireland as the state tried to 'patrol the borders' of people's minds via the media.[16] Three notorious examples of programmes within different series – *Real Lives*, *This Week* and *Nation* – are historically significant to illustrate the tightening censorship on broadcasting. Firstly, in 1985 the BBC's *Real Lives* episode, 'At the Edge of the Union', was attacked prior to transmission (and unseen) by the British prime minister Margaret Thatcher, and interfered with directly by Leon Brittan, the minister with responsibility for broadcasting. The programme presented in parallel two Derry-based MPs, Martin McGuinness (Sinn Féin) and Gregory Campbell (Democratic Unionist Party), showing their domestic lives and work and allowing them to voice opinions. The programme, shaped by its proximity to the BBC ethos, was 'impeccably balanced'[17] and had followed 'reference upwards' scrupulously. But Thatcher's government was increasingly worried about the growing electoral mandate of Sinn Féin. It was felt that showing McGuinness bouncing his baby on his knee at home normalised him whereas Campbell seemed more extreme and (legally) kept a gun in his kitchen cupboard. The BBC governors – some of whom aired such objections – capitulated to political pressure and banned the broadcast. Journalists were angry that the BBC's independence had been compromised and went on strike causing a twenty-four hour news blackout. The programme was eventually shown later in the year with minor amendments. Secondly, Thames TV's 1988 *This Week* episode, 'Death on the Rock', probed into the circumstances of the SAS killings of IRA members in Gibraltar and asked searching questions of the government's sanctioning of counter-insurgency tactics by security forces. It was a

37 Sub-titling Bernadette McAliskey on *Nation* (1991).
Courtesy of David Miller

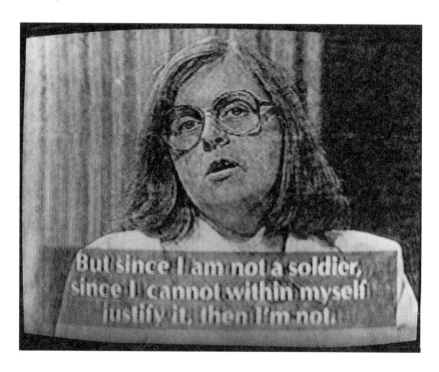

model of event-based investigative journalism. It used tightly organised material in the standard illustrative mode (images matching commentary), reconstructive sequences, interview and analysis to pose piercing questions of the state. The transmission of 'Death on the Rock' was defended by the IBA against government attack and tabloid press opprobrium. *This Week* editor Roger Bolton has described how footage of a car being exploded and the horrific effects of IRA's Enniskillen bombing were deliberately placed at the start of the filmed report in order to show his programme's condemnation of the IRA in anticipation of accusations of pro-IRA bias.[18] The British state's accountability and its definition of SAS actions in the national interest were the main targets of the programme's critique. *Death on the Rock's* methods were vindicated by an independent inquiry headed by a prominent lawyer, later published as *The Windlesham/Rampton Report* (1989).

The government's response to what it termed 'irresponsible journalism' was to introduce a set of broadcasting restrictions on 19 October 1988, which prohibited the broadcasting of 'any words spoken' where 'the person speaking the words represents or purports to represent' a proscribed organisation, or 'the words support or solicit or invite support for such an organisation'.[19] While not as self-evidently stringent as Section 31, the prohibition was sufficiently imprecise to induce reflexive caution among some broadcasters. Others saw that reported speech over visual images or subtitled or voice-over words could circumvent the restriction and even draw attention to the censorship process. The restrictions did not just apply to news and current affairs reportage; historical documentary footage and people stating views construed as support for Republicanism were also silenced. The editorial implications of this were graphically illustrated in a studio discussion programme, 'Killing for a Cause', part of the *Nation* series, produced independently for the BBC and shown in 1991. Bernadette McAliskey, a former MP known for republican socialist views, was part of a panel assembled to debate the issue of whether or not violence was justifiable for a political cause. Cases discussed included South Africa (ANC), Sri Lanka (Tamils) and Ireland (IRA), and views from the audience were actively sought. McAliskey's carefully nuanced answer and the articulate exposition of an elderly man (Tom Durkin) in the audience were subtitled even though the BBC *Guidelines* on factual programmes stated at that time that 'generalised comments about or even in favour of terrorism in Ireland or about Irish Republicanism are not prevented'.[20] As David Miller has commented, the idea 'that understanding the actions of the IRA could apparently be construed by the broadcasters as being identical to support for the IRA',[21] shows how paranoid, two-dimensional thinking breeds in a culture of censorship.

Channel Four's alternative Irelands

Since its inception in 1982, Channel Four TV has been a significant source of finance and exhibition for documentary films and videos about Ireland. Part of its distinctive remit was to represent alternative perspectives in the media, but its documentary output soon fell foul of broadcasting restrictions discussed above. *Mother Ireland* (1988), produced by Derry Film and Video Collective, a workshop initiative financially assisted by Channel Four in the mid-1980s, had the dubious honour of being the first programme to be banned under the 1988 restrictions. Researched, narrated and directed by Anne Crilly, the video examines the role and image of women in Irish history and culture from an interrogative position. It tackled some of the thorniest issues in the relationship between feminism and nationalism, republicanism and violence, without endorsing a particular viewpoint.[22] Produced on video to broadcast standards, it was a relatively cheap, easily distributed format and ideally suited for an alternative circulation at festivals, in community groups and colleges.

From collective, workshop origins, *Mother Ireland* is individually authored, oppositional in its political perspective and expositional in relation to its material. Its formal elements are conventionally recorded and assembled to maximise clarity: commentary and image are closely linked. A variety of images of 'mother Ireland' are shown (paintings, cartoons, statues, film footage), interwoven with popular song and music, and contextualised historically by Crilly's commentary and by a talking-head academic (Margaret MacCurtain). However, the strongest feature of the documentary is the set of diverse views given by Crilly's interviewees, including Bernadette McAliskey (political activist), Nell McCafferty (journalist), Pat Murphy (film-maker) and the Peppard sisters (women photographed for an Irish advertising campaign). These are contrasted with Sighle Humphries and Miriam James, surviving members of Cumann na mBhan, a women's organisation trained in arms, the former active during the 1916 Rising, along with present day Sinn Féin member, Rita O'Hare, and IRA member, Mairéad Farrell (who by the time the film was shown had been shot in Gibraltar by the SAS). The value of the video is to see women give their views on how they identified with the image of 'mother Ireland' and its links with nationalism. Some found it had positive qualities, others found it regressive or irrelevant. Editorial juxtaposition brought out the contestation and disagreement. The thing that the women had in common was a Catholic/nationalist upbringing in which Marian iconography proved influential in shaping their attitudes and behaviour. It has been suggested that the absence of Protestant/unionist women is an Achilles heel of the video,[23] but rather than a kind of spurious inclusivity it might be a more valuable project for a group of Protestant/unionist women to make a video about their attitudes to female figures produced in Irish and British culture.[24]

A year later in its 'Eleventh Hour' slot, *Trouble the Calm* (1989) was broadcast, though some sections were subtitled. This film was significant firstly for its indirect, expressive mode of representation as a documentary but also for its trenchant critique of the Fianna Fáil republicanism and corporate capitalism's domination of Ireland. Made by Dave Fox at the London-based Faction Films, its oppositional analysis is unashamedly socialist republican, its documentary method is visually and aurally highly associative, the voice-over commentary subjective and dead-pan. The central image suggested by the title itself is of the deceptiveness of an apparently smooth surface, contemporary Ireland's modernity, progressiveness and business potential. Beneath the preferred image of Ireland compliant to corporate financial interests, Fox's film argues that the implications of partition and civil war conflict remain unresolved. The state oppresses its own citizens and assists in extraditing them to British jurisdiction. The state dupes the population with a combination of media manipulation, advertising hype and political rhetoric, which has distorted its own historical origins in republicanism. A memorable image is repeated in the film showing a group of children being led across a road tied together for their safety but suggesting authoritarian shepherding. In another sequence, Taoiseach Charles Haughey (Fianna Fáil) is seen and heard making an annual commemorative speech over Wolfe Tone's grave in Bodenstown. Shot at a distance from among the tombstones at the back of the crowd, Haughey's cliché-ridden speech is intercut with shots of two gravediggers about their work while the head of government speaks. As an edited sequence it works beautifully. Haughey's rhetoric is undercut by the image of disinterested workers and Fox's dead-pan commentary. The fact that the diggers were filmed on the day *before* the speech – not during it – and edited in afterwards[25] does not invalidate the integrity or documentary truth of Fox's film. It is a healthy reminder that alternative and oppositional representations are no purer or less constructed than the audio-visual elements of documentary endorsing a dominant politics.

38 *Trouble the Calm* (1989).
Courtesy of Dave Fox/Faction Films

As a final example of Channel Four's record in commissioning material on Ireland that offered alternatives to the political consensus, Mary Holland and Michael Whyte's *Shankill* (1994) was the best newly-commissioned programme within 'The Long War', a season of programmes that explored the Troubles.[26] The makers of the award-winning *Creggan* (1980), about a nationalist housing estate, Holland and Whyte had considerable reputations. Their combined journalistic and film-making experience was brought to bear in representing on film a group of working-class Protestants from the Shankill Road in West Belfast. Although the early 1990s had witnessed more loyalist paramilitary killings than IRA, the film sympathetically reflected on the tragic loss to relatives of those killed by the IRA's Shankill bomb in November 1993 and the relative optimism created by the Downing Street Declaration.[27] *Shankill* used many of the audio-visual signifiers associated with Northern Ireland and loyalism. The exterior sequences are accompanied by a synthesised, melancholic pipe leitmotif music; visually the sequences comprise car-mounted tracking shots through urban wasteland or stationary, long takes in which children wander by, self-conscious of the camera. The film's structural logic is to alternate between exterior location sequences and interviews. Filmed against a whited-out studio, some of the interviewees are trained communicators, but most are ordinary people relating to an off-screen Holland. The film has a measured quality that presents a range of testimony from local people in the Shankill area that is moderate, reasonable, non-sectarian, compassionate and articulate. It did not include the voices of militant loyalists on the Shankill who supported the UVF and the UFF,[28] a telling absence chillingly corrected in Peter Taylor's BBC film *Loyalists* (1999). The Shankill is presented as a synecdoche for loyalism in crisis: 'It's a community in retreat, on almost every front', as Jackie Redpath explained, 'territorially, politically, economically, and culturally'. In a film that seeks to offer itself as a dispassionate study using restrained techniques, one brief shot in the film's opening sequence is slipped in between the predictable sights and sounds of marching bandsmen, flute music, streets, soldiers and children. A static medium shot of three elderly people in their back yard, looking at a large gold crown on a velvet pillow, is a bizarre, non-naturalist, richly associative image. It is not referred to in Holland's sparse, neutral commentary but is suggestive of unionism's symbolic political source: the British Crown.

Locally, transatlantically Irish? *Out of Ireland* (1994) and *The Uncle Jack* (1996)

Much contemporary documentary does not directly address the Troubles but deserves no less attention. In this section we examine two very different films that attempt to define personal material, which is shaped by local and global perspectives on Irish identities by their respective film-makers. Paul and Ellen Wagner's *Out of Ireland* (1994) is a feature-length documentary about the great historic drama of emigration to the USA that examines the causes and consequences of this transatlantic journey of Irish people, concentrating on the experience of Catholic émigrés. The film received a theatrical release in the USA,[29] was transmitted on local PBS cable TV in Boston and went to video sell-through, available for example in Irish airport retail outlets, intended for returning US visitors. The film production and educational informational values were high; its academic credentials were impeccable.[30] It featured well-known Irish and US talent, with Kelly McGillis narrating and Liam Neeson and Aidan Quinn, among others, reading in voice-over the emigrant letters. Writer John B. Keane and musician Michael Maloney appeared as native cultural experts. Paul Wagner's concept skilfully knitted together personal documentation of letters, individual and family stories, but traced these local origins on to a US national narrative that typified Irishness as an exemplar of modernity.

Structurally, the film is composed of fifteen segments, each varying in length from two to twelve minutes, organised chronologically but with a theme based on the letters of particular emigrants. Segment eight, 'Miraculous energy' – taking a phrase from a letter – dealt with the arrival and subsequent flourishing of Irish emigrants at the turn of the nineteenth century. Film footage of the Statue of Liberty and Ellis Island Immigration Centre is accompanied by the story of Annie Moore, the first immigrant to use the new reception centre.[31] McGillis's expositional commentary gives way to first the voice, then the talking heads of Dennis Clark and Hasia Diner, intercut with still period photographs. For these academics, there is a clearly articulated agenda for historical study at a time when the USA is absorbing a new generation of Asian and Latin American immigrants. Clarke states: 'America is not sure what it thinks and feels about these new immigrants. For us to understand their predicament, their problems in this fast-paced society, it's necessary for us to study the immigration of the past.' Hasia Diner's views in voice-over and to camera are used to reinforce the idea that 'if we can come to an understanding of one group who was compelled to leave its homeland … we have gone a long way to not only understanding American society … but a fundamental human experience'. These ideas articulate an educated, liberal humanitarian view, which seeks to be inclusive of different ethnicities by considering their experience as universally human. But modernity's fast-paced social and cultural movements test the limits of the concept of nation, referred to at the end of the film when Miller concedes that 'it is very difficult for us to deal with the reality of change using the ideas, concepts and rhetoric of the past'. Jarring with Clark and Diner's apparently postnationalist ideas, Richard O'Gorman's late-nineteenth-century letter (voiced by Gabriel Byrne) underpins the idea that the miraculous energy of the 'Celtic *race*' will fulfil a destiny in the USA. The visual track is bridged aurally from the black and white still to contemporary film with the sound of the sea, and McGillis's voice-over exposition is visualised by a sequence of individual shots: a shoreline, a dog running away from the camera up a lane ('nineteenth-century history'), a ploughshare foregrounded ('grinding poverty'), a castle ('landlord oppression') and a ruined, overgrown cottage ('horrors of the Great Famine'). Over a beautifully framed shot of a crucifix on a hill looking out to sea at dusk, the narrator explains that in response to their historical conditions the Irish 'created a transatlantic solution'; the traffic of people westwards and money eastwards. The segment closes looking forward to the early twentieth century and the next generation for whom emigration was 'not so much a refuge from disaster but a promise of fulfilment'.

Out of Ireland organises its audio-visual elements to evidence the idea that Catholic Irish immigrants have constructed a valid place for themselves in the USA such that subsequent generations ought to feel at home in, rather than hanker nostalgically for 'mother Ireland'. Its preferred reading of history attempts to revise traditional nationalism but in so doing mobilises the Irish case to allude to related debates about modernity and current xenophobia about Asian and Latin American immigration. Miller's reflection that 'in a sense we are all exiles', alternates between himself as interviewee in a head-and-shoulders shot and an associative image of a bird flying over the ocean (a wild goose?). He offers the idea that the Irish experience of emigration might provide a key for understanding the sense of rapid social change and uprooting, which he sees as typical of modern life: 'Like the Irish immigrants we all – or most of us – yearn nostalgically for some sort of fancied security that we had in childhood'. Miller's personalised delivery leaves it open at least to think that a lingering nostalgia for certainties may still lie at the heart of some inflections of 'postmodern Irishness'; an insecurity that the film's final narration tries to smooth over and assuage in its invocation to Irish migrants to 'come home – home to America'. If the Irish-American experience has been to wrestle with such contradictions, within Ireland itself home, childhood and the past have been increasingly subjected to searching reappraisal in indigenous documentaries, redefining the co-ordinates of what it is to be Irish.

The Uncle Jack (1996) is an intensely personal film in terms of subject matter but also in its method of production and the subjective mode of address that dominates. Although it is concerned with the emotional bond between John T. Davis (film-maker) and his uncle, Jack McBride – a leading cinema architect of his day – Davis has also created a visual history of Northern Ireland's cinema culture,[32] and a reflexive meditation on the nature of his own film-making. His films defy simple classification both as to their genre, but also in the range of subject matter.[33] He made a brilliant opening with *Shell Shock Rock* (1978), a film about punk rock in Northern Ireland, has made films in the USA like *Route 66* (1985) and *Hobo* (1991), and about Evangelism in Ireland like *Power in the Blood* (1989)[34] and *Dust on the Bible* (1990). In his own inimitable way, Davis's work explores fundamentalist, lonely or obsessed individuals, like Jack McBride (and Davis's own artistic and spiritual obsessions). In this respect his films offer insights into his native surroundings, Ulster Protestantism and 'that treacherous country of the past', that startle and penetrate in ways that escape the exposition and interview of institutionalised documentaries.[35]

39 A film-maker's reflexive look: *The Uncle Jack* (1996). Courtesy of John T. Davis

The film opens with a reconstructed scene from Davis's childhood, a boyhood epiphany, a vision of a bright yellow Texan Trainer aircraft over Belfast Lough. This changes to a darkened studio containing scale models of Jack McBride's cinema designs, the yellow Texan Trainer and Davis himself talking direct to camera. We learn that design, model aircraft, photography and film-making were the connections between uncle and nephew at the expense of the boy's paternal relations. Davis assembles a melange of drawings, family photos, amateur video footage of *The Tonic* cinema burning, archive footage from *Devil's Rock* (1938), Davis's own film recording of his parents' memories of cinema, Jack McBride's 8mm home movies from the postwar period, Davis's own first film (*Transfer*, 1975), actuality of a plane crash and Davis's short experimental films made from Jack's photograph collection. In one haunting image – a photo booth self-portrait – Jack had scratched out the eyes – representing his deterioration into paranoid obsession and breakdown. Davis's skilful, visually eclectic compilation is linked by his reflexive voice-over, snatches of music (some composed by his uncle) and even tape recordings made by his dead relative. Davis muses that his uncle repressed much of his creative and sexual expression to familial and class propriety; even the affection given to his nephew was a form of control from which the adolescent Davis was repelled. To

Davis, gazing at aircraft over Belfast Lough, 'flight was the most enduring inspi-
ration ... vapour trails to the USA, escape to North America ... clear from
cramped judgements and a way out of the claustrophobia which had smoth-
ered Jack'. He made his first film with Jack's own movie camera, passed down to
him at his uncle's death, and showed it in the USA, 'the gateway through which
I first escaped'. He regrets the neglect of George (his blood father) who died
during the production of *The Uncle Jack*, but takes solace from his memory
being recorded on film. Davis completes his film by flying the scale replica of
the Texan Trainer we saw at the opening. He acknowledges the influences of
both paternal figures to his life and the closing voice-over speaks of film-
making's intellectual, spiritual and physical freedoms to an evocative 'Yippee-
ah-ay' reprise of the soundtrack from '(Ghost) Riders in the Sky'.

Forbidden territories of the past? RTÉ and contemporary documentary

RTÉ has a considerable institutional pedigree in television non-fiction genres
and has produced many accomplished journalists and documentarists. Since
the establishment of the Independent Production Unit (IPU) in 1993, RTÉ has
commissioned work that has been significant in wider cultural initiatives to
explore sensitive areas of Irish society and history, including the Catholic
church, taboos concerning sexual identity and exploitation and the Irish civil
war. Whereas RTÉ had suppressed Cathal Black's *Our Boys* (1980) for over a
decade, the IPU was prepared to commission, co-fund with the Irish Film
Board and broadcast Louis Lentin's *Dear Daughter* (1996). In a society in which
mass attendance is high, respect for the Church traditionally strong and the
value placed upon motherhood and family historically prioritised by the state,
Dear Daughter's account of the systematic physical abuse of illegitimate babies
and children under the care of the Sisters of Mercy nuns in Goldenbridge
(Dublin) could not be anything but disturbing and controversial. A veteran
television producer and director,[36] Lentin became interested in this subject
following Christina Buckley's revelations about her childhood on Gay Byrne's
radio show in 1992. Shot on Beta SP video, *Dear Daughter* used a compelling
mix of documentary techniques intercut with extended dramatised sequences
to render childhood experiences from the 1950s and 1960s. Buckley[37] and other
female interviewees presented disturbing accounts of cruelty and criminal
abuse by particular nuns, allegations which have not been refuted by the
order.[38] The programme's broader narrative – Buckley's search for her white
Irish mother and black African father (a Nigerian medical student) – was given
fuller treatment in a longer proposal that was initially turned down by RTÉ. In
the fifty-eight minute broadcast version, costing £100,000, the emphasis falls
more on the presentation of the women's experiences and a calling to account
of the nuns. The parental search narrative is provided by the programme's
opening hook, Buckley's own direct-to-camera statement: 'I wanted to find my
parents and kill them ... [to say] ... see, what I'm suffering for the likes of you'.

At the start, the film uses a mediating male voice-over (Bosco Hogan) to set the scene but this gives way to the strength of the subjective, personal narratives of the women themselves, none of which was formally scripted. The documentary combined dramatised reconstruction sequences, slow motion and affective incidental piano music to evoke Buckley's childhood memories of her beatings, abuse and humiliation. From these monochrome sequences using a child actress (Jasmine Quinlan) to signify the past, the film then bled back to colour and the other surviving women as interviewees in the present. With the women's consent, Lentin chose a disjunctive technique whereby Buckley and other *adult*, surviving victims were filmed in a Dublin priory architecturally similar to Goldenbridge. At workroom benches the women re-enacted their childhood actions while speaking to camera, in an experience of reliving and telling that was particularly arresting to the viewer. They recounted how as young girls they were forced to string rosary beads on wire for long periods even while their fingers were lacerated. Paradoxically, at a time when the church extolled the virtues of mission work for black babies in Africa, Buckley recalls in the film that she was called a 'black bastard' and Lentin has noted that her 'skin colour was a reason for even more brutal treatment'. Racist phobia about miscegenation and a warped Christian morality clearly justified sadistic abuse in some nuns' minds. Indeed, one reviewer felt that 'still hanging unaddressed

40 Race and religion in *Dear Daughter* (1996).
Courtesy of Louis Lentin/Crescendo Concepts/*Film Ireland*

in the aftermath of the programme is the issue of race in Irish society'.[39] While the film concentrated on the personal experiences of half a dozen women (out of some twenty contacted by Lentin), these were presented as not untypical, as the response to the broadcast and the programme's extra-textual life subsequently indicated.

The Sisters of Mercy had declined to participate in the programme except for a statement given on-camera by a spokeswoman, Helena O'Donoghue, at the end of which she said the order was 'deeply distressed, deeply disturbed by these stories, these recollections [and asked] in some way for forgiveness … it was a dark side of our history that we deeply regret'. *Dear Daughter* was broadcast on RTÉ1 on 22 February 1996, watched by 940,000 viewers (remarkably, nearly a third of the country's *total* population), capturing 76 per cent of the TV share figure (all those watching television, including satellite).[40] It prompted hundreds of calls to a telephone help line set up by the Sisters of Mercy and a considerable degree of debate was generated in the press and other media. In *The Irish Times*, Michael Foley questioned the dramatising methods employed by Lentin, said that the film was unbalanced and suggested that some of the testimonials needed more rigorous substantiation and that media journalists should be sceptical of claims being made.[41] As if to provide a right of reply, *Prime Time* (RTÉ's own current affairs programme) did a programme on *Dear Daughter* and the ageing Sister Xavieria was interviewed. She denied the substantive points, was not pressed by the interviewer and came out of the report quite favourably from other interviewees' testimonies. The women in *Dear Daughter* were deeply hurt, Buckley felt the Sisters were being let off the hook and Lentin felt that *Prime Time's* report was institutionally calculated, not as a 'right of reply, [but] was a deliberate undermining of *Dear Daughter*'. He has repeatedly called for a public inquiry to be set up by the government to assemble evidence for a file that could be presented to the director of public prosecutions, although this has not taken place to date.[42] Although the Irish public witnessed a greater degree of media exposure and examination of institutional abuses of authority during the early 1990s,[43] the debate and discomfiture produced by *Dear Daughter* showed this kind of documentary to be socially significant. It also seems to indicate tensions within RTÉ itself and Irish society more widely as to the extent to which the collective past should be opened up. Despite Lentin's view that 'TV is no longer allowed to articulate popular feeling', other commentators see dramatised documentary modes and 'trauma drama'[44] based on disputed events as being effective means of articulating *already existing* popular frustrations about corruption or lack of accountability within powerful social and political establishments such as the church, governments, the police or corporate business.

A week later in the same slot on RTÉ1, Liam McGrath's *Male Rape* (1996) presented a documentary on criminal sexual deviance. The potential for voyeuristic reception if not style was an issue anticipated by one interviewee who said that for viewers unfamiliar with the topic, the 'main interest is graphic details – not how you felt afterwards'. The film presented the experiences of six men who had been the victims of rape and sexual abuse by gangs of school peers, an elder female sibling, adults in trust and anonymous, random attacks. That such crimes and their long-term after-effects were insufficiently recognised in Irish society was attested by the closing caption that informed viewers that 'over 800 men contacted Irish Rape Crisis centres in the six months it took to complete this film'. McGrath, following a method he employed with *Boys for Rent* (1995),[45] investigating male prostitution, married the five to eight minute interviewee voice tracks with two kinds of arresting visual sequences; some were black and white and reconstructive, others were associative, grainy and, at times, surreal. Personal testimony was paramount, carried by the different voices – sometimes cracked with emotion, at other times clear, angry and articulate – which moved between recalling events and reflective thoughts about those memories. Added to this subjective voice track, sound effects (breathing, traffic sounds, car door, undergrowth, wind) were used to reinforce the short, acted sequences. While the first five interviewees were shot variously (silhouetted, back lit, in extreme close ups) to maintain anonymity, the final, oldest interviewee was seen full-face in a head-and-shoulders shot, reporting that he had learned with time to 'sever the grip of the abuser' by sharing his memories with his wife.[46] This programme, more so even than *Dear Daughter*, aimed to 'break the silence'[47] about contemporary social life and presented aspects of what we have termed an Irish subaltern history, the kind of experience that is missing from official accounts, that in its utterance is disruptive of the dominant, national discourses of church and state institutions but also the gendered discourses of Irish sexuality.[48]

The final example from RTÉ's contemporary production returns us to the public debate about the significance of the civil war in Ireland, popularised beyond academia by Neil Jordan's film, *Michael Collins* (1996). The documentary, *Ballyseedy* (1997), was a project researched, scripted and presented by Pat Butler, directed and produced by RTÉ's Frank Hand. Although set in a national context, it pivots on the juxtaposition of a folk memory of a local incident in March 1923 at Ballyseedy, County Kerry, with official state documentation from the period.[49] It set out to remind RTÉ's viewers of atrocities carried out by soldiers of the Free State army as reprisals against the IRA's use of booby-trap mines during the civil war. It made a case to indict senior military men and politicians for a cover up of what would now be considered war crimes perpetrated by the national army.

Despite this topic and the revelatory rhetoric of its pre-publicity[50] and commentary ('documents in our possession', 'until *now*'), *Ballyseedy* was cumbersome, laboured and old-fashioned in its methods. The controlling narrator (Butler himself) was both a voice-over and an on-screen, on-location, story-telling presence.[51] The documentary made some use of talking-head academics and a local historian in a field, but much weight was given to eye witnesses and other interviewees (children at the time or present-day relatives of protagonists), including retrieved footage from a BBC TV history first shown in 1981. Actors (dressed in period costume) were used to read from official state papers, published memoirs and private papers. Still photographs, newspaper cuttings and newsreel footage were the visuals that connected extensive and repeated sequences of dramatic reconstruction (sepia-tinted monochrome), framed by narrative voice-over, map graphics and on-screen captions. The RTÉ Orchestra punctuated this panoply of visual evidence and documentation with an affective incidental music score.

Ironically, *Ballyseedy* is a victim of its own thoroughness, over-burdened by minutiae in both its research synthesis and production details. The dramatised sequences often labour already-established points without adding insight and some are even repeated from a different angle or in slow motion. At one level, the film simply exhausts the viewer's attention and becomes tedious, but at another level, as Harvey O'Brien has argued, the film failed to demonstrate contemporary historiographical awareness, it 'failed to stretch the conventions of docudrama to explore the subjectivity of personal history' and was 'unlikely to contribute significantly either to the consideration of Irish history, or to the advancement of docudrama as a medium of historical reconstruction'.[52] While the civil war remains sensitive territory in Irish history, *Ballyseedy's* five-year production gestation made it seem curiously out-of-joint at the moment of its broadcast. It struggled to be convincingly even-handed about the exigencies of civil war and the repressed unconscious of an older republicanism bubbled up through the script and visualisation. That it looked and sounded old-fashioned in the wake of Ireland's political and televisual developments in the 1990s is not to dismiss its significance as a piece of cultural history. It demonstrates that historical and aesthetic progress is rarely linear and that folk memory retains a potency despite the forensic claims of revisionism.

In this chapter, we have explored how documentary has developed in the television era, transforming and hybridising forms that existed in film documentary to produce texts that are increasingly more reflexive, formally variegated and discursively dramatic. Technical innovation, coupled with particular social uses – that are themselves determined by wider political ideologies and trends in cultural production – have produced a diverse range of non-fiction material broadly called documentary, which has been examined in selected case studies. This chapter has argued that responsible, investigative and informative films retain the capacity to be a progressive force within the societies in which they are made and shown. While contemporary documentary is no longer associated with – nor perhaps is capable of producing – the kinds of national social cohesion envisaged by some of its earliest film practitioners, it can powerfully articulate the histories, identities and aspirations of what we have elsewhere in this book called the subaltern in Ireland's past and present culture. We have seen how documentaries about unresolved and awkward political, social and ethical issues have been subject to different kinds of censorship on public service television in Ireland as well as in Britain. In certain periods, the corrosive combination of self-censorship and statutory legislation made it difficult for certain topics and social taboos in Irish life to be easily and honestly represented on television. Even though in the 1990s there may have been a spirit of opening up Ireland's past to investigation and documentation, market-driven commissioning policies within British and Irish television acted to limit the parameters for contemporary documentary both in terms of subject matter and style.

Notes

1 Paul Rotha, the BBC's first head of documentaries for television, in an unpublished memorandum, 'Television and the future of documentary' (1954), quoted in E. Bell, 'The origins of British television documentary: The BBC 1946–1955', in J. Corner (ed.), *Documentary and the Mass Media* (London, Arnold, 1986), 71.

2 D. Butler, *The Trouble with Reporting Northern Ireland* (Aldershot, Hampshire, Avebury, 1995), 116.

3 R. Kilborn and J. Izod, *An Introduction to Television Documentary: Confronting reality* (Manchester, Manchester University Press, 1997), 66–71.

4 This distinction was first proposed by John Caughie in 'Progressive television and documentary drama', *Screen*, 21:3 (1980). P. Kerr, 'F for fake? Friction over faction', in A. Goodwin and G. Whannel (eds), *Understanding Television* (London, Routledge, 1990), 76, insists that as such drama-documentary is not 'a universal or ahistorical programme category, but a historically specific controversy about such categories, not so much a distinct genre as a debate about genre distinctions'. D. Paget has skilfully integrated theoretical debates and current developments in practice for both the USA and British television in *No other way to tell it: Dramadoc/docudrama on television* (Manchester, Manchester University Press, 1998).

5 J. Corner, *The Art of Record* (Manchester, Manchester University Press, 1996), 32.

6 B. Winston, *Claiming the Real* (London, British Film Institute, 1995), 237.

7 R. Cathcart explains the historical circumstances for this in *The Most Contrary Region: The BBC in Northern Ireland* (Belfast, Blackstaff Press, 1984), 278–81. This veto remains in the current *Producers' Guidelines* (London, BBC, 1996), 134–6. Thanks to Professor Olga Edridge for supplying a copy.

8 This censorship has been analysed in detail in a range of influential work, including L. Curtis, *Ireland: The propaganda war* (London, Pluto Press, 1984); C. Ó Maoláin, *No Comment: Censorship and the Irish Troubles* (London, Article 19, 1989); D. Miller, *Don't Mention the War: Northern Ireland, propaganda and the media* (London, Pluto Press, 1994); Butler, *Trouble with Reporting Northern Ireland*; A. F. Parkinson, *Ulster Loyalism and the British Media* (Dublin, Four Courts Press, 1998).

9 M. Kelly and B. Rolston, 'Broadcasting in Ireland: Issues of national identity and censorship', in P. Clancy *et al.* (eds), *Irish Society: Sociological perspectives* (Dublin, Institute of Public Administration, 1995), 577.

10 B. Rolston, 'Political censorship', in *Let in the Light* (Dingle: Kerry, Brandon, 1993), 161–5, argues that the British Official Secrets Act (1911) and the Police and Criminal Evidence Act (1984), the Northern Irish Criminal Law Act (1967) and the Republic of Ireland's Official Secrets Act (1963) were used to threaten, dissuade and convict journalists.

11 Cited by B. Purcell, 'The silence of Irish broadcasting', in B. Rolston and D. Miller (eds), *War and Words: A Northern Ireland media reader* (Belfast, Beyond the Pale, 1996), 255.

12 Cited in Ó Maoláin, *No Comment*, 34.

13 P. Feeney, 'Censorship and RTÉ', *The Crane Bag*, 8:2 (1984), 64.

14 The above points are made in Purcell, 'Silence of Irish broadcasting', 258–64.

15 L. Curtis, *Ireland: The propaganda war* (Belfast, Sásta, 1998), 173–96.

16 G. Murdock, 'Patrolling the border: British broadcasting and the Irish question in the 1980s', *Journal of Communication*, 14:4 (1991), 104–15.

17 Butler, *Trouble with Reporting Northern Ireland*, 125.

18 R. Bolton, *Death on the Rock and Other Stories* (London, Optomen/W. H. Allen, 1990), 220–1.

19 BBC, *Producers' Guidelines* (London, BBC, 1989), Appendix 5.

20 BBC, *Producers' Guidelines*, 40, cited in Miller, *Don't Mention the War*, 57.

21 D. Miller, 'Censoring Northern Ireland', in G. Philo (ed.), *Glasgow Media Group, Volume 2: Industry, economy, war and politics* (London, Routledge, 1995), 60.

22 S. Edge, 'Representing gender and national identity', in D. Miller (ed.), *Rethinking Northern Ireland* (Harlow, Essex, Longman, 1999), 221.

23 B. McIlroy, *Shooting to Kill*, (Trowbridge: Wiltshire, Flicks Books, 1998), 133.

24 See B. Loftus, 'Mother Ireland', *Circa*, 44 (March/April 1989), 33–4; and B. Loftus, '"Mother Ireland" and loyalist ladies', *Circa*, 51 (May–June 1990), 20–3. For signs of debate among unionist women and those in the loyalist community, see Rhonda Paisely, 'Feminism, unionism and "the brotherhood"', *The Irish Reporter*, 8 (1992), 32–3. See also the interviews in M. Hyndman (ed.), *Further Afield: Journeys from a Protestant past* (Belfast, Beyond the Pale, 1996).

25 Fox was challenged on the production of this sequence at a conference in Ulster as reported in Butler, *Trouble with Reporting Northern Ireland*, 128.

26 L. Pettitt, 'A camera-woven tapestry of Troubles', reviews the BBC and Channel Four output in July and August 1994, *Irish Studies Review*, 8 (Autumn 1994), 54–6.

27 Desmond Bell's ethnographic video work is worth considering for its examination of Protestantism, especially its youth culture. *Redeeming History* (1991) and *Out of Loyal Ulster* (1993) are available at the Film and Sound Resource Unit at the University of Ulster, Coleraine. See also his book, *Acts of Union: Youth Culture and Sectarianism in Northern Ireland* (Basingstoke, Hampshire, Macmillan, 1990)

28 R. Bennett, 'Hearing voices', *Sight and Sound*, 4:7 (July 1994), 22–3.

29 For a review of its initial release see, *Variety* (31 October 1994), 91, and its video release, *Variety* (5 June 1995), 27. *Out of Ireland* had a theatrical release in Dublin and was favourably reviewed by P. Power, *Film West*, 20 (Spring 1995), 36.

30 Kerby Miller and Paul Wagner, *Out of Ireland: The story of Irish emigration to America* (London, Aurum Press, 1994) was published to accompany the film. Miller is a respected specialist in the field, author of *Emigrants and Exiles: Ireland and the Irish exodus to North America* (Oxford, Oxford University Press, 1985). The principal historical consultant, Miller assisted with the script and appeared as a talking head. The research for the film was assisted by a grant from the District of Columbia's Community Humanities Council; scripting and production received funds from the National Endowment for the Humanities; and post-production was done at the Media Centre of the Virginia Foundation for the Humanities. The film's commentary was incorrect in one detail, however, in that it stated (87 minutes) that the treaty

of 1921 caused the partition of Ireland. In fact, this was achieved by the Government of Ireland Act (1920) and a separate parliament for Northern Ireland had already been formally opened before the treaty was signed in late 1921. US film students may wish to refer to *The Long Journey Home: The Irish in America*, funded by Walt Disney, whose four-part structure titles suggests an upward trajectory of immigrant achievement: 1) Great Hunger, 2) All Across America, 3) Up from City Streets, 4) Success.

31 While the film shows immigrants disembarking, it must post-date 1892 as moving images did not exist until three years later.

32 The UTV/Channel Four series *A Seat Among the Stars: The cinema and Ireland* (1984) did weave Ulster into a history of cinema in Ireland. See also M. Open, *Fading Lights and Silver Screens* (Antrim, Northern Ireland, Greystone Books, 1985).

33 'I don't know what my films are. I don't think of them as documentaries and they're not fiction, but there's drama in them and some description even though they are not acted', as quoted in McIlroy, *Shooting to Kill*, 147.

34 For a review of this film about a US country singer turned evangelist who visits paramilitary converts in prison in Northern Ireland, see T. Sheehy, 'Northern skyline', *Film Base News*, 12 (April–May 1989), 16.

35 McIlroy's (1998) recent consideration of Davis's oeuvre in a chapter called 'Protestant visions', 149–51, could be extended to encompass *The Uncle Jack* (1996). For an excellent Davis interview, see D. Lavery, 'Power in the lens', *Film Ireland*, 32 (November–December 1992), 18–21.

36 Lentin was responsible for RTÉ's highly acclaimed and formally innovative *Insurrection* (1966), shown over eight consecutive nights during Easter week 1966 to commemorate the fiftieth anniversary of the Rising. It presented historical events in a nightly live news reportage format, freely combining imitation actuality, documentary conventions and extensive dramatised reconstruction. Non-referenced quotations in the text are taken from a detailed fax (2 March 1999) and subsequent telephone interview with Lentin about the production.

37 L. Kavanagh, 'Christine's tale', *RTÉ Guide*, 20:8 (16 February 1996), 64–5.

38 At the insistence of the Sisters of Mercy, a particular nun in question, Sister Xavieria, was not named in *Dear Daughter*. It is worth knowing that Channel Four TV's series, *Witness*, broadcast 'Love in a Cold Climate' (16 March 1998), which examined the cases of women abused and psychologically damaged while at institutions in Ireland run by nuns. Such places were repositories for illegitimate children, unmarried mothers, prostitutes and other 'fallen women' ostracised by society, condemned by the Catholic church and barely provided for by the state. A recent *60 Minutes* documentary (3 January 1999) in the USA reported on the Magdelene laundries in Dublin. Videotape orders can be made at '60 Minutes', 524 West 57th Street, NY 10019. Telephone 800–848–3256. Testimony Films can be contacted at 12 Great George Street, Bristol BS1 5RS, England. Telephone 0117–925–8589.

39 T. Sheehy, *Film Ireland*, 52 (April–May 1996), 33.

40 Statistics kindly provided by RTÉ Audience Research Unit.

41 'Lack of balance in coverage of "Dear Daughter"', *The Irish Times* (19 March 1996), 12.

42 L. Lentin, 'Doubting the orphanage victims' truthfulness only betrays them again', *The Irish Times* (5 April 1996), 12. See also Lentin's letter, 'Silence after "Dear Daughter"', *The Irish Times* (17 March 1998), 15, which chastised the police for only being interested in sexual abuse cases.

43 For instance, Cardinal Cathal Daly's attempted explanation of the church's cover up of the paedophile priest, Brendan Smyth.

44 Jane Feuer's term is cogently discussed in Paget, *No other way to tell it*, 171.

45 For an analysis of the representation of sexuality in *Boys for Rent*, see L. Pettitt, 'Pigs and prostitutes, provos and prejudice', in E. Walshe (ed.), *Sex, Nation and Dissent in Irish Writing* (Cork, Cork University Press, 1997), 275–7.

46 For a programme with such unfamiliar subject matter, it attracted an audience share of 11 per cent or 370,000 viewers, comprising 217,000 female and 153,000 male viewers. Statistics from the RTÉ Audience Research Unit.

47 F. Walsh. 'Breaking the silence', *RTÉ Guide*, 20:9 (23 February 1996), 8.

48 T. McAdam's three-part film, *Hoodwinked* (1997), a recent attempt to document the history of women in post-1922 Ireland, was produced independently for RTÉ. Copies available from East Lane Films, 6 Sandycove East Lane, Sandycove, County Dublin.

49 Shown on RTÉ1 in November 1997, *Ballyseedy* was watched by 411,000 viewers (12 per cent of the TV audience), most of whom were in the 55 and above age group category, with a distinct provincial weighting to the figures towards Munster. Clearly, this programme attracted close relations and participants from the region in which the events depicted took place. Statistics from the RTÉ Audience Research Unit.

50 P. Kehoe, 'Tragedies of Kerry', *RTÉ Guide*, 21:46 (7 November 1997), 18 and 44. This publicity misleadingly, in my view, labels the programme as a drama-documentary. While there were substantial sequences of dramatised reconstruction and shorter inserts in which costumed actors assumed the roles of historical figures to read from their letters or diaries, it does not constitute drama-documentary as I have defined it nor as exemplified in chapter 11.

51 For a similar presentational device, see Kenneth Griffith's to-camera delivery of Michael Collins' life story in ATV's, *Hang up Your Brightest Colours* (1973), which was banned from British television until 1993 for its partisan eulogy to Collins. It is available on video in the USA from The Cinema Guild, New York, and distributed in the UK and Ireland (along with *Curious Journey*) by Global Visions, London. For an example of a more conventional on-screen historian in expositional, interpretative mode, see Robert Kee's thirteen-part BBC historical series, *Ireland: A television history* (1980–81). Researchers and students might also wish to compare the representational strategies of RTÉ's *The Shadow of Béal na Bláth* (1988) in reconstructing the still-disputed circumstances of Michael Collins' death in Cork in 1922. Thanks to Nessan Danaher for a copy of this film.

52 H. O'Brien, *Film Ireland*, 62 (December 1997–January 1998), 39–40. Following O'Brien's review, a terse exchange of letters between film-maker and critic was published. See P. Butler, *Film Ireland*, 63 (February–March 1998), 46, and H. O'Brien, *Film Ireland*, 64 (April–May 1998), 45.

CHAPTER 11

TELEVISION DRAMA AND THE TROUBLES

- What role does drama have within public service television?
- What have been the dominant formats and themes in Troubles dramas on TV?
- Has TV fiction followed the Troubles or imagined its future turns?

Television drama in a dramatised society[1]

Television is no subversive demon . . . [its] . . . function has been to reinforce the central value system of the society it serves and the dominant mode it has used has been primarily dramatic.[2]

The TV news coverage of the civil rights march attacked by the RUC on 5 October 1968 was filmed by RTÉ and UTV camera teams. Overnight Northern Ireland became an international media story. News editors at the BBC opted to buy the RTÉ footage for that evening's programme because it was 'much more dramatic film'.[3] Even for ostensibly factual programmes, the political conflict in Northern Ireland presented itself to broadcasters as requiring dramatic treatment. Since then, television drama departments have produced a considerable volume of material on the Troubles, creating a sub-genre whose significance has yet to be fully evaluated.[4] The aims of this chapter are to make an argument for the significance of drama, to provide a concise history of Troubles drama production by the BBC and British independent companies, and to present selective analyses of the key productions in different formats ranging from the single play (both as adaptation and original screenplays), series drama and prime-time drama-documentary.

Much of this fictional exposition has, however, struggled in an institutional environment circumscribed by periodic direct censorship, restrictive codes of practice and a deeper cultural myopia. Unsurprisingly, television drama about Northern Ireland has tended to endorse the political status quo. On occasion the hegemonic views of political and cultural élites have been challenged, but effective interventions using drama from within influential cultural institutions such as the BBC have been intermittent, not an organised campaign by 'the Brits Out of Telly Centre'.[5] Nor have individual programmes 'glorified the IRA'[6] at the expense of the RUC. Nor has there been, as McIlroy has claimed, a 'masked posture' against the British presence in Northern Ireland.[7] However, the creative dissidence of many writers and directors tends to lead them away from received ideas and formal political ideologies, to the possibility of imagining situations and emotions beyond mere verisimilitude, historical fact or autobiographical experience. Many of the writers discussed in this chapter have offered qualified questioning if not radical revisions of their cultural inheritances and political ideologies. This chapter argues that in some cases TV drama has pre-empted political events of the future, allowed fresh insights into the past and displayed the capacity to make people interrogate received ideas. Moreover, drama can be a means whereby 'you can vicariously live the lives of people that you wouldn't normally expect to know or understand. That's why drama is important – it's a journey of the imagination'.[8]

Understanding contexts for TV drama production

However, television drama is not made in a creative free space but is shaped by the economic, cultural and ideological forces within broadcasting's institutions and routines of production that have developed historically. British television has been funded by a mixture of public money in the form of a licence fee and commercial investment, deeply imbued with a public service ethos that remains but is being forced to reinvent itself in circumstances over which it has lessening control. Since the neo-liberal economic changes of the 1980s, television has become more commercialised. In particular, the BBC operates in an international audio-visual market but remains a national institution. One of the cornerstones of public service television has been its avowed commitment to the cultural value of drama within a mixed schedule of programmes. However, national institutions like the BBC contain both conservative and progressive currents, which are reflected in tensions between programme-makers and managerial executives, and on another level between the institution and the state. Television drama is no less prone to such tensions. A residual, patrician strain conservatively argues for drama on TV, stressing the educative benefits of high cultural traditions that are brought to a large audience. Another broadly progressive current tends to see the role of TV drama – particularly in contemporary work – to challenge as well as entertain millions of viewers in their own homes. Within commercial television companies, the market-driven production of inoffensive, popular drama series compete with writing that seeks to engage broad audiences with controversial topics. A progressive view, epitomised by, for example, Granada TV, advocating both single drama and series/serials is set against a degree of conservative, institutional inertia and commercial imperatives, which work to absorb, incorporate and contain radical ideas and new ways of making drama. These tensions are particularly highlighted in TV drama related to Northern Ireland.

Aesthetically, TV drama has evolved from its origins in radio and influences from theatre to a much closer set of links with the medium of film and the institution of cinema. This has had consequences for the visual look or aesthetics of drama on television. TV drama from the 1950s and 1960s tended to be studio-bound by cumbersome equipment, featured ponderous long-takes and was broadcast live. This tele-theatre retained the sense that it was a one-off theatrical performance on a small screen for quite some time after videotape became available for use in Britain in the late 1950s.[9] The relatively new medium of television employed technical and creative personnel from radio and the theatre, in particular, bringing their habits and prejudices with them. But television also gave opportunities for rank beginners to experiment with and shape the medium. Studio scenes were sometimes mixed with telecine inserts of sequences shot on film but it was not until the 1970s that TV drama was being routinely shot on 16mm film, usually for prestige productions, such as the BBC 'Play for Today' series (1970–84), making full use of locations. The idea of an absolute distinction between television drama and cinema film was further complicated after 1982 with Channel Four's pioneering 'Film on Four' initiative, which accelerated television's involvement in financing, commissioning and showing film. The economic and political contexts for TV production altered during the 1980s and, in a decisive initiative to make the corporation a leading producer of films, the BBC appointed Mark Shivas as head of drama in 1988, indicating that 'there was indeed a period of revolutionary change in the two or three years around 1990'.[10] Under legislation of that year, the BBC was forced to engage in commissioning programme material from sources outside the corporation. It set itself targets for programme production from the BBC's regional centres and under the ethos of 'Extending Choice' (1993), changed its budgeting arrangements to create an internal market within the institution. One of the BBC's most successful drama departments in the 1990s was that based in Northern Ireland under the leadership of Robert Cooper. In the relationship between British television and film, which has undergone a series of difficult negotiations since the 1960s, it may be argued that 'film opened out the televisual experience and that it rescued television drama from its theatrical influences'.[11]

At moments of extreme crisis, politicians resistant to change have questioned the BBC and ITV companies for making exploratory TV dramas about Northern Ireland. But a variety of counter-arguments have been set out over the years by television executives, producers and TV commentators about the importance of drama in television schedules. To some, the production of television drama from within Northern Ireland itself demonstrates that not all the forces in the province are destructive. Drama becomes 'a way of representing the creative vitality of two communities [and this is] one way in which the BBC may play a constructive role in Northern Ireland's divided society'.[12] Others again, perhaps mindful of the censorship of news, current affairs and documentary programmes, are alert to the idea that fiction may potentially provide more engaging forms of television, arguing that 'drama can paint a more accurate picture of the situation in Northern Ireland'.[13] Drama is not required to be balanced or impartial like news and may engage a wider audience through its dramatic rather than documentary conventions to afford 'imaginative insights into the complexity of the situation'.[14] It would be a mistake, however, to believe that television drama is inherently challenging. Much of it may in fact reinforce received ways of seeing a situation and 'defining "normality" – that most powerful of concepts in a frightened society'.[15] The specific conditions at the heart of political difference and social conflict may be dissolved or transformed into narratives and images that appeal to so-called universal, human qualities or individual character traits, especially when produced for audiences outside Northern Ireland in Britain, Ireland and international TV markets.

Traditionally, the credibility of TV drama has been underpinned by the idea that it allows individual authors to express their personal convictions, rather than in cinema, which tends to prioritise the creative influence of the film's director. This privileging of the TV dramatist is due in part to the particular antecedents of television, the initial need felt in the 1950s and 1960s to justify television as a worthwhile medium by its attachment to the high cultural values of theatre. Whereas much of the non-fiction output of television is explicitly conditioned by guidelines and institutionalised discourse, drama is valued not only for its entertainment but its ability to 'say the unsayable, think the unthinkable',[16] as Ann Devlin has put it. The BBC and commercial television alike have nurtured the idea of creative authorship in drama for commercial reasons but also importantly for cultural kudos. The BBC, Channel Four and some long-standing ITV companies actively court particular writers and commission innovative, controversial or new writing talent to prove their critical independence, demonstrate their role as cultural leaders in new ideas and maintain ratings or serve niche audiences. However, if a drama does challenge a consensual view, it is usually carefully tagged by pre-publicity and continuity announcements as personal; that is, distanced from the institution itself. There are, then, three different kinds of tensions at play in drama production. First, writers insist on their right to creative expression, facilitated and defended by commissioning editors, progressive directors and producers. But executive controllers, senior management and governors tend to be more conservative and cautious. Second, it is important to realise that the institutions – BBC, ITV and, since the early 1980s, other independent producers – exist in competition with each other to produce the most popular and critically-acclaimed drama. Third, these institutions are also in a dynamic relationship with governments, their ministers and authorities representing the state, such as the police and the armed forces. All these parties seek to manage the media representation of Northern Ireland through overt and covert means, and, while 'the media operate within a set of constraints in which power is clearly skewed towards the state',[17] the state does not enjoy an absolute monopoly that is invincible to challenge, particularly if it is internally divided at moments of crisis. TV drama then, is intrinsically *political*, through each of the commissioning, writing, production, transmission and reception phases. The task of cultural analysis of television drama about Northern Ireland is to assess the extent to which particular productions confirm, revise or seriously challenge consensus views. This chapter argues that not only does the political history of the Troubles need drama, but that dramatic representation needs to be criticised politically. What follows is a selective analysis of Troubles television drama, starting in the early 1960s, showing that significant fictional images predated the dramatic news actuality that hit the screens at the end of the decade. Basically chronological, this selection has been made to emphasise the point that a discernible line of drama exists, which represents the deeply problematic relations between loyalism and the British state, that goes to the heart of a postcolonial understanding of Northern Ireland. Indeed, it might now be argued that it is more important to find ways of exploring this relationship than that between the state and Irish republicanism. Secondly, we can define a series of plays which probe the nature, limits and potential of liberal democratic ideals in Britain and Northern Ireland. In the narratives of single plays and popular series (often in a thriller format) that are concerned with Northern Ireland, agents and institutions of the British state, such as the security forces and the judicial system, are exposed as corrupt or falling short of traditional ideals.

Early images: one-off plays from the 1960s

Some of the most significant images of Northern Ireland on British television, which pre-date the heavy news coverage of 1968–72, were provided by the drama of John D. Stewart and Sam Thompson. Both were brought up within Protestant communities but Stewart came to term himself an 'independent socialist [and] ill-constructed Presbyterian humanist', while Thompson was a shipyard socialist and Labour Party candidate in Belfast. In Stewart's *Danger, Men Working* (1961) and Thompson's *Over the Bridge* (1961) and *Cemented with Love* (1965), changes in industrial labour conditions and Ulster politics are clearly differentiated from other social-realist British drama of this kind in the 1960s. Both writers unequivocally expose sectarianism, *Over the Bridge* being a powerful indictment of the failure of labour politics against religious fundamentalism in a Belfast shipyard.[18] But Stewart's plays are equally percipient in their emphasis on the fractious relations between Britain and Northern Ireland's unionist population. Set on a Belfast building site, ATV's *Danger, Men Working* (1961),[19] dramatises the process of how British postwar modernisation affected Northern Ireland. The central conflict of the play is between Protestant building workers and a newly arrived English manager, Major Trumball, 'a tough, go-getting managing director (the perfect Irishmen's view of an English boss)'.[20] The unsympathetic characterisation of Trumball can be read as symptomatic of the resistance in some quarters at attempts to apply welfare capitalism, to make Northern Ireland more like the rest of the United Kingdom. While the nationalist minority would focus on this as commitment to equal civil rights from the mid-1960s, popular Protestant reaction was to reject the old-style, patrician Unionist Party and take up a more populist, fundamentalist politics and paramilitary organisation, which involved both the reformation of the UVF in 1966 and Ian Paisley founding the Democratic Unionist Party (DUP) in 1971. In *Boatman do not Tarry* (1968),[21] the tensions brought about by a reformist unionist government's plans to develop

41 Early images of the Troubles: *Boatman do not Tarry* (1968).
Courtesy of BFI Special Collection/Ulster Television

Northern Ireland cause resentment and violent protest. Set on a fictional penin-
sular (actually shot in Bannfoot, County Armagh), John Corby's ferry links an
isolated rural community to the larger world. In response to government plans to
develop the area, he goes on strike, supported by the local community who are
shown in a location-shot telecine sequence marching on Stormont's government
buildings. Corby's claim for compensation eventually results in a fatuous title
('Royal Boatman') and a cash payment. To the metropolitan disdain of a reviewer
in London, it seemed 'an amateurish drama of parish-pump politics',[22] but the
play's contemporary parallels would have carried an important local political
charge. Here was a play broadcast on the ITV national network that portrayed the
growing sense of dissatisfaction among grassroots unionists with their own leadership[23] and interference from London. While many commentators have justifi-
ably focused on the impact and significance of newsreel images of aggrieved civil
rights marchers, three months earlier this drama had presaged events that would
take place in the near future, including the suspension of Stormont and the impo-
sition of Direct Rule in 1972 and the spread of popular reactionary organisation
like the Ulster Workers' Council, which brought the province to a standstill in
1974.

Casualties in the long war, 1972–85

There was an institutional reluctance to address the issue of Northern Ireland
during this period indicating a sense of war-weariness but also war-wariness.

There were several instances of direct censorship intervention by executives under political pressure or a paranoid self-censorship of the kind discussed in chapter 10.[24] Apart from occasional individual plays or episodes of series featured on commercial television in Britain, the bulk of the TV drama about Northern Ireland came from the BBC, particularly in the single drama strand called 'Play for Today' (1970–84). Even though the BBC's output did not amount to much in the 1970s,[25] it did provide a few opportunities for writers to address a national television audience on the topic of Northern Ireland, which to a TV news agenda by mid-decade 'had become a routine story. Tragic certainly, but now somewhat boring.'[26] Two productions stand out: Colin Welland's *Your Man from Six Counties* (1976) and Derek Mahon's adaptation of the Jennifer Johnston novel, *Shadows on Our Skin* (1980). They were typical in that they focused on the impact that street violence, bombings and militarisation had on children in Northern Ireland. Both were shot on film rather than videotape but were different in that Welland's screenplay featured a boy sent away over the border to the Republic to recover from the trauma of Belfast, whereas Mahon's film captured the oppressive, grim and claustrophobic atmosphere of Derry city at the height of the street war between the IRA and the British Army in the early 1970s. Welland's film was significant for its exploration of Irish nationalist attitudes south of the border, whose differences might have surprised some English viewers. While *Shadows* is essentially a humanist presentation of a young Catholic boy's upbringing, it did strike a chord with a populist sentiment, supported in *The Daily Mirror* at that time, that the army should withdraw from Ireland.

Indeed, several plays in this period dealt with the predicament of British soldiers stationed in Northern Ireland. Unlike the political establishment's endorsement of their role as peace-keepers and the public's support for their welfare, writers drawn to this topic tended to be critical of the military presence and the security forces in general. A Belfast writer like W. J. Haire, a socialist keen to show the alternative possibilities, produced for the BBC *Letter from a Soldier* (1975). Writers of the British Left like Howard Brenton and David Leland produced one-off dramas such as *The Paradise Run* (1976) and *Psy-Warriors* (1981). The first examined despondency and desertion among the troops, while Leland's play indicted the training techniques of the army anti-terrorist units.[27] Brian Phelan wrote *Article 5*, which dealt uncompromisingly with the brutal interrogation techniques employed by the security forces on suspected terrorists, and, although produced, it has never been transmitted nor allowed to be viewed by researchers. Some anti-establishment feeling could be tolerantly absorbed and even in the mid-1980s a degree of freedom still remained for the individual, established writer or director on British television. Alan Clarke's *Contact* (1985) was a gripping BBC film that featured the lives of soldiers on undercover night surveillance duties in rural south Armagh. As a production it is virtually without dialogue, its sound recording quality eerily heightens natural noises, there is little narrative direction and it features long sequences of soldiers' point of view, sometimes through a green filter to imitate their infra-red night sights. Clarke's dogged and dispassionate camera captures the alternating monotony and tension of patrols, its bleakness and beauty, and we often get the sense that the soldiers are being spied on too. The lasting impression of the film was a compelling insight into soldiers' lives, their vulnerability and exhaustion and frustration and the platoon leader's (Sean Chapman) disillusionment back at barracks is communicated with great economy.

By contrast Mike Leigh's *Four Days in July* (1985), again made for the BBC, portrayed the parallel lives of two couples expecting their first babies in urban Belfast between the tenth and thirteenth of July. Leigh's characteristically improvised rendition of two parallel lives in Belfast is full of meandering natural talk and several wonderful set-piece speeches and exchanges. Eugene (Des McAleer) and Colette (Bríd Brennan) are the Catholic couple, while Billy (Charles Lawson) and Lorraine (Paula Hamilton) are Protestant. They seem to be materially a bit more well-off and Billy is a part-time soldier in the UDR, while the Catholic couple seem warmer together and are surrounded by supportive neighbours (including a cameo performance by Stephen Rea as Dixie). Critics have differed on whether or not Leigh's film invites a viewer to favour the Catholic couple over the Protestant one,[28] but we are meant to realise that despite some similarities in their ordinariness, there are a host of specific cultural and political differences between them. Leigh cuts back and forth between the couples as each day follows (signalled by date intertitles) and the understated domestic details accumulate, interspersed with conversations that define the profoundly different views of history, which each couple articulates. The onset of labour suggests a sense of the couples converging as they go to the non-sectarian institutional space of the hospital. But neither fathers in the waiting room nor mothers in the post-delivery ward meet on the common human ground of parenthood. In the concluding scene, an exchange of looks between the women accompanies their discussion of the babies' names: 'Billy, after his daddy', Lorraine informs Colette; Lorraine herself has just learned that Colette's baby is to be called Mairéad, 'coz Mairéad is the Irish for Margaret'. Leigh switches at this point from the close-up reverse angles of conversation to a wide, two-shot at a distance in which mothers and babies are separated at the edges of the frame. Unlike much of the analgesic drama that stresses a common humanity at the expense of material, political differences, Leigh deliberately refuses any easy reconciliation in the final scene. *Four Days in July* presents us with ordinary people who rhetorically or actually support political violence; in Billy's case the UDR on behalf of the state, and in the case of the Catholic community surrounding Eugene and Colette, the republican movement in opposition to the state.

In fact, most Troubles drama skirted round the representation of paramilitaries in all but a few productions during this period. Notably, the best attempts came from writers within Northern Ireland itself. Martin Dillon, journalist with the BBC who went on to write important studies of loyalist paramilitary activity, wrote a half-hour studio play, *Squad* (1976), significant as the first BBCNI television drama production in Belfast. Dillon's tense play followed a paramilitary hit squad on the night of an operation, delineating the different personalities and motivations for their involvement. It was a subject close to the concerns of people's everyday lives in Northern Ireland. Without the same budget, it anticipated *Resurrection Man* (1998) and was a brave opening for a station that went on to develop a prestigious fiction output over the following decades. Harry Barton's *Fire at Magilligan* (1984) is significant in a post-hunger strike (1980–1981) context since it featured the sympathetic portrayal of a republican prisoner. It featured flashbacks of HM Magilligan Prison – a hut and barbed wire prison for paramilitaries in the 1970s – which showed prisoners (loyalist and republican) in free association, with status as political prisoners not criminals (a situation that changed after 1976). Inmates are seen watching television clips of *Colditz* (a popular drama series about a German World War II prisoner-of-war camp), which also analogously inferred the paramilitaries' political status. Far from being a republican sympathiser, Barton was an ex-British navy officer of Ulster Protestant background, who was intent on articulating that undertow of dissidence that was to surface more forcibly in the decade after the Hillsborough Agreement.

Ulster soaps won't wash? The *Billy* plays (1982–87) and *Lost Belongings* (1987)

By the mid-1980s two Northern Irish writers, Graham Reid and Stewart Parker, had begun, through their radio, stage and television work, to define the contours of a middle-ground of Troubles representations in drama. Graham Reid established his reputation with *Billy: Three Plays for Television* (1982–84), with a young Kenneth Branagh playing the lead role, supported by the stalwart James Ellis as his father, Norman Martin, and Bríd Brennan as Lorna, Billy's long-suffering sister.[29] Set in fictional Coolderry Street in loyalist Belfast, Reid's script and the BBCNI treatment combined to produce a kind of working-class realism familiar to viewers in Britain. Accents aside, much of the specificity of Belfast was effaced, it 'could equally have been located, with variations, in a working class ghetto *anywhere in Britain*'.[30] The plays are strong on delineating the generalised socio-economic conditions that produce filial conflict, wife beating, male street violence and unemployment, but few links are made between character and the wider community or the political contexts of their environment. Given the prominence of republicanism following the Hunger Strikes, interest in and exploration of Ulster loyalism was not to the fore in the minds of viewers and critics in the early 1980s. But, by the mid-1980s, reviewers' remarks about *A Coming to Terms for Billy* (1984) betray a discernible change in perceptions: 'How authentic the production was to the street values of Protestant Belfast: *how like the rest of Ireland the North really is*'.[31] Suddenly, Reid's Belfast is not similar but different to the 'mainland'. At the end of the trilogy, some kind of peaceful resolution has been achieved between Billy and his father. Norman and Mavis (his second wife) depart for her native Manchester in a taxi. In a final, slow crane shot looking down across the roof tops, Coolderry Street is filled with an Orange marching band 'really banging out Derry's Walls by this stage'.[32] The camera lingers to frame an image of what amounts to a defiant emergence of a loyalist identity that was submersed in earlier episodes. The Hillsborough Agreement signed a year later angered loyalists who saw it as a deal done between London and Dublin, a sell-out to nationalism. *Lorna* (1987) focused on the future for Bríd Brennan's character, a young woman left behind in the old family home, eager for independence and change. She chooses to join the RUC and sell the house (it is unable to sustain change) much to the dismay of Billy and Norman. But her bid for a new start away from 'home and the responsibilities that have imprisoned her' is coloured by 'the sadness of the men that the house is abandoned'.[33] Powerful memories and sense of irrevocable change closed this drama – beautifully conveyed by James Ellis's voice-over during the credits – and it struck an emotional chord with an Ulster loyalist sense of abandonment post-Hillsborough.

Stewart Parker's work is characterised by a humane openess to change and accommodation, the reinvention of inherited cultural histories, particularly those of his native Northern Ireland.[34] His single most ambitious television project was a six-part thriller, *Lost Belongings* (1987), set in 1980 between Belfast and London, made for Euston Films and Channel Four. It was made with a considerable budget as a prime-time television film for the ITV network (with repeat broadcast on Channel Four). *Lost Belongings* featured two main plot lines suggested by the title. The first concerns Deirdre Connell's (Catherine Brennan) past. A product of a mixed marriage she is orphaned and is brought up by her evil Uncle Connell (Harry Towb). Her family history – her lost belongings – repeats itself as she becomes emotionally involved with Niall Usher (Gerard O'Hare), a Catholic lad in a band struggling to make it. Alongside this love across the sectarian divide narrative, a more interesting line contrasts the lives of two boys, neighbours from Protestant Belfast, Craig Connell (Colum Convey) and Alec Ferguson (Oengus Macnamara), whose lives have diverged. Flashing back to the 1960s, Craig and Alec became involved in the UVF, but Alec is whisked away to a music academy in London before he is interned like Craig. Back in the present, Alec returns to Belfast to give a concert but is confronted by his memories. In Craig and Alec, Parker dramatises the conflicts within a loyalist history of Northern Ireland. Past loyalties – Alec's 'lost belongings' – like the UVF tattoo on his arm, remain to trouble the returned migrant. Aiming this drama first and foremost at 'my own people of Northern Ireland', Parker intends the audience to understand his series as a modern reworking of 'Deirdre of the Sorrows'[35] and embrace the idea that Ulster's (pre-Christian) past reveals a shared heritage, more complicated than contemporary political ideologies allow. In an assessment of Troubles drama on television, the representation of loyalist paramilitaries, evangelist churches and Orange Order meetings is important to Parker, who observes of previous drama that 'not only do you not see Protestant paramilitaries and their ideologies but you only see the IRA in stereotyped versions'.[36] Relishing the popular medium, Parker's television plays engaged in rewriting contemporary Ulster protestantism from a humanist standpoint inflected with the traces of a Christian ethos. The posthumous television production of *Pentecost* (1990), set in the unrest and mayhem of the 1974 UWC strike, epitomises this stance. The play's message of personal redemption was carried in its dramatic intensity. Under more forensic analysis, the increased activity of loyalist paramilitaries in the early 1990s tended to indicate that Christian individuals would still a generation later tacitly support paramilitary groups in their midst.

Extending and reacting to TV's middle-ground, 1984–89

Anne Devlin's screen work provided a moderate nationalist and female perspective on Northern Ireland during the 1980s. In *A Woman Calling* (1984), *The Long March* (1984)[37] and *Naming the Names* (1987), the effects of childhood trauma, political upheavals and violence of the 1960s are explored in young female characters, but it is in the latter two plays that Devlin focuses more specifically on the problematic relations between women, nationalism and republicanism. 'The Long March' refers to a march from Belfast to Derry in January 1969 led by People's Democracy, a radical socialist group, and others involved in civil rights activism. The violent clash between marchers and counter-protesting loyalists at Burntollet Bridge is etched into Helen Walsh's (Marcella Riordan) childhood memory as a defining moment in her life. She has returned to Belfast from England, so the play's title also refers to her own personal journey and development. She has to negotiate both her father's (James Ellis) labour politics and the more militant views of the Molloy family in the West Belfast community about the moral ethics and political significance of the republican hunger strikes against which the play is set. Networked on the BBC, the play creditably attempted to dramatise the internal debates and differences within a broad Irish nationalist spectrum, which the one-dimensional media view of Northern Ireland in Britain often fails to recognise. For instance, one reviewer argued that *The Long March* was presented entirely from a republican point of view in a crass misinterpretation of Devlin's work. Indeed, Devlin herself is adamant that as a dramatist she is 'interested in individual, personal dramas and personal tragedies which may be more important than the vast political tragedies going on around them'.[38] The play ended in reconciliation between the Molloys and Walshes, and with false neatness as Father Oliver brings news of the hunger strike's end. Devlin thus avoids the major issue of the second hunger strike in 1981, which brought the deaths of ten male strikers and was of lasting political significance to republicanism and feminist republicans in particular. Yet, in an interview for the *Radio Times* (London), Devlin explained that her play 'wasn't a refusal to take sides. It was objectivity'. Two years later, commenting more generally about Northern Ireland in *The Irish Independent*, she claimed, 'I find it impossible to take sides. It's a tragedy for all sections of the community'. Far from being republican, such remarks outline the broadly apolitical, liberal stance, of a middle-ground female writer acceptable to the BBC.

Her *Naming the Names* (1987) tells of how Finn's (Sylvestra Le Touzel) life is shaped by her experience of the Protestant pogrom of 1969, in which her granny died, and the subsequent arrival of the British troops. The narrative is structured through flashbacks or dream sequences during her interrogation by an RUC officer (Ian McElhinney). She has been arrested for her part in luring Henry Kirk (Michael Malone) to a park where he has been shot by the IRA. Henry, the son of a judge and from a unionist background, was studying Irish history at Oxford, and became sexually involved with Finn after visiting the book shop in which she worked. Repeat broadcast in 1989 to commemorate the twenty-fifth anniversary of the troops' arrival in Northern Ireland, *Naming the Names* gave little credible motivation for Finn's involvement with the IRA (except the fatherly influence of James Ellis's character) nor did it clarify the historical role of the British army. Finn's voice-over of a sequence showing soldiers setting out barbed wire in August 1969 is typically vague: 'They were here. They will not go until it is over.' Under interrogation in the present, Finn recites the street names of West Belfast, very possibly a trained response. As she does so she suffers a catatonic fit. Other sequences from her past sexual encounters hint that she is mentally unstable, that she is bitter towards men or revengeful over her granny's death. Ambiguously freeze-framed in a spider's web image at the end, Finn's predicament seems to be that – although like a female spider that lured her male lover to his death – she herself is trapped by history's web of male republicanism. Finn's representation is open to being interpreted as a psycho-femme terrorist like Miranda Richardson's Jude in *The Crying Game*; a representation which seeks to deny that ordinary women can be republican *and* remain rational.

Adaptations of fiction and drama by established fiction writers continued to attract drama resources in the BBC. Productions such as Maurice Leitch's *Chinese Whispers* (1989),[39] about an orderly in a mental hospital, provided a scenario in which the Troubles impinge on a world of institutionalised madness within a state that is itself unstable. Use of indirect parallels and understated observation is characteristic of William Trevor's fiction, much of which he has adapted for the screen. *Beyond the Pale* (1989)[40] tells of an English middle-aged, middle-class foursome holidaying at a hotel in Northern Ireland. One of the group, Cynthia (Annette Crosbie), suffers a breakdown brought on by seeing the ghost of a young man who committed suicide for his co-religious lover. The production values enhanced the excellent ensemble acting that is a hallmark of British TV drama. Trevor, nevertheless, exposed the complacency of English attitudes to Ireland, even if in doing so, he reinforced other stereo-types about Irish character.

Loyalist anger at English ignorance, wilful or due to laziness, is the prime target of one of this decade's most acerbic television dramas, Ron Hutchinson's

Rat in the Skull (1987)[41] made for Central TV. It is set in a London police cell during the interrogation of Roche (Colum Convey), an IRA suspect, by RUC detective Nelson (Brian Cox), under the supervision of P. C. Naylor (Gary Oldman) and his superior, Superintendent Harris (Philip Jackson). In a moment when they are alone, Nelson assaults Roche, fouling up the prosecution's case and allowing Roche to go free. The heightened stage language, the studio-bound production, with plenty of long takes, big close-ups of faces and little incidental music lent itself to the claustrophobia inherent in the dramatic situation but also expressed the intimate hatred shared by opposing traditions within Northern Ireland. The play was structured through a series of flashbacks to Nelson's inter-rogation observed by Naylor and the debriefing between Harris and Nelson. Harris needs to know why Nelson hit Roche for his incident report and as part of his 'specialisation in Anti-Terror'. Nelson will only refute that it was 'a straight brutality', simply sectarian hate. It points up an English, colonial tendency to define problems within a limited framework. Naylor is a vulgar version of the more senior professional Harris. Nelson punctures the racist attitudes of English people and British institutions for failing to recognise the Irish as anything but 'paddies', of failing to differentiate Ulster protestants from nationalists and republicans. Moreover, Nelson observes that in loyalism the English 'see the worst of yourselves in us. The Brit boiled down. The bollock-bare, the stripped and stinking. Not comfortable to live with, are we? The clockwork Orangemen, bob-bing along behind our tribal banners, our ranting reverends, wa-hooing down the street, so damn confusingly loyal to you.' Nelson's attempt to get 'behind Roche's eyeballs', like a rat in the skull, becomes a process of self-interrogation about his own father's generation of 'stick-up Orange men' and, ultimately, the nature of loyalism that will define his future. Understood in this way, *Rat in the Skull* is a searching revision of loyalism's core beliefs and attachments to British values and as such is a rare piece of TV drama. Over the last generation, the fabric of Britain's postcolonial identity has come apart at the seams. Many of the sym-bolic threads of Britishness – such as its unwritten constitution, its legal and judicial systems – were seen to stretch and snap under strains the source of which lay in Northern Ireland.

Blind Justice (1988), conceived by Scottish barrister Helena Kennedy with dramatist Peter Flannery, was produced for the BBC out of the conviction that 'the 1980s was not a decade we will come to associate either with justice in our courts or with outspokenness in television drama'.[42] The series of six films was not a drama-documentary as such, more a faction, a creative conflation in dramatic terms of the recent past with reference to actual events and the process of justice in Britain, but with fictional figures and narrative. According to Helena Kennedy, 'an Irish case had to be at the core of the series'[43] and episode three, 'The One about the Irishman', sought to address the issue that Irish suspects could not expect fair trial in British courts due to political pres-sure and racial prejudice. It starred Jack Shepherd as Frank Cartwright, a barrister who successfully acquits Eamon Hand (Colum Convey) of conspiracy to blow up the Cenotaph[44] in Westminster while six other suspects are found guilty. Frank's fellow law partner, James Bingham (Julian Wadham) unsuccessfully defends Ruari McFadden (Frank Grimes), a leading republican, but earns himself career points with a passionate speech about the nature of British justice. In a series of cleverly worked plot twists, it emerges that the crown prosecution's case against Hand was rigged because he had offered to be a police informer on the fringes of the IRA's bombing of Brighton in 1984, but was turned down at the time. In conversation with Frank about his charges in the present case, Hand claims he had a deal with the police. He is supposed to withhold bogus information in order to get a lesser sentence, while actually providing real information to sink the others, but not disclosing this to his defence lawyer. Frank realises that Hand is being used by the police and MI5 (the British security service) and that, ultimately, he too is being used by the judicial system. In court, the prosecution deliberately spikes its own guns following collusion between MI5 and the office of the director of public prosecutions, in order to cover up the mistake of 1984 and the use of an informant in the present case. Frank muses how the state and its apparatus operates: 'There are moments when you actually feel the monster roll its muscles underneath your feet; and you've suddenly been moved, you're not standing where you thought you were'.

42 Honest Jack, corrupt legal system? Jack Shepherd in *Blind Justice* (1988). Courtesy of the BBC Picture Library

The episode ends with Hand contacting a newspaper to give them the real story, but he is shot in a pub toilet – by the IRA as an informant, or could it just possibly be MI5 anxious to silence any further revelations? The constraints imposed on independent thinking within the media in the 1980s, culminating in the Douglas Hurd legislation of 1988, had particular impact on investigative journalism but anxieties about litigation also affected the commissioning of dramatic work too.[45] However, journalists' projects began to find their way into dramatised productions as a means of circumventing full-on censorship and further changes to broadcasting guidelines. For example, in the IBA's *Television Guidelines* (April 1985), paragraph 6.2, it is made clear that 'the due impartiality required of a play by an independent dramatist is *not identical* to that required of a current affairs programme'.[46] But under the Broadcasting Act (1990), the new ITC's *Guidelines* were significantly altered so that 'dramatised documentary which lays claim to be a factual reconstruction of a controversial event covered by the Act *is bound* by the same standards of fairness and impartiality as those that apply to factual programmes in general'.[47] It was in such increasingly constrictive conditions that film-makers attempted to use drama-doc to create space to imagine alternatives. Their aim was to question authorised versions of the recent past and attack state authorities in whose name injustices were carried out.

Drama-doc or drama in the dock?

1990 stands out as a vintage year in drama-documentary, the hybrid genre which, although it is based on journalistic research, documentation and evidence like a documentary, uses the aesthetic and dramatic codes of fiction film to mediate the real world to which it specifically refers. There were no less than three films that dealt with the cases of innocent people charged by the state and wrongly convicted for crimes they did not commit. In March, *Who Bombed Birmingham?*[48] (Granada TV) brought the appeal cases of the Birmingham Six to the attention of huge television audiences. A pre-broadcast furore in parliament saw Conservative ministers faced with awkward questions and Prime Minister Thatcher assert: 'A television programme alters nothing. We do not have trial by television here'.[49] Mary Holland, an experienced newspaper commentator on Irish affairs, insisted that 'it is vital for all of us that this kind of expensive, irritating journalism continues' since it overcame the switch-off reaction produced by current affairs programming about Northern Ireland.[50]

This was proved in June with *Shoot To Kill* (Yorkshire TV), which portrayed the investigation of the RUC's counter-terrorist activities and MI5 involvement in Northern Ireland during the early 1980s.[51] This investigation was carried out by a Manchester-based chief constable, John Stalker, whose extensive report was never finally published since he was removed from the case. Documentary film-maker Peter Kosminsky commissioned screenwriter Mick Eaton[52] to produce a two-part, £1.5 million thriller because he encountered difficulties obtaining the interview and film evidence usual in the investigative research for a straight documentary. The result was compelling: four hours of prime time fiction broadcast over two consecutive evenings. It was introduced as a drama-documentary, the action was date captioned 1982 and characters bore the names of real figures, but it used the full repertoire of TV drama conventions, visual cues and incidental music score to convey the covert war of surveillance, the paranoid foreboding and suspense surrounding Stalker's investigation team. Having played a similar role in *Blind Justice*, the casting of Shepherd was perfect as the plain-speaking Yorkshire policeman, John Stalker, doggedly applying his objective English policing ethics in the face of Sir John Hermon's (T. P. McKenna) dour obstructionism. The film indicted a special anti-terrorist unit within the RUC for unlawfully killing six unarmed terrorist suspects, the RUC's fabrication of evidence and perpetrating a cover up in the subsequent inquiry. Stalker's investigation was itself spiked because he came close to revealing that operations in Ulster were authorised by MI5 and senior members of the British government. UTV refused to screen the programme in Northern Ireland on legal advice, owing to the sensitivities of the security forces and families affected. The broadcast was attacked in advance by John Hermon himself and in a post-transmission discussion programme on the issues raised. Ian Gow, for the government, and Unionist David Trimble claimed the film was inaccurate and misleading to viewers; an example of how objections to content and viewpoint in drama-documentary are often 'strategically displaced into … objections about the unacceptability of the form itself'.[53] But Kosminsky, Seamus Mallon and Amnesty International defended the veracity of the research, stressing the importance for democracy of questioning decisions made by authorities purportedly in the national interest.[54] A memorable year in television drama-doc production ended with a co-production called *The Treaty* (Thames/RTÉ). This was a kind of television film forerunner to *Michael Collins*, which marked the seventieth anniversary of the treaty that ended the Anglo-Irish war in 1921. Based on a meticulously researched and documented script by Brian Phelan, it represented an important intervention in the political context of the early 1990s. Although historical, this dramatisation of the past ghosted the secret negotiations between Sinn Féin and the British government that were taking place during the production of *The Treaty*.[55]

The BBC continued to commission work that shaped the Troubles within a tragic template, usually in a thriller format, like the series, *Children of the North* (1991). It also produced a rare sitcom series, Alomo Productions' *So You Think You've Got Troubles?* (1991), in which a London Jew (Warren Mitchell) is transferred by his company to manage the take-over of a tobacco manufacturer in Belfast.[56] *Breed of Heroes* (1994) told the story of a group of young British army officers on a tour of duty in Belfast in 1971, but only rehearsed the well-worn idea that the army were reluctantly sent to keep apart what liberal journalism was still calling 'the two white tribes of Ulster'[57] over two decades later.

Proving again the worth of work from within Northern Ireland itself, Bill Morrison and Chris Ryder's *Force of Duty* (1992) was carefully produced by BBCNI under Robert Cooper. Although based on Ryder's journalistic research, it was a conventional drama that focused on the pressurised lives of RUC officers. Simpson Gabby (Donal McCann) is a middle-aged, married police detective with a good service record, who ends up committing suicide following the assassination of his detective colleague, Billy (Adrian Dunbar). Badly traumatised and guilt-ridden, Gabby becomes emotionally detached from his loving family, finds little solace in drink and the pious invitations to prayer from his boss. Although early in the film he has resisted the pressure of Orange Order marchers within his own community to move outside the law, the generic requirements of the police genre do show Gabby pushed to the brink in his desire to see justice done after Billy's funeral. The play captured the paranoia within the ranks of the RUC. One uniformed officer even comments, 'We know what they've done and we can do nothing about it. Well, there are men who *will* do the job'. He has leaked photos of IRA suspects to loyalist paramilitaries, which Gabby condemns with the classic liberal defence against extra-legal action: 'You can't take the Law into your own hands, or there is no Law'. Often viewed in long-shot from a hidden camera (under surveillance by the enemy?), Gabby and Billy are observed going about their thankless duty engaging in a grimly humorous repartee. Gabby's expression is reduced to taciturn 'ayes' and the music score signifies aurally the tragic inevitability of Gabby's suicide. While Brian McIlroy has praised the script as one that actually gives voice to members of the RUC and humanises them, this is to miss the point that, however accurately represented, the film dramatised Gabby's destruction as a personal response to his job; the force of duty broke him. It did not explore the idea of *institutional* failure, where a consensual society does not exist to be policed in an ordinary way. The limitations of British law enforcement traditions in Ulster were exposed in Morrison's screenplay, but this film was more significant for its portending portrayal of RUC and grassroots Orange protesters clashing, one of whom asks Gabby to his face: 'What kind of Protestant are you?' Here, drama pre-empted the test of loyalty that became known as the 'spirit of Drumcree'[58] after 1995 as Ulster loyalism reinvented its fundamentalism in the middle of the peace process.

Peace drama – and after?

The key factors in furthering the peace process in Northern Ireland have been the paramilitary ceasefires, and the issues of prisoner release and decommissioning of arms. Ronan Bennett's intensely involved thriller, *Love Lies Bleeding* (1993), about Conn (Mark Rylance), a Republican prisoner out on twenty-four hour home leave, anticipated some of these developments. While trying to find the killers of his girlfriend, he becomes embroiled in an internal battle for power within the IRA. Fellow prisoner Thomas (Brendan Gleeson) has been instrumental in the pro ceasefire campaign, opposed on the outside by the hard-line Armagh faction led by Ruairi (Bosco Hogan). The film ends in bloody carnage as Gleeson's men slaughter the hard-liners allowing Sinn Féin to enter political negotiations with the British government. Formally, *Love Lies Bleeding* adhered to the generic conventions of the TV film thriller, but in fictionalising a ceasefire it did offer an alternative position, anticipated that republican politics could be engaged in negotiations and presaged the ceasefire that was declared in August 1994.

In a typically sombre fashion, Graham Reid's *Life after Life* (1995) showed further ramifications, portraying the problems of a republican prisoner (Lorcan Cranitch) trying to acclimatise to life after long-term imprisonment. He finds out that family, former lover and republican politics have all moved on and that the lasting significance of his heroic sacrifice is questioned by those around him. In *The Precious Blood* (1996), Reid takes a similar theme with Billy McVea (Kevin McNally), a Protestant paramilitary turned evangelist preacher in East Belfast, living his faith empowered by the 'Power of the Blood'. McVea's religious conversion took place while serving a sentence for the killing of Paul Willis, a small-time UVF man, allegedly an informer. McVea now runs a local boxing club but by fateful coincidence becomes a surrogate father and trainer to John Willis

43 Terrorist, teen, UVF widow: *The Precious Blood* (1996). Courtesy of the BBC Picture Library

(Michael Legge), the teenage son of the man he shot, and befriends the widowed Rosie Willis (Amanda Burton). When Rosie finds out about her former husband's unknown UVF connections from the RUC and tells John, the boy reacts badly. He is stoned in a street incident and critically injured. At the hospital bedside, McVea confesses his crime to Rosie, and the closing shot is of McVea entering an RUC station, suggesting that he is going to give himself up.

Drama since the late 1960s has not only reflected the political shifts in Northern Ireland, but it has in certain instances explored some of the deepest fears of those embroiled in conflict. The political, security and legal apparatus of the British establishment has been most effectively critiqued at different junctures in the drama-documentary format. There has been a line of drama that has interrogated the problematic relationship of unionism within Anglo-Irish politics and the increasingly attenuated sense of Ulster loyalism.[59] Little drama exists to explain how and why many 'ordinary' people would join or support – even passively – paramilitary organisations involved in killings and punishment beatings. This limitation is only of television's making in the sense that its restricted range is an historical index of British political and cultural shortcomings. While most drama has followed the terrain of the Troubles, marking out a representational middle-ground, in a few cases drama has challenged viewers' minds by imagining events that could not be countenanced by factual television. Fictional representations, therefore, have played a major role in the maintenance and reshaping of perceptions about the Troubles and to this extent they have performed a political function.

Notes

1 R. Williams, *Writing in Society* (London, Verso, 1984), 11–12.
2 B. Winston, *Misunderstanding the Media* (London, Routledge & Kegan Paul, 1986), 5–6.
3 R. Cathcart, *The Most Contrary Region: The BBC in Northern Ireland 1924–1984* (Belfast, The Blackstaff Press, 1984), 208. Stills taken from RTÉ and UTV are reproduced in T. Downing (ed.), *The Troubles* (London, Thames TV International/Macdonald Futura, 1989), 143.
4 H. Sheehan's does address the topic within *Irish Television Drama* (Dublin, RTÉ, 1987). L. Pettitt's 'A Box of Troubles' (Dublin, unpublished Ph.D, NUI, 1991) focuses on British television drama and Northern Ireland. M. McLoone provides an incisive essay, which is restricted to BBC television drama, 'Drama out of a crisis', in M. McLoone (ed.), *Broadcasting in a Divided Community* (Belfast, The Institute of Irish Studies, 1996). B. McIlroy devotes two short chapters to British television drama and TV film in his wide-ranging book, *Shooting to Kill* (Trowbridge, Wiltshire, Flicks, 1998).
5 R. Last, *Daily Telegraph* (7 January 1985), 10.
6 BBCNI controller James Hawthorne's comment about the thriller, *Crossfire* (1988), a series which was censored and delayed in transmission, was reported in 'BBC halts "Glorifying" IRA film', *The Times* (16 February 1987), 2.

7 McIlroy, *Shooting to Kill*, 100. David Butler insists that 'there is no organised conspiracy for or against unionism in the broadcast media ... they have been persistently ignored, misrepresented and, at times, maligned', in his 'Ulster Unionism and British broadcast journalism', in B. Rolston (ed.), *The Media and Northern Ireland: Covering the Troubles* (Basingstoke, Hampshire, Macmillan, 1991), 117.

8 BBCNI drama producer Robert Cooper as quoted in A. Crilly, 'Stories for television', *Film Ireland*, 42 (August–September 1994), 22.

9 J. Caughie, 'Before the golden age: Early television drama', in J. Corner (ed.), *Popular Television in Britain: Studies in cultural history* (London, British Film Institute, 1991), 30–40. This technological lag was both cultural and political. Studio technicians' trade unions resisted videotape as a threat to its members' livelihoods.

10 J. Tunstall, *Television Producers* (London, Routledge, 1993), 11.

11 M. McLoone, 'Boxed in? The aesthetics of film and television', in J. Hill and M. McLoone (eds), *Big Picture, Small Screen: The relations between film and television* (Luton, John Libbey Media, 1996), 86.

12 Cathcart, *Most Contrary Region*, 261–2.

13 K. Cully, 'Nationalist attitudes', *The Tribune* (23 February 1979), was comparing Ron Hutchinson's bizarre comedy, *The Last Window Cleaner* (1979), which was screened after the BBC's flagship current affairs programme, *Panorama*, had presented a report on US attitudes to the 'Blanket Protest' in Long Kesh (The Maze) by republican prisoners.

14 R. Hoggart, 'Is TV drama a switch-off subject?', *The Listener* (27 March 1980), 390–1.

15 J. McGrath, *A Good Night Out: Popular theatre, audience, class and form* (London, Methuen, 1981), 113.

16 She was speaking on BBC2's arts programme, *The Late Show*. The programme's report, 'Telling the Troubles', examined fictional representations of the Troubles and was broadcast on 21 September 1993.

17 D. Miller, *Don't Mention the War: Northern Ireland, propaganda and the media* (London, Pluto Press, 1994), 277.

18 See Paddy Devlin, 'First bridge too far', *Theatre Ireland*, 3 (June–September 1983), 122–4; Hagal Mengal, 'A lost heritage: Ulster drama and the work of Sam Thompson', *Theatre Ireland*, 2 (January/May 1983), 2 ; S. Parker, 'The tribe and Thompson', *The Irish Times* (18 June, 1970).

19 *Danger, Men Working* was originally commissioned by CEMA (Council for the Encouragement of Music and the Arts) as a stage play for the Festival of Britain celebration in 1951; part of an attempt at popular, cultural morale boosting in the nadir of postwar exhaustion. The festival sought to have every region represented and acknowledge the cultural and historic achievement of the United Kingdom. First staged in Belfast in 1951, the BBC in London broadcast it on radio in April of the same year.

20 *The Times* (8 May 1961).

21 It is significant that this play was produced locally by Ulster Television not a company in England. A copy of the play is extant at UTV's archive though not for viewing purposes.

22 *The Daily Telegraph* (9 July 1968).

23 Captain Terence O'Neill's Unionist Party government collapsed in the 'cross roads' election of 1969, failed to secure stability and increased political fragmentation.

24 Liz Curtis's invaluable 'Appendix' to her *Ireland: The propaganda war* (Belfast, Sásta, 1999), lists those dramas and non-fiction television programmes affected by censorship of different kinds since 1959.

25 Hoggart, 'Is TV drama a switch-off subject?', 390–1.

26 P. Schlesinger, *Putting 'Reality' Together* (London, Methuen, 1987), 206.

27 Analysed in P. Schlesinger, P. Elliott, and G. Murdock, *Televising Terrorism* (London, Comedia, 1983), 104–8.

28 McIlroy seems to think that Leigh is biased against Billy and Lorraine, *Shooting to Kill*, 92. My own view, supported by that of Paul Clements, 'Four Days in July', in G. Brandt (ed.), *British Television Drama in the 1980s* (Cambridge, Cambridge University Press, 1993), 174, is that Leigh's carefully structured paralleling in the film does not conclusively invite sympathy either way. Leigh himself has declared his own interest in republicanism as a political philosophy. See R. Comiskey, 'The two sides of Belfast', *The Irish Times* (29 January 1984), 10.

29 Much could be discussed in the histories of these three Northern Irish actors. Ellis, a contemporary of Sam Thompson, was part of the cast in the original stage version of *Over the Bridge* (1960) and recently appeared as a detective in *Resurrection Man* (1998). Branagh's Ulster protestant background is discussed in his biography, telling how he moved to Reading, near London, in 1969 and quickly lost his Belfast accent. A graduate of RADA, he has been styled as an English director and actor comparable to Laurence Olivier. Bríd Brennan has worked steadily in theatre, television and film in a restricted repertoire of roles, consistently producing strong performances. She took the lead in a coda to the *Billy* trilogy, entitled *Lorna* (1987).

30 H. Kretzmer, *The Daily Mail* (17 February 1982). My italics.

31 J. Naughton, *The Listener*, 111:2847 (1 March 1984), 30. My italics.

32 G. Reid, *Billy: Three plays for television* (London, Faber, 1984), 117.

33 H. Herbert, *Guardian* (3 June 1987), 9.

34 *Catchpenny Twist* (1977), *I'm a Dreamer Montreal* (1979) and *Iris in the Traffic, Ruby in the Rain* (1981).

35 As Parker points out in the introduction to the screenplay of *Lost Belongings*, this tale is a revised version of an earlier prose narrative in Old Irish (8–9th century A.D.) called 'Longes mac n-Uislenn' or 'The Exile of the Sons of Uisliu (or Uisnech)'. See T. Kinsella (tr.), *The Tain* (Oxford, Oxford University Press, 1969).

36 Quoted in S. Lane, 'Shared heritage of Northern Ireland', *Morning Star* (4 April 1987), 8.

37 The screenplays of *A Woman Calling* and *The Long March* have been published along with *Ourselves Alone* (London, Faber, 1986).

38 *Belfast Telegraph* (18 April, 1984), 10.

39 M. Leitch, *Chinese Whispers* (London, Arena, 1988).

40 W. Trevor, 'Beyond the Pale', in *Collected short stories* (London, Penguin, 1991), 64–86.

41 R. Hutchinson, *Rat in the Skull* (London, Methuen, 1984). This is the original text for the stage version.

42 P. Flannery, 'Introduction', *Blind Justice* (London, Nick Hern Books, 1990), viii. My thanks to Peter Flannery for supplying me with a videotape of this episode for viewing purposes.

43 H. Kennedy, 'Introduction', *Blind Justice* (London, Nick Hern Books, 1990), vii.

44 The Cenotaph is a monument that commemorates the British military war dead and is the centre piece of the annual Armistice Day service in November. Located very close to Downing Street, the office of the British prime minister, it would provide a symbolic and sensitive target.

45 Flannery, *Blind Justice*, ix–x.

46 Quoted in P. Bonner (with L. Aston), *Independent Television in Britain, Volume 5* (Basingstoke, Hampshire, ITC/Macmillan, 1998), 68. (My italics).

47 Bonner, *Independent Television in Britain*, my italics.

48 Granada sold the film to HBO, the movie channel in the USA, retitled as *Investigation: Inside a Terrorist Bombing*. The other productions were *Shoot to Kill* and the much more quietly received *A Safe House* and *Dear Sarah*, based on the experiences of the Guildford Four and the Maguire Seven.

49 Quoted in *The Financial Times* (4 April 1990), 21. J. M. Wober's study of viewers concluded that the 'evidence is that watching *Who Bombed Birmingham?* probably did alter viewers' perceptions and attitudes to agree more with those put forward in the programme'. See J. M. Wober, 'Effects on the perceptions of viewers of the TV drama-documentary *Who Bombed Birmingham?*' (London, ITC Research Paper, September 1990), 8.

50 M. Holland, '"Faction" on the six beat the turn-off factor', *The Irish Times* (4 April 1990), 10.

51 In my view, *Shoot to Kill* had far more credibility and impact than the more well-known *Hidden Agenda* film by Ken Loach.

52 Mick Eaton came to the project three years into its documentary research phase and has said that this kind of screen adaptation work does not constitute the authorship associated with single drama or film scripts: 'We are … structuralists rather than dramatists – producers want us to supply form and structure'. As quoted in D. Paget, *No other way to tell it Dramadoc/docudrama on television* (Manchester, Manchester University Press, 1998), 176.

53 J. Corner, *The Art of Record: A critical introduction to documentary* (Manchester, Manchester University Press, 1996), 39.

54 A recent audience study of *Shoot to Kill* found that 'in its presentation of the RUC the drama-documentary provided a site within which some viewers re-negotiated some of their common sense notions concerning the definition and usage of the term "terrorism"', but also found that such oppositional readings were actively delegitimated by other viewers' discursive strategies. See J. Roscoe, 'Contesting the term "terrorism": audience interpretations of the drama-documentary *Shoot to Kill*', paper presented at 'Discourse and cultural practice conference', University of Adelaide, February 1996. Research was carried out in London.

55 I discuss this production more fully in L. Pettitt, 'Troubles, Terminus and *The Treaty*', in C. Graham and R. Kirkland (eds), *Ireland and Cultural Theory: The mechanics of authenticity* (Basingstoke, Hampshire, Macmillan, 1999). RTÉ had produced an innovative fiftieth-anniversary dramatisation of the Easter Rising in 1966 called *The Rising*, which employed news reportage conventions in its re-enactment; an example of the docu-drama form.

56 For my analysis of these two productions, see L. Pettitt, 'Situation tragedy? British television drama and Northern Ireland', *Irish Studies Review*, 1 (Spring 1992), 20–2.

57 R. Malan, 'The white tribes of Ulster', *Guardian Weekend* (3 April 1993), 6–9, 13–14 and 16.

58 The opposition by 'Spirit of Drumcree' loyalists like Joel Patton to any appeasement with local nationalist residents and the divisions within the Orange Order and unionism have been a feature of Northern Ireland politics since 1996. BBCNI's current affairs programme, *Spotlight*, covered this issue in a special programme on 6 May 1997, and Margo Harkin captured marching conflict in *Twelve Days in July*, made for Besom Productions and Channel Four, and broadcast on 21 July 1997.

59 It is reported that BBC2 has commissioned a six-episode series from BBCNI called *Six into Twenty-Six Won't Go*, a chronicle 'about three Protestant friends living through the Troubles over the past thirty years'. See *Inproduction* (2 May 1998), 8.

CHAPTER 12

SCREENING IRELAND IN THE 1990S

- What is the nature of the audio-visual environment in Ireland?

- Which films are significant to understanding Ireland in the 1990s?

- Have Irish films extended and transformed the idea of national(ist) cinema?

Mapping Ireland's changing audio-visual space

Having been on the receiving end of images of Ireland and Irishness for the past century, film-makers are now able to speak directly to an audience at home and our best work can be exported abroad in an epoch of increasing globalisation.[1]

Ireland's audio-visual environment in the 1990s, characterised by diversity of format, complexity of interaction and technological flux, has the potential to provide both narrowcast and global reach. Cinema attendance revived somewhat in many European countries in the mid-1990s, assisted – not curtailed – by increased use of home video and the broadcast of films on TV. In 1996, Ireland had the highest cinema attendance rate in Europe, experienced a burst of cinema-building activity and also had the highest use of video rental in the EU.[2] Indeed, in Ireland, watching films is the most popular form of arts event, whether at home or in the cinema.[3] Film production in Ireland, north and south, became extremely buoyant, funded from a variety of state, private and EU sources, British TV and Anglo-American film backers. While the Hollywood product dominates the box-office in Europe, Ireland's films have been successful at festivals and box offices in countries like France, Spain and Germany as well as the USA. Irish audiences flocked to see *Michael Collins*, taking a record IR£4.0 million (10 per cent of the year's total gross), and indigenous films have attained healthy ratings when shown on RTÉ and on BBCNI.[4] Accompanying cinema's ebullience, European public service broadcasting (PSB) television was rapidly transformed in the course of the 1990s. Under regulatory regimes favouring privatisation, the development of satellite and digital telecommunications was shaped by government policies that advocated economic liberalism within the EU while continuing to defend an internal market in a global context from complete 'Los Angelesation'.[5]

In the first section of this chapter, the key events in audio-visual policy in Ireland between 1995 and 1998 are examined, arguing that while cinema and television remain distinctive, they are irrevocably interdependent. We will also examine the increased productivity of the short film and assess its part in revitalising new Irish cinema and television. In the second section, the different kinds of films made since 1993 are analysed. To what extent are they different in theme and style from what went before? In what ways do they represent the subaltern in postnational cinema?

Co-existence and creativity in Irish cinema and television

After the bonanza of 1995, a note of realism has arrived, shifting the emphasis away from the taxi rank of slavering foreign producers, queuing for crews and services, back on to Irish producers creating and developing a successful indigenous industry.[6]

In 1995 the Irish government published a discussion document (or Green Paper), *Active or Passive? Broadcasting in the Future Tense*,[7] which outlined its ideas for developing broadcasting legislation in an era of technological convergence and global telecommunications. Its introductory analysis addressed the cultural effects of the US audio-visual sector's 'unassailable global dominant vantage point' (133) and questioned whether the EU 'liberal free market approach' (134) was the most effective strategy against US and Japanese penetration. The document went on to acknowledge that it was now difficult to find 'a consensus on what is "national" about the output of cultural industries [in Ireland and the EU], given the contemporary economic and pragmatic realities of the co-production format in film and television production' (135). The document asked: 'Will we be able to inject Irish cultural production with a *critical regional self-confidence*, secure in its identity in a peripheral nation, that contributes to the promise of a European space that is not bland, monolithic and claustrophobic?' (my emphasis, 136). This question carries the inimitable signature of Michael D. Higgins, steeped in the terminology of postnational and postmodern debates discussed at the end of chapter 1.

As for its concrete proposals, the Green Paper suggested that with RTÉ's monopoly effectively broken, public service broadcasting needed to be legally defined so that providers could be held to account. The Green Paper (Ch. 5, 5.10) went on to propose that a 'Super Authority' be set up by legislation to organise, oversee and develop broadcasting and telecommunications in Ireland, in effect merging the RTÉ Authority (in place since 1960), the Independent Radio and Television Commission (IRTC; instituted in 1988) and the Broadcasting Complaints Commission (166). RTÉ's response betrays how it is caught between the language of national service and that of the market place, not unlike the BBC in Britain.[8] RTÉ firmly asserted its own role in promoting 'the principle that public communication is a public good', arguing that broadcasting should remain a service for citizens of the state and that with secure funding, RTÉ as the historic institution in the state was best placed to provide this service. It rejected the idea of merging existing bodies into a super authority, suggesting instead a less powerful National Broadcasting Commission. It argued that there had been fruitful relations, for example, between the independent production companies, the Irish Film Board and RTÉ; that co-existence within the audio-visual industry needed to recognise its different elements and not have these strategically developed by one single body.

In the budget of 1996 changes were made to Section 35 (S.35) of the Finance Act, which would remain in place until 1999. S.35 provides tax relief to individual and corporate investors in film production in the Republic of Ireland. Originally conceived in 1987, the Act was revised in 1993, providing very favourable terms to foreign investors. It was instrumental in attracting inward investment which, in conjunction with the relaunch of the Film Board, helped boost film production in the Republic from twelve in 1993, to thirteen in 1994 and twenty-two in 1995.[9] It was generally perceived that the changes made in 1996 favoured the smaller budgeted, indigenous productions and were something of a disincentive to the larger Anglo-American backers and production companies courted in the early 1990s.

Originally envisaged in the Fianna Fáil–Labour coalition 'Programme for Partnership' (1993), a national television broadcasting service called Telefís na Gaeilge (TnaG) went on air at the end of October 1996, operating as a publisher broadcaster like Sianel Pedwar Cymru (SC4), the Welsh language station. TnaG installed digital production studios at its Spiddal headquarters in County Galway, to make its own news programmes, but the majority of its material is commissioned, like the soap opera, *Ros na Rún*, co-made by Tyrone/Eo Teilifís. It received IR£6.1 million in start-up funds from the state and has annual running costs of IR£10.2 million. It has been nurtured under the wing of RTÉ, taking a quota of its programmes at no charge. Its Connemara location encouraged independent producers to set up businesses in the underdeveloped west of Ireland, joining earlier pioneers like Bob Quinn's Cinegael. TnaG has a small core staff of thirty people with an average age of twenty-four. TnaG's viewers are estimated to be about 280,000 or 7–9 per cent of the national adult TV audience.[10]

The European Commission (EC) based in Brussels continued to be a vital factor in shaping Ireland's audio-visual environment through its MEDIA programme.[11] Active between 1996 and 2000, MEDIA II is an EC initiative that continues some of the work of earlier MEDIA projects, which between 1991–95 spent ECU (European Currency Units) 200 million on the audio-visual sector in the Europe. Although its funding is considerable – ECU 310 million (or approximately $380 million) – the range of its remit is more modest. It supports training, development and the distribution and promotion of audio-visual projects. This includes setting up training schemes for skills, assisting development of individual production companies and their films and programmes, nurturing audio-visual heritage projects (MAP-TV) and promoting the screening European films around Europe. The Irish Film Board received 48 per cent of its income via the EU Structural Fund in 1997.[12]

After a period of consultation, the government published a White Paper, *Clear Focus: The Government's Proposals for Broadcasting Legislation* (1997), in an election year in the Republic, which saw Síle de Valera replace Higgins in the newly-coined portfolio as minister for arts, heritage, the gaeltacht and the islands. *Clear Focus* went into abeyance with the new administration and the new minister became preoccupied with digital TV. *Clear Focus*'s proposals included the clear, legal definition of 'public service broadcasting', the establishment of an Irish Broadcasting Commission (IBC), a single regulatory and policy-making body to oversee broadcasting (including cable, satellite, local and community services), the abolishment of the IRTC and the conversion of the RTÉ Authority and TnaG into statutory corporations under the new IBC. RTÉ's editorial independence from the state would be guaranteed by virtue of the proposed commission acting as a buffer (46–47). However, *Clear Focus* does point out that RTÉ needed to be much more accountable since it was a publicly-owned institution financed by viewers' licence fees. It also needed to show clearly how it would balance serving the public interest as a broadcaster with its competitive role alongside other broadcasters in the future, such as the new private station, TV3.[13] While the White Paper insisted that this balance should be 'the subject of rigorous scrutiny' (51) its own proposed commission was envisaged as both judge and jury in subsuming the role performed by the separate Broadcasting Complaints Commission (BCC).

Although much fictionalised on film,[14] Northern Ireland had long been a desert for film production. Channel Four TV had funded workshop initiatives since the early 1980s, like the one in Derry that produced *Mother Ireland* and *Hush-a-bye-Baby*. There was meagre support provided through the Northern Ireland Arts Council (in 1994–95 just £50,000), but the majority of fiction film being produced in the early 1990s was from BBCNI. Local pressure for initiatives to bolster independent production in Northern Ireland led to the formation in 1989 of the Northern Ireland Film Council, a voluntary organising and lobbying body.[15] In 1991, ending an anomalous but revealing cultural exclusion, the British Film Institute (BFI) altered its charter to include Northern Ireland within its remit to promote film along with England, Scotland and Wales. The NIFC's *Strategy Proposals* (1991) shaped its work to create and enhance a 'vibrant indigenous film and video culture, which is held to be the basis for a thriving industry in NI'.[16] The NIFC worked with BBCNI's dynamic producer, Robert Cooper, to organise the production of 'Northern Lights' in July 1995, a season of short films, some of which are discussed later in this chapter. The NIFC disbursed over £350,000 of National Lottery Arts Fund money to develop film between November 1995 and mid-1996. In July 1997 the NIFC became a higher profile commission, with a remit to receive and channel funds amounting to £4 million (1997–2000) from a variety of sources including the Arts Council (NI) National Lottery Arts Fund, government departments for economic development and education in NI, and an EU fund for 'Peace and Reconciliation' matched with money from the British government. 1997 brought changes to British tax legislation, which mimicked aspects of S.35 in the Republic and the year saw a flurry of production activity in Northern Ireland, including Tim Loane's short, *Dance Lexie Dance* (1997), as well as cinema features like *Divorcing Jack* (1997) and *Titanic Town* (1998) and a series of shorts for cinema under the NIFC's title 'Premiere', most with BBCNI's involvement since it commanded the largest single source of finance on the island of Ireland for fiction film.

Some of these productions have been in conjunction with RTÉ, which has considerably smaller budgets at its disposal. RTÉ has respectably produced serial dramas, *Glenroe* and *Fair City,* to fairly high standards but has neglected its output of single television drama and filmed fiction. As an institution, RTÉ was slow to adapt to the changing climate. Despite the hint in the 1990 Broadcasting Act that RTÉ should commission a 'reasonable level of independent production', it took statutory amendment in 1993 to require the broadcaster to set up a separate budget to finance commissioned production from the independent sector. RTÉ appointed Claire Duignan in 1993 to head up the Independent Production Unit (IPU) to help develop, fund and produce independent material. Restrictions to RTÉ's advertising revenue generation were lifted in 1993, and the IPU was able to budget over a five-year period to spend as follows (all figures are in IR£ millions): 1994, 5.5; 1995, 6.0; 1996, 7.0; 1997, 8.0; 1998, 10.0; 1999, 15.[17] RTÉ runs 'Script Awards' for new directors, has showcased the work of college graduates and short films in series called *Short Cuts* (in conjunction with the Irish Film Board since 1995) and *Frame Works* (for animation).

The short film surge of the 1990s should be seen as part of a longer, vital element running through contemporary Irish film culture, from experimental, formalist films such as *A Pint of Plain* (1975) and *Waterbag* (1984), right up to contemporary work like Carol Moore's *Gort na gCnámh* (*Field of Bones*, 1997) and animations like Joel Simon's *Ciderpunks* (1997) and Maria Murray and Edith Pieperhoff's *An Bonnán Buí* (1995). Many within the current wave of short film-makers tend to come from an art college or film school background with the cinephile's passion for film as an artistic endeavour. However, with the development of graduate shows since the late 1980s at Dun Laoghaire College of Art and Design, National College of Art and Design and Rathmines College (Dublin Institute of Technology), younger practitioners are encouraged to think that being involved in film, television and animation is also a viable way to make a living. As has been detailed, film festivals in Ireland and abroad provide a showcase for new talent and the number of short film slots on television has increased on both Irish and British networks, providing opportunities for experiment, training and discipline within confines of resources and time. Short and no-budget films constitute a significant part of film culture in contemporary Ireland in which perennial subjects feature, but the short film has explored a range of themes and styles. Damien O'Donnell's brilliantly conceived and executed *Thirty Five Aside* (1995), makes hilarious and sympathetic comedy out of a boy from a dysfunctional family who is bullied at school, while John Moore's unique, *He Shoots, He Scores* (1995), is set in a monochrome futuristic world.[18] Brendan Bourke's slowly-paced *Fishing the Sloe-Black River* (1995, 15 mins.) attempted to film Colum McCann's spare, heavily-metaphorical short story allegory about emigration. Stephen Burke's *After '68* (1994, 26 mins.) and *81* (1996, 26 mins.) sensitively explored the history of the Troubles, managing to be inclusive without being anodyne and a clutch of films came out of the north, including *The Cake* (Nylin, 1995, 12 mins.), *Skin Tight* (Forte, 1995, 15 mins.) and *Dance Lexie Dance* (Loane, 1997, 20 mins.), nominated for an Oscar in 1998,[19] which skilfully probed the nature of sectarianism. Despite the tradition of formal experimentation associated with short film, social realism has been effectively deployed to explore how homophobia affects teenagers growing up in Ireland post-1993, with Orla Walsh's *Bent out of Shape* (1995, 20 mins.) and Eve Morrison's *Summertime* (1995, 28 mins.) being notable examples. Maverick film-makers, Enda and Michael Hughes produced a schlock horror spoof called *The Eliminator* (1996) made for £8,000.[20] Overrunning at eighty-three minutes and in some ways victim of its own inventiveness, it was enthusiastically received, won awards and was quickly followed up with the short, *Flying Saucer Rock 'n' Roll* (1997), a science fiction story set in 1950s Ireland. Despite these encouraging developments, the younger independent producers, like Ed Guiney, are reluctant to get carried away by media hype about the current situation in Ireland:

44 Des O'Byrne and Stuart Donnell in *Bent Out of Shape* (1995).
Courtesy of Orla Walsh/Roisín Rua Films

Remember that things are still at a relatively early stage in terms of development of a real Irish film industry. In terms of facilities, infrastructure and track record, the Irish film industry is still among the least developed industries in Europe.[21]

Re-inventing national cinema?

In this section we pick up some of the debates discussed at the end of chapter 1 and in chapter 2 to examine selected examples from the growing number of feature-length films produced in and about Ireland since 1993. Although output continued to be dominated by Anglo-American finance, productions often had significant Irish creative and technical influence. From a very rich talent pool, Irish actors like Gabriel Byrne, Stephen Rea, Liam Neeson, Brenda Fricker and Brendan Gleeson stood out and began to achieve an international screen presence, but also appeared in smaller budget films and numerous TV projects.[22] Post-1993, indigenous films might have two or three European sources of finance but, despite the risk of turning out 'Euro-puddings', memorable Irish films have been made, which interrogate Ireland's political past, the legacy of its cinematic domination and offer more complex versions of Ireland's present social, political and cultural life. As John Hill has defined it, a '"national" cinema which is properly "national", must be capable of registering the lived complexities of "national" life, be sensitive to the realities of difference (of nation, region, ethnicity, class, gender and sexual orientation) and alert to the fluidity, as well as assumed fixity, of social and cultural identities'.[23] With this in mind, the films discussed next have been divided into three broad groups: (a) films that represent the political conflict in Ireland – particularly Northern Ireland – most of which (with the exception of *Michael Collins*) are set in the recent past;[24] (b) 'heritage cinema' often based on literary or dramatic adaptations, which continued to find audiences; and (c) mostly original screenplays that dealt with the diversity of contemporary Ireland or its recent past, often exploring social problems, migration and the marginalised histories of the subaltern nation.

Troubles, ceasefires and peace?

The history of Anglo-Irish political conflict, particularly in relation to Northern Ireland, remained a rich source of material for film in the 1990s. In this section we examine a selection of films that addressed the conflict, ceasefire and peace-making episodes of this decade. Most films dealt with contemporary history, but *Michael Collins* (1996) went into production (with Warner's $25 million budget) during the longest period of paramilitary ceasefire (1994–96) in the present generation. Jordan's film elevated the events of the historical period 1916–23 to an epic scale, creating, according to one eminent reviewer, 'the most important film made in or about Ireland in the first century of film'.[25]

It was a phenomenal success in Ireland,[26] attracted vituperative criticism in much of the British press and a poor reception in the USA (in terms of box office and Oscars).[27] The epic dimensions of *Michael Collins* generate a tremendous narrative momentum as one's experience is keyed into the intense pace of events portrayed. Apart from the opening, closing and occasional graphic titles there are few concessions made to viewers who are unfamiliar with the period.[28] Jordan compressed the events and key figures of a remarkable seven year period into just over two hours, cutting out the sedentary Treaty negotiations. He conflated historical figures into single characters such as Ned Broy (Stephen Rea) and, to the horror of some historians, the film contains anachronisms (the IRA did not use car bombs in this period), elisions and creative licence (such as the 'Bloody Sunday' massacre). None of these are indefensible. Jordan was not bound by broadcasting's impartiality and balance strictures nor the objectivity claimed by some historians. But it is significant that, like the TV film, *The Treaty* (1991), Jordan provides only a brief, grimly comic moment for Ulster Protestantism (Ian McElhinney's Belfast detective character), indicating a reluctance or inability on the part of many film-makers from the Republic to engage with Unionism, past or present. *Michael Collins*, however, is not a film that glorifies violence as some Irish – as well as many English – critics in the media inaccurately tried to imply.[29] True, Jordan shows that Collins (Liam Neeson) was driven to devise his terrorist methods as a logical strategy to counter the systematic violence of the British Crown forces in Ireland. Perhaps most important for audiences in the Republic was that Jordan took his film past the Treaty, beyond the immediate withdrawal of the British and into the more uncharted cinematic territory of the Irish Civil War that followed independence. Jordan's film probes the postcolonial psyche of the still relatively young state, whose emergence was still within the living memory and whose political configurations had largely followed those set down in the enmity of 1922–23. The scenes in which Collins' assassin (Jonathan Rhys-Meyers) talks with Collins and then Dev (Eamonn de Valera played by Alan Rickman), are suggestive of the young state torn between two versions of its postcolonial future. In an unprecedented, explanatory press statement, the Irish Film Censor, Seamus Smith noted that such was the historical significance of *Michael Collins* that he wished 'to make the film available to the widest possible Irish cinema audience' – despite the graphic violence portrayed – and issued the film with a PG (parental guidance) Certificate.[30] Jordan's film unquestionably favours Collins over de Valera and in the film's pre-credit coda, de Valera's own captioned words ('History will record the greatness of Collins ... at my expense'), the monochrome newsreel footage of Collins' funeral and Elliot Goldenthal's score bring the film to an impressive, elegiac conclusion.

Michael Collins is doubly significant because, as the centenary of world cinema was being celebrated in 1996, Jordan's film is a bravura essay on the nation's *cinematic* past too, pointing up Ireland's particular experience of that 'universal' history. Integral to the political history of violence, Jordan's screenplay engages with the history of US cinema's cultural domination of Ireland through the cinematic medium. Exemplifying the process of postcolonial mimicry outlined earlier in this book, Jordan appropriates the epic bio-pic, film noir and the gangster movie – popular genres themselves reworked by the independent directors of the New Hollywood – for the present-day concerns of Irish audiences saturated in US cinema. The influence of *The Godfather* (1972) is clear in Jordan's film, most notably in the sequences showing the killings of the Cairo gang (British secret service men) by the Apostles (Collins' gang) and the Tans' reprisal killings at Croke Park, known as Bloody Sunday.[31] Jordan's intercutting of intimacy and violence, sanctity and savagery, imitates Coppola's masterpiece.[32] Visually, the desaturated colour palate and lighting by Chris Menges may be seen to borrow from *The Godfather* and noir lighting, making silhouetted figures a 'signature for the film'.[33] There are also touches in the screenplay that suggest Jordan was consciously working in visual references to the Western genre, some of which made the final cut, like the Irregular ambush of Collins at Béal na mBláth, for example.[34] In an era of digital special effects, Jordan's film was old-fashioned in that the magnificent shelling of the Four Courts, Dublin, was achieved on location, in real time before the cameras.

The film was a massive logistical undertaking; the crew and cast working quickly in difficult locations. The whole process became a highly publicised and very public occasion in Irish cinema. Open calls for unpaid extras produced thousands eager to re-enact their country's past and the filming coincided with the 'Forum for Peace' meeting in Dublin Castle. The circumstances of the film's production, eventual release and reception could not have been more propitious. It marked the seventy-fifth anniversary of the foundation of the state, becoming a prism through which Northern Ireland was discussed.[35] *Michael Collins* demonstrated that film had become the pre-eminent medium through which Ireland both examines itself and projects its image to the wider world.

Tripping up the empire: contemporary Troubles films

In a subversive, comic scene from *In the Name of the Father* (1993), falsely-accused Gerry Conlon (Daniel Day-Lewis) and a black prison-mate drop LSD secreted in a jigsaw puzzle map of the British empire. Irish and Afro-Caribbean are criminalised by the state but the ex-colonial from its incarcerated position is still capable of tripping up the empire. Indeed, the dissensual contemporary history of Britain and Ireland has provided rich subject matter for popular films.[36] The British state is shown to have underwritten miscarriages of justice, remained unmoved by the political gesture of self-willed starvation and has only recently established a fragile peace in Northern Ireland at great cost to the lives of civilians and combatants, as well as corrupting the institutions and values it seeks to uphold.

In the Name of the Father (1993), *Some Mother's Son* (1996) and *The Boxer* (1998) constitute a trilogy of films, based on a productive collaboration

45 Filial conciliation: *In the Name of the Father* (1993).
Courtesy of Universal Pictures

between Jim Sheridan and Terry George. The first of these, adapted from the autobiography of Gerry Conlon,[37] one of the people who subsequently became known as the Guildford Four, wrongly convicted for IRA bombs in 1974,[38] is a narrative about innocent individuals overcoming racism and criminal misdemeanours within the British police and judicial system. The heart of the film was the exploration of the difficult relationship between Giuseppe Conlon (Pete Postlethwaite) – who tragically died in prison before a judicial appeal was upheld in 1989 – and his wayward son. Critical flak was directed at the film, for the script's factual errors – such as having Giuseppe and Gerard share a prison cell. Attacking a film for its standards of journalism, accusing it of distortion, was a deliberately inappropriate, indeed, pre-emptive strike by a hostile British news media. The power of the underlying truths portrayed in the film required damage-limitation strategies. Most of the British press, government and legal establishment disliked the film because it rekindled the outrage felt by the Irish community in Britain at an appalling miscarriage of justice; it raised awareness of the case among the wider population in Britain; and it undermined the credibility of the English legal system at an international level and provided further momentum to similar cases, such as the Birmingham Six.[39] The screenplay's dramatic licence is justified in that it told the essential truth of the case. It did not distort the fact that innocent people were wrongly convicted. In terms of what it contributed to Irish film, it imaginatively focused on a redeemed father-son conflict and the implications of this as a metaphor for contemporary Ireland. In the mild-mannered, stoical and loving Giuseppe, Sheridan was attempting to provide Ireland with a good father figure, rare enough in Irish culture. As one critic has suggested, it constitutes as an imaginative attempt by a postcolonial cinema to redefine colonial fatherhood models that are characterised by authoritative paternalism.[40]

A common ploy to attack *In the Name of the Father* in both Britain and the USA was to smear it by association as 'pro-IRA',[41] a gross distortion of the screenplay that carefully distanced Giuseppe and Gerry from the republican movement in Belfast and from the sadistic IRA prisoner (Don Baker) in prison itself. Similar strategies were used to marginalise *Some Mother's Son* (1997),[42] an $8 million film based on a screenplay by Terry George that ambitiously reimagined for the first time on screen a key event of the contemporary Troubles. The hunger strikes of 1979–81 saw ten republican prisoners starve themselves to death for political status and, like *Michael Collins*, the past was projected in the present with IRA and UVF prisoners a crucial factor in peace negotiations. Its release was allegedly delayed in Britain and Ireland because of its possible destabilising effect on negotiations. Hostile reactions in the British press were predictable, but criticism from republicans were less expected. Two mothers, Kathleen Quigley (Helen Mirren) and Annie Higgins (Fionnula Flanagan), are brought together when their sons, Gerard (Aiden Gillen) and Frank (David O'Hara), are imprisoned as IRA volunteers. In the focus on the mother-son relationship, George was tapping into a strong mythos within traditional Irish nationalism, but he chose the

46 Mothers united: *Some Mother's Son* (1997).
Courtesy of Castle Rock Entertainment/Turner Entertainment

womens' perspective as a lens through which to investigate the complexities of
the hunger strike; something hitherto portrayed as a narrative of Irish male sacrifice. There was republican discomfort at how it showed divisions within communities and church, between politicians and relatives, and less than unified
opposition to British intransigence.[43] *Some Mother's Son* focuses on mothers who
differ in class, personality and attitudes. The film tries unconvincingly to hold
them together in maternal unity until the end, when Kathleen decides to sign her
son off the strike. Annie is compelled by her long-held republicanism to let her
son kill himself and the British are shown to be duplicitous in negotiations to end
the protest. *Some Mother's Son* is a fast-paced, convincingly-acted film, which,
through the star-persona of Mirren, compels us to imagine a dilemma few of us
would ever contemplate. It allowed its audiences to experience what popular history must feel like to its participants and 'in an age of images, traditional historians may feel especially threatened by efforts at popular history', which these
films constitute.[44]

Reservoir Prods? Recent images of loyalist paramilitaries

American-Irish and English-based film producers have been castigated by
newspaper critic Alexander Walker for making films that were allegedly IRA
propaganda, while academic Brian McIlroy argues that most films about the
Troubles reproduce – deliberately or naively – what he terms 'the innate intellectual weakness in the dominant nationalist cinematic heritage of Ireland – its
exclusionary aesthetics'.[45] According to him, the majority population of
Northern Ireland, who support political unionism, remain misrepresented,
leaving Ulster loyalist viewers to masquerade the pleasures of imaginary narratives in which their own cultural identity is degraded, rendered problematic or
absent.[46] Two recent productions allow us to consider these ideas. *Nothing
Personal* (1995)[47] and *Resurrection Man* (1998) focused on the urban Protestant
working class of Belfast and proved to be highly contentious films. Based on
Northern Irish literary sources,[48] they were directed by Thaddeus O'Sullivan,
Dublin-born but long resident in London, and Welshman Marc Evans. Made in
the interregnum of peace in 1994–95, the historical setting of *Nothing Personal*
is the short-lived truce between the republican and Ulster loyalist paramilitaries of 1975. It attempts, like *Resurrection Man*, to render the social lives and
psychology of working-class men involved in the UDA and UVF.[49] Both films
focus on killings periodically organised by these paramilitaries to out-terrorise
the terrorists (that is, the IRA). Tapping into serial killer and new gangster
movies, these films focus on the sadistic sectarianism of individuals like Lennie
Murphy, who led a maverick UVF gang known as the Shankill Butchers,
responsible for brutal, ritualistic murders of Catholics (and some Protestants
who were deemed disloyal).

In *Nothing Personal*, Ginger's (Ian Hart) actions are tolerated within an
embattled community of crime, unemployment and political powerlessness

overseen by godfathers like McLure (Sean McGinley). However, virtually nothing beyond an enclosed, dimly lit world of loyalist drinking clubs and the mean streets of Belfast is suggested to contextualise the killings. If the film says little about politics in a formal sense, it is more insightful about the psycho pathology of male paramilitary gangs and their associates. Ginger's sadism towards Catholics is an extreme version of his attitudes towards women; the outcome of a sub-culture of guns is prefigured in Tommy's (Ruaidhrí Conroy) adolescent attempts to impress girls. Liam (John Lynch) is tortured by Ginger's gang and only spared because Kenny (James Frain) happened to know him from their boyhood days, a time when such connections between communities could exist. Without calling for anodyne solution story lines, the possibilities of this past have yet to be explored outside the 'love across the barricades' treatment, familiar in much TV drama. As it is, the weakest part of *Nothing Personal* is its foray into a relationship between Liam and Ann (Maria Kennedy) a Protestant nurse, who takes him in after his beating. As we have seen with other representations, a tension between imperatives to verisimilitude or historical realism on the one hand, and on the other, dramatic or aesthetic concerns, often shows itself within a film. While *Nothing Personal* used an explanatory caption to open the film, O'Sullivan has talked of filming the setting to present it 'in a way that is really more theatrical than naturalistic',[50] and that he is more concerned about dramatising conflict visually than giving sociological reasons for it. Nevertheless, it is difficult to accept his claim that he did not have a political position to take on the film. O'Sullivan is rare among Irish film-makers in that he has made a concerted attempt to put southern and Ulster Protestants on screen, as in *The Woman who Married Clark Gable* (1985) and *December Bride* (1990). But his basically humane desire for the film to be understood in 'human terms and not in terms of Northern Ireland politics'[51] did not satisfy critics from a unionist viewpoint.

Such a viewer might find even less comfort in *Resurrection Man*, the early 1998 release of which provoked protest in Northern Ireland, caused some British critics to walk out of previews[52] and was poorly reviewed in *The Irish Times*. Victor Kelly (Stuart Townsend), the eponymous 'resurrection man', is brought up by an over-zealous, protective mother-figure, Dorcas Kelly (Brenda Fricker), and a weak father (George Shane). The controlling framework for the film are snippets of interviews given to a journalist by people who knew Victor, a moody, sharply-dressed sadist who is alluring to the local women. His formidable mother maintains her boy's innocence after he has been gunned down in an ambush set up by Jimmy McLure (Sean McGinley), evangelist preacher by day and perverse gang leader by night. Pierre Aim's cinematography is excellent in capturing the look of seventies Belfast (actually shot in north-west England) and the ambient soundtrack of period pop choices is informed by the grisly wit of an Ulster radio DJ, David Holmes. In one scene, 'Tiger Feet' (by Mud) accompanies the sickeningly casual kicking of a Catholic by a group of men in the Gibraltar Bar, a loyalist drinking club.[53]

Early on in the film, Victor, as a child (Lee Mulrooney) is seen identifying with Jimmy Cagney's character in *Public Enemy* (1931) and, as a young man, slashing his victims mercilessly to a slow death, he seeks the recognition of the media, represented by Ryan (James Nesbitt) and Coppinger (James Ellis). Ryan has been violent towards his partner, hospital doctor, Elizabeth (Zara Turner) and the young reporter is unusually fascinated with the killings, a trait correctly observed by Herbie (Derek Thompson), Ryan's superior officer. The film probes the discomforting idea that Victor's psychosis is intimately connected with the normality of a dysfunctional society, heavily militarised and suffocating under surveillance. Victor moves between the authoritarian austerity underlying Dorcas's domestic doting and the manipulative McLure who steers his principal 'resurrection man' only as long as it is useful to him to maintain his local power base. In one of the more bizarre moments in the film, McLure is seen surrounded by Nazi memorabilia, snorting cocaine, listening to 'Jerusalem' and flirting with young Victor. This confection of McLure's evangelism, neo-Nazi nationalism, decadence and hint of homosexuality is a cinematic caricature of the right-wing undercurrents of loyalist 'ultras'. In one of the film's most memorable images, Victor's mental state is represented by a shot of a mirror in which his reflection is distorted by the blood of a victim streaming down it. Ryan is set up by McLure not only to witness Victor's last victim plead for death – the film also hints that Ryan actually finishes him off – but is made complicit in his silence about McLure's part in the killing of Victor. The 'resurrection man' had become a danger to McLure who goads the reporter: 'I knew

47 Stuart Townsend as Victor in *Resurrection Man* (1998).
Courtesy of Polygram Filmed Entertainment

you wouldn't say anything … congratulations, Ryan, you're one of us now', which suggests a wider dilemma for media reportage to avoid the seductions of 'the durable rhythms of violence'.[53] 'The Shankill Butchers' killings are shocking and, even if the film explored rather than exploited the topic, it is perhaps understandable that *Resurrection Man* might anger Gary Mitchell, a playwright from a loyalist background who criticised the film.[54] But it is worrying that a kind of paranoia – expressed by Brian McIlroy when he states that: 'The unionist case … cannot be trusted to be put by Protestants themselves'[55] – would have film-makers hold back from unflinchingly reimagining a Protestant past, including its villains as well as its heroes.

Heritage and literary adaptation films

Considerable Anglo-American investment in Irish-themed films continued throughout the 1990s, despite the changes made to S.35 funding in 1996. Many of these films used literary and theatrical sources as the basis for screenplays and often cast US stars in lead roles supported in depth with Irish talent. Film deals were put together involving television broadcast rights and some were able to make use of MEDIA support. Typically such films adopted an approach to an Irish screen past, which was defined in chapter 6 as 'heritage cinema'. Notable films did buck this trend: Cathal Black is content with smaller budgets (under a million) and self-distribution because it ensures his control of the finished product; Mary McGuckian, Ed Guiney and Paddy Breathnach are new directors and producers who have attempted to make films not just with EU money but within an (Eastern) European film tradition, ever conscious of Hollywood's domination of European cinemas.

Directors like David Keating and Pat O'Connor have created films that are essentially rites of passage narratives aimed at youth audiences, epitomised in *Last of the High Kings* and *Circle of Friends* both of which were released in 1995. Keating's film (co-scripted with executive producer and actor, Gabriel Byrne) was based on a short novel by Ferdia MacAnna, starred American Jared Leto as Frankie Griffin coming to terms with life after the Leaving Certificate (pre-university) examinations during a long, sunny summer in 1977. Frankie's voice-over conventionally allows us access to his adolescent worries about exam results, his family and his nascent sexuality. His family are a bunch of loveable eccentrics: Ma (miscast and poorly performed by Irish-American Catherine O'Hara) is an implausible character who spouts half-baked nationalism and claims the family to have a blood line to the High Kings of Ireland; Da (Gabriel Byrne) is an actor, often away on tour. The Irish elections of that year form a background to the film but only intrude in so far as to provide a politician (Colm Meaney) with an opportunity to seduce Ma. Frankie's sexual urges culminate in a conventional bedroom scene with Jayne Wayne (Lorraine Pilkington) set to 'Parisienne Walkways'. Playing with masculinity's representational ambiguities in 1990s cinema, the film consistently frames the young male lead's body 'to-be-looked-at'. This potential to be simultaneously an object of desire for straight female and gay viewers is most explicit in the image of Leto's bare backside as he descends from Jayne's bedroom window. However, narrative heterosexuality is reaffirmed by Frankie's romantic interest in Romy Thomas (Emily Mortimer). The film's other pleasures come from the beautifully filmed summery locations in Howth and the expertly deployed music of Thin Lizzy, Rory Gallagher and David Bowie, period sounds adding to the golden glow of the cinematography.

The USA features significantly in the film in terms of narrative, theme and character. Da's tour to New York produces Erin (Christina Ricci), a teenage visitor who tries unsuccessfully to woo Frankie, but teaches him how to express his feelings and kiss. At the end of the film, he uses Erin's exact words to convince Romy that he fancies her, and not her best friend Jayne with whom he has lost his virginity. A large part of Jayne and Romy's appeal is their Protestantism and supposed sexual liberalism. Through Frankie's confrontation with his mother the film gently points to Ireland's growing maturity and social liberalism. Within comfortable middle-class suburbs, old-fashioned Fianna Fáil politics and the church – personified by the out-of-touch Father Michael (Mark O'Regan) – are gently satirised. If the American Erin is a catalyst for change in Frankie, then the death of Elvis Presley in August 1977 is seen to prefigure the passing of an era in Ireland's popular culture. Frankie and his mates stage a beach party ('What do you think this is … California?' asks one doubter) at the summer's close, which becomes a wake for Elvis – his image is projected on to an out-door film screen singing 'Blue Suede Shoes'. The narrative is perhaps too neatly tied up with the return of Da, and the fact that Frankie gets his exams and his girl (Romy) at the end of the party. But in its confident positioning of Thin Lizzy – an Irish rock band fronted by Phil Lynott, a mixed-race Dubliner – between Elvis and Bowie, and the preferred values of liberal reform, the film found 1970s sources for the progressive 1990s.

Circle of Friends, based on Maeve Binchy's popular novel and adapted for screen by Andrew Davies, opens with a long-shot of the green, rural surrounds of Knockglen (filmed in Kilkenny) and Irish pipe music. Starting in 1949 – the year in which Ireland's status as a Republic separate from the British Empire was achieved – the film traces the lives of three girls, Benny (Minnie Driver), Eve (Geraldine O'Rawe) and Nan (Saffron Burrows), from confirmation to coming of age. The film jumps forward to the year 1957–58, showing the girls going up to college in Dublin, the excitement of the city and boys, particularly Benny's infatuation with Jack Foley (Chris O'Donnell), a handsome medical student and rugby-player. Benny strains at the leash of small-town life. Her parents run a haberdashery and imagine Benny will become engaged to the obsequious Sean Walsh (Alan Cumming). Further narrative hurdles are put in the way of Benny and Jack's union as Nan becomes pregnant by Simon Westward (Colin Firth), the caddish Protestant of the Big House, but blames it on Jack. Benny is deeply upset, returns to Knockglen, where she has to repel

Sean's attempted rape. At a party at Eve's cottage in the woods (left to her by her dead father), Nan's lie is exposed. She leaves for England by boat and Benny's voice-over explains how Jack and herself fall in love again. The film closes with the couple secretly entering Eve's cottage and Benny's voice-over – 'Bless me, Father, for I *have* sinned' – cues the credits. The film provided a highly conventionalised narrative of love and courtship triumphing against the constraints of small-town rural life. It coyly captured the sense of Ireland on the cusp of change in the late 1950s. The pleasures of the film come more from the sumptuousness of Frank Conway's design and Pat O'Connor's direction of good-looking young stars than from its rather predictable narrative resolution. It was a winning box-office formula in the USA, taking $15 million dollars in its first six weeks of release.[56]

Mary McGuckian's *Words Upon the Window* Pane (1995) is atypical in that she took a 'difficult' W. B. Yeats play and made a film with a European art film sensibility for her debut feature.[57] Set in Dublin in the late 1920s, it tells the story of a group of disparate people meeting to conduct a seance in a Georgian house, which it transpires is haunted by the spirit of Dean Jonathan Swift's secret wife, Stella, who had died two centuries earlier. It is a slow-paced, deliberate film that manages to convey the play's sense of forbidding disturbance. In McGuckian's view her film, through its use of Anglo-Irish architecture, Georgian streets and the organising presence of Swift (Jim Sheridan), sought to address the marginalisation and rejection of Ireland's Anglophile cultural heritage in traditional nationalist versions of the past: 'I think we're over it now and should be able to address it and celebrate it'.[58] Funded, filmed and post-produced variously in Germany, Luxembourg, the UK, France and Ireland, McGuckian has pointed out that 'it was made as a European film for a European audience. It was intended to be a departure from this 1950s Irish look'.[59]

Cathal Black co-wrote and directed *Korea* (1995), a short feature that tackled the 1950s in a way that avoided the pitfalls that McGuckian rightly identifies in some heritage films of the 1990s. Based on John McGahern's short story of the same title, *Korea* contains the stock-in-trade ingredients of a father-son conflict, an absent mother, tradition versus modernity, emigration, the vestiges of civil war rivalry between neighbours and a rites-of-passage romance concentrated in seventy-five minutes.[60] Black's achievement in the film is (like O'Sullivan in *December Bride*) to marry characters to place and create a narrative whose unfolding has a measured, almost restrained pace. Shot in Bawnboy, on the Cavan border the story tells of John Doyle (Donal Donnelly) and his son Eamon (Andrew Scott) who fish the lake for eels. Doyle senior is in conflict with his neighbour, Ben Moran (Vass Anderson) both about the past (Doyle was a Republican, Moran a Free Stater during the civil war) and the present. Moran is a modernist. He accepts that the lake must take on tourism, while Doyle fights to defend tradition and his eel-fishing livelihood. The neighbourhood believe Moran's recent affluence is US government compensation money,

48 The 'American' hero, dead and buried in Ireland: *Korea* (1995).
Courtesy of Cathal Black. Photo reproduction by Blowup

paid for the death of his son, a soldier-emigrant killed in Korea. Caught up in this feud, Eamon falls in love with Moran's daughter, Una (Fiona Maloney). Eamon is reluctant to carry on his father's bitterness but is undecided about his future. In an effort to break up the young lovers, and with half a mind to the money that might come back in post-office money orders (or military compensation?) Doyle buys his son a ticket for the USA. In the end, father and son are reconciled, but the best feature of *Korea* is its superb handling of the complexity of this period's interconnections. In the USA, Ireland's contradictory soul is laid bare: it is the source of opportunity and wealth during a time of economic stagnation, an outlet from repression, but also a source of tragedy, loneliness and the ultimate loss. This is captured memorably in the image of young Moran's coffin draped in the 'Stars and Stripes' being rowed across the lake to a watery burial

Frank McGuinness's screen adaptation of Brian Friel's internationally acclaimed drama, *Dancing at Lughnasa* (1998), set in 1936, recreates this period through the meticulous elegance of Pat O'Connor's direction and Kenneth MacMillan's photography.[61] The five Mundy sisters subsist on a desolate small-holding in Donegal, bringing up Michael (Darrell Johnston), the illegitimate son of Christina (Catherine McCormack). Their fragile economy is threatened when school-mistress sister Kate (Meryl Streep) is made redundant and the cottage knitting industry of the area is absorbed by the opening of a textile factory. The emotional stability of the family unit is shaken by the return after twenty five years of their brother, Jack (Michael Gambon), a missionary priest in Africa; the re-appearance after two years absence of Gerry (Rhys Ifans),

Michael's father, and Rose's (Sophie Thompson) secret dalliance with Danny Bradley (Lorcan Cranitch) – separated but still married – who wants to emigrate with her. Its narrative – framed by the voice-over of Michael as an adult (Gerard McSorley) – explores the tensions within the forced stoicism of rural Irish life. Ireland's connections with colonialism and internationalism are teased out in several ways. Father Jack's feathered tricorn hat (from the last governor of Uganda) signifies Irish involvement in political forms of imperialism. Some see that he has had 'his head turned completely' in Africa, devout Kate resents his 'own distinctive spiritual search' and the local Irish hierarchy are suspicious that he has 'gone native' on the African mission, Catholicism's part in a kind of spiritual colonialism.

Devout christianity's 'contamination' from overseas is an index of the threat represented by indigenous popular passions, namely the pagan god, Lug. Celebrated in August in the dancing of Lughnasa, Irish Lug is likened to the African earth goddess, Obi. The most resonant audio-visual image is of the Marconi wireless set in the Mundy's kitchen. Radio Éireann's transmission signal is symbolically weak, subject to interference and oral competition (Gerry singing Cole Porter's 'Anything goes' to Christina). While radio schedules in the 1930s attempted to endorse a staid version of post-independence Irish music culture, it was potentially the harbinger of momentary passions: the five sisters give themselves to the mood of near hysteria induced by the Irish dance music (composed by Bill Whelan). However, Noel Pearson's production has a downbeat ending: Agnes and Rose emigrate to London and destitution; Gerry becomes accidentally injured in the International Brigade in Spain fighting Franco; and Jack dies an apostate while the remaining sisters eke out their dreary and inconsolable lives.[62]

Imaging contemporary Ireland

Some of the most recent low-budget independent productions from Ireland tackle contemporary society, its problems and transitional crises, including damaging marital relations, separated spouses, social exclusions based on poverty and prejudice and disenchantment with the new Ireland without its anchoring institutions. This cinema of the have-nots and the left-outs, the criminals, losers and misfits, is often bleak and disturbing but also memorable and sometimes surprisingly funny. Gerry Stembridge's debut feature, *Guiltrip* (1995), benefited from EURIMAGE funding and came about after tricky financial deals were struck across Europe.[63] This did not seem to have a detrimental effect on the treatment of the subject matter – the domestic abuse of Tina (Jasmine Russell) by her soldier husband, Liam (Andrew Connolly). Shot in Maynooth and Leixlip, and taking place on one day in the week of imaginary 'Anytown Ireland',[64] the setting is claustrophobic, characters criss-cross a narrative that is played back through a complex series of flashbacks to earlier in the day. Liam is obsessive about hygiene, order and discipline at work and in his marriage. He is a domestic control freak who insists Tina accounts for her every action in a ledger-book. Although Liam never hits her or their child, he mentally tortures her and tries to cut her off from her one friend, Joan (Pauline McLynn), their neighbour. His warped kind of 'loving' behaviour (neatly captured in the lyric from the Joe Dolan CD she plays for him: 'I love you in my own peculiar way') is rooted in emotional insecurity and sexual inadequacy. An after-work drink with his soldier friends gets out of control. The town's electronics shop salesman (played well by Peter Hanley), tries unsuccessfully to use his inane sales patter in the bruising environment of the bar. While he is painfully inept and socially clingy, it also becomes clear that his marriage to Michelle (Michelle Houlden) is flawed and she resents his presence. Observing this weakness and spurred by sexual attraction, Liam takes Michelle back to the army base for sex. But his impotence provokes momentary anger and frustration, and he batters her to death. As with Kevin Liddy's accomplished short film, *The Soldier's Song* (1997), this film examines how the training of service men conditions them to bully and dehumanise in the name of discipline and manliness. It also has similarities with Paddy Breathnach's *Ailsa* (1994) in which a man (Brendan Coyle) obsessively stalks a woman who shares his house. It is perhaps no surprise that Ed Guiney produced both *Ailsa* and *Guiltrip* with the European art film in mind. In *Guiltrip*, Stembridge has explained how he wanted to avoid the urban–rural divide often portrayed in Irish film and show what he sees as the small-town life of Ireland where 'city and country collide'.[65] On a limited budget of IR£800,000 ($1.2 million), this nuanced sense of place, along with Tina's domestic confinement and Liam's menacing emotional limitations, is well conveyed.[66]

The mid-1990s saw the emergence of women film-makers. Mary McGuckian followed up *Words* with a contemporary love story set in Northern Ireland, *This is the Sea* (1997). Trish McAdam, followed her debut feature, *Snakes and Ladders* (1995),[67] with the three-part documentary, *Hoodwinked* (1997), charting the role of women in the Irish state post-1922. *Snakes and Ladders* is an assured thirtysomething comedy set in a vibrant, slightly bohemian Dublin that focuses on the lives, love and friendship of two female street performers, Jean (Pam Boyd) and Kate (Gina Moxley). Jean's engagement to a musician, Martin (Sean Hughes), has unconventional origins (a proposal scene in a toilet) and the idea of marriage is more enthusiastically embraced by Jean's eccentric mother (Rosleen Linehan) than it seems to be by the couple themselves. Jean's ambition leads her to fall out with Kate to take a tacky job as a youth TV presenter. Martin and Kate sleep together and she becomes pregnant. Jean soon becomes disillusioned with the world of TV, her marriage to Martin goes ahead because Kate refuses to name the father of her child, and the two women become best friends again. The ending is comically well-poised with Martin left awkwardly holding the baby on the day of his wedding in the traditional photograph. *Snakes and Ladders* is a refreshing, light-hearted film in which character and performance take precedence over what is on the surface

49 Jean (Pam Boyd) and Kate (Gina Moxley) in *Snakes and Ladders* (1997).
Courtesy of Trish McAdam

an unremarkable narrative of contemporary life. The female characters are
complex, funny and interact well together. The atmosphere of 1990s Dublin is
well conveyed in the club venues, street theatre and the 'Left Bank on the Liffey'
redevelopment, but this is neatly off-set by the suburban sequences showing
Ma's older generation caught between Joe Dolan and keep-fit aerobics. It was
not a film that declared issues but it did buck Irish cinematic convention and
contributed to a more diverse representation of contemporary Ireland.

    Geraldine Creed's debut feature, *The Sun, the Moon and the Stars* (1996), is
one of the more accomplished coming-of-age Irish screen stories about women
that is not set in the north.[68] The film tells of Mo (Gina Moxley), confronted by
a boss who will not promote her because of her 'family commitments' – she has
two daughters, Dee (Aisling Corcoran) and Shelley (Elaine Cassidy) – and is
separated from her husband. Mo hurriedly books a holiday in a small seaside
town, which provides time and space for self-assessment and exploration for
the three women. They come into contact with new age American, Abbie
(Angie Dickinson), and travelling Australian, Pat (Jason Donovan). The quirky
humour, engaging performances and a plausibly happy ending were only
marred, according to one reviewer,[69] by the uneven editing of the material.
Thematically, however, it addressed the difficulties faced by some women in
Irish society, despite supposed advances over inequalities. In interview, Creed

has commented on the relative immaturity of Irish cinema and notions of film politics defined restrictively – according to her – by Kevin Rockett at a conference in Virginia in May 1996. Creed asserts that 'there are personal politics as well as social politics. Not everyone is talking about 1916 and the fucking formation of the State and the mother figure in the household, you know?'[70] Her remarks indicate a disenchantment with a screen politics defined in male terms at a national level, which is perhaps best addressed not only in films by women, but in shifting the focus to the sub-national, to individuals and groups who are the losers, the victims, the criminalised or the insane; in other words, what we have been terming the subaltern in Irish society.

Billy Roche's first venture into screen writing produced *Trojan Eddie* (1997), which makes excellent use of a small-town environment (probably based on his native Wexford) as a setting for his eponymous, unlikely 'hero' (Stephen Rea). Eddie prides himself on his market trader patter to earn a living. He has separated from his wife, is bringing up two children, is perpetually planning to start out on his own and genuinely wants to do the best for his kids. Humour and sympathy are generated by seeing an essentially inoffensive, harmless character getting out of his depth in the nefarious activities of the informal economy of temporary market fairs. He sells cheap (possibly stolen) household goods for John Power (Richard Harris), the ageing patriarch of a settled Traveller family. This widowed man mourns his wife and, deep-down, his own betrayal of the travelling life. He attempts to rekindle his passion and

50 Reluctant hero: Stephen Rea in *Trojan Eddie* (1997).
Courtesy of Channel Four Films. Photo: Jonathan Hession

status by an inappropriate match to Kathleen (Aislinn McGuckian), a young girl from another Traveller family. She skips off with Eddie's 'assistant', Dermot (Stuart Townsend), on the wedding night, taking a case of cash. Long-suffering Eddie covers for his mate's recklessness much to the annoyance of Power. The film unsentimentally portrays the place of the Travellers in Ireland's marginal economy, the underbelly of the Celtic Tiger. The scenes of formal courtship and the wedding itself ring true and Harris is awesome as a man of injured pride. However, Eddie's understated but endearing character is the emotional centre of a film that is dark but wryly humorous and leaves us thinking Eddie finally has got a lucky break to start up his own business.

Johnny Gogan's first full-length feature, *The Last Bus Home* (1997), spans a period between 1979 and 1993 and is set in the imaginary McDonagh Heights in Dublin's northside suburbia. Its principal characters are Reena (Annie Ryan), Jessop (Brian F. O'Byrne), Petie (John Cronin), and Joe (Barry Comerford). They are Ireland's inner exiles, finding no connection with the mass observance of John Paul II's visit to Dublin in 1979. The colour tones of Dublin's skyscape, its stillness and the silence away from Phoenix Park are eerily arresting after the film's energetic opening to 'Teenage Kicks' by The Undertones. Gogan's film captures an astringent confrontation – crystallised in Irish youth culture – the division that opened up at the end of the 1970s between tradition and iconoclasm, between the Pope and punk. *Last Bus* taps into this alternative undercurrent – rather like the skilful use of Lynott and Bowie in *Last of the High Kings* – making Alan Parker's dalliance with Dublin soul in *The Commitments* look shallow and exploitative by comparison. The four disaffected youths form a band, 'The Dead Patriots', subverting its nationalist connotations and reinventing popular song with their own punk rendition of 'Are you there, Moriarty?' during a power cut at a gig. They use Dublin public buses to get around Dublin and slowly begin to attract a following. While Reena and Paul explore sex openly on the back seat of the bus, the young drummer Petie is painfully coming to terms with his own homosexuality. He is assaulted by skin heads but also has to endure Paul's casual intolerance. Petie confides in Reena and things look up when he catches the eye of Billy (Anthony Brophy), just back from London. The two lads covertly flirt with each other under the noses of an unknowing Paul and later, in one of Irish cinema's rare gay bed scenes, Petie says: 'My only regret is that this didn't happen sooner'. In a rush, Petie comes out to his parents in the belief that he will go to London with the band since they have attracted the interest of Steve (Brendan Coyle), largely due to Reena. However, the band stalls at the decision to go to London, Paul lacks self-confidence, feels cut out of Petie's life and is jealous about Reena's fling with Steve. At their farewell gig, Paul cruelly humiliates Petie by 'outing' him to a vociferous crowd. Afterwards, Petie is killed by the last bus home in circumstances that suggest suicide. The film comes forward to 1993. Reena has been away to the USA and Paul has set up a club in which Billy, in a kind of Marc Almond torch-song, remembers Petie and we learn that homosexuality has just been decriminalised in Ireland. The film captures a transitional moment in the late-1970s, but it also questions the extent to which 1990s reforms have delivered gays from insidious homophobia. The film is 'postgay', that is, it extends beyond the 'good gay movie' syndrome of the early 1990s, since Petie does not happily survive the film. This is less a negative image than a reminder that teenage gays are disproportionately represented in Irish suicide figures, still get 'gay-bashed' and feel compelled to emigrate despite law reform and Ireland's relative economic prosperity.[71]

The lives of Irish emigrant building workers in the USA are confronted head on in *2by4* (1997), a narrative about alienated men escaping from problems of a social and psychological kind. Jimmy Smallhorne – born and bred in Dublin's northside – wrote the screenplay (with Fergus Tighe and Terry McGoff), took the lead role as Johnny, and directed the action in an independent US film that disturbed any nostalgia about emigration, US immigrant groups and liberal gay rights voices in America and Ireland.[72] Its frank portrayal of a young man literally scarred by sado-masochistic sex abuse by his uncle (Chris O'Neil) also highlighted the Irish workers' incipient racism against Jews and Hispanics. As Smallhorne himself said: 'I don't make fuckin' political correct films'.[73] Johnny is a foreman of a gang of Irish workers subcontracted to refurbish a Jewish office development (*2by4* refers to the size of the wood used in construction). While it provides some giddying, lyrical sequences of the cityscape from the point of view of the workers, the film gives us intimate access to the social and psychological realities of life for illegal immigrants. The gang is being ripped off by the uncle, who uses their wages to pay for a muscled male black prostitute to whip him. The gang also has no security and gets by on cocaine and the camaraderie of desperation. In a truly moving scene, one workman (Joe Hollyoake) is forced by his mates to read a poem that unbeknownst to them he has had published. It articulates his loneliness and homesickness, which silences them in recognition. It is a rare, reflective moment in a film that conveys the pace, liveliness and activity of the city at work and play. Johnny's sexually alternative lifestyle is not so far removed from the alcohol and drug hedonism of his work mates. In an improbable plot-line, Johnny meets up with a young, good-looking Australian street-hustler, Christian (Bradley Fitts), whose drug addiction and insecurity make him cling to Johnny following a tender love-scene in a brothel. The film is punctuated with surreal flashback or dreams from Johnny's past, which hint at the abuse by his uncle and these memories come back to him in a climatic breakdown on the dance-floor of a night club, after which he begins to confront his past. Johnny is a complex personality brilliantly portrayed by Smallhorne. He is racist towards a Hispanic shop-keeper and gets beaten for his abuse. Although he is a deeply troubled person he exhibits some degree of empathy to care for his work mates, his girlfriend Maria (Kimberley Topper) and Christian. He also ends up forgiving his abuser. The flashback device[74] linking his mental state and sexual identity to sex abuse sits awkwardly in a film that is otherwise an impressive debut that even manages to use 'Danny Boy' unsentimentally over the closing credits.

Ireland went through a period of rapid transition in the 1990s, especially in Dublin and other cities like Cork, Limerick and Belfast. Ireland became more internationalised, urbanised, cosmopolitan and materialistic. Socio-economic poverty in regions outside Dublin became more pronounced with the corollary of a growing illicit economy and crime, both petty and serious organised activity, increasingly violent and drugs-related. The news media investigated and increased awareness of crime, and the contract killing of journalist Veronica Guerin in 1996 shocked Ireland. But the media also exposed major business fraud within the Irish beef industry and among government ministers, which led to a judicial tribunal of inquiry in 1991–92. The political effect of the 'Beef Tribunal' was to bring down the Fianna Fáil government, but its wider significance in the 1990s was to confirm popular doubts about certain Irish politicians, the process of government itself, and increase scepticism about the probity of corporate business activities in Ireland. Against a background in which distinctions between gangsters and governors became blurred, and in the cinematic context of a vogue for US and British gangster movies – from Scorsese's *Goodfellas* (1990) and the Coens' *Miller's Crossing* (1990) to *Lock, Stock and Two Smoking Barrels* (1998) – it is interesting to consider two award-winning Irish films that tap into this genre.

The General (1997), by veteran film-maker John Boorman, an Englishman resident in Ireland for nearly thirty years, deals with the life of Martin Cahill (Brendan Gleeson), a notorious Dublin figure who graduated from house-breaking as a young man to become 'The General' of an extremely powerful gang perpetrating major organised crimes during the 1970s and 1980s, often with seeming impunity from Gardaí and the law.[75] The film was shot in colour but released in stunning black and white, 'so you would look at contemporary Ireland in a slightly different way. It's a way of revealing'.[76] Cahill was an ingenious, iconoclastic, charismatic figure, but macabre in his principled brutality. Boorman's insight that 'it's comforting to think of criminals being completely different from us' helps to explain what he was attempting in the portrayal of Cahill: 'To demonise him is one thing, to humanise him is both legitimate and also deeply disturbing'.[77] While we witness him nail a man to a table, he is also seen as a protective, family man – despite a strange *menage à trois* with his wife and her sister – loyal to his working-class roots, a pigeon-fancier who is belligerently anti-authoritarian from a young age and against the drugs-related crime in which the film alleges the IRA became involved. Despite some shared interests, he refuses to deal with the IRA on their terms, thus bringing about his nemesis. Rerunning the opening sequence, the film comes full-circle to show Cahill shot at the wheel of his car outside his home by an IRA hit-man. As Paul Duane suggests, *The General* struggles to reconcile the contradictions of Cahill's persona, relishing the comic scenes in which Gleeson excels as a popular hero against the 'keystone cop' Gardaí, but unable in the end to fully

51 Crime behind the clown: Brendan Gleeson as Martin Cahill in *The General* (1997).
Courtesy of John Boorman/Merlin Films

examine the motivations of Cahill's violent non-conformity or unable to
ground his actions in Irish political life.[78] Ted Sheehy has sought to link
Michael Collins and *The General* by suggesting that they are about the loss and
debasement of male leadership in contemporary Irish society.[79] Boorman was
attracted to Cahill, feeling that he 'represented the pagan characteristics of a
Celtic chieftain' in modern-day Ireland.[80]

Making a film based on 'Dis-organised Crime' was the idea of director and
producer team, Paddy Breathnach and Robert Walpole. They felt a comic
'hood' genre movie[81] would strike a chord with cinema audiences and commissioned a screenplay from Conor McPherson, whose stage play, *The Good Thief*
(1994), had been successful in Dublin. The result was *I Went Down* (1997), a
spoof crime movie starring Brendan Gleeson and Peter McDonald as Bunny
Kelly and Git Hynes, a pair of incompetent minor criminals reluctantly sent on
a job by Tom French (Tony Doyle) to recover Frank Grogan (Peter Caffrey),
being held hostage by a rival gang in Cork. As a genre movie, character and
scene take precedence over plot. The film deftly and comically handles the
iconography of gangster movies: Bunny instructing Git how to use a firearm
concludes with a wonderful sight gag with a balaclava. It was also an Irish road
movie in which the buddies are reluctantly brought together, much of the
comedy generated from their contrasting personalities and reactions to situations. The film also effectively contrasts Dublin and Cork as distinct cities

52 *I Went Down*: An Irish caper movie? Git (Peter McDonald) and Bunny (Brendan Gleeson) contemplate their predicament (1997).
Courtesy of Paddy Breathnach/Robert Walpole/Buena Vista International (Ireland)

and captures regional differences of dialect, attitude and behaviour in McPherson's acute, witty dialogue. Equally, the midlands of Ireland and in particular the bogland scenes provide a location that is at once identifiably Irish yet also shot to look like a US prairie. In genre, iconography and landscape, *I Went Down* demonstrates how contemporary Irish film is imbued with, yet gives a localised inflection to, US film genres. This film is unconcerned with sociologically-driven naturalism; its world of bars, shady criminal activity, prison, betrayal and revenge takes reference from other cinematic representations and is true to this medium rather than reality. What is refreshing, and indeed, pleasurable about the film is to see its conventions being skilfully tried out on its hapless characters, transforming the conventions in the process.[82] The screenplay successfully realised the working methods of the creative team and the decision of Treasure Films to make and market (via Buena Vista) a commercial, unselfconsciously Irish movie within a receptive network of festivals in Europe, the USA (for example, at the Sundance Film Festival) and commercial cinemas.

A similar maturity and cinematic self-confidence underpins Neil Jordan and Pat McCabe's *The Butcher Boy* (1998), which, although it is an adaptation of a book that dips back into the early 1960s, is far from heritage cinema and closer instead to a postmodern conception in Irish film. From the animated opening credit sequence, to the medley of music, the screen's luminous colour tones, the characterisation and performance of familiar Irish actors from film, television personalities and pop music icons, *The Butcher Boy* engages us in an experience which 're-imagines Ireland in a profoundly challenging manner'.[83] We see small-town Ireland in 1962 through the consciousness of Francie Brady (Eamonn Owens), a boy who becomes progressively more disturbed by his circumstances and eventually becomes a psychotic killer. Jordan cast his long-standing actor alter-ego, Stephen Rea, as Francie's trumpet-playing alcoholic father; Rea also doubled-up doing the adult voice-over of Francie. This choice set Rea's screen familiarity against the freshness of an unknown schoolboy playing the central role of Francie. From Francie's obsessive, depressive, suicidal mother (Aisling O'Sullivan) to the entire town's millenarian belief in the coming of Our Lady, *The Butcher Boy* is an attempt to find a film language to articulate altered states of mind, a heightened perception that borders insanity. Indeed, Jordan's film pushes us to question how society distinguishes between sanity and madness, and how we care for those it defines as mentally ill. In this it contributes to the Irish cinema's exploration of the margins of society, which Joe Comerford believes to be the key to understanding a culture.[84] But the film also celebrates the creative potential of madness, embodied in Francie's incur-able optimism and openess, which Jordan sees as characteristic of an Irish imagination.[85] The film also furthers Jordan's project to debunk the shibboleths of de Valera's Ireland. Sinead O'Connor's Irish maiden playing the harp in front of Francie's model white cottage is hardly comely and the picturesque backdrop of the lake in a rural setting is literally exploded by an atomic bomb before

53 Irish boyhood, playing 'Indian': *The Butcher Boy* (1998).
Courtesy of Geffen Pictures. Photo: Pat Redmond

Francie's (and our) eyes. Harking back to the hysteria of the Cuban missile crisis and the perceived threat of modernity via television, *The Butcher Boy* forces us to reconsider the debates discussed at the end of this book's opening chapter about Ireland's recent economic, cultural and political development. Ireland's position is summed up by Mrs Canning's (Rosaleen Linehan) dooms-day observation that 'it'll be a bitter day for this town if the world comes to an end'. This comic inversion contains a defiant, parochial worldliness that acknowledges Ireland's in-between status, its cultural location between the local 'Beautiful Bundoran' and the rapacious globalisation of US culture. The product of such a conjunction is a kitsch, cartoon world that imbues the child-hood imaginations of Francie and his friend, Joe (Alun Boyle), whose 'cowboys and indians' game blurs into sci-fi horror. The mass media culture of comic books and television westerns mixes with a communal lore of priests, police and psychiatrists. This cultural mix is negotiated by individuals living through that conditioning aggregate, but at the same its very heterogeneity allows for imaginative connections to be made, the activity of resistant defiance in a post-modern world. Screening disturbing yet fresh and exhilarating images of Ireland, Jordan's film brings down the curtain on the first century of Irish cinema as it suggestively ushers in the next.

Notes

1 R. Stoneman, '44 and counting', *Ireland on Screen 1997–98* (Dublin, Film Base Publications, 1998), 5. Stoneman is the chief executive of the Irish Film Board.

2 See Appendix A. For comment on building of cinemas in Ireland, see C. Hogan, 'Heavy marketing planned for new cinemas', *Sunday Business Post* (11 October 1998).

3 These are the findings of a survey conducted by the Graduate School of Business at University College, Dublin, *The Public and the Arts: A survey of behaviour and attitudes in Ireland* (Dublin, UCD, 1994), 34–43.

4 For example, see 'Ireland on screen', *Film Ireland*, 65 (June–July 1998), 7, which features a table of viewing figures produced by RTÉ Audience Research.

5 The EU directive, 'Television without Frontiers' (1989), embodied this framework, which was endorsed by the GATT agreement (1993). The EU directive, 'Strategy options to strengthen the European programme industry' (1994), led to a less ambi-tious but better funded MEDIA II programme. M. Mac Conghail robustly questions the future of broadcasting in Europe in 'Trash is trash in any language', *Film Ireland*, 55 (August–September) 1996, 25–7.

6 Emma Burge, an Irish producer, commenting on effects of changes to S.35 in *Film Ireland*, 53 (June–July) 1996, 25.

7 Government of Ireland, *Active or Passive? Broadcasting in the future tense* (Dublin, Stationery Office, 1995). References are shown in parentheses in the main text.

8 RTÉ, *Response to the Government's Green Paper on Broadcasting* (Dublin, RTÉ, 1995).

9 *Film in Ireland – The role of the Arts Council* (Dublin, The Arts Council, 1998), 10.

10 For a pre–launch assessment and 'Fact file' of TnaG, see J. Gogan, 'Ar aghaidh linn', *Film Ireland*, 52, (April–May 1996), 12–16; and S. McBride's assessment after two months of broadcasting, *Film Ireland*, 57 (February–March 1997), 31–3. Up to date

information on TnaG can be found on the Irish Film and Television Network (IFTN) web site.

11 J. Trappel, 'EU media policy', *Irish Communications Review*, 6 (1996), 75.

12 *Film Ireland*, 60 (August–September, 1997), 8. *Film Ireland* carries full details of the opportunities provided by MEDIA and the IFTN carries up-to-date information on all aspects of media activity in Ireland.

13 This station began broadcasting in September 1998. It is owned largely by CanWest, a Canadian company.

14 B. McIlroy extensively examines 'Filmmaking and the "Troubles" in Northern Ireland', in *Shooting to Kill* (Trowbridge, Wiltshire, Flicks Books, 1998).

15 Two reports from this period give clear insights into the independent sector in Northern Ireland. The NI Film and TV Working Group produced *Media Express: The journey to media education and film training in Northern Ireland* (1988), while the Independent Film and Video Producers Association published *Fast Forward* (1989), on the funding of grant-aided film and video, based on three years research. This made a cogently argued case for a properly organised and funded strategy for audio-visual training, production and exhibition within Northern Ireland.

16 NIFC, *Strategy Proposals* (Belfast, NIFC, 1991), 1.

17 RTÉ, 'Response to the government's Green Paper on Broadcasting', 24. Originally the figure for 1999 was 12.5 million but RTÉ subsequently managed to find extra money for the IPU in 1998.

18 A. O'Keefe, 'They shoot, They score', *Fortnight*, 20:369 (March–April 1998).

19 *The Cake* and *Skin Tight* were part of the 'Northern Lights' project (BBCNI/NIFC). A. O'Keefe, 'The Village Voice', on the Galway Film Fleah, 19:366 (November 1997) and 'Lights, camera – Oscar', on *Dance Lexie Dance*, 34.

20 *Fortnight*, 19:360 (April 1997), 39–40, on the Dublin Film Festival and a review of *The Eliminator*, 19:364 (September 1997), 28–9.

21 E. Guiney, 'Film and television in Ireland: Building a partnership', in J. Hill and M. McLoone (eds), *Big Picture, Small Screen: The relations between film and television* (Luton, John Libbey Media, 1996), 210.

22 Frederic Jameson contends that one of the prerequisites for a national cinema is a vibrant theatre and strong acting tradition with which to supply the screen personae of a national imagination. A second prerequisite is to construct an 'other' against which to define oneself: in Ireland's case this has historically been Britain and the USA. Jameson's remarks, part of an address at the Irish Film Institute's centenary conference, 'Projecting the Nation' (November 1996), are reported and discussed by F. O'Toole, 'A national cinema: is it possible?', *The Irish Times* (13 November 1996), 1–4.

23 'The future of European cinema?', in J. Hill, M. McLoone and P. Hainsworth (eds), *Border Crossing: Film in Ireland, Britain and Europe* (Belfast, Institute of Irish Studies, 1994), 72.

24 For example, *A Further Gesture* (Dornhelm, 1996) and *The Devil's Own* (Pakula, 1997).

25 Michael O'Dwyer, *The Irish Time* (31 August 1996), 1.

26 It made £3 million in Ireland alone where perhaps an average Irish film would make between £350,000–£500,000.

27 J. Dean, '*Michael Collins* in America', *Film West*, 27 (February 1997), 16–17.

28 Jordan has conceded in interview that 'if the film has a fault, it may be difficult for American audiences to approach', S. McSwiney, *Cineaste*, 22:4 (1997), 20.

29 Ruth Dudley Edwards in *Daily Mail* (5 November 1996); Brenda Maddox, *The Times* (6 November 1996); and 'Editorial', *Daily Telegraph* (15 October 1996), which called for Warner Brothers to 'withdraw this inflammatory film from circulation – forthwith'. Alexander Walker, film critic of the London *Evening Standard*, known for his belligerent attacks on so-called 'pro-Republican' films, defended Jordan's work: 'It isn't a film intended, or likely, to incite violence'. For further quotations from the British press, see *BFI Viewing Notes – Michael Collins* (London, BFI, 1997), compiled by the author.

30 This meant that children under twelve were required to be accompanied by an adult to see the movie. Seamus Smith, 'Film Censor: Press Statement' (20 September 1996).

31 N. Jordan, *Michael Collins: Film diary and screenplay* (London, Vintage, 1996), scenes 130–49.

32 L. Gibbons makes an astute point that Jordan's film unsettles what appears to be an absolute distinction between state violence and terrorist 'godfathers' favoured by a dominant political discourse, thus reminding the Irish state of its foundations in violence, 'Framing history: Neil Jordan's *Michael Collins*', *History Ireland*, 5:1 (Spring 1997), 51.

33 Jordan, *Michael Collins*, 38.

34 Jordan, *Michael Collins*. Sc. 185: 'EXT. FOUR COURTS. NIGHT. Republican sentries stand on the Four Courts roof, like Indians out of a Western' (147). Sc. 239: 'EXT. BÉAL NA MBLÁTH ROADSIDE. DAY. O'Reilly's covering fire is ferocious. Collins pulls two pistols from his belt and stands, firing both simultaneously' (163). The ambush was filmed just outside Hollywood, County Wicklow.

35 *The Irish Times* (5 June 1998), 13, reported that Ken Loach was writing a screenplay about the 1916 Rising called, *Stolen Republic*, a title that suggests that the pure line of unreconstructed republicanism remains attractive to some on the British left.

36 Loach's *Hidden Agenda* (1989) is not discussed here.

37 G. Conlon, *Proved Innocent* (London, Penguin Books, 1993).

38 R. Kee, *Trial and Error* (London, Penguin Books, 1989).

39 The Birmingham Six were also wrongly convicted by falsified police evidence for bombings in 1976 and eventually released in 1990.

40 J. Nugent, 'The remains of Empire: Conflicting representations in contemporary film', *Irish Studies Review*, 7 (Summer 1994), 23–7.

41 J. Dean appraises *In the Name of the Father*'s reception in the US, 'The Far Side – American Letter', *Film West*, 18 (July 1994), 14–15.

42 For an excellent, lengthy interview, see S. MacSwiney, 'From Hollywood barracks … to Hollywood boulevard', *Film West*, 25 (Summer 1996), 10–17.

43 G. Crowdus and O'Mara Leary, 'The Troubles he's seen in Northern Ireland: Interview with Terry George', *Cineaste*, 23:1 (1997), 24–9.

44 B. Neve, 'Cinema, the ceasefire and the Troubles', *Irish Studies Review*, 20 (Autumn 1997), 5. In *The Boxer* (1997), Sheridan and George take a story of a released IRA man and boxer, Danny (Daniel Day–Lewis), to investigate the tensions within the republican movement leading up and into a ceasefire. Danny represents another in a long line of principled IRA men in Irish cinema who try to move on from the violence of the past. In Danny's case, he re-establishes the non-sectarian Holy Family boxing gym for the local community and intends to get back to the career cut short by political violence. *The Boxer* shows Day-Lewis's character sparring with his personal and political past but it lacked the urgency and clear-sightedness of the previous films. Both *In the*

Name of the Father and *The Boxer* show that the IRA – whether on 'war footing' or
ceasefire – needed punishment shootings (knee-capping) and beatings; that is, coercive force in addition to the tacit support it received within nationalist communities.

45 McIlroy, *Shooting to Kill*, 16–17.

46 McIlroy, *Shooting to Kill*, 15–21.

47 This film was released in the US with the title *Fanatic Hearts*.

48 Daniel Mornin's *All Our Fault* (London, Arrow Books, 1996) and Eoin McNamee's
    Resurrection Man (London, Picador, 1995).

49 For a concise history of the UVF, the oldest twentieth-century paramilitary grouping
    in Northern Ireland, pre-dating the IRA, see J. Cusak and H. McDonald, *UVF* (Dublin,
    Poolbeg Press, 1997), particularly Ch. 6, 'Cutting throats: Lennie Murphy and the
    Shankill UVF', which situates these films in historical context.

50 N. Fennell, 'Fanatic heart', interview with O'Sullivan, *Film West*, 22 (July 1995), 17.

51 Fennell, 'Fanatic heart', 17.

52 K. Holland, 'Troubles film sickens critics', *Sunday Tribune* (1 February 1998), 7.

53 McNamee, *Resurrection Man*, 1995, 58.

54 As cited in D. Traynor, *Film Ireland*, 64 (April–May 1998), 32–3. Mitchell's review, 'Red,
    white and very blue', appeared in *The Irish Times* (27 March 1998). From a loyalist
    background, Mitchell has written a radio play, *Stranded*, for the BBC, several stage
    plays, including *Tearing the Loom and A Little World of Our Own* (London, Nick Hern
    Books, 1998) and a TV screenplay, *The Officer from France* (RTÉ, 1998), about Wolfe
    Tone, leader of the United Irishmen in the 1798 rebellion.

55 McIlroy, *Shooting to Kill*, 145.

56 J. Dean, *Film West*, 21 (Summer 1995), 35. For a fuller account of the funding and mar-
    keting strategy behind the film, see A. Finney, *The State of European Cinema: A new
    dose of reality* (London, Cassell, 1996) 245–7.

57 John Huston's *The Dead* (1987) is a consummate example of adapting a literary text, in
    this case a short story from Joyce's *Dubliners*. It starred Donal McCann as Gabriel and
    Angelica Huston as Gretta in a film that was shot mostly in California but beautifully
    recreates its period and distils the emotional essence of a great short story.

58 Quoted in P. Collins, *Film West*, 20 (Spring 1995), 19.

59 P. Collins, *Film West* 20 (Spring 1995) 20.

60 V. Brown interviews Black at length in *Film West*, 24 (Spring 1996), 18–22. Shane
    Barry's review picks up on 1950s materialism in Ireland, *Film Ireland*, 50 (December
    1995–January 1996), 35.

61 E. Lennon, 'Inventing the director', *Film Ireland*, 58 (April–May 1997), 12–17, provides a
    sound interview and retrospective of Pat O'Connor's career.

62 For contrasting reviews of the film, see M. Mac Conghail, *Film West*, 34 (October 1998),
    16–17; and D. Clarke, *Film Ireland*, 66 (August–September 1998), 32–3.

63 These are usefully detailed and analysed in Finney, *State of European Cinema*, 230–9.

64 M. Collins, 'Guiltrip', *Film Ireland*, 50 (December 1995–January 1996), 35.

65 S. Barry, 'Family affair', *Film Ireland*, 50 (December 1995–January 1996), 25.

66 Similar themes were explored in Roddy Doyle and Stephen Frears' four-part BBC TV
    film, *Family* (1994), a dark examination of contemporary, urban life in Dublin.

67 *Snakes and Ladders* is favourably reviewed by Ruth Barton, *Film Ireland*, 63
    (February–March, 1998), 37.

68 Stephen Burke's short film, *After '68* (1994), economically and sensitively deals with a
    young girl's coming of age in a Northern Irish setting.

69 Katie Moylan, *Film Ireland*, 56 (December 1996–January 1997), 29–30.

70 As quoted in P. Power, 'Night and day', *Film Ireland*, 53 (June–July 1996), 12.

71 For a fuller argument about the 'postgay' and Irish film, see L. Pettitt, 'The construction site queered', *Cineaste*, 24:2–3 (Spring 1999), 61–3.

72 H. Linehan, 'Long way from Clare to here', *The Irish Times* (31 July 1998), 13.

73 G. Killilea, '*2by4* knocks Irish America flat', *Sunday Independent* (2 August 1998).

74 Smallhorne claims in interview that these were added after test-screening feedback, 'Odd man out', *Filmmaker*, 6:2 (Winter 1998), 90.

75 Boorman's screenplay source was Paul Williams' best-selling account of Cahill, *The General: Godfather of crime* (Dublin, The O'Brien Press, 1998).

76 Boorman quoted in T. Sheehy, 'General Boorman', *Film Ireland*, 65 (June–July 1998), 18. Boorman has also suggested that 'a black and white film approaches the condition of a dream, of memory, reaches out into the audience's unconscious. There was often a mythic dimension to black and white movies. They presented a familiar yet alien world, a contiguous reality', *The General* (London, Faber, 1998), xvii.

77 Sheehy, 'General Boorman', 19.

78 P. Duane, *Film Ireland*, 65 (June–July 1998), 34–5.

79 Sheehy, 'General Boorman', 14.

80 Boorman, *The General*, viii.

81 C. McPherson, *I Went Down: The shooting script* (London, Nick Hern Books, 1997), 113.

82 Gerry McCarthy, *Film Ireland*, 61 (October–November 1997), 34, gives the film high praise in contrast to Derek O'Connor's more critical review, *Film West*, 30 (October 1997), 60.

83 M. McLoone, 'The abused child of history: Neil Jordan's *The Butcher Boy*', *Cineaste*, 23:4 (1998), 36. For example, Sinead O'Connor as BVM; Stephen Rea; Ardal O'Hanlon from *Father Ted*; veteran screen actor Milo O'Shea as the paedophile priest; the ubiquitous Brendan Gleeson as a Christian Brother; Fiona Shaw as Mrs Nugent; and even Patrick McCabe in a cameo.

84 J. Comerford, 'The sanitisation of Irish art', *Film West*, 27 (February 1997), 25.

85 T. Sheehy's interview with Jordan, *Film Ireland*, 63 (February–March 1998), 14–15.

SELECTED STATISTICS

Number of TV households[a] in Republic of Ireland

Year	No. (thousands)
1984	929
1985	941
1986	954
1987	975
1988	979
1989	992
1990	1020
1991	1047
1992	1069
1993	1078
1994	1102

Source: Eurostat (1996)
[a]at least one TV

VCR households[a] in Republic of Ireland

Year	No. (thousands)
1987	210
1988	383
1989	453
1990	512
1991	564
1992	606
1993	644
1994	678

Source: Eurostat (1996)
[a]at least one VCR machine

Value of rental of video cassettes in Republic of Ireland

Year	Value (millions of ECU)[a]
1988	49
1989	48.9
1990	58.6
1991	56
1992	46
1993	45
1994	50.4

Source: Eurostat (1996)

[a]An ECU is equivalent to approximately st£0.66.

Note: The 1998 Eurostat pamphlet points out that 'Irish households with VCRs were the most active video rental customers in the EU in 1996', renting a video on average thirty-seven times per year. (p. 13)

Comparative percentage of satellite/cable penetration in private households (1996)

	Ireland	UK	Highest	EU	Lowest	EU
Satellite	10	18	Austria	34	Italy	4
Cable	40	8	Netherlands	96	Greece	1

Source: Eurostat (1998)

Number of cinema screens in Republic of Ireland

Year	No.
1980	163
1985	135
1990	171
1991	173
1992	164
1993	182
1994	190

Source: Eurostat (1996)

Number of cinema admissions in Republic of Ireland, 1980–98

Year	Admissions (millions)
1980	9.5
1985	4.5
1990	7.4
1995	9.8
1996	11.5
1997	11.1[a]
1998	12.5[a]

Source: Eurostat (1998)

[a]These estimated figures are based on January to June figures cited in *Inproduction,* 3 September, 1998, p. 23.

Note: The average individual annual attendance rose from 2.1 to 3.2 times per year during 1990–1996, giving Ireland the highest frequency of cinema attendance in Europe. The average attendance in the EU is 1.9 times per year. In the USA the figure is 4.6 per year.

Cinema income from gross box-office receipts, 1985–96

Year	No. (IR£ millions)
1985	16
1990	19
1994	27
1995	28
1996	32

Source: Eurostat (1998)

Note: Combined box office value of cinema in the EU is 3.29 million ECU. The EU market is 71% the size of the USA market.

Age profile of audience at the cinema in Republic of Ireland

Age	%
15–19	45
20–24	54
25–34	28
35+	8

Source: *MAPS* (Media Advertising Promotions Sponsorship) *Directory*, 1997–98

Box office figures for Irish films in the 1990s

Film (year)	Distributor	Ir.£ (US dollars)
Michael Collins (1996)	Warner Bros	4.0m ($5.6m)
In the Name of the Father (1994)	UIP	2.4m ($3.3m)
The Commitments (1991)	Fox	2.2m ($3.1m)
Circle of Friends (1995)	Abbey Films	1.4m[c] ($1.9m)
The General[a] (1998)	Warner Bros	1.3m ($1.8m)
The Butcher Boy (1998)	Warner Bros	1.1m ($1.5m)
Into the West (1992)	Clarence Pictures	1.0m ($1.4m)
The Boxer (1998)	UIP	0.8m ($1.1m)
The Crying Game (1992)	Warner Bros	0.8m ($1.1m)
Some Mother's Son (1996)	Abbey Films	0.75m ($1.0m)
I Went Down (1997)	Buena Vista International	0.6m ($0.8m)
Eat the Peach[b] (1986)	Strongbow	0.3m ($0.4m)
The Snapper (1994)	Fox	0.3m ($0.4m)
The Nephew[b] (1998)[a]	UIP	0.27m ($0.37m)
Last of the High Kings (1996)	Dublin Film Distributors	0.24m ($0.3m)
Dancing at Lughnasa (1998)[a]	Clarence Pictures	0.18m ($0.25m)
December Bride (1990)	Clarence Pictures	0.17m ($0.2m)
The Run of the Country (1995)	Abbey Films	0.17m ($0.2m)
Guiltrip (1996)	_____	80,000 ($100,000)
Broken Harvest[b] (1994)	Buena Vista International	80,000 ($100,000)
Nothing Personal (1995)	Clarence Pictures	70,000 ($97,700)
A Man of No Importance (1994)	Clarence Pictures	60,000 ($83,700)
Korea (1995)	_____	40,000 ($55,800)
Space Truckers (1996)	Abbey Films	40,000 ($55,800)
Trojan Eddie (1996)	Clarence Pictures	30,000 ($41,850)
Moondance (1995)	Clarence Pictures	20,000 ($27,900)
The Disappearance of Finbar (1997)	Buena Vista International	17,296 ($24,133)
Gold in the Streets (1997)	Abbey Films	10,387 ($14,492)
Snakes and Ladders (1998)	Dublin Film Distributors	9,054 ($12,633)
The Boy from Mercury (1996)	Clarence Pictures	6,457 ($9,009)
This is the Sea (1998)	_____	6,241 ($8,708)
All Souls Day[b] (1997)	_____	3,328 ($4,643)
A Further Gesture (1997)	Clarence Pictures	3,048 ($4,252)
The Sun, The Moon and The Stars (1996)	_____	2,899 ($4,044)
Words Upon the Window Pane (1995)	Clarence Pictures	2,100 ($2,930)
Ailsa (1995)	_____	1,300 ($1,813)

[a] Film still on release, [b] Film financed entirely in Ireland, [c] estimated figure

Note: Figures relate to Ireland, North and Republic.

Source: Ted Sheehy, *Screen International*, 1179, 9-15 October 1998, 16

Censorship and Irish cinema, 1984–93

Year	Submissions	Cut	Rejected	Appeals	Upheld
1984	181	20	3	1	0
1985	172	18	1	0	0
1986	153	7	0	0	0
1987	162	2	2	2	1
1988	159	1	1	1	0
1989	152	0	0	2	1
1990	153	2	0	3	2
1991	175	1	1	6	3
1992	145	0	0	2	1
1993	129	1	1	2	1

Source: Shane Barry, *Film Ireland*, 44 (December 1994/January 1995), 18

SELECTED VIDEO AND ELECTRONIC RESOURCES

It has become easier to research, teach and study the moving image culture of Ireland over the last decade. The films and programmes discussed in this book have been viewed in different kinds of cinemas, at festival screenings, by appointment at film archives, resource centres and RTÉ, on home videos available by retail and post, generously supplied VHS copies from individual film-makers and from personal off-air video recordings. With ingenuity, perseverance and a modest outlay, university departments can build up a workable resource base for teaching and learning.

Video resources

The list below is of VHS (PAL) titles available (February 1999) in the UK and Ireland, though this is obviously subject to change.

Title (date of original)	Distributor (reference number)
Angel (1982)	Channel Four Films (VA 30592)
Ballykissangel (1997)	BBC Video (BBCV5985)
Barry Lyndon (1975)	Warner Home Video (PEV61178)
The Butcher Boy (1998)	Warner Home Video (V015522)
Circle of Friends (1995)	Polygram Filmed Entertainment (PG1072)
The Courier (1987)	Palace Video (PVC2119A)
The Crying Game (1992)	Polygram (088 902 3)
Dancing at Lughnasa (1998)	Clarence Irish Classics (forthcoming)
The Devil's Own (1997)	Columbia Tristar Home Video (CVT24773)
Eat the Peach (1986)	Columbia Pictures International 1987 (CVT11203)
Guiltrip (1995)	Metrodome (SE 2404)
I Went Down (1997)	Buena vista (forthcoming)
The Informer (1935)	Polygram UK (055 5483)
In the Name of the Father (1993)	Universal (VHA1720D)
Into the West (1992)	Miramax (EW1239)
Joyriders (1988)	Warner Home Video (LBV1)
The Last of the High Kings (1996)	First Independent (VA30729)
Man of Aran (1934)	Rank British Classics/VCI (VC3472)
Michael Collins (1996)	Warner Home Video (V014205)
Mise Éire (1959)	Gael Linn (GLV001)
Out of Ireland (1995)	Shanachie Home Video (SH948)

Reefer and the Model (1988)	reVision (MJ012)
Ryan's Daughter (1970)	MGM/UA Modern Classics (SO50163)
Resurrection Man (1998)	Polygram Film Entertainment (PG1197)
Saoirse? (1961)	Gael Linn (VGL002)
Some Mother's Son (1996)	Columbia Tristar Home Video (CVR 76035)
Trojan Eddie (1997)	Film Four/VCI (VC3628)

Electronic resources

CD-Roms

Filmscan 1999: Ireland's film, TV and video directory (1999) is a trade directory for Ireland's film, TV and video industry; *Videologue* can be otained from Trade Service Information Ltd, Cherryhold Rd., Stamford, Lincs PE9 2HT, England (Telephone: 01780-64331) and lists VHS cassettes for rental or purchase; *Ireland on Screen: 1898-1986* (1996) is a text-only CD, with a listings compiled by Robert Monks and is available from the National Library of Ireland (Telephone: 00-3531-6618811).

Web sites

http://www.rte.ie/
RTÉ's website has useful documentation and latest information.

http://www.iftn.ie
Irish Film and Television Network provides up-to-date information and contacts for organisations within Ireland. Highly recommended as a starting place for research and contacts.

http://avc.ucd.ie/wftv/main/background.html
Women in Film and Television is a professional, international forum for women working in the industry.

http://www.tnag.ie
Telefís na Gaeilge is Ireland's national, Irish-language broadcaster.

http://www.searcs-web.com/cinema.html
SERCS Guide to Irish Resources Online. A comprehensive and easy to use site.

http:www.acisweb.com
The American Conference for Irish Studies web site has several links to other sites of Irish interest, academic and cultural.

http://www.heanet.ie/EFACIS/
The European Federation of Associations and Centres of Irish Studies is an organisation of academics interested in Irish Studies.

Suppliers of videos and video catalogues in UK and USA

http://www.flf.com/
Fine Line Features is a supplier of videos in the USA that has Irish titles.

http://www.newline.com/
New Line Home Video Store (USA).

http://ukstuff.com/vdocmdy.htm
Supplies NTSC videos of *Father Ted*.

www.blackstar.co.uk
Based in Northern Ireland. Supplies Clarence Pictures videos plus other Irish titles available in UK.

Other contacts in the USA include: The Cinema Guild, 1697, Broadway, Suite 506, New York, NY10019; National Video Resources, 73 Spring Street, Suite 606, New York, NY 10012; University Film and Video Association, P.O. Box 69799, Los Angeles, CA 90069.

Select bibliography

Unpublished material

Cornell, J. (1991), 'Different countries, different worlds: A study of the images of Northern Ireland in contemporary British TV drama', MA Peace Studies, University of Ulster.

Doyle-O'Neill, F. (1997) 'Challenging Irish society: *The Late Late Show* 1962–1997', Ph.D, NUI, Cork.

Hanlon, P. (1991), 'How valid is Paul Hill's assessment of the media coverage of the "Guildford Four" case throughout the 1970s?', MA Irish Studies, University of Liverpool.

Negra, D. (1999), 'The greening of the screen: American television and the possessive investment in Irishness', ACIS Conference, Roanoke, VA.

Neve, B. (1994), 'Film and the Northern Ireland conflict', EFTSC Conference 'Turbulent Europe: Conflict, Identity and Culture', London.

Pettitt, L. (1991), 'A box of Troubles: British television drama and Northern Ireland', Ph.D, NUI, Dublin.

Richards, S. (1993), 'Aeschylus in Ulster: A reading of the TV play *In the Border Country*', BAIS conference paper, Oxford.

Official reports, publications and statistical sources

AAI (1997–98), *Media Advertising Promotions Sponsorship (MAPS) Directory*, Dublin, Association of Advertisers in Ireland.

Arts Council Ireland (1998), *Film in Ireland – The role of the Arts Council*, Dublin.

An Roinn Ealaíon, Cultúir, Gaeltachta/Department of Arts, Culture and the Gaeltacht (1995), *Active or Passive? Broadcasting in the future tense*, Green Paper on Broadcasting, Dublin, The Stationery Office.

An Roinn Ealaíon, Cultúir, Gaeltachta/Department of Arts, Culture and the Gaeltacht (1997), *Fócas Géar/Clear Focus: The Government's Proposals for Broadcasting Legislation*, Dublin, The Stationery Office.

BBC (1996), *Producers' Guidelines*, London, BBC.

Coopers & Lybrand (1994), *The Employment and Economic Significance of the Cultural Industries in Ireland*, Dublin, Coopers & Lybrand.

Couling, K. and Grummitt, K. (1998), *Cinema-going in Europe: UK and Ireland*, Leicester, Dodonna Research.

Eurostat (1996), *Audio-Visual Statistics Report 1995*, Brussels, Office of the Official Publications of the European Community.

Eurostat (1998), *The Audio-Visual Sector in the European Economic Area in the 1990s*, Brussels, Office of the Official Publications of the European Community.

Graduate School of Business (1994), *The Public and the Arts: A survey of behaviour and attitudes in Ireland*, Dublin, UCD.

Inproduction (1998), Caherdaniel, Co. Kerry, J. R. Publications

Independent Television Commission (1993), *The ITC Programme Code*, London, ITC.

Irish Government (1993), *Fianna Fáil and Labour Programme for a Partnership Government 1993–1997*, Dublin, Stationery Office.

Northern Ireland Film Council (1991), *Strategy Proposals for the Development of the Film, Television and Video Industries and Culture in Northern Ireland*, Belfast, NIFC.

OECD (1997), *Economic Surveys: Ireland*, Paris, OECD.

Rice, T. C./Irish Film Board (1995), *North American Distribution of Irish and Low Budget European Films*, Dublin, Irish Film Board.

RTÉ (1995), *Response to the Government's Green Paper on Broadcasting*, Dublin, RTÉ.

RTÉ (1995), *Annual Report*, Dublin, RTÉ.

Special Working Group on the Film Production Industry (1992), *The Film Production Industry*, Dublin, The Stationery Office.

Statistical Year Book (1997), 'Ireland', *Cinema, Television, Video and the New Media*, Strasbourg, European Audiovisual Observatory.

Books, chapters and journal articles

Adams, G. (1995), 'Speaking of peace', *Index on Censorship*, 24:2, March/April, 50–3.

Aldgate, A., (1983), 'British domestic cinema of the 1930s', in Curran, J., and Porter, V. (eds), *British Cinema History*, London, Weidenfeld and Nicolson, 257–71.

Anderson, B. (1991), *Imagined Communities: Reflections on the origins and spread of nationalism*, London, Verso.

Barbrook, R. (1992), 'Broadcasting and national identity in Ireland', *Media Culture and Society*, 14:1, 203–27.

Barnouw, E. (1993), *Documentary: A history of the non-fiction film*, Oxford, Oxford University Press.

Barrett, P. (1994), 'Pure genius', *Screen International*, 965, 8 July, 11–12.

Barrett, P. (1997), 'The trying game', *Screen International*, 1097, 28 February, 21–4.

Barry, S. (1994/95), 'Who's protecting who?', *Film Ireland*, 44, December/January, 16–18.

Bartlett, T., Curtin, C., O'Dwyer, R. and Ó Tuathaigh, G. (eds) (1988), *Irish Studies: A general introduction*, Dublin, Gill & Macmillan.

Bell, D. (1988), 'Ireland without frontiers? The challenge of the communications revolution', in Kearney, R. (ed.), *Across the Frontiers: Ireland in the 1990s*, Dublin, Wolfhound, 219–30.

Bell, D. (1990), *Acts of Union: Youth culture and sectarianism in Northern Ireland*, Basingstoke, Hampshire, Macmillan.

Bell, D., and Meehan, N. (1989), 'Cable, satellite and the emergence of private TV in Ireland', *Media Culture and Society*, 1:1, 89–114.

Bell, E. (1986), 'The origins of British television documentary: The BBC 1946–55', in Corner, J. (ed.), *Documentary and the Mass Media*, London, Arnold, 65–80.

Bell, G. (1982), *Troublesome Business: The Labour Party and the Irish Question*, London, Pluto Press.

Bell-Metereau, R. (1993), *Hollywood Androgeny*, New York, Columbia University Press.

Benjamin, W. (1973), *Illuminations*, Glasgow, Fontana/Collins.

Bhabha, H. K. (1994), *The Location of Culture*, London, Routledge.

Bizot, R., and Shout, J. D. (1997), 'New Approaches to "Irish" Film', Fort Lauderdale, Nova Southeastern University Working Papers in Irish Studies.

Boland, E. (1995), *Object Lessons: The life of the woman and poet in our times*, Manchester, Carcanet.

Bolton, R. (1990), *Death on the Rock and Other Stories*, London, Optomen/W. H. Allen.

Bonner, P., with Aston, L. (1998) *Independent Television in Britain, Volume 5: 1981–92*, Basingstoke, Hampshire, ITC/Macmillan.

Boorman, J. (1998), *The General*, London, Faber.

Bordwell, D. and Thompson, K. (1990), *Film Art: An introduction*, New York, McGraw-Hill Publishing, 3rd ed.

Boyce, D. G. (1984), 'Marginal Britons: The Irish', in Colls, R. and Dodd, P. (eds), *Englishness: Politics and culture, 1880–1920*, London, Croom Helm, 1984, 230–53.

Brandt, G. W. (ed.) (1993), *British Television Drama in the 1980s*, Cambridge, Cambridge University Press.

Brennan, P., and de Saint Phalle, C. (eds) (1997), *Arguing at the Crossroads: Essays on changing Ireland*, Dublin, New Island Books.

Briggs, A. (1961), *A History of Broadcasting in the United Kingdom, Volume 1: The birth of broadcasting*, London, Oxford University Press.

Brouder, A. (1995), 'The history of cinema-going in Galway', *Film West*, 22, July, 20–3.

Brown, T. (1981), *Ireland: A social and cultural history, 1922–79*, Glasgow, Fontana.

Brownlow, K. (1996), *David Lean: A biography*, London Richard Cohen.

Burns-Bisogno, L. (1998), *Censoring Irish Nationalism*, Jefferson: North Carolina, McFarland & Co.

Burns, R., and Kenneally, M. (eds) (1999), *The Irish Overseas in Fact and Imagination*, Amsterdam, Rodolphi Press.

Burrowes, W. (1977), *The Riordans: A personal history*, Skerries, Co. Dublin, Gilbert Dalton.

Butler, D. (1991), 'Ulster Unionism and British broadcasting journalism, 1924–89', in Rolston, B. (ed.), *The Media and Northern Ireland: Covering the Troubles*, Basingstoke, Hampshire, Macmillan, 99–121.

Butler, D. (1995), *The Trouble with Reporting Northern Ireland*, Aldershot, Avebury Press.

Byrne, G. (1972), *To Whom it Concerns: Ten years of The Late Late Show*, Dublin, Torc Books.

Byrne, H. (1997), '"Going to the pictures": The female audience and the pleasures of the cinema', in Kelly, M. J., and O'Connor, B. (eds), *Media Audiences in Ireland*, Dublin, University College Dublin Press, 88–106.

Byrne, T. (1997), *Power in the Eye: An introduction to contemporary Irish film*, Lanham, Maryland, Scarecrow Press.

BFI (Annually), *BFI Film and Television Handbook*, London, British Film Institute.

Burrows, E., Moat, E., Sharp, J. and Wood, L. (eds), *The British Cinema Source Book: BFI archive viewing copies and library materials*, London, British Film Institute.

Cairns, D., and Richards, S. (1988), *Writing Ireland: Colonialism, nationalism and culture*, Manchester, Manchester University Press.

Calder-Marshall, A. (1963), *The Innocent Eye: The life of Robert J. Flaherty*, London, W. H. Allen.

Carty, C. (1995) *Confessions of a Sewer Rat: A personal history of censorship and the Irish cinema*, Dublin, New Island Books.

Cathcart, R. (1984), *The Most Contrary Region: The BBC in Northern Ireland 1924–1984*, Belfast, The Blackstaff Press.

Caughie, J. (1991), 'Before the golden age: Early television drama', in Corner, J. (ed.), *Popular Television in Britain*, London, British Film Institute, 22–41,

Caughie, J., with Rockett, K. (1996), *The Companion to British and Irish Cinema*, London, Cassell.

Clayton, P. (1996), *Enemies and Passing Friends: Settler ideologies in twentieth century Ulster*, London, Pluto Press.

Clements, P. (1993), 'Four Days in July', in Brandt, G. (ed.), *British Television Drama in the 1980s*, Cambridge, Cambridge University Press, 162–77.

Collins, P. (1981), *It Started on The Late Late Show*, Dublin, Ward River Press.

Conlon, G. (1993), *Proved Innocent*, London, Penguin.

Connolly, J. (1988), 'Labour and the proposed partition of Ireland', in Beresford Ellis, *James Connolly: Selected writings*, London, Pluto Press.

Corner, J. (ed.) (1991), *Popular Television in Britain: Studies in cultural history*, London, British Film Institute.

Corner, J. (1995), *Television Form and Public Address*, London, Edward Arnold.

Corner, J. (1996), *The Art of Record: A critical introduction to documentary*, Manchester, Manchester University Press.

Coulter, C. (1990), *Ireland: Between first and third worlds*, Dublin, Attic Press.

Coulter, C. (1993), *The Hidden Tradition: Feminism, women and nationalism in Ireland*, Cork, Cork University Press.

Crawford, M. (ed.) (1999), *Green Screen: The state of the contemporary Irish film industry*, Belfast, Fortnight Educational Trust. Supplement to *Fortnight*, 379, June.

Crick, B. (1988), 'An Englishman considers his passport', *The Irish Review*, 5, Autumn, 1–10.

Crissell, A. (1997), *An Introductory History to British Broadcasting*, London, Routledge.

Crowdus, G. (1997), 'The screenwriting of Irish history', *Cineaste*, 22:4, 14–19.

Crowley, E. and MacLaughlin, J. (eds) (1997), *Under the Belly of the Tiger: Class, race, identity and culture in global Ireland,* Dublin, Irish Reporter Publications.

Cullingford, E. B. (1998), 'Gender, sexuality and Englishness in modern Irish drama and film', in Bradley, A., and Valiulis, M. G. (eds), *Gender and Sexuality in Modern Ireland*, Amherst, University of Massachusetts Press/ACIS, 159–86.

Curran, J. M. (1989), *Hibernian Green on the Silver Screen: The Irish and American movies*, Westport, Connecticut, Greenwood Press.

Cusack J., and McDonald, H. (1997), *UVF*, Dublin, Poolbeg.

Curtis, L. (1984), *Ireland: The propaganda war*, London, Pluto Press.

Curtis, L. (1994), *The Cause of Ireland: From United Irishmen to Partition*, Belfast, Beyond the Pale.

Curtis, L., and Jempson, M. (1993), *Interference on the Airwaves: Ireland, the media and the broadcasting ban,* London, Campaign for Press and Broadcasting Freedom.

Deane, S. (ed.) (1990), *Nationalism, Colonialism and Literature*, Minneapolis, University of Minnesota Press.

Devereux, E. (1998), *Devils and Angels: Television, ideology and the coverage of poverty*, Luton, University of Luton/John Libbey Media.

Devlin, A. (1986), *Ourselves Alone*, London, Faber.

Doherty, H. (1993), 'Images of protestant identity', *Film Ireland*, 33, February/March, 30.

Doolan, L (ed.) (1997), *Cinemobilia: Memoir of a travelling cinema along the Irish border*, Dublin, Bord Scannán na Éireann.

Doolan, L., Dowling, J., Quinn, B., and Leonard, M. (1969), *Sit Down and Be Counted: The cultural evolution of a television station*, Dublin, Wellington Publishers.

Downing, T. (1979/80), 'The Film Company of Ireland', *Sight and Sound*, 49:1, 42–5.

Doyle, R. (1993), *The Barrytown Trilogy*, London, Minerva.

Dully, H. (1992), 'Mná na hÉireann and their screen sisters', *Film Ireland*, 30, July/August, 20–1.

Dunn, J. (1986), *No Tigers in Africa: Recollections and reflections on 25 years of Radharc*, Dublin, The Columba Press.

Dyer, R. (1992), *Only Entertainment*, London, Routledge.

Edge, S. (1995), 'Women are trouble: you know that, Fergus?', *Feminist Review*, 50, Summer, 181–6.

Edge, S. (1999), 'Representing gender and national identity', in Miller, D. (ed.), *Rethinking Northern Ireland*, Harlow, Essex, Longman, 211–27.

Ellis, J. (1982), *Visible Fictions: Cinema, television, video*, London, Routledge & Kegan Paul.

Fanon, F. (1985), *The Wretched of the Earth*, Harmondsworth, Penguin.

Fanon, F. (1986), *Black Skin, White Masks*, London, Pluto Press.

Farrell, B. (ed.) (1984), *Communications and Community in Ireland*, Cork, Mercier Press.

Feeney, P. (1984), 'Censorship and RTÉ', *The Crane Bag*, 8:2, 61–4.

Felice, J. de (1975), *Filmguide to Odd Man Out*, London and Indiana, Indiana University Press.

Fennel, D. (1989), *The Revision of Irish Nationalism*, Dublin, Open Air Books.

Ferguson, B. (1985), *Television on History: Representations of Ireland*, London, Institute of Education, University of London/Comedia.

Film Comment (1994), 'Irish cinema', May–June, 24–41.

Finn, E. (1998), *Irish History and the Troubles*, NFTA Filmographies, 7, London, BFI.

Finney, A. (1996), *The State of European Cinema: A new dose of reality*, London, Cassell.

Fisher, D. (1978), *Broadcasting in Ireland*, London, Routledge & Kegan Paul.

Flannery, P. (1990), *Blind Justice*, London, Nick Hern Books.

Fleeton, G. (ed.) (1984), *A Seat Among the Stars: The cinema and Ireland*, Belfast, UTV/Channel Four.

Flynn, A. (1996), *Irish Film: 100 years*, Bray, Co. Wicklow, Kestrel Books.

Foster, J. W. (1988), 'Culture and colonialism: A view from the North', *The Irish Review*, 5, Autumn, 17–26.

Foster, H. (ed.) (1985), *Postmodern Culture*, London, Pluto Press.

Foster, J. W. (1989), Radical regionalism, *The Irish Review*, 7, 1–15.

Foster, R. F. (1986), 'We are all revisionists now', *The Irish Review*, 1, 1–5.

Foster, R. F. (1989), *Modern Ireland: 1600–1972*, Harmondsworth, Penguin.

Foster, R. F. (1995), *Paddy and Mr Punch: Connections in Irish and English history*, Harmondsworth, Penguin.

Frey, L. H. (1995), 'Two studies of Irish myth and film: "Odd Man Out" and the "Death of Cuchulain", "The Quiet Man" and its unquiet mythic background', *Études irlandaises*, Fall, 67–75.

George, T. (1996), *Some Mother's Son*, New York, Grove Press.

Geraghty, C. (1991), *Women and Soap Opera: A study of prime time soaps*, London, Polity Press.

Giannetti, L. (1981), *Masters of the American Cinema*, New Jersey, Prentice Hall.

Gibbons, L. (1990), 'Fragments into pictures', *Film Base News*, 20, November/December, 8–12.

Gibbons, L. (1991), 'Challenging the canon: Revisionism and cultural criticism', in Deane, S. (ed.), *The Field Day Anthology of Irish Writing: Volume 3*, Derry, Field Day, 561–6.

Gibbons, L. (1996), *Transformations in Irish Culture*, Cork, Cork University Press.

Gibbons, L. (1996), 'Framing the family: national narratives in recent Irish film and fiction', *Actas XVI Encontro do APEAA*, Vila Real, Portugal, APEAA (Portuguese Association for Anglo-American Studies), 155–65.

Gibbons, L. (1996), 'The esperanto of the eye? Re-thinking national cinema', *Film Ireland*, 55, October/November, 20–2.

Gibbons, L. (1996), 'Engendering the state: Narrative, allegory, and *Michael Collins*', *Éire-Ireland* (Fall/Winter), 261–9.

Gibbons, L. (1997), 'Framing history: Neil Jordan's *Michael Collins*', *History Ireland*, 5:1, Spring, 47–51.

Giles, J. (1997), *The Crying Game*, London, BFI.

Gill, A. (1998), 'Dear Daughter', in *Orphans of the Empire: The shocking story of child migration to Australia*, London, Vintage, 552–7.

Gorham, M. (1967), *Forty Years of Irish Broadcasting*, Dublin, Talbot Press.

Gribben, A., Wilson, T. and MacKillop, J. (1987), *Images of the Irish and Irish-Americans in Commercial and Ethnographic Films*, Fort Lauderdale, Nova Southeastern University Working Papers in Irish Studies.

Graham, C. (1994), 'Post-nationalism/post-colonialism: Reading Irish culture', *Irish Studies Review*, 8 Autumn, 35–7.

Graham, C. (1994), 'Liminal spaces: Post-colonial theories and Irish culture', *The Irish Review*, 16, Autumn/Winter, 29–43.

Graham, C. (1996), 'Subalterity and gender: problems of post-colonial Irishness', *Journal of Gender Studies*, 5:3, 363–73.

Gramsci, A. (1971), 'Notes on Italian history', in Nowell-Smith, G. (ed.), *Selections from Prison Notebooks*, London, Lawrence & Wishart.

Gramsci, A. (1985), *Selections from Cultural Writings*, London, Lawrence & Wishart.

Gray, F. (1994), *Women and Laughter*, Basingstoke, Hampshire, Macmillan.

Green, F. L. (1991) *Odd Man Out*, London, Sphere Books.

Guiney, E. (1996), 'Film and television in Ireland: Building a partnership', in Hill, J., and McLoone, M. (eds), *Big Picture, Small Screen: The relations between film and television*, Luton, John Libby Media, 210–14.

Hall, S. (1994), 'Notes on deconstructing "the popular"', in Storey, J. (ed.), *Cultural Theory and Popular Culture*, Hemel Hempstead, Harvester Wheatsheaf, 459–66.

Hall, S. (1996), 'When was the post-colonial? Thinking at the limit', in Chambers, I., and Curti, L. (eds), *The Post-Colonial Question: Common skies, divided horizons*, London, Routledge, 242–60.

Hanna Bell, S. (1990), *December Bride*, Edinburgh, Mainstream Publising.

Hardy, F. (ed.) (1979), *Grierson on Documentary*, London, Faber.

Harkness, D. (1996), *Ireland in the Twentieth Century: Divided island*, Basingstoke: Hampshire, Macmillan.

Hayward, S. (1993), *French National Cinema*, London, Routledge.

Hazelkorn, E. (1996), 'New technologies and changing work practices in the media industry: The case of Ireland', *Irish Communications Review*, 6, 28–38.

Hazelkorn, E. and Smyth, P. (eds) (1993), *Let in the Light: Censorship, secrecy and democracy*, Dingle, Kerry, Brandon.

Hedeman, M. P., and Kearney, R. (eds) (1984), 'The Media and Popular Culture', *The Crane Bag* (Special Issue), 8:2.

Hennessy, P. (1996), *The Hidden Wiring: Unearthing the British constitution*, London, Indigo.

Hickey, K. (1984), 'The cinema and Ireland: A short history', in *Green on the Screen*, Dublin, Irish Film Institute, 6–16.

Hill, J., and Gibson, P. C. (eds) (1998), *The Oxford Guide to Film Studies*, Oxford, Oxford University Press.

Hill, J., McLoone, M., and Hainsworth, P. (eds) (1994), *Border Crossing: Film in Ireland, Britain and Europe*, Belfast, Institute of Irish Studies.

Hill, J., and McLoone, M. (eds) (1996), *Big Picture, Small Screen: The relations between film and television*, Luton, John Libby Media.

Hollows, J., and Jancovitch, M. (eds) (1995), *Approaches to Popular Film*, Manchester, Manchester University Press.

Hutchinson, R. (1984), *Rat in the Skull*, London, Methuen.

Hyndman, M. (ed.), *Further Afield: Journeys from a Protestant past*, Belfast, Beyond the Pale.

Ignatiev, N. (1995), *How the Irish Became White*, London, Routledge.

Irish Communications Review (1991–99), Dublin, Dublin Institute of Technology.

Irish Museum of Modern Art (1993), *Hindesight*, Dublin, IMMA.

Irish Review, The (1997), 'Film and the Visual Arts in Ireland', 21 (Special Issue), Autumn/Winter.

Jackson, A. (1989), 'Unionist history', *The Irish Review*, 7, Autumn, 58–65.

Jordan, N. (1993), *The Crying Game: An original screenplay*, London, Vintage.

Jordan, N. (1996), *Michael Collins: Film diary and screenplay*, London, Vintage.

Keane, J. B. (1991), *The Field*, Dublin, Mercier Press.

Kearney, R. (1988), *Transitions: Narratives in modern Irish culture*, Dublin, Wolfhound Press.

Kearney, R. (ed) (1988), *Across the Frontiers: Ireland in the 1990s*, Dublin, Wolfhound Press.

Kearney, R. (ed.) (1990), *Migrations: The Irish at home and abroad*, Dublin, Wolfhound Press.

Kearney, R. (1992), 'Modern Irish cinema: Re-viewing traditions', in M. Kenneally (ed.), *Irish Literature and Culture*, Gerrards Cross, Buckinghamshire, Colin Smyth, 144–57.

Kearney, R. (1997), *Postnationalist Ireland: Politics, culture and philosophy*, London, Routledge.

Kee, R. (1989), *Trial and Error*, London, Penguin.

Kelly, M., and O'Connor, B. (eds) (1997), *Media Audiences in Ireland*, Dublin, University College Dublin Press.

Kelly, M., and Rolston, B. (1995), 'Broadcasting in Ireland: Issues of national identity and censorship', in Clancy, P., Drudy, S., Lynch, K. and O'Dowd, L. (eds) *Irish Society: Sociological perspectives*, Dublin, Institute of Public Administration, 1995, 563–92.

Kennedy, L. (1993), 'Modern Ireland: Post-colonial society or post-colonial pretensions?', *The Irish Review*, 13, Winter/Spring, 107–21.

Kennedy, L. (1996), *Colonialism, Religion and Nationalism in Ireland*, Belfast, Institute of Irish Studies.

Kiberd, D. (1995), *Inventing Ireland: The literature of the modern nation*, London, Jonathan Cape.

Kiberd, D. (ed.) (1997), *The Media in Ireland*, Dublin, Four Courts Press.

Kirkland, R. (1996), *Literature and Culture in Northern Ireland since 1965: Moments of danger*, Harlow, Essex, Longman.

Kilborn, R., and Izod, J. (1997), *An Introduction to Television Documentary: Confronting reality*, Manchester, Manchester University Press.

Lee, J. J. (1989), *Ireland 1912–85: Politics and society*, Cambridge, Cambridge University Press.

Lennon, M., and Diski, R. (1991), *The Treaty*, London, Thames TV/Screen Guides.

Lindsay, P. (ed.) (1993), *The Media and Modern Irish Society in Ireland*, Celbridge, Co. Kildare, The Social Study Conference.

Longley, E. (1994), 'From Kathleen to Anorexia: The breakdown of Irelands', in *A Dozen LIPs*, Dublin, Attic Press, 162–87.

Longley, E. (1994), *The Living Stream: Literature and revisionism in Ireland*, Newcastle upon Tyne, Bloodaxe.

Loomba, A. (1998), *Colonialism/Postcolonialism*, London, Routledge.

Lourdeaux, L. (1990) *Italian and Irish Filmmakers in America*, Philadelphia, Temple University Press.

Luddy, M., and Murphy, C. (eds) (1989), *Women Surviving: Studies in Irish women's history in the nineteenth and twentieth centuries*, Dublin, Poolbeg.

Lusted, D. (1998), 'The popular cultual debate and light entertainment', in Geraghty, C., and Lusted, D. (eds), *The Television Studies Book*, London, Arnold, 175–90.

Lyons, F. S. L., (1973), *Ireland Since the Famine*, London, Fontana.

McBride, S., and Flynn, R. (eds) (1996), *Here's Looking at You, Kid! Ireland goes to the movies*, Dublin, Wolfhound.

Mac Conghail, M. (1984), 'The creation of RTÉ and the impact of television', in Farrell, B. (ed.), *Communication and Community in Ireland*, Cork, Mercier Press, 64–74.

MacCurtain, M., and O'Dowd, M. (eds) (1991), *Women in Early Modern Ireland*, Edinburgh, Edinburgh University Press.

McGrath, J. (1981), *A Good Night Out: Popular theatre, audience, class and form*, London, Methuen.

McGuinness, F. (1998), *Dancing at Lughnasa*, London, Faber.

McIlroy, B. (1988), *Irish Cinema: An illustrated history*, Dublin, Anna Livia Press.

McIlroy, B. (1993), 'The repression of communities: Visual representations of Northern Ireland during the Thatcher years', in L. Friedman (ed.), *British Cinema and Thatcherism*, London, University College London Press, 92–108.

McIlroy, B. (1996), 'When the Ulster Protestant and Unionist looks: Spectatorship in (Northern) Irish cinema', *Irish University Review*, 26:1, Spring/Summer, 143–54.

McIlroy, B. (1998), *Shooting to Kill: Filmmaking and the 'Troubles' in Northern Ireland*, Trowbridge, Wiltshire, Flicks Books.

MacKillop, J. (ed.) (1999), *Contemporary Irish Cinema: From The Quiet Man to Dancing at Lughnasa*, Syracuse, Syracuse University Press.

MacLaughlin, J. (1995), *Travellers and Ireland: Whose country, whose history?*, Cork, Cork University Press.

McLoone, M. (ed.) (1991), *Culture, Identity and Broadcasting in Ireland: Local issues, global perspectives*, Belfast, Institute of Irish Studies.

McLoone, M. (1992), 'Funding an identity crisis', *Film Ireland*, 30, July/August, 12–13.

McLoone, M. (1993), 'A little local difficulty? Public service broadcasting, regional identity and Northern Ireland', in Harvey, S., and Robins, K. (eds), *The Regions, the Nations and the BBC*, London, British Film Institute, 38–48.

McLoone, M. (1996), 'Boxed in? The aesthetics of film and television', in Hill, J., and McLoone, M. (eds), *Big Picture, Small Screen: The relations between film and television*, Luton, John Libbey Media.

McLoone, M. (ed.) (1996), *Broadcasting in a Divided Community: Seventy years of the BBC in Northern Ireland*, Belfast, Institute of Irish Studies.

McLoone, M. (1998), Ireland and cinema, in Hill, J., and Gibson, P. C. (eds) *The Oxford Companion to World Cinema*, Oxford, Oxford University Press, 510–15.

McLoone, M., and MacMahon, J. (eds) (1984), *Television and Irish Society*, Dublin, RTÉ/Irish Film Institute.

McNamee, E. (1995), *Resurrection Man*, London, Picador.

McNee, G. (1990), *In the Footsteps of 'The Quiet Man'*, Edinburgh, Mainstream Publishing.

McPherson, C. (1997), *I Went Down: The shooting script*, London, Nick Hern Books.

Memmi, A. (1990), *The Colonizer and the Colonized*, London, Earthscan Publications.

Meaney, G. ([1991]1994), 'Sex and nation: Women in Irish culture and politics', in *A Dozen Lips*, Dublin, Attic Press.

Miller, D. (1994), *Don't Mention the War: Northern Ireland, propaganda and the media*, London, Pluto Press.

Miller, D., and McLaughlin, G. (1996), 'Reporting the peace in Northern Ireland', in Rolston, B., and Miller, D. (eds), *War and Words: A Northern Ireland media reader*, Belfast, Beyond the Pale, 421–40.

Miller, D. (1995), 'The media and Northern Ireland', in Philo, G. (ed.), *Glasgow Media Group Reader: Volume 2*, London, Routledge, 45–75.

Miller, D. (ed.) (1998), *Rethinking Northern Ireland: Culture, ideology and colonialism*, Harlow, Essex, Longman.

Miller, K. (1985), *Emigrants and Exiles: Ireland and the Irish exodus to North America*, Oxford, Oxford University Press.

Miller, K., and Wagner, P. (1994), *Out of Ireland: The story of Irish emigration to America*, London, Aurum Press.

Modleski, T. (1982), *Loving with a Vengence*, New York, Methuen.

Moore-Gilbert, B. (1997), 'Crises of identity? Current problems and possibilities in post-colonial criticism', *The European English Messenger*, 6:2, Autumn, 35–43.

Mornin, D. (1996), *All Our Fault*, London, Arrow.

Mulryan, P. (1988), *Radio Radio: The story of independent, local, community and pirate radio in Ireland*, Dublin, Borderline Pubications.

Murdock, G. (1991), 'Patrolling the border: British broadcasting and the Irish question in the 1980s', *Journal of Communication*, 2:4, 104–15.

Murphy, R. (1983), 'Rank's attempt on the American market, 1944–49', in Curran, J., and Porter, V. (eds), *British Cinema History*, London, Weidenfeld and Nicolson, 164–78.

Nairn, T. (1977), *The Break-Up of Britain*, London, Verso.

Nairn, T. (1990), *The Enchanted Glass: Britain and its monarchy*, London, Picador.

Nandy, A. (1983), *The Intimate Enemy: Loss and the recovery of self under colonialism*, Oxford and Dehli, Oxford University Press.

Neale, S., and Krutnik, F. (1990), *Popular Film and Television Comedy*, London, Routledge.

Nelson, T. G. A. (1990), *Comedy: The theory of comedy in literature, drama and cinema*, Oxford, Oxford University Press.

Neve, B. (1997), 'Cinema, the ceasefire and the Troubles', *Irish Studies Review*, 20, Autumn, 2–8.

New York Times (1970), *Film Reviews, Volume 1: 1913–31*, New York, Arno Press.

Nichols, B. (1991), *Representing Reality: issues and concepts in documentary*, Bloomington and Indianapolis, Indiana University Press.

O'Connor, B. (1984), 'Aspects of representation of women in Irish film', *The Crane Bag*, 8:2, 79–83.

O'Connor, B. (1984), 'The presentation of women in Irish television drama', in McLoone, M., and MacMahon, J. (eds), *Television and Irish Society*, Dublin, IFI/RTÉ, 123–32.

O'Connor, B. (1990), *Soap and Sensibility: Audience response to Dallas and Glenroe*, Dublin, RTÉ.

O'Connor, B. (1998), 'Riverdance', in Peillon, M., and Slater, E. (eds), *Encounters with Modern Ireland*, Dublin, Institute of Public Administration, 51–60.

O'Donnell, D. (1992), 'Cinema film distribution and exhibition in Ireland', *Irish Communications Review*, 2, 8–19.

O'Dowd, L. (1990), 'New introduction', in Memmi, A., *The Colonizer and the Colonized*, tr. H. Greenfeld, London, Earthscan, 30–66.

O' Dowd, L. (1995), 'Development or dependency? State, economy and society in Northern Ireland', in Clancy, P., Drudy, S., Lynch, K. and O'Dowd, L. (eds), *Irish Society: Sociological perspectives*, Dublin, Institute of Public Administration, 132–77.

O'Dowd, L. (ed.) (1996), *On Intellectuals and Intellectual Life in Ireland*, Belfast, Institute of Irish Studies.

O' Dwyer, M. (1997), 'Ten days that shook the Irish film industry', *Film West*, 30, August, 24–8

Ó Gráda, C. (1997), *A Rocky Road: The Irish economy since the 1920s*, Manchester, Manchester University Press.

O'Hearn, D. (1994), *Free Trade or Managed Trade? Trading between two worlds*, Belfast, CRD.

O'Leary, L. (1980), *Rex Ingram: Master of the silent cinema*, Dublin, The Academy Press.

O'Leary, L. (1990), *Cinema Ireland 1896–1950: From the Liam O'Leary Archives*, Dublin, The National Library of Ireland.

Ó Maoláin, C. (1988), *No Comment: Censorship, secrecy and the Irish Troubles*, London, Article 19.

Open, M. (1985), *Fading Lights and Silver Screens: A history of Belfast cinemas*, Antrim, Northern Ireland, Greystone Books.

O'Regan, T. (1995), *Australian National Cinema*, London, Routledge.

O'Shaughnessy, M. (1990), 'Box Pop: Popular television and hegemony', in Goodwin, A., and Whannel, G. (eds), *Understanding Television*, London, Routledge, 88–102.

O'Sullivan, T., Dutton, B. and Rayner, P. (1998), *Studying the Media*, London, Arnold.

Ostergaard, B. S. (ed.) (1995), *The Media in Western Europe: The Euromedia handbook*, London, Sage.

O'Toole, F. (1990), *A Mass for Jesse James: A journey through 1980s Ireland*, Dublin, Raven Arts Press.

O'Toole, F. (1994), *Black Hole, Green Card: The disappearance of Ireland*, Dublin, New Island Books.

O'Toole, F. (1997), *The Ex-Isle of Erin: Images of a global Ireland*, Dublin, New Island Books.

Paget, D. (1990), *True Stories? Documentary drama on radio, screen and stage*, Manchester, Manchester University Press.

Paget, D. (1998), *No other way to tell it: Dramadoc/docudrama on television*, Manchester, Manchester University Press.

Parker, S. (1987), *Lost Belongings*, London, Euston Films/Channel Four.

Parkinson, A. F. (1998), *Ulster Loyalism and the British Media*, Dublin, Four Courts Press.

Parry, B. (1994), 'Resistance Theory: Theorising resistance', in Barker, C., Hulme, P., and Iverson, M. (eds), *Colonial Discourse/Postcolonial Theory*, Manchester, Manchester University Press.

Patterson, H. (1989), *The Politics of Illusion: Republicanism and socialism in modern Ireland*, London, Hutchinson Radius.

Peillon, M., and Slater, E. (eds) (1998), *Encounters with Modern Ireland*, Dublin, Institute of Public Administration.

Pettitt, L. (1992), 'Situation Tragedy? The troubles in British TV drama', *Irish Studies Review*, 1, Spring, 20–2.

Pettitt, L. (1994), 'A camera-woven tapestry of Troubles', *Irish Studies Review*, 8, Autumn, 54–6.

Pettitt, L. (1997), 'Pigs and provos, prostitutes and prejudice: Gay representation in Irish film, 1984–1995', in Walshe, É. (ed.), *Sex, Nation and Dissent in Irish Writing*, Cork, Cork University Press, 252–84.

Pettitt, L. (1999), 'Troubles, terminus and *The Treaty*', in Graham, C., and Kirkland, R. (eds), *Ireland and Cultural Theory: The mechanics of authenticity*, Basingstoke, Hampshire, Macmillan, 1999, 119–35.

Pettitt, L. (1999), 'A construction site queered: Gay images in new Irish cinema', *Cineaste* 24:2–3, 61–3.

Porter, B. (1984), *The Lion's Share: A short history of British imperialism, 1850–1983*, Harlow, Essex, Longman.

Porter, V. (1993), 'Broadcasting pluralism and the freedom of expression in France, Germany and Ireland', in Drummond, P., Patterson, R. and Willis, J. (eds), *National Identity and Europe: The Television Revolution*, London, British Film Institute.

Purcell, B. (1996), 'The silence in Irish broadcasting', in Rolston, B., and Miller, D. (eds), *War and Words: A Northern Ireland Media Studies Reader*, Belfast, Beyond the Pale, 253–64.

Reid, G. (1984), *Billy: Three plays for television*, London, Faber.

Richards, J. (1997), *Films and British National Identity: From Dickens to Dad's Army*, Manchester, Manchester University Press.

Richards, S. (1999), 'Breaking the "cracked mirror": binary oppositions in the culture of contemporary Ireland', in Graham, C., and Kirkland, R. (eds), *Ireland and Cultural Theory: The mechanics of authenticity*, Basingstoke, Hampshire, Macmillan, 99–118.

Roberts, J. (1988), 'Sinn Féin and video: notes on a political pedagogy', *Screen*, 29:2, Spring, 94–7.

Roche, B. (1997), *Trojan Eddie: A screenplay*, London, Methuen.

Rockett, K. (1979/80), 'Irish cinema: Notes on some nationalist fictions', *Screen*, 3–4:20, Winter, 115–123.

Rockett, K. (1980), 'Film censorship and the state', *Film Directions*, 3:9, 11–15.

Rockett, K. (1991), 'Aspects of the Los Angelesation of Ireland', *Irish Communications Review*, 1, 20–5.

Rockett, K. (1994), 'The Irish migrant and film', in O'Sullivan, P. (ed.), *The Creative Migrant: The Irish world wide, Volume 3*, London, Leicester University Press, 170–91.

Rockett, K. (1996), *The Irish Filmography: Fiction films 1896–1996*, Dublin, Red Mountain Press.

Rockett, K., Hill, J., and Gibbons, L. (1988), *Cinema and Ireland*, London, Routledge.

Rockett, K., with Finn, E. (1995), *Still Irish: A century of the Irish in film*, Dublin, Red Mountain Press.

Rolston, B. (ed.) (1991), *The Media and Northern Ireland: Covering the troubles*, Basingstoke, Hampshire, Macmillan.

Rolston, B., and Miller, D. (eds) (1996), *War and Words: The Northern Ireland media reader*, Belfast, Beyond the Pale Publications.

Roscoe, J., Marshall, H., and Gleeson, K. (1995), 'The television audience: A reconsideration of the taken-for-granted terms "active", "social" and "critical"', *European Journal of Communication*, 10:1, 87–108.

Rowthorne, B. (1987), 'Northern Ireland: An economy in crisis', in Teague, P. (ed.), *Beyond the Rhetoric*, London, Lawrence & Wishart, 111–35.

Ryan, L. (1990), 'Irish emigration to Briain since World War Two', in Kearney, R. (ed.), *Migrations: The Irish at home and abroad*, Dublin, Wolfhound Press, 45–67.

Ryan, P. B. (1991), *Jimmy O'Dea: The pride of the Coombe*, Dublin, Poolbeg.

Said, E. (1985), *Orientalism*, Harmondsworth, Penguin.

Said, E. (1994), *Culture and Imperialism*, London, Vintage.

Sarris, A. (1975), *The John Ford Movie Mystery*, London, Secker & Warburg.

Savage, R. (1996), *Irish Television: The political and social origins*, Cork, Cork University Press.

Scannell, P. (1990), 'Public service broadcasting: The history of a concept', in Goodwin, A., and Whannel, G. (eds), *Understanding Television*, London, Routledge, 11–29.

Scannell, P., and Cardiff, D. (1991), *A Social History of British Broadcasting: Volume 1, 1922–39 – Serving the nation*, Oxford, Basil Blackwell.

Schlesinger, P. (1987), *Putting 'Reality' Together*, London, Methuen.

Schlesinger, P., Elliott, P., and Murdock, G. (1983), *Televising Terrorism*, London, Comedia.

Sendall, B. (1982), *Independent Television in Britain: Volume 2, 1958–68 – Expansion and change*, London and Basingstoke, Macmillan.

Sewell, T. (1998), *Keep on Moving: The Windrush legacy, the black experience in Britain from 1948*, London, Voice Enterprises Ltd.

Sharkey, S. (1997), 'Irish cultural studies and the politics of Irish studies', in McGuigan, J. (ed.), *Cultural Methodologies*, London, Sage Publications, 155–77.

Sheehan, H. (1987), *Irish Television Drama: A society and its stories*, Dublin, RTÉ.

Sheehy, T. (1998), 'Tax player', *Screen International*, 1179, 9–15 October, 14–16.

Slide, A. (1988), *The Cinema and Ireland*, North Carolina, McFarland & Co.

Spivak, G. (1990), *The Post-Colonial Critic: Interviews, strategies, dialogues*, London, Routledge.

Stalker, J. (1988), *Stalker*, London, Penguin.

Stoneman, R. (1996), 'Nine notes on cinema and television', in Hill, J., and McLoone, M. (eds), *Big Picture, Small Screen: The relations between film and television*, Luton, John Libbey Media, 118–32.

Street, S. (1997), *British National Cinema*, London, Routledge.

Strinati, D. (1995), *An Introduction to Theories of Popular Culture*, London, Routledge.

Synge, J. M. (1982), 'The Aran Islands', in Price, A. (ed.), *Collected Works: Volume 2*, Gerrards Cross, Colin Smyth, 47–184.

Thomas, M. (ed.) (1983), *Stories and Songs: The films of Philip Donnellan*, London, BFI.

Tobin, F. (1984), *The Best of Decades: Ireland in the 1960s*, Dublin, Gill & Macmillan.

Tulloch, J. (1990), *Television Drama: Agency, audience, myth*, London, Routledge.

Tunstall, J. (1993), *Television Producers*, London, Routledge.

Turner, G. (1993), *Film as Social Practice*, London, Routledge.

Variety's Film Reviews (1983–99), New York, R. R. Bowkers.

Vaughan, D. (1995) *Odd Man Out*, London, BFI.

Vincendeau, G. (ed.) (1995), *Encyclopedia of European Cinema*, London, Cassell/BFI.

Wagg, S. (ed.) (1998), *Because I Tell a Joke or Two: Comedy, politics and social difference*, London, Routledge.

Walker, B. (1990), Ireland's historical position – 'colonial or European'?, *The Irish Review*, 9, 36–40.

Wallace, M. (1966), Northern Ireland, in J. Hawthorn (ed.), *Two Centuries of Irish History*, London, BBC, 122–30.

Walshe, É. (ed.) (1997), *Sex, Nation and Dissent in Irish Writing*, Cork, Cork University Press.

Ward, K. (1984), 'Ulster terrorism: The US network news coverage of Northern Ireland 1968–1979', in Alexander, T., and O'Day, A. (eds), *Terrorism in Ireland*, London, Croom Helm, 201–12.

Ward, M. (1991), *The Missing Sex: Putting women into Irish history*, Dublin, Attic Press.

Watts, J. F. (1996), *The Irish Americans*, New York, Chelsea House.

Whelan, C. T. (1995), 'Class transformation and social mobility in the Republic of Ireland', in Clancy, P., Drudy, S., Lynch, K. and O'Dowd, L. (eds), *Irish Society: Sociological perspectives*, Dublin, Institute of Public Administration, 324–57.

Whyte, J. (1990), *Interpreting Northern Ireland*, Oxford, Clarendon.

Wilkins, G. (1994), 'Film production in Northern Ireland', in Hill, J., McLoone, M., and Hainsworth, P. (eds), *Border Crossing: Film in Ireland, Britain and Europe*, Belfast, Institute of Irish Studies, 140–5.

Whooley, S. (ed.) (1997), *Neil Jordan*, in conversation with Michael Dwyer, Galway, Film West Publications.

Williams, P. (1998), *The General: Godfather of crime*, Dublin, The O'Brien Press.

Williams, R. (1984), *Writing in Society*, London, Verso.

Williams, R. (1990), *Television: Technology and cultural form*, London, Routledge.

Windlesham and Rampton, R. (1989), *The Windlesham/Rampton Report on Death on the Rock*, London, Faber.

Winston, B. (1995), *Claiming the Real: The documentary film revisited*, London, BFI.

Wober, J. M. (1990), 'Effects on perception on seeing the drama-documentary *Who Bombed Birmingham?*', London, IBA.

Woodman, K. (1985), *Media Control in Ireland*, Galway, Galway University Press.

Woll, A. L. and Miller, R. M.(eds) (1987), 'Irish', in *Ethnic and Racial Images in American Film and Television*, New York, Garland, 261–74.

Wyver, J. (1989), *The Moving Image: An international history of film, television and video*, Oxford, Basil Blackwell.

Young, L. (1996), *Fear of the Dark: 'Race', gender and sexuality in the cinema*, London, Routledge.

Index of film and television titles

Index

Note: 'n' after a page reference indicates a note number on that page